With best wishes,

Ian Scalor

December 2008

The Story of the
Palace Theatre
Watford

The Story of the
Palace Theatre
Watford

IAN SCLEATER

ATLANTIC PUBLISHING

Dedication

This book is dedicated to the Anonymous Donor
without whose generosity the Palace Theatre, Watford
would not exist today. It is my dearest hope that one day
the identity of the Donor will be revealed and the
gratitude of Watford can be properly expressed.

OPENING NIGHT AT THE PALACE THEATRE WATFORD, DEC 14. 08.

First published in 2008 by
Atlantic Publishing

Atlantic Publishing
38 Copthorne Road, Rickmansworth,
Hertfordshire, WD3 4AQ

© Ian Scleater

Designed by Judy Linard
Production Cliff Salter
Printed in Great Britain by
Biddles Ltd, King's, Lynn, Norfolk

ISBN 978-0-9558298-4-0

Contents

Bibliography

A Century of Service by John N. Young
(The National Amateur Operatic & Dramatic Association)
Mrs. Fuller's Free School by Neil Hart
Hut 40 Scrap Book by David Windsor
CHAPLIN Stage by Stage by 'A.J' Marriot
Laurel and Hardy – The British Tours by 'A.J' Marriot
Watford Past by Robert Bard
The Book of Watford by J.B. Nunn
Tearing Tickets Twice Nightly by John Alexander
My Autobiography by Charles Chaplin
A Stupid Boy by Jimmy Perry
A Last Complete Performance by Ivor Buckingham
Watford – The Official Guide
British Theatres and Music Halls by John Earl

Sponsors

The sponsors of this book include:-
The Mayor of Watford's Community Fund

107. PALACE THEATRE. WATFORD

Acknowledgements

Watford Borough Council
Watford Observer
Watford Museum
Watford Central Library
Watford Operatic Society
Watford Palace Theatre
Gardiner & Theobald
Mary Forsyth
Abbots Langley Gilbert &
Sullivan Society
Ian Robertson

Norman Tyrwhitt
Cassio Operatic Society
University of Kent
Angela Edmonds
Giles Croft
Lou Stein
Jane Williams
Grelle White
Roy Hudd
Gabrielle Drake
Chris Emmett

Jimmy Perry
Andrea Bath
Kirstie Davis
Andrew Robertson
Roger Vaughan Picture Gallery
Amanda Arnold
(Mercury Theatre,
Colchester)
Greg Child
John Ausden
David Huggins

Acknowledgements of Photographs

Original façade of the Palace Theatre Watford 1909 by courtesy of the Watford Central Library
Giles Croft by Robert Day
Children queuing by T.H. Greville
1982 Auditorium photograph by J.B. Nunn
Photographs of Gertie Gitana, Harry Lauder, Nellie Wallace, Lily Morris
reproduced from the collection of Terry Lomas of The British Music Hall Society
Gayle Hunnicutt by Universal Pictorial Press & Agency Limited
Brigit Forsyth by Vincent Abbey
The Denville Premiere Players by Greville of Watford
Donald Edwards and Betty Nelson by Greville of Watford
Chris Emmett by Sarah Woodward
Gloria Grahame by Roy Blakey
Roy Barraclough by Adrian Gatie
Jo Jenkin and Brian Abell by Graphic Photos
Derrick Phoenix by T.H. Grevillle
Belinda Lang by Charlie Carter
Stephen Fry by Johnny Boylan
Mr. Meadows's Mausoleum by Frederick Downer
Many of the other photographs were taken by the author. For some the name of the
photographer has not been discovered; others are out of copyright. Any identification of the
photographer subsequently discovered will be included in any future edition of this book.

Foreword

I have deliberately entitled this book 'The Story of the Palace Theatre'. To employ the word 'History' might engender in the minds of some that it is to be a dull treatise. It has been anything but 'dull' to write. It has been an adventure and on occasions, exciting.

I am indebted to the many people who have encouraged me. More than once I thought that the story was complete only to stumble upon an interesting clue, which after research, revealed a story well worth including.

There were instances when I received a telephone call from a complete stranger, like, for example Mr. Baldwin, who told me that his maternal grandmother had been employed at the theatre from its opening in 1908, as a dresser, right up until her death on her way to the theatre in 1952.

The research and writing of this book has been a 'Labour of Love' and has taken me three years.

My association with the Palace Theatre, Watford started in March 1935 when I was taken as a small child to see my father play the comedy lead in an amateur production of *The Desert Song* performed by Watford Operatic Society. He was a founder member of that society and my mother joined the society a year or two later. They were married in 1929 and I was born the following year. I believe that I was the first child to be born as a result of two people meeting as members of Watford Operatic Society.

I believe that on the occasion of my first visit I fell under the spell of the Palace Theatre and it is a spell that has never been broken.

I saw every production by Watford Operatic Society from 1935 up until now, except for the production of *The Boy Friend* in 1990, many of them from the orchestra pit.

In 1963 I was elected by the members of the society to succeed the late Allan

Baldwin as Hon. Musical Director, a position I held until 1982. In that year I felt that the society was looking to perform musicals of less musical content than I enjoyed rehearsing and performing. I believed, therefore, that it was time to make way for a younger man who would lead the society forward on its chosen path.

After a year or two, I started to miss the 'glamour' of performing and this feeling increased and so my long-suffering wife suggested that I might let it be known that I was available to resume my amateur musical activities, if any society wished to avail themselves of my services. To my delight and not inconsiderable surprise it was not long before various local amateur operatic societies complimented me with invitations to musically direct a performance. To them all I shall forever be grateful.

In 1994 I found myself appointed to the Board of Directors of the newly privatised Palace Theatre. This was a position in which I delighted. It gave me an opportunity to input a contribution to the administration of my local theatre and an opportunity to repay some of the debt I owed it.

I served the full term permitted under the Articles of Association of The Palace Theatre Watford Limited. During my tenure of office I had the privilege of participating in the decision-making process of rebuilding the theatre. At times not an enviable responsibility but looking back on it, and savouring the retained beauty of the theatre, a thoroughly worthwhile interlude in my life.

After my retirement from the Board I was invited to take an interest in the archives of the theatre. Sadly, although records of recent years have been meticulously preserved, the archives do not go back very far.

Research has involved trawling through back numbers of the *Watford Observer*, studying the contents of many programmes which have been a source of enormous quantities of information and talking with many people who were not only able to tell me stories about the theatre but were able to provide corroborative proof of their authenticity.

Throughout the book I have referred to the building as the Palace Theatre, Watford, the name by which it has been known since it was opened in December 1908 and for a good ninety per cent of its time, otherwise I have referred to it as 'the Palace' or simply as 'the theatre'. To change from that name to its two brief periods when it was officially referred to as the Watford Palace Theatre makes the whole story confusing. In any case I am not comfortable calling it the Watford Palace Theatre. To my pedantic mind this title implies that it is the theatre attached to the Watford Palace but I am not convinced that Watford has ever boasted a palace. As mentioned above, the name of the company which today operates the theatre is 'The Palace Theatre Watford Limited' and the words 'Palace Theatre' are emblazoned across the façade. I live in hope that the historic name will be reverted to before too long.

This book is published to coincide with celebrations of the centenary of the Palace Theatre. Pains have been taken to ensure its authenticity but I should welcome any relevant information regarding its history for any future edition. Otherwise it is my hope that it encapsulates an accurate history of the building.

To conclude the preamble, I have many people to thank for their encouragement, support and assistance in so many ways.

First I must thank members of my family. I have earlier referred to my 'long-suffering' wife. She has endured the various passions and interests in my life. For most of our married existence she has been tolerant of my abiding joy in performing as musical director with amateur operatic societies in and around Watford, the Home Counties and London. There is, to me, no atmosphere to compare with the anticipation of entering the orchestra pit for a performance. The sound of the orchestra tuning up brings about an adrenalin rush with which nothing can compare. Having now 'hung up my baton' has given me more time to concentrate on the writing of this book. At least I have been at home in the evenings. She has actively encouraged me in what I called at the top of the page a 'Labour of Love' and was tolerant when I found excuses not to mow the lawn.

I should like to express special thanks to Greg Child who some years ago arduously ploughed through the pages of back issues of the *Watford Observer* and compiled an exhaustive list of productions and other performances at the theatre. This saved me hours of work and I have merely updated the list from where he left off in 1992.

My thanks are also due to many staff members of the Palace Theatre, past and present and their anticipation of the result of my labours has driven me on. I am particularly grateful to Lawrence Till and Mary Caws and, more recently, by their successors Brigid Larmour and Anne Gallacher. Throughout the preparation, research and writing Val Heyden has keenly followed progress and I thank her. We have known each other many years. There are too many members of staff at the theatre to be mentioned by name. They know who they are and they know how much I appreciate their encouragement but may I mention Craig Titley, Jane Foy, Sally Wilson and Sue Evans who were subject to much pestering by me but invariably responded to my cries for help and information with great patience and kindness.

I am also indebted to many actors and actresses (although it seems that ladies prefer to be described as 'actors' these days). It is a sadness to me that Sir John Mills did not stay with us long enough to have made what would have been a considerable contribution to the content. He also liked to refer to the

Palace Theatre as his 'local theatre'. Jimmy Perry, also, has been an inspiration and so helpful in reading and checking those part of the book which refer to him.

I have sought and obtained permission of a number of our contemporary actors to include pictures of them in the book and it has been significant that each of them when writing to give me their consent have invariably included a compliment, 'I have such happy memories of appearing in…..' or 'it is such a beautiful theatre'. Such comments have been an added inspiration. I have even received offers of any help I need and all have wished me luck with the project.

Most of the photographs in the book come from my own collection. Some portraits of early music hall performers were taken from picture postcards and the reproduction is not quite as clear as I might have wished.

Marion Duffin and Mary Forsyth have been of immeasurable help, finding for me items of relevance and interest at the Watford Museum. Without their help the factual authenticity of this volume would have been seriously lacking. Similarly, I have been given much help by the staff at Watford Central Library which has included making available to me some of their archives concerning the theatre.

Greg and Beryl Child have proofread this book and to them both I extend my deepest thanks. I have already expressed my gratitude to Greg. He will never know the extent of that gratitude which started when I presented myself at Watford Central Library intent upon compiling, from back copies of the *Watford Observer*, a comprehensive list of all productions at the theatre, only to be told that he had already done the job.

My thanks are due to A.J Marriot whose encyclopaedic knowledge of the life of Charles Chaplin convinced me, with regret, that the fact that the great man played at our theatre was no more than a myth.

To Greg Hill of Atlantic Publishing, I am also immensely obligated. I have never written a book before. He led me through the intricacies of publication and has produced what I believe is a book that will grace any bookshelf, irrespective of its content.

An enormous 'thank you' is also due to the sponsors of this book. Some of whom wish to remain anonymous.

This has been quite an undertaking, a larger one than I envisaged when I started. On the other hand I have discovered so much about the Palace Theatre and the journey through the research has been, as I have said, exciting. The spell has still not been broken.

Thank you for reading my book. I hope you will derive as much enjoyment from it as I did in researching it and writing it.

IAN SCLEATER

CHAPTER 1

Watford Gains a Theatre

Early in the twenty-first century, Watford is not over-endowed with historical buildings of architectural interest. Predominant among those that possess these attributes is St. Mary's Parish Church in the centre of the town and the oldest building in the town, then the Old Free School in St Mary's Churchyard. This was built in 1704 to house Mrs. Elizabeth Fuller's Free School which was to evolve into today's Watford Grammar School for Boys and Watford Grammar School for Girls.

Of similar interest is Watford Place in King Street, today occupied by Messrs Sedgwick, Kelly, solicitors, but at one time, early in the eighteenth century, the home of Mrs. Fuller and her third husband, the previous two having died.

Today another extant building to qualify is the younger, but no less interesting, Palace Theatre in Clarendon Road with its beautiful Edwardian auditorium.

These buildings have a tenuous connection.

The theatre occupies part of the site of what was known as the Watford House Estate. It, and Watford House, an imposing three-storey residence, which was a part of it, were owned and occupied in the eighteenth century by Mr. Thomas Meadows, for forty years a trustee of Mrs. Fuller's Free School, and a philanthropist, who made a grant to the school of £400 in 1767. A princely sum in those days, equivalent to some £50,000 in today's money.

In 1781, after his death, a pyramid was erected in the grounds of Watford House which served as Mr. Meadows's mausoleum. At the base of the pyramid there was an entrance to a second chamber which connected with a short passageway leading to the Watford Ice House.

Watford House subsequently passed into the ownership of the

Above: *Watford House*

Right: *Mr Meadows's Mausoleum*

Below: *Longitudinal drawing of Mausoleum*

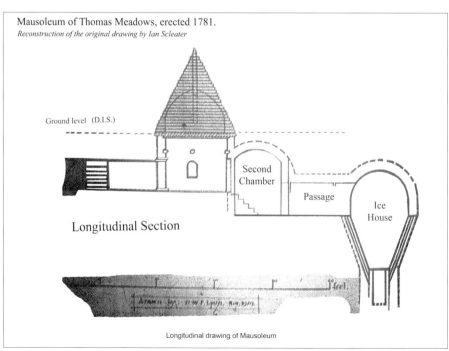

Mausoleum of Thomas Meadows, erected 1781.
Reconstruction of the original drawing by Ian Scleater

Ground level   (D.I.S.)

Second Chamber

Passage

Ice House

Longitudinal Section

Longitudinal drawing of Mausoleum

Clutterbuck family who were prominent in the town and eventually it became the home of Dr. Brett. On his death it was sold and demolished and the land became part of the 'Parade'.

Ice houses were a feature of many large houses. They were situated away from the house. Ice was collected during the cold winter months from frozen ponds and rivers and put into the ice house which was some way under ground. The ice was then insulated with straw and other such materials and was available during warmer weather for cooling purposes. The pyramid and its adjoining ice house occupied a position behind the site where the theatre was built in 1908.

Clarendon Road was not cut through until 1864 and to make way for it, the entrance gates to Watford House had to be removed. Watford House stood where the building stands which today houses T.J. Hughes, and before that for more than one hundred years, Clements, who traded from 1898 until 2004. Later, in another part of the former Watford House Estate, the Lime Tree Hotel was erected. This was to the south of Clarendon Road, on a site now occupied by Woolworths and immediately next to the premises which today are occupied by the Halifax. The hotel fronted onto Watford High Street. It was a long and relatively narrow building which ran back from the High Street, parallel with Clarendon Road, extending almost to where the theatre is now situated. Behind the hotel was a meadow upon which, to the consternation of the residents in Clarendon Road, there was erected from time to time a marquee in which a troupe of pierrots gave performances.

This was not the only place of entertainment in Watford. In the lower High Street, behind the Wheatsheaf public house close to Bushey Arches there was an open space and from time to time portable theatres were erected, one of which was 'Holloway's portable theatre'. The Holloways were one of the most famous portable theatre companies in the nineteenth and early twentieth century (their last show was as late as 1938). There were, in the early/mid-nineteenth century a few cast iron, nominally portable, theatres that actually served more or less static companies, but the Holloways were completely peripatetic, setting up wood and canvas booth theatres, mainly but not exclusively in fairgrounds. They had their own travelling company of actors presenting brief seasons of heavily abbreviated classics and blood-and-thunder melodramas, repeated many times a day until the time came to move on to their next venue. It is said that Henry Irving played with Holloway's Portable Theatre behind the Wheatsheaf in 1856 and again in 1857. This would have been very early in his acting career.

A playbill exists dating from 1803 which advertises a benefit performance for Mr. Barry and Miss Draper to take place on Saturday the 16th July 1803 at 'Theatre, Watford'. The programme presented was of two plays, *Folly As It Flies*, a five-act comedy written by Frederick Reynolds who was a well-known playwright in his day, followed by *Tale of Mystery*, by Thomas Holcraft, described on the playbill as a 'Favourite new Melo Drama' (*sic*). In fact historians have credited this play as being the first melodrama to be put on the English stage. It is generally believed that the performance of these plays was staged at a portable theatre behind the Wheatsheaf.

The residents of Watford were treated to various forms of entertainment. The diary of Henry Lomax '2 19th Century Herts Diaries' (*sic*) records that on 5th August 1822 'Saunders Company of riders performed at Watford for 3 nights. On the last night they sent up a fire balloon'. This was probably Saunders' Equestrian Circus which the actor Edmund Kean had joined around 1804. Mention of the fire balloon may be evidence that this performance took place in the open air.

As well as the portable wooden theatre at the bottom of the town, entertainment was also available at the Corn Exchange. The entrance to the Corn Exchange was sited between Cawdells Department Store and the Essex Arms Hotel in the High Street, approximately where the JJB Sport shop stands at present. A long passageway led up to a large hall which was variously used for entertainment. In 1909 the Kinetic Picture Company rented the building and, although a degree of ambiguity surrounds the use of the building thereafter, it appears that it became Watford's first cinema and became known as the Kinetic Picture Palace, known to the public by the abbreviated title of 'The Kinetic'. Its use as a cinema ended in 1914. Old photographs of the High Street show a temporary platform which was erected outside the entrance to the Corn Exchange from which election results were announced.

There exists in the Watford Museum the tattered remains of the programme of a 'Pianoforte, Violin and Song Recital' given at the Corn Exchange on Monday, November 18th 1895 at eight o'clock, by Miss Marie Olson (piano) Miss Ethel Barns (Violin) and Mr. Charles Phillips (Vocalist). Mr. Cyril Miller was the accompanist.

From the programme notes we are told that Marie Olson was making her first visit to Watford and that she had been 'a most successful pupil of Madame Schumann'. This must have been Clara Schumann, wife of the composer Robert Schumann. Of Ethel Barns the programme note stated in unequivocal terms 'Miss Ethel Barns has already appeared several times in Watford and her playing has always excited enthusiasm. Last year she took

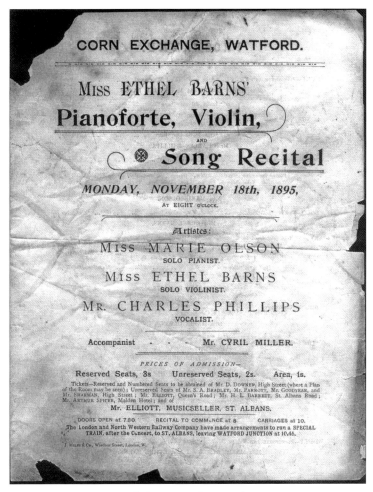

Barn's Concert at Corn Exchange

Lady Halle's* place at the Ballad Concerts, St. James's Hall [Piccadilly] and this season Miss Barns is playing at the Crystal Palace Saturday Classical Concerts. That this gifted young violinist is only at the commencement of a brilliant career is apparent to all.' Praise indeed and it was to prove justified but today she is remembered as a composer of songs, instrumental pieces and violin concertos. Ethel Barns died in 1948. The 1895 concert included two of her works which were sung by Charles Phillips one of which bore the strange title *With gloomy sails my ship doth fly.*

---

* Lady Halle was the wife of Sir Charles Halle, founder and conductor of the famous Manchester-based Halle Orchestra.

Tickets for reserved seats for the concert were priced at 3s and the unreserved seats at 2s or, in decimal currency 15p and 10p, respectively. They could be obtained from Mr. Elliott, Musicseller, who kept a shop in Queens Road, Watford. W.J. Elliott was a piano maker in the first half of the twentieth century and he was also a seller of sheet music at his shops in St. Albans, Watford and Harrow. Later a music shop was opened on the corner of Upton Road and Watford High Street and of this we shall hear more in a later chapter.

At the end of the concert the London and North Western Railway Company ran 'a SPECIAL TRAIN to ST. ALBANS leaving WATFORD JUNCTION at 10.45.'

We can go back even earlier to find evidence of the provision of entertainment in Watford. *The Times* of the 7th July 1790 carried the following announcement:

BY DESIRE OF
Mr. and Mrs. B U X T O N,
The laft N I G H T.
Mr. J O N E S's *B E N E F I T*
Tuesday June 4, at Watford new Theatre,
Will be held up to view, the Mirror of Nature;
JONES takes for his Benefit.

What the 'new Theatre' looked like and where it was situated, no one today knows. Certainly not in Clarendon Road which was not to exist for another 75 years. It predated the Holloways by many years. Most towns of any size were building little barn-like theatres about this time and they were often built behind inns. Perhaps the 'new Theatre' was one of these and occupied the same site which Holloways were to use at a later date. No records have been found to confirm this. On the other hand reference is made in historical documents to the 'Bijou Theatre', this may have been one situated behind the Wheatsheaf and it is known that the one-time landlord of the Wheatsheaf, George Barnes, had his own portable theatre behind his inn.

In 1908 Watford was still a relatively quiet market town, situated in Hertfordshire about twenty miles northwest of London. Not the County Town nor the Cathedral City but then and still the largest town in Hertfordshire with a population, in 1908, of some 20,500 inhabitants.

At the turn of the century, Music Hall was the craze. Performances took place in public houses and other such establishments frequented by the 'lower orders'. The middle class and even more so the aristocracy were not in the habit of patronising such places and so it became necessary to erect convivial places of entertainment more acceptable to all classes of society. Even then it took some time for an entertainment which, traditionally, had been more popular with the 'working class' to become acceptable to those who considered themselves superior. Some of the 'middle' and 'upper' classes, however, *did* attend musical halls. It is said that King Edward VII used to attend *incognito*.

Few provincial towns of standing were without their music halls and Watford was not out to be an exception. The people living in Clarendon Road, which at the tail end of the nineteenth century consisted of imposing residences occupied by personages of quality and substance, were accustomed to the presence of the Agricultural Hall, by this time renamed the Clarendon Hall. The consternation they felt at the erection of the marquee in the meadow at the High Street end of the road turned to indignation when they heard of proposals to erect a permanent theatre. Opposition to the project was organised but to no avail.

The Clarendon Hall, where magic-lantern lectures were given, stood close by the site proposed for the theatre. It was used, on occasions, by the Watford School of Music for concerts and there were also evenings of light entertainment. On Friday and Saturday, the 18th and 19th December 1908, for example, at the end of the week in which the new Palace Theatre opened, there was presented at the Clarendon Hall an evening consisting of a 'Medley of Melody & Movement'. This was given by Miss Miriam Freshwater (Soprano), Madame Hortense Samuelson (Contralto), Mr. F.G. Hind (Tenor) and Mr. R. Butler (Baritone). A string orchestra was conducted by Miss Marianne Radford and pupils of The Royal Caledonian School, Aldenham Road, Bushey (by special permission) performed their National Dances. It is intriguing to speculate as to which of the two venues attracted the larger audience, the newly opened theatre or the familiar hall. The Clarendon Hall eventually became the Territorial Drill Hall and was not demolished until the Ring Road was constructed in the 1960s. The buildings once occupied by The Royal Caledonian School are today occupied by the Purcell School, the oldest specialist music school in the country.

Mr. Meadows's pyramid, the Ice House and the Lime Tree Hotel survived into the early 1930s. The pyramid was demolished because children were in the habit of playing in the structure and it had become unstable. The Ice House, however, was yet to feature in the rebuilding programme of 2002. When the foundations were being excavated for the extension to the stage house at the rear of the theatre, part of the remains of the roof of the second chamber and a section of the roof of the Ice House, were uncovered. The significance of the uncovered brick culverts was not realised at the time, resulting in an expensive delay to the rebuilding programme while it was being decided what to do.

The foundation stone of what was to become the Palace Theatre was laid on 3rd June 1908. It is not known who performed the ceremony. It might have been the Earl or Countess of Essex who resided at Cassiobury House or one or other of their neighbours at The Grove, the Earl and Countess of Clarendon. In all probability, even if invited, they would have declined for fear of upsetting friends residing in Clarendon Road. Furthermore both families were represented on the Board of the Clarendon Hall, almost next door to the proposed theatre and, at times, in competition with the new venture.

The question is sometimes asked: was the Palace Theatre a Matcham theatre? Frank Matcham was arguably the greatest of the English theatre architects and was responsible for many of the surviving theatres of that period. His greatest success being the London Coliseum, home today of English National Opera, but 'No' the Palace was not designed by Frank Matcham but by H.M. Theobald.

Five days after the laying of the foundation stone, on 8th June Mr. H.M. Theobald, the architect of the theatre, lodged the notification of his intention to build the theatre. There were certain requirements which seem to have centred largely on the number of 'Water Closets' provided and drainage. In a statement, which in modern terms amounted almost to effrontery, the application said 'I hereby give you notice that I intend after one month from the date of submitting this notice to erect a Building namely the New Palace of Varieties situate at Clarendon Road in accordance with the Public Health Act and the Bye-laws now in force within your District and I send herewith as required by Bye-law 90...'. Planning control was not introduced until 1947. The only application that would have been required in 1908 concerned structural safety and means of escape.

In 1873 Mr. William Gardiner took into partnership a Mr. Henry Wells Dewhurst Theobald to found the now internationally renowned firm of Chartered Surveyors, Gardiner & Theobald. The family name of the Theobalds was originally Medows but in 1776 John Medows changed his name to John Medows Theobald 'pursuant to the Will of Elizabeth Theobald'. Many members of the now Theobald family were given their

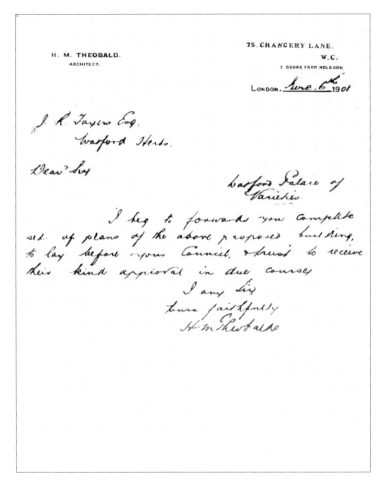

Application for planning permission

original family name as a baptismal name. It is likely that the 'M' in the architect's name stood for 'Medows' but no proof of this fact can be found. H.M. Theobald was clearly not the same man who was a partner of William Gardiner although it is probable that they were cousins. It must be more than a coincidence that the two men were engaged in connected professions. Henry W.D. Theobald, in due time, succeeded William Gardiner as senior partner and in 1896 his son John Medows Theobald became a partner in the firm and much of the success it subsequently enjoyed was achieved by his endeavours. In 1936, he was elected President of the Royal Institution of Chartered Surveyors.

By pure coincidence the quantity surveyors to the rebuilding programme in 2002 were Gardiner & Theobald.

The *Watford Newsletter* in its issue of the 10th December 1908 included a line-drawing by 'A. Mills' of the interior of the theatre from the Circle. This drawing presents something of a mystery. It gives an artist's impression of what the interior was like but it should not be relied upon for detailed accuracy. The caption which accompanied it also contains a number of inaccuracies. The architect of the theatre is referred to as 'Mr. Brown', No initials or first name being given. The drawing appears to include a sunken orchestra pit complete with music stands and behind the conductor's position a rail which never existed and was unnecessary. These various inaccuracies may be attributed to 'artistic licence'. The architect's original longitudinal drawings did incorporate an orchestra pit, but for whatever reason, the pit does not appear to have been excavated at that time. Instead there seems to have been a space left between the stage and the front row of Stalls to accommodate the orchestra. This was certainly the case up until the early 1950s.

Perhaps, when the theatre was first built, it was decided that in view of the downward rake of the seating in the Stalls, giving a clear uninterrupted view of the stage, a pit was not necessary, thereby saving expense, The pit which existed in 2002, prior to the rebuilding, was constructed in the early 1950s.

The caption under the drawing reads:

NEW PALACE THEATRE, WATFORD.

Above we reproduce a sketch from the Circle of Watford's theatre, which opens on Monday next. Without making any pretensions as regards the exterior the architect, Mr. Brown, has lavished his constructive and decorative ability, on the interior, which is very pleasing indeed. We cannot here give details; let it suffice to say that in the matters of safety, comfort, elegance and uninterrupted view of the stage, the building is as near perfection as any we have ever entered. Fitted with handsome tip-up plush seats in almost every part, with floors covered with rich-coloured carpets – even the 'gods' having warm cork lino – the whole scheme marks a new era, so far as Watford is concerned.

Note the comment that 'Mr. Brown, has lavished his constructive and decorative ability on the interior.' This is fundamentally untrue. The drawing shows an elaborate interior decoration, and immediately in front of where the artist drew his picture, six rows of comfortable seats where in reality, in that position, there were only three. The photograph taken from the stage

Drawing of auditorium in 1908

on the opening night shows the front of the Circle which is plain and devoid
of any decoration. Perhaps the line drawing and its caption should be taken
with more than a pinch of salt, unless, of course, the artist was aware of what
the interior decoration was intended to look like when eventually the
auditorium was completed. The claim that the auditorium was fitted 'with
handsome tip-up plush seats in almost every part' was a flagrant distortion
of the facts. Most of the seating in 1908 was hard wooden forms without
backrests. The photograph taken from the stage on opening night clearly
shows, on both levels, five rows on which are seated members of that first

audience in comparative comfort and behind them the occupants of the wooden forms jammed together in what must have been considerable discomfort.

Why, if a photograph was taken on the opening night, one might ask, was there not a photograph of the interior rather than the line drawing? The explanation must be that the interior at that time did not resemble what the drawing portrayed and this leads on to the conclusion that perhaps the theatre was deliberately built in two stages and the line drawing was showing what the auditorium would eventually look like.

It is a matter for conjecture whether the writer of the caption had, in fact, seen inside the new theatre or whether he was simply judging its internal appearance from the hearsay evidence of the line drawing

If the audience had expected to find themselves in a lavishly appointed auditorium as shown in the line drawing, they were in for a surprise, not to say a considerable disappointment. The interior at that time was somewhat basic and almost devoid of decoration. When it was eventually completed it came to be regarded as an outstanding example of an Edwardian auditorium, one which to this day is regularly described as one of the most beautiful auditoriums, of its period, in the country. Indeed, Dame Anna Neagle, when she played at the Palace said that she thought it was one of the most beautiful theatres she had ever seen.

In 1920 the *Watford Newsletter* (which by coincidence was founded in 1908) amalgamated with the *West Herts Post* to form the *West Herts Post and Watford Newsletter*.

So, when was the richly modelled plasterwork around the front of the Circle added? Did 'A. Mills', the artist, know what the interior of the theatre was *eventually* going to look like? If so, was the interior as we know it today completed in 1911 when the Gallery and the new façade were added? It seems highly likely.

For many years there has persisted a myth that the theatre opened under the name of 'Watford Palace of Varieties' and that its name was changed, one week after the opening, to 'Palace Theatre'. Like all the best myths this one is founded on fact. To accompany his planning notification, Mr. Theobald was required to submit drawings of the proposed building and there is no question that the name by which the new building was intended to be known was 'Watford Palace of Varieties'. In his drawing of the façade, for example, the intended name 'Palace of Varieties' is picked out in raised and contrasting coloured brickwork. What then went wrong?

On the front page of the edition of the *West Herts and Watford Observer* for 28th November 1908 an advertisement announced that the 'NEW THEATRE, Watford, will in future be known as Watford Palace of Varieties' but only a week later, on 5th December the same newspaper carried another front page advertisement announcing the opening of the PALACE THEATRE, Watford. Had someone taken a look at the façade of the new building and discovered to their no small dismay that the wording built into the external fabric was not PALACE OF VARIETIES but instead PALACE THEATRE? This might be the reason for the sudden and unexplained change of name. What is certain is that for most of its existence it has been known as the 'Palace Theatre, Watford' but there have been brief interludes when the order of the wording has been changed round and it has been called the 'Watford Palace Theatre'. To some this might imply that it is the theatre attached to, or part of, the Watford Palace but there has never been such a building in Watford.

Construction of the theatre, which was undertaken by Barker Brothers of Maidenhead, had taken just six months. Most of the labour employed was local. The front elevation of the building, facing Clarendon Road, was simple, but somewhat uninspiring, in design. It resembled a child's drawing of a house, or even one end of a warehouse, a rectangle with triangular gable and eaves on top. Within the eaves was a seven pointed star surrounding a circle which contained the date, 1908.

The stage itself was of an irregular shape, being deeper on the right-hand

Architect's drawing of façade

Watford Observer 28.11.08

side as faced by the audience and having an increased slope towards the audience halfway across. This shape was unavoidable because of the existence of Mr. Meadows's pyramid situated at the rear of the site which prevented construction of a rectangular stage. A photograph of the rear wall of the theatre taken in 2001 makes the irregular shape very clear.

The accompanying reproduction of a map of the junction of the High Street and Clarendon Road dating from the 1880s with the position of the theatre superimposed, clearly shows how close to the rear wall of the theatre the pyramid was situated.

It seemed surprising that the stage was never made into a regular shape,

Watford Observer 5.12.08

even after the demolition of the pyramid in the early 1930s. A story used to circulate to the effect that the stage of the theatre could not be extended or 'squared up' because the land behind the theatre was consecrated and contained the remains of French soldiers, prisoners from the Napoleonic wars. This story was not considered to have a basis in fact, but, as in other instances in the theatre's history, there was a strong element of truth in the story. One may assume that the pyramid which was also Mr. Meadows's mausoleum would have been consecrated.

A book published in 1885 entitled *History of Watford and Trade Directory* by Henry Williams speaks of the Pyramid erected over a hundred years earlier in

Above:
*Completed theatre
in 1909*

Left: *Palace
Theatre 1909*

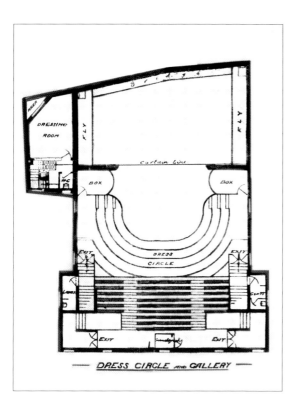

Left: *Plan of circle*

Below: *Rear wall showing its irregular shape*

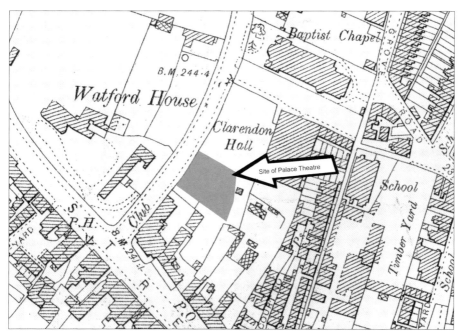

Plan of site

memory of Thomas Meadows. It goes on to say that 'The house occupied for many years by Mr. Charles Moore was once a malting belonging to Mr.Clutterbuck (a brewer), and previous to that a prison in which many French soldiers were confined during the wars between England and France. These unfortunate men employed a portion of their time in cutting toothpicks, tobacco stoppers, and other things from bone, which they sold to the inhabitants, and I understand there are still some in existence. Death put an end to the sufferings of some of the men while confined here, and they were buried in the garden at the back of the building, and I am told there still exists a mark showing the place of interment.'

But for the fact that it is known that the pyramid incorporating the Watford Ice House was behind the theatre, the location of the graves of the French Prisoners of War, could have been true and is likely to be the fact which gave rise to the myth. Either that or, simply, with the passing of the years the two stories became confused. Nevertheless, it would seem that the ground immediately behind the rear wall of the theatre was consecrated ground but to Thomas Meadows not to French Prisoners of War.

When the present ring road was being constructed in 1963 Beechen Grove Baptist Church Hall and Sunday School were demolished and a number of coffins buried in regular rows were revealed. These were not the graves of French soldiers. The interred remains with English sounding names were deceased previous worshippers at Beechen Grove Baptist Church.

From further description of the area it would seem that the house occupied by Mr. Moore stood to the south of the present day Clarendon Road and nearer to the centre of the town. We are told that 'outside Mr. Moore's house stood a fine chestnut tree'. Today Lime trees stand in this part of the High Street, no doubt the Lime Tree Hotel derived its name from these trees. Watford House was, as previously mentioned, a residence of size, surrounded by a large garden. It is probable that the house next to it was of similar dimensions and if so, we may wonder whether, in 1885, it was the only house occupying the land between Clarendon Road and today's Charter Place.

It is worth noting that the alley immediately opposite the theatre which is now used as an access to the car park behind T.J. Hughes was, until recently, known as Watford House Lane.

The irregular shape of the stage remained until the rebuilding in 2002/2004. Today the stage is a perfect rectangle and has increased depth.

There was a fly tower above the stage into which scenery could be hoisted when not required on stage. The roof above the fly tower, however, was triangular in shape which reduced the effectiveness of the tower. Scenery had to be hauled up physically on hemp ropes by stage hands who were positioned at the sides of, but above, the stage and out of sight of the audience.

The architect's longitudinal drawing showed that the stage was on the same level as Clarendon Road, outside. The ground floor, or Stalls, sloped downwards towards the stage. To assist in visibility the stage had a modest rake downwards from the back to the front.

In 1908 there were only two floors. From the architect's drawings it is apparent that on the ground floor there were five rows of comfortable seats at the front, described as Orchestra Stalls and behind those the Pit Stalls which consisted of ten rows of benches. The total ground floor seating capacity was 372. The floor above consisted of a Circle containing five rows of comfortable tip-up seats accommodating 125 people and behind the Circle seats was positioned the Gallery. This consisted of nine rows of wooden benches without backrests, similar to the Pit Stalls below, into which could be crammed 250 people.

The theatre was built for The Watford Hippodrome Co., Ltd but history does not reveal who they were or how much the theatre cost to build. At the opening the proprietors were the Watford Palace of Varieties Co., further evidence of the intended name of the theatre. The *West Herts and Watford Observer* announced to the populace that the Managing Director was Mr. T.M. Sylvester, Acting Manager: C. Mason, Assistant Manager: H.G. Wright and Director of the orchestra: G. Whittington. It is interesting to note that only T.M. Sylvester qualified for a prefix.

The theatre duly opened on Monday 14th December 1908. Advertisements in the local press announced that:

'The Programme will be of such as to be found in the Metropolis but without the inconvenience of an irksome train journey.

'The soundness, repleatness and safety of the structure has been certified by experienced architects and engineers.'

The photograph taken from the stage on the opening night provides valuable information. First of all, it is amazing that so many people could be crammed in. Not only were they seated close to each other but they can have had very little leg room. It is interesting to note that there was no centre aisle in the Circle. The rail separating the Circle from the Gallery behind it can be seen. There is no relief decoration around the front of the Circle and there is corroborative evidence that the orchestra pit did not exist at that time because the conductor and the double bass player, who are both standing, and the heads of two seated members of the orchestra, are clearly visible above the level of the stage. It is

Lime Tree Hotel

reasonable to assume that the orchestra were seated, or standing, on the same floor level as the audience behind them.

The programme on the opening night included:-

- *The Melody Makers* – Six men and 4 pianos in a high class speciality called 'The Burglar's Dream'.
- *John Tucker and 8 Ladies* – in refined entertainment introducing songs and dances.
- *The Denaro Brothers* – Juvenile equilibrists and acrobats. These young artists are the most wonderful performers the world has ever produced.
- *Oliver Conroy* – London's favourite eccentric comedian.
- *The Palace Pictures* – Giving an interesting panoramic exhibition of animated pictures.

The advance publicity, if repeated today, would, it is suggested, cause consternation within the offices of the Advertising Standards Authority, especially that advertising the *Denaro Brothers*.

As if to gild the lily, a later programme was to assure the audience that 'The theatre is disinfected throughout with Jeyes's Fluid.'

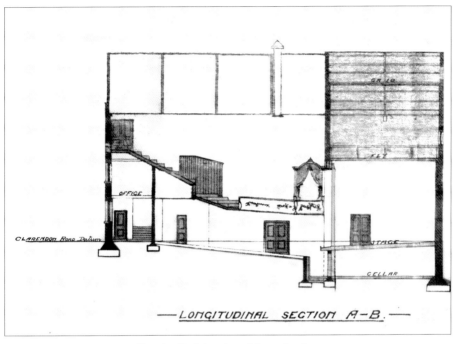

Longitudinal drawing of the auditorium

Opening night 1908

The advent of a permanent theatre in Clarendon Road was surely not the start of the decline in status of the road but by the time of World War II many of the residences had become doctors' or dentists' surgeries. Today it consists almost entirely of the offices of insurance companies and banks. It also includes an office of the Inland Revenue.

The entertainment offered in the early years was by no means restricted to Variety. Certainly Variety played a large part but plays were also presented, almost exclusively imported from other theatres, including the West End of London. This intention was proclaimed in the advertisement on the front page of the *West Herts and Watford Observer* of the 28th November 1908, in which it was stated 'Mr. T.M. SYLVESTER wishes to make it clearly understood to the inhabitants of Watford and District that although he is catering for the two Performances Nightly, he is also going to make a special effort to secure all the London No.1 Musical Comedy and Farcical Productions, which will be produced in due course.' The Variety shows were timed for 7.00 and 9.00 p. m. and lasted for one and three quarter hours. Mr. Sylvester did not lack ambition and to a great extent his ambitions were realised.

The prices of admission for Variety shows were set at 4d to 1/6 (in decimal currency 1.6p to 7.5p) but Mr. Sylvester reserved the right to vary the prices during the 'Theatrical Entertainment Season' for these productions only one performance nightly was proposed.

Mr. Sylvester made a further well-intentioned announcement in the same edition of the newspaper. An announcement which, had today's climate of political correctness prevailed in those days, might well have caused raised eyebrows, in the following terms: 'He [Mr. Sylvester] also wishes to mention that in running the High-class Vaudeville Entertainment, facilities are offered to every Class, as the Two Performances Nightly are arranged to suit the Working Man as well as the Tradesman; the First Performance will commence precisely at 7 o'clock and will terminate at 8.45, thus allowing for the Working Man who has to rise early in the Morning and the Residents of the surrounding Villages to enjoy a rational Entertainment without interfering with their daily toil; whilst Tradesmen, who are occupied in their businesses until 7 or 8 o'clock, can attend the 9 o'clock Performance which will finish at 10.45.'

Of all those who have worked at the theatre during its first century, surely the longest-serving member of staff must have been Mrs. Kate Wareham. In her younger days she had been an acrobatic dancer and a singer on the music halls under her maiden name, Kate Lewis. She joined the theatre in 1908 as a 'Dresser' assisting the performers into their costumes, carrying out running repairs or adjusting costumes so that they fitted. She also made it her business to supply them with food and coffee from one or other of the neighbouring establishments.

During her time at the theatre Kate Wareham compiled autograph albums which tell their own story. Many of the artistes she served contributed and the books contain the signatures and tributes of many illustrious theatrical and music hall performers. Her achievements and services were aptly summed up by Phil Ray who was in the cast of *Beauty and the Beast* in 1939-1940. He wrote in her album:

> If pantomime dresses get caught up
> And you're afraid you'll tear 'em
> Just yell out 'Dresser' who will show
> The proper way to 'Wareham.'

Marie Lloyd once asked Kate, who possessed rosy-coloured cheeks, 'What colouring do you use?' adding, 'If you will give me the correct answer I'll give you a quid.' Kate did not use make-up and so she answered' 'Nature's colouring.' Marie duly handed over the £1.

In 1938 Kate Wareham celebrated thirty years of employment at the theatre and to mark the occasion she was presented with an illuminated address, which read:

WATFORD THEATRE CO. LTD.
MRS. K.D. WAREHAM
It affords me very great pleasure to congratulate you
on behalf of the Directors and myself on this the 30TH ANNIVERSARY
of your faithful services as Dresser commencing with the opening on 14th
December 1908. During this period it has been my privilege, as Secretary
to be in close contact with those whom you have served, and who have
frequently commented upon the courtesy and respect shown to them by
you.
The Directors ask your acceptance of the enclosed cheque
in recognition of your long association with the Theatre and
hope that this may continue for many years to come.

THE WATFORD THEATRE COMPANY LTD
Frank Roberts Secretary, December 14th 1938.

Kate Wareham

The hope expressed by Mr. Roberts was fulfilled. Mrs Wareham continued as Dresser until 1952 when she was 82 years old. She lived in Southeron Road, only a 'stone's throw' from the Palace, and she was on her way to the theatre when she collapsed and died. She had served the theatre for 44 years and during that time, it is said, she had never taken a holiday.

Right at the outset, in January 1909, the first production was a play entitled *The Diver's Luck*. History leaves us in suspense as to the nature of the luck he enjoyed. The following week was Variety, followed by a production of *Raffles* and between Acts 3 and 4 of that play, scenes from the 'Earthquake in Italy' were shown on the Cinematograph. This was also being shown in the Clarendon Hall next door. Also on the bill at the Clarendon Hall during the week commencing on the 19th January 1909 was a performance by the 'Famous Animals Entertainment'. This is presumed to be the explanation for the presence of an elephant, horse and pony in the famous photograph taken at the front of the theatre?

It may be noted that *Raffles* was to be presented again in 1910 but by a different company.

The promoters were not afraid to give their products a good boost. At the end of March 1909, there was presented *An Englishman's Home* by Major du Maurier. This was described as 'London's Latest and Greatest success'. The effusive publicity went on to declare that 'Watford is the only town in the provinces of its size which can boast of *An Englishman's Home* being performed at its theatre. The management after long and tedious efforts, congratulate themselves on bringing to Watford a production which cannot fail to appeal to all patriotic Englishmen.'

1909 also saw the first 'big name' on the Palace stage. George Robey, the self-styled Prime Minister of Mirth visited the theatre on 12th April, the first comedian ever to visit Watford commanding a salary of £300 a week. It seems he gave only one performance at what was described as a 'flying matinee'. His famous remark to an appreciative audience was 'Kindly temper your hilarity with a modicum of reserve'. Of course, the more he admonished the audience the louder their laughter.

A fortnight later and for a full week, this time, Harry Tate came to the theatre. He was born Ronald Hutchinson in 1872. He started his career as an impressionist, impersonating, among others, George Robey. He made his name performing a sketch entitled *Motoring* in which he appeared as a chauffeur having difficulty starting the car. He died in 1940 as a result of injuries sustained during an air raid in WWII.

True to his word, Mr. Sylvester did not disregard musical comedies and *Miss Hook of Holland* was given in February 1909. This was followed two months later by *The Cingalee*, with music by Lionel Monckton. *The Cingalee* was described in advance publicity as a brilliantly successful musical comedy and for this the entire production from Daly's Theatre in London with a full chorus and increased orchestra was transported to Watford. The theatre possessed its own orchestra which played at all performances at that time. *The Belle of New York*, another popular musical comedy, was given in November of the first full year of performances, by Bannister Howard's No.1 London Company – from the Shaftesbury Theatre, London.

Many music hall artistes and other entertainers who were well known at the time but have today largely been forgotten visited the Palace. Some of these are listed in Chapter 11.

A Girl's Cross-roads presented on 5th February 1910, was written and produced by Walter Melville. Surely a portent of the part to be played in the story of the theatre by other members of this distinguished theatrical family. Walter was an uncle of Andrew Melville who, as we shall see, was the lessee of the theatre from 1939 until 1956.

During the month of July, 1910 the theatre was used as a 'High Class Picture Palace at popular prices'. Prices must indeed have been popular. A seat in the Gallery, which please remember was on the same level but behind the Circle, cost 1d or in today's metric currency 0.4p.

Audiences got their money's worth. In August 1910 there was a production of *The Silver King*, a melodrama by Henry Arthur Jones. It was publicised as the 'Greatest Drama of the Past and Present Century'. The critic reported that it represented 'Twenty-four years of unbroken popularity. Only fault to be found was that the curtain came down at nearer to 11.30 p.m. than 11.00.'

Pantomimes have also featured regularly but not in every year. The first pantomime was *Aladdin* which opened on Boxing Day 1908. It played for seven days, twice nightly at 7 and again at 9 p.m. plus three matinees. There was no interval. By the end of the week the cast must have been exhausted. This was the first production after the opening week of Variety performances. It is strange to note today that *Dick Whittington* was performed for a week commencing on 22nd March 1909, but most productions in those days were imported and so were presented by different companies, whereas today the majority of productions, including pantomimes, are 'home produced'. In some years more than one panto was presented,:for example, in 1913 there were three pantomimes in consecutive weeks, *Cinderella, Aladdin* and *Sinbad the Sailor* and again in 1914 *Aladdin*, followed by *Robinson Crusoe* and *Cinderella*. The management had a clear understanding of which pantomimes were the more popular.

There was a long-held belief that the celebrated comedian and inventor of the pantomime 'Dame', Dan Leno, real name George Galvin, played at the Palace. This is not so. Dan Leno is acknowledged as the greatest of the Victorian comedians. He may have appeared at the wooden theatre at the lower end of the town. Some authorities say that he was so overworked that he lost his reason and ended his days in an institution. It seems more probable that he suffered a brain tumour. Sadly, he died in 1904, at the exceptionally early age of 44, four years before the Palace Theatre was built. However, his son Ernie Leno was in a Variety programme during the week commencing 20th March 1911 and another son who went by the name of Dan Leno Jnr. played at the theatre in 1923.

Many entertainers who were celebrities in their day are almost, or completely, forgotten today. One such was Sam Mayo who appeared on several occasions at the Palace Theatre, the first being in a Variety Week commencing on the 8th October 1910.

He was born Sam Cowan, He had an elder brother, Ted, who was already established as a musical hall entertainer. A member of the company of which Ted was a member was taken ill while they were playing at the Alhambra, Sandgate. Ted suggested to the manager that Sam would be suitable to fill the vacant slot but the manager, a Mr. Fisher, was not favourably inclined to the employment of relatives. Ted invented the name Sam Mayo for his sibling and secured his employment. Sam Mayo became known as 'The Immobile One', a title which belied his lifestyle, and became a star almost overnight. He sang humorous songs with a 'deadpan' expression.

He was an accomplished pianist and song writer. In an article which appeared in the *West Herts Post* in 1910 it was recorded that 'The celebrated Sam Mayo, who is appearing at the Watford Palace Theatre this week, has achieved a marvellous and unique record. In order to fulfil his engagements in London and the provinces, a powerful motor car was bought into requisition. Starting from Brixton, where he resides, he travels on to Watford for the first performance. Re-entering his car he returns to London where he is appearing at the Metropolitan music hall, thence to the Standard Theatre, Pimlico and on to the Oxford Theatre (which was situated on the corner of Tottenham Court Road and was described as the 'most important music hall in London') back to the Metropolitan, on to Watford for the second show and finally returning home to Brixton. This smart performance covers between 90 and 100 miles nightly and about six turns at the various theatres.'

Sam was also an excellent billiards and snooker player. He returned to the Palace the following year and again in January 1922. Sadly, he is little remembered today.

Some accounts of the theatre's history report that in 1909 a major reconstruction of the theatre began. The date is incorrect. It was on the 12th June 1911, only two and a half years after it was opened, that the theatre closed for structural alterations. The alterations consisted of the construction of a new façade onto Clarendon Road. The façade, with a few minor alterations, is the one with which we are familiar today. The weight of the masonry in the new façade allowed, on the cantilever principle, for the addition of a third tier above the Circle. A comparison of the photograph taken on opening night and that taken after the 1967 redecoration indicates that there was sufficient height in the auditorium to accommodate a third floor. Although it seems probable that while the new façade was being built the opportunity was taken to raise the height of the ceiling over the new Gallery. Visitors to the theatre today will observe that the ornate ceiling above the Stalls and Circle terminates at this position and that it is higher above the Gallery.

No record exists of the reason for these alterations but it is not unreasonable to assume that the theatre was doing good business. It was at this time that theatres generally had achieved an unprecedented level of popularity and profitability. The success of the new theatre was evidenced by a comment by the critic in the local newspaper, regarding the Variety programme which ran for a week commencing on the 15th November 1909, '…probably one of the best that has been given since

Dan Leno

the theatre was opened. Really the show is so good, that on leaving the first "house" one *almost*★ envied those waiting for the second'. A comment rather spoiled by his qualification. If the review of the Variety programme given during the week of the 23ʳᵈ January 1911 was written by the same journalist, he may have been trying to redeem himself by saying of George Leyton, Massona and the Lyric Hummers, three of the acts performing that week, that the show was 'Very good this week – one might be tempted to go three times'. Another reason for the alterations may have been that the seating capacity was insufficient to accommodate audiences in comfort. Added together, it could have been, quite simply, that it was always intended that the construction in 1908 was merely the first stage of the building of the theatre. Probably we shall never know for certain the true reason for the construction work that took place in 1911, but it is an historical fact that theatres were being built all around the country. By 1916 the demand had been satisfied and theatre construction came to a virtual halt.

The critics were not invariably generous. In May of the same year, there took place a production of an entertainment entitled *A-LAD-IN. And Well Out Of It* by W. Bruce Smith, which was performed by the children of Drury Lane Theatre. The critic observed 'Mr. Smith's rhymed couplets however are somewhat tedious. For one thing puns occur with such exasperating frequency that they cease to amuse'.

The seating capacity in the auditorium, even with the additional tier, was

★ the author's italics

not substantially increased but there were many more comfortable tip-up seats than before, especially in the Circle, and this justified an increase in ticket prices and a corresponding increase in profitability. Converted to modern decimal currency, the new ticket prices were fixed at: Stalls 10p; Circle 7?p and Gallery 1.6p. It is interesting to note that seats in the Circle were cheaper than those in the Stalls. When the theatre was first constructed there were five rows of comfortable seats in the Circle, providing no more than 125 comfortable seats on that level and a similar number in the Stalls. After the 1911 reconstruction two more rows were added in the Circle making for some 170 comfortable seats on that floor and seating in the Stalls was increased to about 225. Approximately 180 could be accommodated in the new Gallery on the wooden forms which were moved up, all of those previously in the Circle and some from the Stalls. The surplus wooden forms remained as the Pit Stalls until 1930.

For some years now the seats in the Circle have been more expensive than those in the Stalls but even in the 1940s seat prices in the Stalls retained the same nominal differential, namely 2½p in decimal currency (a premium of 6d over those in the Circle at 4/- and 3/6 respectively).

Seats in the Gallery were not numbered. It was a case of 'first come first served'. The new Gallery was reached by climbing sixty concrete steps entered by doorways on either side of the theatre at ground level. The Gallery itself was entered at its highest point and the audience made the precarious way to their seats by descending a precipitous staircase equipped with handrails. For occasions when it was known that the theatre would be well supported the Gallery audience would queue outside. One further addition was made, that of the covered passageway along the left of the theatre which led to the doorway to the dressing rooms. It is probable that the Scenery Dock, on the other side of the theatre was also added at this stage.

The theatre re-opened on the 16th October 1911. Top of the bill was a Military Band – 'The Legion of Frontiersmen' conducted by Lt. Insen. The West Herts and Watford Observer reported that the theatre, although enlarged, was 'now cosy and beautiful'. Reference to the beauty of the theatre may be taken as evidence that much of the decoration of the auditorium, including the embellishment of the Circle and Gallery balustrades, was added at this time.

A major undertaking to improve the theatre had taken just four months.

The theatre was now very much in the form in which it was to remain until the rebuilding project which lay some ninety years ahead, except that the canopy over the main entrance, fronting on Clarendon Road and another on the right-hand side of the building to shelter those queuing for the Gallery, were not added until the following year, 1912.

CHAPTER 2

The Second Phase

After the new façade was built and the upper and final tier was completed, the theatre settled down to the next phase of its popularity with the residents of Watford and neighbouring towns and villages. Apart from periodic redecoration and minor modifications, it was to stay, largely, in this form until the major rebuild in 2002.

Following the Variety programme which re-opened the theatre in October 1911, there was the first of eight visits over the coming years by Fred Karno and his Popular Company of Comedians.

The four most celebrated names that have, in recent times, been regularly mentioned as appearing at the theatre are: Charlie Chaplin, Stan Laurel, Gracie Fields and Bob Hope, yet, in the commemorative programme celebrating the half-century of the theatre in 1958 the only names mentioned are: Marie Lloyd, Gracie Fields and Flanagan and Allen. There is irrefutable evidence that these four artistes did indeed play at the Palace.

It is only in recent years that the legend has circulated that Charlie Chaplin appeared at the Palace Theatre, Watford. In the souvenir programme for *Mrs Dot* in 1988, the play by Somerset Maugham which celebrated the eightieth anniversary of the construction of the theatre, although the names of several artistes who have appeared at the theatre are listed, there is no mention of Chaplin.

So what are the facts regarding Chaplin?

Charlie's half-brother, Sydney, was a member of the Fred Karno Company of Comedians and in 1908 he persuaded Karno to employ Charlie, who, after the end of a national tour of a play entitled *Sherlock Holmes*, in which he played the part of 'Billy', and a short period subsequently in the cast of *Casey's Circus*, had found himself unemployed. He was then 19 years of age.

Fred Karno, real name Frederick John Westcott, ran several companies and over the period 1911 to 1930 a Fred Karno troupe appeared at the Palace on eight occasions. The first one was during the week beginning 23rd October 1911.

On 3rd January 1910, Charlie Chaplin was playing the part of 'Stiffy' in *The Football Match* with a Karno company at the Metropolitan Theatre, Edgware Road. At one period during the early years of the new Palace Theatre, there was an arrangement with the Metropolitan Theatre in which the two theatres shared acts. Could *The Football Match* have travelled down to Watford and given a performance there during the same week? Well, 'no' is the answer. During the week in question the entertainment at the Palace Theatre was a full-length play entitled *Under Two Flags*.

Later in 1910 Karno sent a troupe to tour America. Charlie Chaplin was a member of that company.

In his autobiography published in 1964 Chaplin says that the company returned to England in 1911 and that 'For fourteen weeks we played the halls around London.' It would be understandable to assume that the Palace Theatre at Watford was one of 'the halls around London'. This, however, is not so. Chaplin is wrong in his dates.

It was not until July 1912 that the American tour ended and the company returned to England.

They were in England for twelve weeks from early July until the beginning of October after which they went back to America. There was no visit to Watford from a Karno company during that twelve weeks 'window of opportunity'. Charlie Chaplin left the Karno company during the second tour of America in 1913, but remained in the USA. He did visit England on a few later occasions but never as a performer.

In his excellent book *Chaplin Stage by Stage*, 'A.J' Marriot has compiled lists of Chaplin's exact whereabouts and in which theatres he was performing.

There were four visits to the Palace Theatre, Watford by a Fred Karno company during the period 1911 to 1913 and during this period Charlie Chaplin was a member of Fred Karno's Company of Comedians but throughout that time, except for the twelve weeks referred to, he was touring in America.

Perhaps the confusion arose because of an interview given by a Mr. William Edward Messenger to the *Watford Observer*, in March 1972, celebrating his Golden Wedding, in which he reflected on the eighteen months he spent as a stagehand at the Palace Theatre, just prior to 1913. 'This was a time when' he says, 'the theatre was frequented by top line music hall artists.' Many names sprang to his mind but 'none more vividly than that of Charlie Chaplin' with whom he said he once appeared on stage as a 'dumb waiter' (*sic*).

This evidence appeared to be supported by another interview reported in the same newspaper with Mrs. Parker who was employed at the theatre as an usherette for fourteen years, rising during that time to be head usherette. She told of her recollections of many star names and claimed to have personal knowledge of Chaplin in *Mumming Birds*, the most celebrated of all the Karno sketches. In this interview, dated 1968, she adds that 'a year or two earlier' Chaplin visited her at her home in Watford while he was in London. The last visit to England that Charlie made was in 1952. Sixteen years earlier, not 'a year or two'.

To put it simply, construction of the Palace Theatre was completed in December 1908 by which time Charlie Chaplin was already employed as a member of a Fred Karno company. He left Fred Karno in 1913. As we have seen, during that five-year period a Fred Karno company played at the Palace on four occasions. On each of those occasions Charlie Chaplin was in America.

On the other hand, there is no question that Sydney Chaplin played with a Karno company at the Palace Theatre, Watford at least twice, the first time in October 1911. The logical conclusion would seem to be that Mr. Messenger and Mrs. Parker confused the two brothers, as the inevitable conclusion is that Charlie Chaplin never appeared at the Palace Theatre, Watford.

But what of Arthur Stanley Jefferson who changed his name to Stan Laurel? The story that he performed at the theatre has been current for longer than the story asserting that Charlie Chaplin performed at the Palace but does that make it any more reliable? Stan Laurel was certainly in the same Karno troupe as Chaplin and was his understudy but if we accept, however regretfully, that Charlie Chaplin did not come to the Palace, it casts doubt on the authenticity of the statement that Stan Laurel came.

Stanley Jefferson, as he was then known, joined Karno in November 1909. In September 1910 he sailed from Southampton for New York aboard the S.S. *Cairnrona* as a member of a Fred Karno touring company. He returned to England after about three months. He was out of work for the whole of 1911. In 1912 he joined a production of *The Waxworks* which he soon left and reformed *The Rum 'Uns* with Ted Leo. Following this he joined Bob Reed and others to become *The Eight Comics*. In the spring of 1912 this group left for a tour of Holland and in September 1912 he returned to America to rejoin Karno, never to return except for professional tours with Oliver Hardy.

If Stan Laurel came to the Palace Theatre it must have been sometime in 1912 but no record exists to confirm this, nor does his name appear in any of the advertisements of forthcoming events or reports of same.

How then did this myth develop? If it did, indeed, only gain any sort of credence within the last twenty years or so, could it have started when a member of the audience gazing around the Edwardian building made a casual remark, such as 'This is the sort of theatre that Charlie Chaplin could have appeared in'? Was this remark overheard by someone else in the audience who misheard it and interpreted it as fact? Could this have led to the legend that Stan Laurel appeared at the Palace? After all, he was Charlie Chaplin's understudy, so, if Chaplin came so must his understudy. We shall never know.

This period was undoubtedly the heyday of the music hall and it is true that many established artists played at the Palace Theatre.

One of the greatest stars of the music hall to appear at the Palace was born Matilda Wood. She changed her name to Bella Delamare for the stage and eventually to the name by which she became famous, Marie Lloyd. She was born in the East End of London, the eldest of nine children. Her three sisters all made a success on the stage. Daisy, Alice and Rose specialised as pantomime principal boys and all took the name Lloyd.

Marie's first appearance at the Palace was not until the 26th April 1915. She was preceded by her sister Rosie three years earlier in Variety during the week of the 22nd January 1912. The Press review referred to Rosie '…who wore a Union Jack (sic) in an unusual position'. Either for reasons of decorum or for some other reason, the article went into no further detail. It would seem that Rosie may have followed the style of her elder sister, much of whose act was spiced up with innuendo. Her most famous songs were probably 'The Boy I Love is up in the Gallery', 'My Old Man Said Follow the Van' and 'Come Into the Garden, Maude'. She was adored by her audiences and was known as 'The Queen of the Music Hall'.

It is said, perhaps not surprisingly, that in terms of today's currency her earnings were approximately £2,500 a week, a substantial sum for an entertainer. In contrast to the pleasure she gave to her audiences her private life was not so enjoyable. She had three unsuccessful marriages and died at the early age of 52.

Reference was made earlier in this chapter to the fact that it seems that

Marie Lloyd   *Evie Green*

there was some kind of informal arrangement with the Metropolitan Theatre in the Edgware Road whereby a number of music hall artistes appeared at both theatres in the same week.

We have seen that Sam Mayo certainly appeared on the bills of both theatres during the same week. In fact he is recorded as playing at four or five theatres in one evening. Marie Lloyd also played at the Metropolitan and the Palace on the same evening.

The story goes that in order to fit in performances at both theatres, she gave her performance as the first act in the first 'house' at the Metropolitan, then, conveyed by her pony and trap, she hared down the Edgware Road, over Stanmore Common, down Bushey High Street, up Watford High Street and into Clarendon Road. At the Palace she was the last act in the first 'house'.

She stayed at the theatre to give the first act in the second 'house'. While she was entertaining the Watford audience a man was detailed to stand outside the theatre holding her pony. As soon as her second performance was concluded she jumped back into the trap and reversed her journey, returning to the Metropolitan in time to give the last performance in the second 'house' at that theatre.

This was no mean feat as the distance between the two theatres must have been about fifteen miles. The Metropolitan was considerably larger than the Palace Theatre and had a seating capacity not far short of two thousand.

With the gradual demise of music hall the Metropolitan Theatre struggled to survive and was eventually demolished in 1963 to make way for a road-widening scheme. The site where it stood is today occupied by the top-security Paddington Green Police Station.

In 1927 audiences at the Palace were entertained by Marie Lloyd's daughter, Marie junior.

During the early years of the Palace Theatre, several performances of plays by Hall Caine (1853-1931) were given. *Ruined by Drink, The Christians*, and *The Prodigal Son* (1909); *The Christians* and *The Eternal City* (1912); *The Manxman* and *The Prodigal Son*, again, (1913); *The Bondman* (1914) and finally *The Christians* again in 1920. This last performance of *The Christians* evoked from the Press review that 'the production reduced young men to tears' evincing the further comment that it was 'UnBritish conduct'. One wonders what effect the play had upon the writer of the review and what effect it would have on today's audiences.

Thomas Henry Hall Caine was one of the most successful novelists of his era. He was a very small man standing only 5ft 3inches tall and a colourful and unconventional character. He claimed to be a Manxman but was actually born in Runcorn, Cheshire although his father was a Manxman.

Hall Caine was acquainted with 'Dr' Francis Tumblety, the self-educated American who some suspect as being the notorious 'Jack the Ripper' but probably the most unconventional aspect of his life was his marriage. In 1882 during a stay in London with a bachelor friend the two young journalists arranged for their evening meal to be brought in by two young girls who worked at the nearby café. This fact came to the attention of the fathers of the two girls who, suspecting that the relationship had gone further than it had, put pressure on the two young men to marry the girls even though their daughters were only 13 years of age.

In the nineteenth century there was nothing illegal about marrying a 13-year-old.

The friend agreed to marry his girl but Hall Caine considered Mary Chandler to be too young. He was more than twice her age at 29. Shortly after, Mary's father threw her out and Hall Caine took her in. Many of his friends concluded that he had succumbed to parental pressure from Mary's father, but this was not so. He showed great kindness to her and paid for her to be educated and in 1886, when Mary was aged 17, although Hall Caine declared that she was 23, they were finally married although she had borne him a son when she was only 14.

Despite his irregular lifestyle, which at times bordered on the scandalous, his popularity as a novelist and playwright won the day and in 1918 Hall Caine was appointed KBE and Mary became Lady Hall Caine.

In 1912, programmes consisted of almost unrelieved Variety and some distinguished Variety artists appeared.

On the 4th March the popular musical comedy star Evie Green took part in a Variety programme.

The year started with another visit from a Fred Karno troupe, presenting their most popular sketch *The Mumming Birds*, amongst others. *The Mumming Birds* has been described as the most successful music hall sketch of all times. It featured a show within a show. The scene consisted of two theatre boxes, one on each side of the stage. One was occupied by an aristocratic drunk and the other by an uncle and his loud mouthed nephew. The performers in the show within a show made the act as bad as was possible and they were constantly heckled by the 'audience'. The sketch ran for forty years in twelve countries.

In a succession of Variety programmes that year there followed during the week of the 5th to the 10th February, Lottie Lennox and Charles Whittle, who was famous for the song 'Let's All Go Down the Strand'. Lottie Lennox was an American who was a popular entertainer, although not regarded as an A-list, vaudeville star.

Then in April there was a visit by the illustrious Scottish comedian, Harry Lauder, later Sir Harry, the legendary 'Laird of the Music Hall', who sang his song 'I Love a Lassie'. He shared the evening with a film of the Boat Race on the Bioscope.

The following week the audience was entertained by Marie Kendall, the maternal grandmother of Kay Kendall who took her grandmother's name and is best remembered for her part in the 1953 feature film *Genevieve*. Marie is renowned for the song 'Just Like the Ivy on the Old Garden Wall'. At the end of April the programme included Charles Coborn – 'The Man Who Broke the Bank at Monte Carlo'.

At the end of April that year, during another week of Variety, the matinee performance on 4th May was given in aid of the *Titanic* sufferers.

Later in May there was presented *How Bill Adams Won the Battle of Waterloo*. This was described as a 'musical extravaganza with no recognisable plot but very funny'. During the performance of *East Lynne*, by Mrs Henry Wood, in July of that year, an actor shot himself in the foot due to a faulty

Lottie Lennox   *Sir Harry Lauder*

cartridge. It cannot be confirmed that this incident gave rise to the popular saying.

The Variety programme during the week of the 5th August included Harry Champion – 'Any Old Iron'.

Fred Karno returned on the 14th October 1912 in a programme which, once again, included *Mumming Birds* as part of the entertainment and towards the end of the year in another evening of Variety the featured comedians were Naughton and Gold who were to become prominent members of the Crazy Gang which appeared for many years at the Victoria Palace in London. Also on that programme was Gertie Gitana, dubbed as 'The Idol of the People'. It is reported that her name on a Variety bill guaranteed a full house. She was possessed of a sweet, clear singing voice.

As 1913 progressed, plays became more frequent at the Palace Theatre but not until after another return visit in March from Fred Karno performing, of course, the ever popular *Mumming Birds*. Four pantomimes were produced starting with *Babes in the Wood* which opened on Boxing Day and this was followed in succession by *Aladdin and his Wonderful Lamp*, *Robinson Crusoe* and *Cinderella*. One must conclude that the scenery for these one-week productions would not have been as lavish as those to which we are accustomed today. Even so, the pantomimes were all given by visiting companies who brought their own scenery.

During the week commencing 23rd March 1914, there took place the first of several presentations of a musical comedy entitled *The Girl in the Taxi*. This was an adaptation in English of the musical *Die keusche Susanne* which was set in Paris. It had been first produced at the Lyric Theatre in London, opening on 5th September 1912, where it ran for 385 performances. Yvonne Arnaud was in the original production in the lead role of Susanne. A film version was made in 1937.

In the spring of 1914 there took place the first of the Shakespearean seasons. On consecutive nights from Monday 20th April there were performances of *The Taming of the Shrew, Hamlet, Romeo and Juliet, The Merry Wives of Windsor, Macbeth, A Midsummer Night's Dream* and on the Saturday *The Merchant of Venice*. These plays were presented by Florence Glossop Harris and Frank Collier and their Company.

The Variety programme during the week of 25th May was headed by Fred Emney, the father of the gruff, monocle-wearing comedian of the same name who was a popular entertainer in the 1950s and 1960s.

In November of this year certain evenings were advertised as Special Military Performances which were given at earlier times than the usual advertised times.

1915 started with an emphasis on plays but in March there was a week of Grand Opera. The theatre was visited by the J. W. Turner English Company and they presented from Monday to Saturday 15th to 20th March, *Maritana, Satanell*, followed by the more familiar *Il Trovatore, Faust, Tannhäuser* and *The Bohemian Girl*.

Variety still featured. Later in the same year Marie Lloyd made her first visit to the theatre and there was a further visit by Fred Karno. By late spring, reflecting the prevalent mood in the country, the entertainment presented took on a more military and patriotic flavour. *In the Ranks* and *Chosen by the People*, both described as Military Dramas, were given in May. This type of entertainment did not swamp the programme and the lighter hearted programmes were also featured. Musical comedies, such as *The Geisha* and *The Quaker Girl* continued to be imported from the London theatres as well as Variety programmes and revues.

The year concluded with *Babes in the Wood* and the first two presentations in 1916 were *Red Riding Hood* and *Dick Whittington*. There then followed a varied programme of revues, musicals and plays. The Lehar operetta *The Count*

Gertie Gitana

of Luxembourg was presented. Also in 1916, as light relief, a second presentation was given of *The Girl in the Taxi*. It is as well to remember that at this stage in its life the Palace Theatre was still importing shows. It was to be some years before it started to produce its own shows but there was a foretaste of the future.

Beginning on the 3rd February for one week a play was performed entitled *Grumpy* with Robertson Hare, famous for his catchphrase 'Oh, calamity', in the lead part but also in the cast was a little known actor called Harold Wilkinson who was to join the Melville players repertory company which occupied the theatre from 1939 until James Perry took over its management in September 1956. Harold Wilkinson, known to his friends as 'Wilkie', was a regular member of 'the rep' for most of that period.

1916 also witnessed return visits by Marie Lloyd and by Fred Karno.

The undated photograph of the façade of the theatre, on page 53, is of keen interest to historians. It probably dates from September 1915, because one of the two placards outside the main entrance announces 'WAR NEWS' and a poster outside the theatre appears to advertise *The Quaker Girl* which was presented at the Palace Theatre in that month. The photograph was produced as a picture postcard and printed by 'Kingsbury Photo Works, Park Street Village, Near St. Albans'. The copyright of the photograph was by Lilywhite Ltd. The other placard signifies that the Box Office is Open. The photograph is of particular interest in two respects, firstly the semi-circular architraves above the three first-floor windows no longer exist and secondly the entrance doors are further into the foyer than they are today, above the three steps.★ It is also interesting to note that the two canopies are in place, one over the main entrance and the other down the alleyway on the right-hand side of the theatre which was erected to afford protection from inclement weather to those queuing for the Gallery. These canopies were not built until 1912.

The year 1917 was memorable for the first of many visits by Henry Baynton. At the time of this first visit he was 25 and his fame as a Shakespearean actor/manager was still in the future. His first appearance at the Palace Theatre, was in *The Importance of Being Earnest*, the Oscar Wilde masterpiece. This was in the week of the 9th August and he was back again on 8th November for a week's run of a play entitled *The Heart of a Hunchback* in which he played the Hunchback.

The Heart of a Hunchback was written by Tom Taylor who was appointed manager of the Palace Theatre in 1917. He remained in that post until 1923 when he became manager of the Central Hall in King Street. The Central Hall operated as a cinema during the week but, it is interesting to note, in 1926 they started Sunday evening concerts. Tom Taylor would have known how popular the Sunday evening concerts were proving to be at the Palace, since it was during his time as manager of the theatre that they had been inaugurated.

Variety at the Palace Theatre was dying out. In 1917 only six weeks were given over to it and a further three to revues. This was the year that Tom Taylor was appointed manager.

In 1918 there were no Variety shows but a return for a four week season of plays presented by Henry Baynton and his company. Included in this season was a play entitled *The Melting Pot* by Israel Zangwill, which was presented in the week of the 15th April. Then on Friday 31st May a single performance

★ See page 94

Postcard

of the play was given as a benefit for Henry Baynton. The same play was back again for a week commencing on the 9th September. *The Melting Pot* had achieved considerable success in America in 1908/09.

A number of writers whose plays were performed at the theatre are almost forgotten toda, Israel Zangwill among them. He was born in the East End of London and rose to prominence as an ardent Zionist who devoted much of his life trying to secure a Jewish homeland. In later life Zangwill counted among his closer friends Jerome K. Jerome and H.G. Wells. He was a mere 62 when he died in 1926.

Several plays were presented, which from their titles appear to have continued the military and patriotic theme of the war years. They included *The Pride of the Regiment, Seven Days Leave, Married on Leave* and *Reported Missing*, the last by Alfred Denville, of whom we shall hear more. Even after the Armistice had been signed a play, which may have been planned for before the cessation of hostilities, entitled *Soldier's Bride* was produced on the 9th December 1918.

At 2.30 p.m. on the afternoon of 5th November 1919 there took place a *Grand Matinee* in aid of St. Dunstan's Hostel. The programme consisted of soprano and baritone solos with piano accompaniment, solo dancers and a ballet, a one-act play presented by The Lady Joan Capel (daughter of the Earl of Essex) and Sergeant Nicholls described the work of St. Dunstans, illustrated by the bioscope.

There were three weeks of opera during the first six months of 1920. The first of these, for just one week commencing on the 15th March, was a return visit by the J.W. Turner Opera Company, presenting *Il Trovatore, Faust, The Bohemian Girl, Pagliacci* and *Cavalleria Rusticana, La Traviata, Tannhäuser* and *Maritana*.

On the 22nd March, the week following the visit by J.W. Turner Opera Company, and as a total contrast, a revue was presented entitled *Mr. Tower of London* starring a then relatively unknown Gracie Fields. It is to be wondered which of the two weeks was the more popular with the Watford audience. Gracie Fields was not to achieve fame until 1925, so it may have been this visit to which Mrs. Parker, the head usherette was referring when she recalled Gracie arriving at her house for a meal and saying that she had nowhere to sleep. Mrs. Parker put her up and fitted her out with a sound pair of shoes. Mrs. Parker recalls that in return Gracie gave her a hat.

Then, after a lapse of ten weeks, during which there was a repeat performance of *The Girl in the Taxi*, performances of the evergreen Northern comedy *Hobson's Choice* and a production of *Maid of the Mountains*, opera returned in the form of the Fairbairn Milne Opera Company for a two-week season. The same operas heard ten weeks earlier were presented together with one performance each of *Rigoletto* and *Don Giovanni*.

Was the theatre at this time attempting to raise the artistic appreciation of its audiences? Henry Baynton was back at the end of November 1920 with his Shakespeare Company for a two-week season of plays by the Bard. It must have been quite an honour to have secured Henry Baynton to perform in a play. He played almost every major Shakespearean role and was highly regarded except in London where he appears not to have quite made his mark. This may have been due to the fact that the role of actor/manager was nearing its end. He died in 1951 at the early age of 59.

By 1920 Variety at the Palace Theatre had become almost 'a thing of the past'. Occasional revues and music–hall–type Variety entertainment was offered, but the hey day had passed.

It was during 1920 that the Roller Skating rink next door to the theatre was converted into a cinema and named the Super Cinema, later to be renamed the Carlton Cinema.

Towards the end of 1920 the Palace Theatre inaugurated Sunday evening entertainment. The first of these occasions occurred on Sunday 28th November when Herbert Butcher's Concert Orchestra took to the stage. It was a 24-piece orchestra. Frequent Sunday shows were given by seaside concert parties, driven inland when holiday resorts were out of season.

Many, if not all, of the Sunday evening entertainments were sponsored by the National Sunday League and were well supported by the public, playing, almost invariably, to capacity or near capacity audiences. Entertainers on Sundays were required to conform to a strict code of conduct. For example, costumes were not permitted. The performing artistes were required to dress in 'ordinary' clothes. Profits were donated to charity.

It is recorded in the local newspaper that the theatre was 'packed out' for a visit on Sunday 3rd April 1921 by H.M. Scots Guards Octette which was given in aid of the Warriors' Day Fund. However, it is reported by the same newspaper that a performance on Sunday 16th October 1921 by Frederick Stock's Octette 'delighted a record audience'; this is surprising if the theatre had already been 'packed out' at a performance six months earlier. During this particular performance a speech was made announcing that a petition was being organised to ban these concerts because the audience had been heard to laugh, sometimes uproariously, on a Sunday. The audience present that Sunday evening were encouraged by the speaker not to sign the petition. It would seem that the petition failed because the National Sunday League Concerts were to continue for some years. Concerts were given by many highly respected performers including the London Orchestral Octette and, a frequent visitor, the Broomwood Octette.

The Romance of the Rosary, by Herbert Shelley, presented on the 14th August 1921 by the Herbert Shelley Company, apparently made a strong appeal to human emotions. The press report tells us that it 'has a great many thrilling moments and an air of mystery. One lady in the Stalls dissolved into tears at frequent intervals and was only brought round by brief spells of rather dull comic relief.' Edwardian melodrama at its best, one assumes.

The critic came down hard on Should a Husband Forgive which played at the theatre during the week of the 29th August. His comment was: 'Some of

Henry Baynton (Hamlet)

the dialogue is unnecessarily sordid and one wonders what purpose the representation of a disagreeable subject on the stage can possibly serve'. However, he was pacified a fortnight later by *A Week End*, a farce, which, we are told, played to capacity audiences and was 'so genuinely funny that one chuckles all the time and roars with laughter frequently'.

The 1921 programme was tempered with a play entitled *Tatters* which was described as a 'musical comedy dramatic play' and the subject was that 'of a child of rich parents brought up in the slums', an unusual subject for a musical comedy. Then on Saturday afternoon the 10th December, organised by Watford Public Library Students' Association, a Shakespearean Lecture-Recital was delivered by the eminent actor Sir Johnston Forbes-Robertson, followed the next evening by the Philip Lewis' Palladium Octette and a programme which included Ronald Gourley, the blind pianist. Mr. Gourley had the astonishing ability of playing the piano standing with his back to the keyboard. This feat was the more astounding when it is remembered that his left hand was being used for what the right hand would play when facing the piano. On this occasion he used this technique to play 'When You Come to the End of a Perfect Day'. He returned to the theatre two months later on Sunday 12th February with the London Orchestral Sextette, demonstrating his skills by impersonating, on the piano, a brass band and again playing with his back to the keys.

1921 ended with the first of four pantomimes. *Little Red Riding Hood* of which the critic wrote that it was 'Almost impossible to get a seat, so heavy was the advance booking. Beautifully staged and dressed but the show needs livening up.' This was followed, in the New Year, by *Little Bo-Peep*, *Aladdin* and finally *Mother Goose* which the critic assessed as the 'Best of the four'.

Sunday concerts commenced at 7.00 p.m. but on Sunday 15th January 1922 a performance was anticipated from The Favourite Octette. Unfortunately the Octette and some of the soloists were stranded at Queen's Park Station because of a blizzard which affected the electric trains. One can imagine the consternation of the management and the feverish activity to keep the audience amused until the arrival of the entertainers engaged for the evening. The audience was entertained by the manager Mr. Tom Taylor who gave recitations and by other local artists who either happened to be in the audience or were summoned at short notice. Two members of the cast of *Mother Goose*, the pantomime scheduled to perform during the following week, also took part. Eventually the stranded performers arrived at 8.45.

In 1922 Watford celebrated the granting of its Charter. Watford Urban District Council became Watford Borough Council and for the first time in its long history the town had a Mayor. The Charter Mayor of Watford was the Earl of Clarendon. The granting of the Charter happened on Wednesday 18th October 1922. Following the ceremony, a banquet was held at Bucks Restaurant in the High Street and in the afternoon the first meeting of Watford Borough Council was convened at the Palace Theatre.

On 22nd January 1923 for one week there were performances of Gilbert & Sullivan's immortal operetta *The Mikado*. Apart from the two Saturday afternoon performances of *Iolanthe* by the Watford School of Music Operatic Society the previous year, this was the first recorded week of performances at the theatre of any of the operettas by G&S. but even this presentation was not a full week. It was given by Watford School Of Music Operatic Society which in 1924 changed its name to that by which it is known to this day – Watford Operatic Society. On this occasion the society was required to share the theatre with Watford Public Library Students' Association who gave afternoon performances of *The Merchant of Venice* on the 25th and *Twelfth Night* on the 27th January.

The season continued in recognisable form, with either an orchestral concert or a visiting, displaced, seaside concert party on Sunday evenings and a play, musical comedy or a Variety show during the week. *The Girl in the Taxi* was back again on the 16th April.

Names which appeared on the 1923 programmes included Nervo and Knox who were later to become another pair of the Crazy Gang veterans.

Nervo and Knox appeared in the Grand Variety Programme on the 22nd October but prior to their appearance, in September, there was an appearance by Dan Leno junior who was the son of the great Dan Leno.

At the end of the year Charles Stafford succeeded Tom Taylor as manager of the theatre.

The next year kicked off with a miscellany of musical revues. Expense became no object when on the 10th March, a company headed by the actor Talbot O'Farrell came to town. It was claimed that Mr. O'Farrell was engaged at the biggest salary ever paid to a Variety artist in Watford.

Even so, he was just a month too early to gain advantage of the new stage lighting. The new lighting doubled the quantity of light on stage and added to the beauty of the theatre shows. This relamping was just in time for another portion of opera. This time the visiting company was the Imperial Opera Company. The programme was much as before: *Maritana*, *The Daughter of the Regiment*, *Lily of Killarney* and repeats of the old favourites *Il Trovatore*, *Faust* and *The Bohemian Girl*, but no Wagner this time.

The record expense of Mr. O'Farrell's engagement was short lived when, on the 5th May, Harry Tate and Company arrived of whom it was said that it was 'The greatest and most expensive Variety programme ever seen in Watford'.

The 25th August 1924 also saw the first visit of Ella Shields, for a week in Variety. She returned for another week in a *Grand Variety Programme* on the 20th June 1927. Ella Shields was an American by birth and enjoyed enormous popularity on the music hall stage. She wore men's attire in her act and was made famous by the song 'I'm Burlington Bertie from Bow' written for her by her husband. Two of the other songs with which she will always be associated were 'Show me the way to go Home' and 'If You Knew Susie'.

In the autumn of that year, the Sunday concerts were revived, provided in the main by the concert party refugees from the seaside resorts. On 9th November, Clarkson Rose and his company provided the entertainment. Clarkson Rose ran his Summer Show *Twinkle* for forty years, starting on Ryde Pier in 1921. If Dan Leno was the first pantomime dame, Clarkson Rose was probably the most famous of all. He was a big man and his dames were masculine. He played his last pantomime in Leicester in 1967. He was also a prolific songwriter.

Talbot O'Farrell and Company returned for another week on the 26th January 1925.

Another significant improvement to the theatre was made in February 1925 when central heating was installed at a cost of £1,000. This installation took place, it would seem, with the minimum of disruption to the theatre's programme of entertainment because it was not found necessary to close the theatre while work proceeded.

Two weeks after the central heating was installed the play produced was *The Outsider* and it is recorded that the production was so popular that people had to be turned away; or was it the prospect of enjoying an entertainment in the warmth provided by the newly installed heating system?

If some of the well-known writers and entertainers of the early part of the twentieth century are almost forgotten today, included in the list must be George Mozart who played at the theatre in June 1925. He was billed as the 'famous comedian'. He was clearly a celebrated performer of that era. His name is be found on many theatre bills as a music hall artiste, frequently 'topping the bill' but, apart from this, it has not been possible to find out anything about him today.

On 2nd November, in the same year, however, Florrie Ford was in the cast of a show entitled *Here's to You* and the *Observer* critic described her as 'very good'. The title of the show was most apt because one of the songs in her repertoire, and which she made famous, was 'The Old Bull and Bush'. This was no fictitious public house. It still stands today, although in a somewhat altered form. Originally built in 1645 as a farmhouse, it is situated in North End Way, Hampstead. It is said that such luminaries as Sir Joshua Reynolds, David Garrick and Thomas Gainsborough drank there. It was substantially rebuilt in 1924 and lost much of its character. It is, however, a Grade II Listed building. Florrie Forde, herself, was born in Australia in 1876. She had a large repertoire of well-known music hall songs and would encourage her audience to sing–along with her. In addition to 'The Old Bull and Bush', she was also well known for such songs as 'Hold Your Hand Out Naughty Boy', 'It's a Long Way to Tipperary', 'I Do Like To Be Beside the Seaside' and many others.

Earlier in the year, a sporting revue *10 – 1 On* was presented. Top of the bill had been Jimmy James. James became a popular turn on radio during and after WWII. He developed the act into a trio of comics with himself in the lead role. The other two were known as Hutton Conyers and Bretton Woods. The great Roy Castle put his own solo career on hold in order to play Hutton Conyers. His famous remark to Jimmy James was 'Are you putting it around that I'm balmy?' to which James would reply, 'Why, do you want to keep it a secret?'

Plays by Noël Coward have always featured in the Palace programmes. In November 1925 the first to be presented was *The Vortex*. Coward, who came from a genteel middle-to-lower-class background had struggled for years to achieve recognition. In 1924 he wrote *The Vortex*. This was his third

Left: *Ella Shields*

Above: *George Mozart*

play and was to mark the turning point in his career. The subject was drug abuse among the wealthy and influential. It scandalised and fascinated society and was the talking point of London. It showed a degree of courage by the management of the Palace Theatre to present a play which was still attracting comment, not universally favourable. It was, however, recognised as a work to be considered seriously.

The first three months of 1926 were distinguished for the separate appearances in Variety of three pairs of female entertainers, two pairs of which were sisters. The first pair was Elsie and Doris Waters. Elsie played the piano and sister Doris played the violin. As comediennes they had a very dry, sophisticated form of wit. They had a brother, Jack, who changed his name from Waters to Warner. He was cast in innumerable popular films, including the Huggetts series but probably the most successful of his films and the one for which he will long be remembered was *The Blue Lamp* in which he played the part of P.C. George Dixon. This was later revived as a highly popular television series in the post war period as *Dixon of Dock Green* and ran on television from 1955 until 1976, a total of 376 episodes which has never been exceeded by any other police series on British television. Also in that series was Moira Mannion as Sergeant Grace Millard. She had been in the Melville Players repertory company in the late 1940s. Warner had earlier achieved success in a Saturday evening radio show *Garrison Theatre* with the catchphrase 'Mind my bike'. There is no record that Jack, himself, ever played the Palace Theatre.

Another pair of sisters were the Houston Sisters, Renee and Billie. They were Scots. Renee became the more well-known of the two. As well as being a comedienne she had a reputation as a character actor and appeared in a number of films of note including a 1944 film entitled *Two Thousand Women*. In the cast Renee Houston found herself in exceptional company, Phyllis Calvert, Patricia Roc, Flora Robson, Jean Kent, Thora Hird and Dulcie Gray.

The third pair of female comediennes were Ethel Revnell and Gracie West. They were billed as 'The Long and the Short of it' due to the disparity in their respective heights. They played the music halls for many years and established a reputation on BBC radio. They also appeared regularly as the Ugly Sisters in *Cinderella*, parts usually played by men. Revnell and West performed at the Palace Theatre on the 29th March 1926 in a revue entitled *Margate Ped'lers* which the newspaper critic regarded as the best entertainment at the Palace for a long time. Whether this show was outstandingly good or whether he considered that there had been some recent performances which, in his opinion, had been short of the mark is not made clear.

March 1926 saw the first visit to the theatre of Captain Clive Maskelyne. He was billed as the 'World Famous Illusionist'. The Maskelyne family were celebrated for their performances as illusionists. One member of the family was Nevil Maskelyne, one half of the celebrated duo Maskelyne and Devant.

In April 1926 Kate Carney made her first visit to Watford. This was in a Variety show. Miss Carney was a cockney comedienne with a wide repertoire of songs with which she delighted her audiences. Her speciality was the portrayal, mostly in song, of typical London characters.

Then in July in another Variety programme the bill was topped by the only recorded visit of one of Britain's greatest film comedians, Will Hay. He was perhaps more a comedy actor than a straightforward comedian. He was born in Stockton-on-Tees in 1888. After a successful stage career he turned to films. His two closest associates in his stage act were Graham Moffatt and Moore Marriott but in his film career they were joined by such luminaries as Charles Hawtry, who appeared in many of the *Carry On* films and who said of Will Hay that he learned more from him than from anyone else on how to play comedy. John Mills and Thora Hird also played in his films along with many other actors who went on to achieve fame. Will Hay was most famous for his performances as a schoolmaster but he also played an incompetent stationmaster and fire officer. The other side of his life was as an astronomer. He was a Fellow of the Royal Astronomical Society and delivered papers to that august body and was highly respected in that field. His garden at home was given over to an observatory. He was offered a knighthood but because his marriage was foundering he never received the accolade. He died in 1949.

During the week of the 28th August 1926 there was a production of a comedy under the title of *What Ho*. This was described as the Golden West musical revue. Horses were included, it is not stated how many but the cast included a young Hylda Baker who was well applauded as a clever comedienne. She was tiny, standing less than five feet tall. As well as being an actress she was also a music hall star in her day. In the 1950s she was part of a double act, her partner 'Cynthia' never uttering a word. Hylda Baker became famous for her catchphrase alluding to 'Cynthia' – 'She knows, you know'. Hylda Baker died in 1986 at the age of 81 having spent the last years of her life forgotten and a victim of Alzheimer's disease. There were only ten people at her funeral, truly a sad ending for a once well-known and popular television personality.

The last quarter of 1926 also saw celebrated artists performing at the Palace, including Will Fyffe, Naughton and Gold, members of the Crazy Gang, and Bransby Williams. At the start of his career Bransby Williams excelled as an impersonator of other music hall stars, including Dan Leno with whom he topped the bill at the London Palladium in 1903. Later he concentrated on portraying Dickensian characters and in this art form he is said to have lifted the quality of music hall to a higher level. With the demise of Variety his career went into a decline but was revived by the advent of television and he appeared on that medium for several years as Scrooge in *A Christmas Carol* on Christmas Eve. He died at the age of 91 in 1961.

Also in 1926, on the 25th October, Seymour Hicks presented *Broadway Jones*, with the part of 'Broadway' being played by Harry Piddock. Any claim to fame that Harry Piddock might have is that he had a vaudeville act with Charlie Chaplin before the latter went to America but, again, no evidence has been found that this act ever came to Watford. During the week after *Broadway Jones*, there was a performance by 'The Famous American Boy Star, Tom Douglas' but it would seem that he was also 'a boy wonder' as no record of who he was or what he did can be discovered today.

The week before *Broadway Jones* had witnessed a visit of *Casey's Circus*. It is another of those strange coincidences that as a child between 1903 and 1907

Charlie Chaplin had been a member of this performing company of children.

The beginning of 1927 saw a return of Henry Baynton and company in a repertoire of Restoration comedies.

Then on the 7th March, for one week, Kate Carney returned to the theatre in a programme of burlesque and comedy. Kate Carney was, at the time, one of the most popular performers on the music hall stage.

The programme for the week starting on Monday the 30th May was heralded as All Star Variety and included Jack Byfield and Albert Sandler who entertained radio listeners on Sunday evenings for many years from the 1920s with the Palm Court Orchestra broadcasting from the Grand Hotel, Eastbourne.

This was a time when the Palace Theatre enjoyed strong support from an appreciative audience. The cinema was in its infancy, television, which was to have a serious impact on the theatre later on, was still in the future and 'live' entertainment either at home around the upright piano or at the theatre was all that was available. The theatre played to full houses and on Saturdays the audiences started to queue, especially for the Gallery, before the afternoon, matinee performance had finished. Buskers did a good trade amusing the queues while they waited.

The week of the 18th July 1927 must have been received as an event not to be missed. It was heralded as 'All Star Variety Programme' and came via the Alhambra, Coliseum and Palladium theatres. The star of the show was Lily Morris, who started her career as a principal boy in pantomime. Her name was included for many years after as one of the music hall 'greats' to grace the stage of the Palace Theatre. Her name may not be overly-familiar to today's audiences, but she was certainly a star in her day, being as popular in the United States as she was in the United Kingdom. She had a big personality and it is said that she had a voice to match. Most notable about her performances was the clarity of her diction. Contemporary reports say that not a syllable of her songs was missed by her audience. Her most famous song was 'Don't Have any More Mrs. Moore'.

Later the same year Talbot O'Farrell was back in a *Gigantic Holiday Programme* and in the autumn the Sunday evening concerts once again resumed.

The same pattern of performances continued in 1928 with return visits by popular acts including Albert Whelan, Bransby Williams, the Houston Sisters and Naughton and Gold amongst others in Variety shows and revues, mixed in with productions of plays by visiting companies. It is interesting to note that on the 24th September a play entitled *The Wreckers* by Arnold Ridley

Above: *Will Fyffe*

Right: *Lily Morris*

was given. Arnold Ridley was to become a member of the BBC repertory company on radio and later was to play the part of Private Godfrey in *Dad's Army* on television. A succession of plays by Arnold Ridley was to follow in subsequent years.

A second visit to the theatre was made on the 28th May by Clive Maskelyne, with a selection of 'Maskelyne Mysteries'.

At the end of October 1928 there was a presentation of *The Demon Barber* but it did not feature Tod Slaughter, who made his name in the role of Sweeney Todd. In this production that role was filled by Bob Morris. Watford audiences had to contain their excitement and anticipation until 1932 for the arrival of Tod Slaughter at their theatre.

A play produced in November 1928, the title and description of which caught the eye, was '*Mrs. 'arris* a family affair in three tiffs'.

As ever, pantomime returned at the end of the year with *Jack and Jill* opening on Christmas Eve, followed by *Dick Whittington* on New Year's Eve and *Aladdin* on the 7th January 1929.

The Sunday concerts were in full swing as the New Year started with several visits by bands and orchestras. These included Hamilton Spencer and the New Plaza Band on the 6th January, Bainbridge Robinson and his band the following week and Haidie Rance and her orchestra on the 20th January. Jimmie Parsons and his band were at the theatre on Sunday the 27th January and by way of contrast on Sunday the 3rd February there was a concert by The Band of the London Fire Brigade and so it continued. In addition to Haidie Rance there were visits by several ladies' bands, led by Dorothy Sturdie, Evelyn Hardy and Peggy Wildon.

A series of plays from London theatres was presented during the year – *Mercenary Mary* from the London Hippodrome, an Edgar Wallace play *The Terror* from the Lyceum Theatre, *Blackmail* from the Globe Theatre, *Whispering Wires* from the Apollo Theatre, *Lost Property* from the Duke of York's Theatre, *Square Crooks* from the Prince of Wales Theatre and several more.

The terminology used is sometimes ambiguous in describing the origin of plays. In the earlier years the production may well have come directly from the theatre mentioned on its closing at that theatre and going 'on tour'. In other, later, cases it may have been an indication that the play had originally been produced at that theatre but not necessarily in the recent past, or with the same cast.

For the week beginning on the 17th June audiences were regaled by another Arnold Ridley play, probably his most famous, *The Ghost Train* which came direct from the Garrick Theatre. Two weeks later there was a play entitled *By Whose Hand* which starred the sculptor Sir Jacob Epstein's celebrated model Dolores and a fortnight later a visit by the Frank Forbes-Robertson company in *The Passing of the Third Floor Back* by Jerome K. Jerome, in which Frank Forbes-Robertson himself played the part for which he was most famous – the Stranger.

On Sunday the 10th March 1929 came the first of two visits by Harry Hemsley who was renowned as an impersonator of his own, imaginary family – Elsie, Winnie, Johnny and the baby, Horace. Horace, being the youngest, was unintelligible, giving rise to Harry Hemsley's frequently asked question of the baby's elder sibling 'What's Horace saying Elsie?' and receiving a translation from Elsie who invariably understood what her younger brother had said.

Bransby Williams was back again on Sunday the 6th October with a full supporting cast.

The programme continued during the year with a mixture of Variety, revues and plays imported from London theatres.

The Sunday evening concerts proceeded with a return of many old favourites. In January Harry Hemsley, on his second visit, was joined by Elsie and Doris Waters. Then on the 10th February 1930, Variety for a week provided by a Fred Karno company perfo...ning *Mumming Birds*. This was to be the last visit by a Fred Karno company.

On the 17th March that year there opened for a week a performance of *The Sacred Flame* by W. Somerset Maugham, with a strong West End cast led by Gladys Cooper, one of England's greatest actresses. She was appointed D.B.E. in1967 and played the role of Professor Higgins's mother in the film of *My Fair Lady*, Higgins being played by Rex Harrison. In real life she was the mother-in-law of Robert Morley. She died at Henley-on-Thames in 1971 at the age of 83.

On the 24th March the theatre received another visit by Henry Baynton and his company performing a different play each evening for a week. The programme contained *Bulldog Drummond*, the Conan Doyle play *The Speckled Band* and *The Melting Pot* by Israel Zangwill.

Three weeks later, on the 14th April 1930, a Variety programme under the title *Rogues and Vagabonds* saw the appearance of Hetty King, another male impersonator. She was a popular entertainer around the world, her most famous song being 'All the Nice Girls Love a Sailor'.

Henry Baynton was back at the Palace, this time on his own, on the 28th July to take part in one of the most famous melodramas ever written, *The Bells* by Henry Irving. By stark contrast, the following week saw a return to vaudeville, featuring Robb Wilton. Born in 1881 as Robert Wilton Smith he made his mark in monologues portraying a series of incompetent public officers. It has been suggested that one of his monologues entitled *The Home Guard* was the source of the inspiration for Jimmy Perry to write *Dad's Army*. He is still famous today for the catchphrase, delivered falteringly, which occurred in many of his monologues – 'The day war broke out'.

From the 11th to the 18th August 1930 the theatre was closed for redecorating and reseating. The remaining wooden forms in the Pit Stalls were replaced by tip-up seats, which could be booked in advance.

In October with the approach of autumn, Sunday evening entertainment returned in the shape of a mixture of musical concerts and lighter entertainment. The Western Brothers, Kenneth and George, were on the bill on Sunday the 16th November and four weeks later a welcome return of Elsie and Doris Waters. In their act the Western Brothers were a pair of 'toffs' attired in 'white tie and tails' and each sporting a monocle. In reality they were not brothers but second cousins.

During the week following this there was a visit by the Folies Bergère Revue, from Paris and the Victoria Palace, London. One assumes that with the censorship of entertainment in place at that time the Lord Chamberlain would have ensured that no infringements of the code of stage conduct or other improprieties occurred. The Lord Chamberlain at that time was the second Earl of Cromer, who was succeeded in 1938 by the sixth Earl of Clarendon, former resident at The Grove, Watford.

Only two pantomimes were presented at the end of the season; *Cinderella* commencing on the 29th December, to be followed by *Goldilocks and the Three Bears* on the 12th January. In between there took place a revue – *Happy Days*.

In 1931 another of Arnold Ridley's plays was produced, *Third Time Lucky* which was described as 'London's funniest play'. On Sunday the 29th March another popular and well-known cockney comedian, Leonard Henry, brought his 'little show' to the theatre. Not to be confused with Lenny Henry, who appeared later in the theatre's history, Leonard Henry was already established as a comedian before he came to the Palace. He made his first radio broadcast in 1926. He was diminutive, standing barely five feet tall. He was an early exponent of zany comedy and achieved notoriety by being the first man to blow a 'raspberry' on radio.

In September, the audience enjoyed the *West End Revue Company* headed by Ethel Revnell and Gracie West. Then at the end of September there was a visit by the *West End Vaudeville Company* headed by Flanagan and Allen. The *West End Vaudeville Company* made a number of visits to the theatre and it would appear that it was a blanket name for a series of shows, each one original and not related to any of the others.

It is an oft-repeated story that Bob Hope appeared on the stage of the Palace Theatre and that he was unceremoniously 'booed' off. In research for this book, no reliable evidence has been revealed to substantiate either of these facts. Indeed, it seems to be improbable. Bob Hope (real name Leslie Townes Hope) was born of an English father and Welsh mother, on the 29th May 1903, in Eltham, South London. One source suggests that he appeared at the Palace Theatre before he went to America. He was aged four years when the family emigrated to Cleveland, Ohio and his father was granted U.S. citizenship. Bob is reported to have said that he left England when he discovered he was not going to be King.

If he did perform at the Palace it must have been sometime in the 1920s or the 1930s. Today it seems quite incredulous that such a celebrated comedian in later life could have been so treated, but the fashion in comedy is subject to change and perhaps the young Bob Hope was ahead of his time.

On the other hand, Bob Hope did appear on a stage in Watford. That stage was at the Regal Cinema in King Street (now the Mecca Bingo Hall) and it happened on Thursday 1ˢᵗ July 1943. By this time Bob Hope was famous and enjoying great popularity on both sides of the Atlantic. There is no suggestion that he did not receive an enthusiastic reception on this occasion, indeed the local press recorded that as he walked to the microphone the audience nearly raised the roof. What made that appearance extra special was the fact that he brought onto the stage his 99-year-old grandfather who lived in Hitchin, Herts. Mr James Hope was just one month short of his centenary. This was the first occasion in which he had ever seen Bob, the stage personality. In fact he had never before been inside a cinema. If Bob Hope played at the theatre when in his teens or even in his twenties, did he come alone? Whether or not he was accompanied, it seems unlikely that his grandfather living but a comparatively short distance from Watford would not have made the effort to come and see his grandson perform. Certainly a long-lived family when one remembers that Bob emulated his grandfather's example and himself lived to the age of 100. At his death flags were flown at half mast and the lights on Broadway were dimmed.

Bob Hope was the most honoured entertainer in the world and in 1998 all his previous awards were capped when he was honoured with the accolade of knighthood, but, because he was no longer a citizen of the United Kingdom he could not be called 'Sir' Bob. On hearing the news of his knighthood he is reported to have said 'I'm speechless. Seventy years of ad lib material and I'm speechless'.

Did Watford really treat such a man so disrespectfully?

The Aldwych Farces by Ben Travers and originally staged at the Aldwych Theatre in London were starting to make their mark on British entertainment and in November 1931 there was a presentation of *Marry the Girl* 'a new farce from the Aldwych Theatre'. The Aldwych Theatre, it is worthy of note, was built by Seymour Hicks in 1905, three years before the Palace Theatre and twelve years before his wife, Ellaline Terriss, played at the Palace.

This production had been preceded on 26th October by a visit from *The Co-Optimists*, a sophisticated revue which included in the company two of its founder members, Phyllis Monkman and Stanley Holloway.

In 1931 productions were still being received from the West End and on the 7ᵗʰ December the audience was regaled with *My Wife's Family*, described in advance publicity as 'The Funniest Play in the World'. This play came to Watford from the Garrick Theatre.

The *West End Vaudeville Company* was back again on the 8th February 1932. The company included Elsie Bowers and Billy Rutherford who had appeared on the bill only two weeks earlier in a vaudeville programme. Elsie Bowers and Billy Rutherford were renowned in their day as vocalists with Dance Bands. They sang with the Maurice Winnick Band, one of the Big Bands which were popular in the 1930s and 1940s.

The *West End Vaudeville Company* came back again on the 4th April, and Jane Ayr and Eddie Leslie are listed as taking part together with a singing and dancing competition for contestants over the age of 15 to be judged by the audience. A relatively cheap way to fill out the programme. The final was judged at the evening performance on the Saturday. Cash prizes of £10, £6, £3 and £1 were awarded.

On the 18th April the famous John van Druten play *London Wall* came to the Palace Theatre from the Duke of York's Theatre, followed the next week by the melodrama *The Crimes of Burke and Hare* from the New Theatre, with Tod Slaughter in the cast. Tod Slaughter is remembered today as one of the earliest proponents of horror. He appeared to revel in the sordid and the play he brought to Watford was no exception depicting, as it did, the activities of the infamous grave robbers.

Almost as if seeking an antidote for what some may have considered the unsavoury nature of the previous week's offerings, the management presented a programme entitled *Springtime Cabaret* on 2nd May. The programme was headed by the world-famous Russian ballerina Lydia Kyasht, with a small corps de ballet. Also on the programme, and it may appear a trifle bizarre, was Tommy Trinder performing burlesque dances.

Ellaline Terriss

Phyllis Monkman

Yet again the *West End Vaudeville Company* was back on 16th May with the audience contributing a major part of the show. A competition was arranged of football on bicycles with a top prize of £3.

On the 6th June 1932 the Premier Denville Players arrived to take up residence at the theatre for forty-seven weeks: their manager was Conrad L. Stratford and the plays were produced by Edwin J. Collins. This visit by the Denville Players was the first time that the theatre patrons were given a foretaste of what was to come: Repertory. Alfred Denville himself was an actor/manager and an impresario.

He was no stranger to Watford. In 1886, at the age of 10, he came to Watford with his parents from the Theatre Royal, Nottingham. He attended the little Church School in the High Street, which occupied the site where 146 and 146A High Street now stand and currently the premises of a sandwich and coffee bar and a newsagent and tobacconist. In the evenings he played children's parts at the wooden theatre behind the Wheatsheaf public house at the lower end of the High Street close to Bushey Arches. This is further evidence that the wooden theatre was in existence at the end of the nineteenth century.

In 1931 he was elected Conservative Member of Parliament for Newcastle-upon-Tyne (Central). In 1925 Denville had purchased Northwood Hall, in Ducks Hill Road, Northwood in memory of his son Jack who died at the age of 26 as the result of an injury sustained on stage which reactivated a wound he sustained during the First World War. The property was renamed Denville Hall and the residents are retired members of the theatrical profession.

It was in Watford that Alfred Denville and Edgar Wallace first met.

Two members of the Denville Players were Donald Edwards and Betty Nelson who were to return later with their own company and for a period, managed the Palace Theatre.

During the time the theatre was occupied by the Denville Players a wide range of plays was presented including the *Story of the Rosary, Paddy, the Next Best Thing*, described as containing 'a thousand laughs without a single blush', *Tillie of Bloomsbury, Spring Cleaning* by Frederick Lonsdale and including the special engagement of Kim Peacock in the cast, *The Squall*, a daringly outspoken play, *The Middle Watch*, a naval comedy by Ian Hay and Stephen King-Hall (who was an officer in the Royal Navy), *Lady Windermere's Fan* by Oscar Wilde, *The Last of Mrs. Cheyney*, another Frederick Lonsdale play *The Fake, A Woman of No Importance* by Oscar Wilde (for which a programme exists in the Palace Theatre archives and is the earliest programme so far discovered), *Miss Hobbs* by Jerome K. Jerome, *A Butterfly on the Wheel* written by Ed. H. Hemmerde, K.C. and

Above: *Programme from 1932*

Above right: *The Denville Players*

Right: *Clarendon Road circa 1932*

Frances Neilson. The great play of the Divorce Court, from which we may deduce that the first-named author was a barrister specialising in divorce. *A Pair of Silk Stockings*, which was described as an 'Excruciatingly Funny Comedy'. Apparently a free pair of silk stockings was presented by Lilley and Skinner, who had a shop in the High Street, to every lady in the audience! Also included in the repertoire was *The Under Dog* – a play of Rhodesian life which included in the cast Peter Murray Hill. He was the husband of Phyllis Calvert and besides being an actor was proprietor of a specialist book shop.

A number of other plays were presented before the year ended, included among them a production in December of *A Sinner in Paradise* which was presented at the special request of a number of patrons. It was stated that it was 'A play that will make you talk for weeks.' There was also a production of the Aldwych Farce *Rookery Nook* by Ben Travers and then a dramatisation of the Charles Dickens novel *A Christmas Carol*.

There were no Sunday concerts in 1932 but they were to be reintroduced in April of the following year.

1933 opened with an entertainment 'specially produced for the delectation of the children', *Tom, Dick and Harry*, followed a week later by a comedy in three acts entitled *Come Out of the Kitchen*.

On the 6th March *Nell Gwyn* was presented. This was described as 'The fascinating romantic play, especially written for Alfred Denville'. Then on 20th March *If Four Walls Told* was produced except on the Friday evening when the programme changed for one performance only of *Jerry the Tramp*, in which Alfred Denville himself appeared in the name part.

By 1933 the Sunday evening concerts had taken on a different character. Gone were the orchestral concerts and performances by Military Bands. The Sunday evening entertainment had become lighter in content. There were still performances by Dance Bands performing the lighter style of music but the programmes had taken on much more of the Variety nature.

The season by the Premier Denville Players came to an end on 6th May 1933. Their final week consisted of *Seven Days' Leave* which played from Monday to Thursday and then on the Friday and Saturday, what was described as an uproariously funny comedy, *Facing the Music*, was presented.

The year continued with a resumption of the customary fare, but dominated by Variety and revues. Notable amongst these must have been *The Spice of Paris* for a week starting on 25th September. We are told that there were thirty-four stupendous scenes with one hundred people on stage. This is a little hard to believe given the size of the stage at the Palace Theatre and the primitive system for changing scenes in those days. Plays were still presented including *While Parents Sleep* by Anthony Kimmins, who, like Stephen King Hall, was an officer in the Royal Navy, in Kimmins's case with the rank of Commander. This was the first of eight separate productions of this play over the next twenty-four years.

On 16th October there was a visit by a *West End Revue Company* which included Jose A'Becket, described as 'Watford's phenomenal girl violinist'. It is sad that nothing about her is known today. Perhaps like so many child protégés she 'burned out'.

Later in the month was seen a production of *Fresh Fields* by Ivor Novello and later still an exotic revue entitled *Paris by Night*. Continuing in this vein, on 27th November for the week was presented *Magic Night*, described as 'A new supreme wonder Pageant with lions, monkeys, birds etc presented by the Great Carma'. *Jack and the Beanstalk* opened on Boxing Day.

1934 dawned with a production of *The Chocolate Soldier* with music by Oscar Strauss and a return to pantomime during the week of the 8th January in the shape of *Robinson Crusoe*.

At the end of January the Arthur Gibbons Popular Players arrived to present a forty-three week season of plays commencing with *Thark*, another of the Aldwych Farces by Ben Travers.

The season continued with performances of *Autumn Crocus*, *Almost a Honeymoon*, *Eight Bells* and *Hindle Wakes*. Plays by Edgar Wallace, Somerset Maugham, P.G. Wodehouse, Charles Hawtrey and others followed. Also in the programme of 1934 was a production of *Daddy Long Legs* by Jean Webster, which subsequently appeared in the guise of a musical as *Love from Judy*. It is worth recording that *East Lynne* had another outing but without the mishap which happened during its earlier performance in July 1912. An adaptation of *Bulldog Drummond* by Sapper, real name Herman Cyril McNeile, and Sir Gerald du Maurier was given in May of that year. This was a popular play in its day, based on the novel of the same name by Sapper, but time has dated it. One wonders what one section of the audience made of the play which was presented during the week of the 6th August, *Are You a Mason?*, which publicity described as 'The World Famous Farcical Comedy'.

Understandably, in 1934 while the Arthur Gibbons Popular Players were in residence at the theatre there were very few Variety shows but soon after their departure there was one such show for a week opening on 10th December. This was another appearance of the *West End Vaudeville Company* and the programme was headed by Anton (later Sir Anton) Dolin and Wendy Toye. Dolin was born Patrick Healey-Kay, his father played cricket for Hampshire. In the 1920s he had been a principal dancer for Diaghilev and in the 1940s he toured with Markova. Wendy Toye had started her career as a dancer but later turned to the theatre, acting and directing. She was destined to direct several plays and a pantomime at the Palace Theatre.

The Assistant Stage Manager at this time was one Michael Wilding. He lodged while in Watford with a Mrs. Sargent at 2 Platts Avenue, which was situated close to where J. Sainsbury's store at the top of the town stands today. The younger and then unmarried daughter of the house told Mr. Wilding that he was so lazy that he would never make anything of himself. He became, of course, a leading man in the British film industry. Among the films he made was *Spring in Park Lane* in which he played opposite Anna Neagle and was also the second husband of Elizabeth Taylor.

In January 1935 Winifred and Andrew Melville managed the theatre as the Watford Repertory Company until 4th May. Were the Melvilles 'testing the water'?

Whatever the intention of this brief visit, they must have been satisfied because they returned to take over the management of the theatre with their company The Melville Players in 1939. The association lasted until 1956. Resulting from this the Palace became, for more than a quarter of a century, a repertory theatre.

During the period the Melvilles spent at the theatre in 1935 there were no Variety or revue performances apart from the Sunday evening concerts. These concerts continued unabated on Sunday evenings and a number of leading personalities from the music hall world took part. On the 10th March the Western Brothers were in the show, two weeks later saw Bertha Wilmot on stage, a week later a return visit by Leonard Henry and then on Sunday 14th April the programme was completed with Stainless Stephen. The latter was originally a schoolmaster and so he remained until 1937 but he was already well known outside the classroom as an entertainer. His real name was Arthur Clifford Baynes. His stage name came from the fact that for his act he wore a stainless steel waistcoat. The other feature of his act was that he spoke the punctuation in his dialogue. Bertha Wilmot was a member of a large family that resided at Aller in Somerset for at least seven generations. She became Queen Ratling of the Grand Order of Lady Ratlings in 1973.

No sooner had the Melvilles departed than the programme reverted to complete weeks of Variety and revues. This was to last for two months and the Palace Theatre was host during that time to the Western Brothers, Robb Wilton, Lily Morris and Claude Dampier and Billie Carlyle. Claude Dampier and Billie Carlyle were a husband and wife team. Claude Dampier portrayed the dim witted provincial and was a popular entertainer on stage and radio. He described himself as a 'professional idiot' and would address remarks to 'Mrs. Gibson', a fictitious member of the audience.

From 15th July that year Donald Edwards and Betty Nelson took leading roles. The company was advertised as the Edward Nelson Players. As mentioned earlier they had both been members of the Denville Players company. They presented a number of plays which had been produced at the theatre before, or were to be produced again in the future; these included among others *While Parents Sleep, The Cat and the Canary, Brown Sugar, Laburnum Grove, The Passing of the Third Floor Back, Charley's Aunt* and *Grumpy*.

Betty Nelson was an outstandingly attractive young woman and she enjoyed the distinction of being photographed in 1924 by the celebrated society photographer Bassano, many of whose sitters were members of the royal families of various European countries, including the British and Russian Royal Families and members of the aristocracy of those countries. Many of his photographs are to be found in the collection of the National Portrait Gallery.

The programme for *The First Year* given during the week commencing 20th April 1936 carried the following announcement:

'THE EDWARD NELSON PLAYGOERS CIRCLE'
'Have you joined the Circle yet, if not, why not? The advantages are with you always whilst the [Edward Nelson] Players are in this theatre. For the modest sum of sixpence you are enrolled and become entitled to o n e free seat in every six that you buy. This is an aid to your making up Theatre parties. Why not make it a regular habit? Get your friends to join. Discuss the plays, players and prices. Get your friends theatre conscious. Discuss us until they are (un)conscious; Keep your own Repertory Theatre alive. Keep the players with you. Help us to make this the FIRST Repertory theatre in the South.'

This was the first recorded move to establish a supporters' club. Others were to follow.

In February 1936 the public welcomed a resumption of the Sunday evening concerts. On 23rd February, the ever popular pianist Ronald Gourley was back and shared the programme with Arthur Askey.

Stainless Stephen was on the bill again on Sunday 22nd March and on 12th April Ronald Frankau paid his first visit. Frankau was possessed of an upper-crust accent and was renowned for his repertoire of risqué songs. His accent contrasted with that of Tommy Handley (It's That Man Again) when they teamed up as Mr. Murgatroyd and Mr. Winterbottom.

The weekly entertainment, during this period, was almost exclusively plays with the occasional revue. On 27th July there was a production of *The Man from Toronto* by Douglas Murray for one week and a performance was broadcast on London Regional Radio on 16th August.

In October there were return visits on Sunday evenings by Ronald Frankau, Lily Morris, and Bertha Wilmot, in November by Stainless Stephen, Talbot O'Farrell, Albert Whelan and Arthur Askey and in December visiting Sunday artistes again included Clarkson Rose and Leonard Henry. The Sunday evening concerts were increasingly drawing the better-known entertainers.

Splinters was the show that opened 1937 at the Palace Theatre. Taking part were Hal Jones, 'Les Rouges et Noires', an all–male chorus from France and on Sunday 17th January there was another visit by Ronald Frankau who must have found considerable favour with Watford audiences to be invited back so frequently. Was it his Etonian accent or his risqué songs, one must wonder? This was followed by a week's run of *The Astonished Ostrich* and it was advertised as the farewell performance of David Shenstone as Licensee and General Manager. Presumably he held the licence for music as there was still no bar at the theatre. He was succeeded by Donald B. Edwards, who had featured in the life of the theatre with Betty Nelson the previous year. Titles of the plays performed had an attractive ring about them: *Peg O' My Heart* by J. Hartley Manners; *Winter Sunshine* by G.A. Thomas; *Sally Who?* by Dion Titheridge; *Mademoiselle* by Jacques Duval and another play with the word rosary in its title but this time simply *The Rosary* by Edward E. Ross.

Through all of this and until April the Sunday evening concerts continued. Among those who appeared was Tessie O'Shea who played a banjo and sang. She had an infectious laugh and was immensely good-humoured. Tessie was a rotund lady and rejoiced in the nickname of 'Two Ton Tessie'.

Also in the Sunday evening entertainment was Vic Oliver. He was born into an aristocratic Austrian family but his father had lost his money during the First World War. Vic Oliver himself was a serious musician, a talented pianist and violinist. It is said that he realised that his future lay in comedy when, acting as accompanist to a singer he followed her on to the stage for a vocal recital and as he sat down at the piano, the piano stool gave way under him. He went on to found the British Concert Orchestra of which he was the conductor. For some years he was in the long-running radio show *Hi, Gang!* with Ben Lyon and Bebe Daniels and, being married to Sarah Churchill, was, for a time, son–in–law of none other than Sir Winston.

Also during this season of Sunday evening concerts there was a return visit from Albert Whelan and a visit in April that year from Peggy Cochrane, a popular cabaret pianist.

Plays took on a more sinister aspect with a production of *Little Miss Bluebeard* by Avery Hopwood and on the 3rd May *The Rotters* by H.F. Maltby. It was during the run of this play that, on the 12th May, the coronation of King George VI and Queen Elizabeth took place. His Majesty's speech to the nation was broadcast throughout the theatre during the evening.

The programme of plays continued for the rest of 1937, this included *Ladies Night* by Avery Hopwood, *The Shadow* by H.F. Maltby, another play by Arnold Ridley, *Keepers of Youth*, followed by *Fallen Angels* by Noël Coward and later in the year *Devonshire Cream* by Eden Phillpotts, *Love on the Dole* by

Arthur Greenwood, *Three for Luck* by Mabel Constanduros, another production of *While Parents Sleep* by Anthony Kimmins and a repeat of Arnold Ridley's *The Ghost Train*.

The licensees of the theatre in 1937 were the New Watford Productions Ltd. The directors of the company were Kenneth Duffield (Managing Director), E.A. Gilham, O.T. Hedges, O.S. Marshall and C.E. Robinson. The chairman and secretary was A.E. Millett.

It is apparent that the theatre still employed a regular orchestra which was under the direction, at this time, of Jack Hall.

Donald Edwards continued as Director and Producer and Betty Nelson, his wife remained in the company as leading lady.

The business manager in 1937 was listed as Nora Gordon. For twenty-two years, she with her actor husband, Leonard Sharp, lived in Cassiobury Park Avenue, Watford. Nora Gordon left Watford in 1958 after the death of her husband. She occasionally took roles in productions at the Palace Theatre herself, see below. She did television work, this included *Z Cars*, the first episode of *Coronation Street* and the role of Queen Victoria in the BBC television series *Gilbert and Sullivan*.

Nora Gordon was a member of the cast of *Tell Me the Truth* which was the play selected for 1st August 1938. A twelve-page programme for this presentation exists in the collection held by Watford Museum. Half of the pages were given over to advertisements. It cost 2d, or less than 1p in modern decimal currency. Prices of admission are shown at the equivalent of 14p for the Orchestra Stalls and 10p for a seat in the Dress Circle. A seat in the Gallery was priced at 3¾ p. A further illustration of what has happened to the British currency is shown on the second page of the programme where houses on the new Durrant's Estate at Croxley Green were advertised at £665.

The storm clouds were gathering over Europe in 1938. The regular Sunday evening concerts had ceased in the previous year and were not to feature in entertainment on offer at the Palace Theatre again. For a number of years the theatre was 'dark' on Sundays but in more recent years there have been occasional, but not regular, performances by visiting entertainers on Sunday evenings.

Throughout 1938 there was a succession of plays by well-known playwrights. Among them *The Late Christopher Bean* and *Night Must Fall*, both by Emlyn Williams, a repeat of *Fresh Fields* by Ivor Novello, *Candida* by George Bernard Shaw, *Eden End* by J.B. Priestley, *The Man Who Changed His Name* by Edgar Wallace and a repeat of *London Wall* by John van Druten. One

Betty Nelson and Donald Edwards

other play is deserving of mention if only because Donald (later Sir Donald) Wolfit was in the cast. This play was *The Three Pigeons* by Anthony Armstrong and Roland Crossley. The year continued on the 1st August with *Tell Me the Truth* by Leslie Howard, *Bird in Hand* by John Drinkwater, *For the Love of Mike* by H.F. Maltby, *The Green Pack* by Edgar Wallace.

Later in the year there were presentations of *Young Woodley* by John van Druten, *Third Time Lucky* by Arnold Ridley and *Whiteoaks* by Mazo de la Roche. Described as 'a new comedy', *George and Margaret* by Gerald Savory was produced in November and was followed by *Time and the Conways* by J.B. Priestley, *Comedienne* by Ivor Novello and *Canaries Sometimes Sing* by Frederick Lonsdale.

1939 was to herald a new phase in the theatre's history. Donald Edwards was still in charge and although programmes for this period have not survived it would appear that the plays presented were of a repertory nature but with the arrival of Andrew and Winifred Melville it was on the verge of becoming a fully fledged repertory theatre with a permanent company of actors and actresses.

CHAPTER 3

Repertory
The Melville years

Although no programmes have come to light for the time that Donald Edwards was manager, it would seem that the Palace Theatre was already established as a repertory theatre but when Winifred and Andrew Melville, the husband and wife team, arrived on the scene the theatre was confirmed in that capacity and under their direction it reached new heights. They took over management of the theatre in March 1939 and it was not until 1956 that Andrew handed over management to James Perry who had joined the company a few years earlier. For three years during the Second World War, Andrew served in the Royal Navy leaving Winifred to run the theatre on her own.

There can have been very few plays in the English language that were not performed at the Palace Theatre during the twenty-six years that it operated as a repertory theatre. A new play was produced each week and while that was in performance in the evenings, during the day the play for presentation the following week was being rehearsed. On average fifty plays a year were produced making a total of some one thousand three hundred. Some of them were repeats but still had to be rehearsed, with a different cast. Winifred and Andrew had given it a try for a spell early in 1935 so they slotted easily back into the life of the Palace. They were an immensely popular and good-looking young couple and everyone wished them well. Andrew was a member of a distinguished theatrical family. He was actually Andrew Melville III, son of Andrew Melville II. His father had two brothers, Walter and Frederick. Walter and Frederick were prolific playwrights as well as actors and at different times were the owners of several theatres, both in London and in the provinces, including the Lyceum in the Strand.

It is interesting to observe that at least five generations of the family were known as Melville, whereas in reality their name was Robbins.

Winifred was known as a pantomime principal boy. She and her husband Andrew had been members of the Edward Nelson players who performed at the theatre in 1935 and they had become engaged to be married shortly before joining that company.

Prior to their arrival in 1939 several old favourites had been given another airing. The pantomime at the end of December 1938 had been an amateur production of *Aladdin*, and *Babes in the Wood* saw in the New Year. This was followed by a visiting production of *Lilac Time* with music by Schubert. *George and Margaret* by Gerald Savory returned for a second presentation, in February 1939. It had received its first performance at the Palace Theatre, Watford only three months earlier. *I Have Been Here Before* by J.B. Priestley was to follow. This was Priestley's favourite of all his plays. The great Jerome Kern, Oscar Hammerstein II musical *Show Boat* presented by Watford Operatic Society, followed. In the cast was Tom Brockless. He possessed a magnificent rich quality in his voice, although he was untrained. He sang the part of Jo made famous by Paul Robeson but Tom's voice was even lower than Robeson's and his rendering of *Ole Man River* was the high mark of the show. It is said that this song was inserted, by the writers, at the last moment to cover a noisy scene change.

The play which followed *Show Boat* was *Touch Wood* by Dodie Smith and it was the first production at the theatre under the management of Andrew and Winifred Melville.

Then came a veritable feast of dramatic fare. *For Services Rendered* by Somerset Maugham, Shaw's *Pygmalion*, *Outward Bound* by Sutton Vane and *Recipe for Murder* from the prolific pen of Arnold Ridley.

A matinee Variety show on Saturday the 8th July was given by an amateur group. This was in aid of the Thetis Fund. *Thetis* was a submarine built by Cammell Laird, which on its first dive, in Liverpool Bay on the 1st June 1939, failed to resurface. This was a disaster which touched the sympathies of the nation. All on board perished apart from four who managed to escape. *Thetis* was eventually raised, refitted and renamed *Thunderbolt*. She served in the war for just one year before she was sunk by an enemy depth charge in the Mediterranean in March 1943.

A succession of three plays followed with titles which strangely reflected the mood of the nation at that time: *The Terror* by Edgar Wallace, *Storm in a Teacup* by James Bridie (although it was anything but that) and *Arms and the Man* by George Bernard Shaw. In August *Private Lives* by Noël Coward was staged.

A month later Britain was at war. The play scheduled for performance on Monday the 4th September was *Baby Mine* but in the turmoil which existed at that time and the uncertainty of what might be about to happen, the play was postponed for one week and the theatre remained closed. That was the only week throughout the duration of the war that it was to be closed.

During the remainder of 1939 audiences were treated to another two productions of Noël Coward plays, *Hay Fever* on the 18th September and *Design for Living* on the 4th December. It was a typical repertory company programme with something for all tastes and must have had an effect on morale. *French Without Tears* by Terence Rattigan, *Goodness How Sad* by Robert Morley, *The Sport of Kings* by Ian Hay and *When We Are Married* by J.B. Priestley, among others, were presented. The Melville Players were off to a good start.

Winifred Melville was in most productions but sometimes under her maiden name of Winifred Wright; others in the company at that time were Arnold Bell, Randolph McLeod, George Selway, Hester Paton Brown, Henry Wright and Donald Finlay.

Opening on Boxing Day, the last production of 1939 was *Beauty and the Beast* by Walter and Frederick Melville, Andrew's two uncles, and it was the programme for this pantomime which famously proclaimed a fact destined to be recorded in the history of the Palace Theatre, 'The theatre is disinfected throughout with Jeyes Fluid'.

The programme in 1940 continued with a selection of well-known plays by a variety of illustrious playwrights. *While Parents Sleep* by Anthony Kimmins made a welcome return as did *Rookery Nook* by Ben Travers, *Pygmalion* made an appearance for the second successive year. *If Four Walls Told* by Edward Percy made its first reappearance since it had been presented during the visit by the Denville Premier Players in 1933. Emlyn Williams's play *A Murder Has Been Arranged* was produced and was followed by *Maid of the Mountains* presented by Watford Operatic Society. This was to be their last annual production until 1946 as most of their male membership was away on active service. In May came *The Astonished Ostrich*, no doubt surprised to be given a second outing. Dodie Smith's *Dear Octopus* preceded *Mary Rose* by J.M. Barrie. In August and September a continuous programme of Variety took place under the title of *Happy Circle* – a new song and laugh show for a summer season (a complete change of show every week).

To complete the year there were plays by Noël Coward and Ivor Novello. Daphne du Maurier's *Rebecca* was given its first performance by a repertory

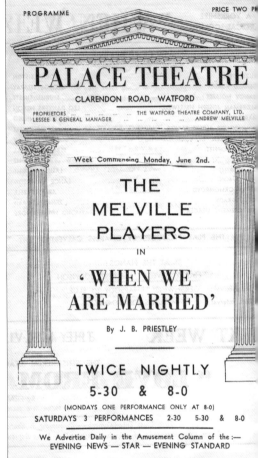

Details of prices

Programme from 1941

company. The Rattigan play *French Without Tears* was repeated as well as *The Light of Heart* by Emlyn Williams. The year ended with a production of *Queen of Hearts* by Walter and Frederick Melville.

By this time, in the interests of economy, the programme consisted of a single sheet of paper in 'quarto' size (that is slightly smaller than A4) folded in half and cost 2d.

The enemy aerial attacks on the United Kingdom which became known as 'The Battle of Britain' started on the 10th July 1940 and during the run of *Happy Circle*, in October 1940, the programme carried the following announcement:

'A.R.P Notice to our patrons

You will be notified from the stage if an air raid warning has been given during the performance. This does not necessarily mean that an air raid will take place. If you wish to leave the Theatre you are at liberty to do so, but if you must go, all we ask is that you depart quietly and without excitement. DON'T FORGET YOUR GAS MASK.'

'A.R.P.' stood for Air Raid Precautions.

It is not recorded that any performance at the theatre was interrupted and this exhortation to the audience, in the event, was scarcely needed. The Battle of Britain ceased on 31st October. However, there were still occasional bombing raids but not with the same intensity as those experienced in 1940 and it was considered advisable to make the audience aware, in as unobtrusive a way as possible, of what was happening outside the theatre so a discreet programme note in 1941, read: 'In the event of an Alert being sounded during a performance the audience will be advised by the two electrical signs either side of the orchestra.' It was not considered necessary on this occasion to give the audience the option to leave the theatre during the performance.

A senior and life-long resident of Watford recalls a performance at which he was present when the air raid warning siren was sounded. The 'All clear' had not been sounded by the end of the play and the audience were asked to remain in their seats until it was sounded. At 2.00 a.m. next morning it had still not been sounded but as there seemed to be little happening outside, the authorities relented and the audience was permitted to leave.

There is no record that the theatre sustained any damage as a result of enemy action throughout the war.

The list of plays in 1941 included the works of many well-known contemporary writers including Emlyn Williams, J.B. Priestley, Dodie Smith, Noël Coward and Ivor Novello. Several plays made welcome reappearances, amongst them, *While Parents Sleep*, *The Importance of being Earnest*, *Whiteoaks*, *Housemaster*, the last of these by Ian Hay, the great George Bernard Shaw play *Arms and the Man* and *Tony Draws a Horse* which was to have repeat performances in later years. The year finished with the pantomime *Puss in Boots*.

The following year, 1942, continued in similar fashion as did 1943. The latter year was memorable for two reasons. The programme for *The Family Upstairs* on the 17th May informed patrons that the theatre was 'under the management of Winifred Melville'. Andrew had left to serve King and

Country in the Royal Navy. Winifred was to manage the theatre by herself for three years until his return. The second event in 1943 worthy of mention was the production in October of that year of a play entitled *Men in Shadow* by Mary Hayley Bell, the wife of Sir John Mills, who was later President of the Palace Theatre for some twenty years right up until the time of his death.

In 1945 Winifred Melville engaged Billy Durrant as resident pianist in the pit at the theatre, a position he held for 16 years. He lived in Hemel Hempstead. Billy used to play the piano for silent movies. From 1930 until 1939 he was resident organist at the former Stoll Theatre, Kingsway. He led the trio at the theatre. He and Lionel Crosse (cello) were two members of the trio but the violin changed until Gae di Vito (violin) joined them. In the programme for *Clutterbuck*, dated the 5th July 1948 the violinist was Ronald Horridge and in the programme for *Trespass* of the 23rd August in the same year, the violinist is listed as Len Newman. The programme for *A Soldier for Christmas* lists for the first time the violinist as Gae di Vito.

Messrs. Durrant, Crosse and di Vito were a trio of exceptional musical ability. Billy Durrant occupied the position of musical director as well as being the pianist of the trio. Lionel Crosse studied music at the London Academy of Music before going on to the Royal Academy of Music. He established a

Lionel Crosse, Billy Durrant, Gae di Vito

reputation for himself while still a schoolboy. In 1914 he joined the army, serving in France where he was seriously wounded. He was appointed assistant music master at Eton College in 1926 where he taught for some twenty years. He played in most of the orchestras of the day and in many London theatres. He took part in more than two hundred broadcasts. Gae di Vito was Italian by birth having been born in Caserto. He played the violin in every country in Europe, including Russia before the 1914-18 war. He played in symphony orchestras under such celebrated conductors as Toscanini and Mengelberg. Surprisingly, he was also a champion swordsman and fenced for Italy in the Olympic Games.

In the late 1940s and into the 1950s the producer for the Melville Players was June Melville. She was the daughter of Frederick Melville and therefore the first cousin of Andrew. From 1939 to 1947 she was the first wife of John Le Mesurier.

On the 20th October 1947 the play was *The Missing Years* by Leslie Sands. Leslie was a member of the Melville Players. He was destined to play the part of Detective Sergeant Caleb Cluff in the 1964/65 television series *Cluff*. In this series he played a Yorkshireman, which was entirely appropriate as Sands himself was born in Bradford. Not only was Leslie Sands a member of the Melville Players but he continued, for a while, with Jimmy and Gilda Perry. He also made his mark as a playwright and several of his plays were produced at the Palace. Following *The Missing Years* in 1947, *Intent to Murder* was presented in 1954, *Beside the Seaside* in 1955 and again in 1961, *Something to Hide* in 1958 and *Basinful of the Briny* in 1960.

The programme for *Hay Fever* which played during the week commencing the 14th February 1949 contained a 'welcome back' for Winifred Wright. It has not been possible to establish the reason for her absence but it is probable that she had been unwell.

The last part she played at the Palace was in *Room for Two* by Gilbert Wakefield. This was in August of the same year, 1949. She had secured a part in *Queen Elizabeth Slept Here* at the Strand Theatre. In anticipation that she was on the verge of stage fame, she and Andrew had left their house in St. John's Road, Watford and moved back to London. Arrangements were in hand for her to play the lead in a new production coming into the West End of London. Cruelly, it was not to be. An illness, as suggested above, for which Winifred had had an operation a few months earlier, flared up again and she was rushed into the Westminster Hospital where she died from cancer of the left lung on the 12th June 1950. She was just 40 years of age.

Watford was devastated. The *Watford Observer* proclaimed that 'Undoubtedly the greatest shock ever received by Watford theatregoers came with the announcement on Tuesday of the death of Winifred Melville'. She was blessed with great beauty and much loved by her public. A Memorial Service was held at St. John's Church, Watford, conducted by Canon Reginald James. The church was crowded and many had to stand at the back as all the seats were occupied. Indeed, in theatrical terms, it could be said to have been a 'full house'.

During the service Milton Swann, a member of Watford Operatic Society, which in those days was the only amateur operatic society which performed at the theatre, sang 'God Be in My Head'. A considerable honour for the society.

In his address, Canon James said, 'For about 12 years Andrew and Winifred Melville — a very devoted pair — have made our local theatre a centre not only of great attraction but of great moral influence in our town and neighbourhood. Plays have been presented which have not only given passing pleasure but have proved that the public are grateful for the high and not low plays. The pantomimes too, have been a joy to grown-ups as well as to children and nothing vulgar or low has ever been presented. It has been hard work requiring great judgement and courage.'

The proceeds of a collection were donated to the Denville Theatrical

Winifred Wright

Retirement Home at Northwood.

But – the show must go on in spite of heartache as Pagliacci knew.

On the cover of the programme of J.B. Priestley's play *Bright Shadow* which was on stage during the week of the 19th to the 24th June 1950 only Andrew's name appeared as manager, just as Winifred's had appeared alone for three years during the war; but Winifred was not coming back

Was Andrew's heart really in it any longer? In the programme of *One Wild Oat* in March 1951, for the first time appeared the name of a young James Perry. It was not until November 1954 that his wife Gilda joined the company. That was in a play entitled *Golden Rain*.

But in 1950, Andrew's reign at the Palace was far from over and a number of exceptional productions lay ahead, and visits from celebrated actors.

In May 1951 there was a visit from the Australian comedy actor Bill Kerr to recreate the role he made in *Harvey*, the story of an imaginary giant rabbit. He was also well known for his television appearances in *Hancock's Half Hour* and many other radio and television comedy shows. He was also a serious actor and was in the cast of *The Dam Busters* and in many other feature films.

In July of the same year a play with the title *But For the Grace of God* starred A.E. Matthews. 'Matty', as he was known, was a long time resident of Bushey Heath. In 1951 he was already 82 and he died at his home in Bushey in 1960 at the age of 91. He was renowned for playing eccentric aristocrats. Almost every part he ever played was a peer, a general or at least a knight. He was to return to the Palace two months later to play the part for which he will forever be remembered, Lord Lister in *The Chiltern Hundreds* by William Douglas-Home.

In the meantime the first of several appearances was made by Jessie Matthews, who was a top musical comedy star in the 1930s. She was born into poverty in Soho, a member of a large family but she cultivated what was described as a 'cut-glass' voice with very clear diction. She had a vivacious personality and was extremely versatile. She was in the film adaptation of the Priestley's play *Good Companions* playing opposite John Gielgud. Her first visit to the Palace was in the play *Larger than Life* and she returned in November the same year for *Love in Idleness*.

Before the return of Jessie Matthews, during the week beginning the 1st October the play was *Many Happy Returns* by Roland Pertwee and Noel Streatfeild. For this play Andrew Melville pulled off an amazing coup; in the cast were two of Britain's most celebrated actresses, Helen Haye and Irene Handl.

Helen Haye must have been one of the most distinguished actresses ever to walk the stage of the Palace Theatre. She was born in 1874 and was often referred to as 'the magnificent Helen Haye'. She toured with Frank Benson and Sir Herbert Beerbohm Tree. Her film career started in 1927 and her last film role was that of the Dowager Empress of Russia in *Anastasia* in 1953. She also taught at the Royal Academy of Dramatic Art (RADA) where two of her students were John Gielgud and Charles Laughton. At the time of her appearance at the Palace she was aged 78.

Irene Handl, by contrast, was a comedy actress and appeared in many British films including the *Doctors* and *Carry On* series. She was also in the original film of *The Italian Job*. Irene Handl was 86 when she died in 1987 and was working right to the end of her life.

The year 1951 was rounded off with a repeat of *Rookery Nook* with the inimitable Ralph Lynn, who was to return in March the following year in *Is Your Honeymoon Really Necessary?*

Gerald Sim joined the repertory company in the week following *Is Your Honeymoon Really Necessary?* in a play with the title *The Duke in Darkness*.

A.E. Matthews

Gerald was to be a member of the company for an extended period. In real life his sister was Sheila Sim, now Lady (Richard) Attenborough and the mother of Michael Attenborough who was Artistic Director of the Palace in the 1980s. Gerald Sim achieved considerable fame playing character parts, frequently members of the clergy, in a range of films and television shows.

If Winifred Wright (Melville) was to be accorded the title 'First Lady of the Palace Theatre', then Gwen Watford would be a close 'Second Lady'. Both were held in high esteem and affection by Watford's theatre-going public. Neither of them achieved their proper life expectancy, their respective lives being shortened by the same dread disease.

Gwen Watford was only 25 when she made her debut on the stage of the Palace Theatre on the 21st April 1952. It was in a play entitled *Anna Christie* by Eugene O'Neill. Later in that same year, 1952, she appeared on Broadway in a play entitled *Women of Twilight*. She remained a member of the Melville Players for several plays. In 1966 she was a member of the cast of *Marriage Go Round* and later that same year she was in *The Queen and the Rebels*. Her husband Richard Bebb also took part in both of these productions.

Although the stage and television were her first preoccupations (she was named television actress of the year in 1958), she also made a career in films. If Winifred's life was cut tragically short when she was on the very threshold of fame, Gwen was spared to achieve her share of success. In the 1963 film *Cleopatra*, in which Elizabeth Taylor played the name part, opposite Richard Burton, Gwen Watford played Calpurnia. It was pure coincidence that her name was Watford and even after she left the resident repertory company at the Palace, she returned regularly in each decade up to the 1980s.

Who can tell what these two fine actresses might have achieved had they lived longer.

From 1976 and for a number of years Gwen Watford was an active member of the Council of Management of the Watford Civic Theatre Trust Limited. In 1982 she won a Laurence Olivier Theatre Award.

Her last recorded appearance at the Palace was in *Toys in the Attic* in 1985. She died in 1994.

The week after Gwen Watford's debut with the Melville Players, the play was *The Shop at Sly Corner* by Percy Edwards and Irene Handl was back in the cast.

It was not long after Gwen Watford's debut at the Palace that in 1953 Ivan Butler joined the company as resident director or, as they were known in those days, the 'producer'. He was to direct the repertory productions at the

Gwen Watford

Palace Theatre continuously up until the time it became a civic theatre. He was very much 'a man of the theatre', his various talents encompassing most facets of repertory. He was himself an actor as well as being a playwright. He shared the task of directing from time to time with another member of the resident company, Richard Dare.

The years 1953 to 1956 continued in the same vein. A typical repertory programme of plays from familiar writers performed by the, by now, firmly established repertory company under the guiding influence of Andrew Melville. For some productions a guest celebrity was included in the cast, for example, Lupino Lane, famous for playing the part of Bill Snibson, the cockney who finds himself heir to an earldom and the wealth that accompanies the title, played this part in a non-musical version of *Me and My Girl*.

Then on the 27th February 1956 the theatre received a welcome return from A.E. Matthews in *The Manor of Northstead*. This was a sequel to *The Chiltern Hundreds* and they were both by William Douglas-Home, the brother of Sir Alec Douglas-Home, the former Earl of Home who renounced his title in order to become Prime Minister. A Member of Parliament may not directly resign his seat, he can only leave the House of Commons by applying for a paid office of the Crown. Steward and bailiff of the Chiltern Hundreds or of the Manor of Northstead are both such appointments and are the procedural method by which a Member of Parliament may resign his seat.

So, on the 20th August 1956 the play presented, *Wagonload o' Monkeys* was the last under Andrew Melville's stewardship. Seventeen years of continuous management came to an end. The Melville's had kept the theatre going throughout the war and had presented plays, alternating between comedies, farces, straight drama and mysteries, much to the liking of their audiences, a total of 791 productions. It was now the turn for two established members of their company to assume control and so on to the stage, as joint managers, as had Andrew and Winifred Melville before them, strode James and Gilda Perry.

Programme of Andrew Melville's farewell production

CHAPTER 4

Repertory

The Perrys

Jimmy Perry was not a native of Watford. His early years were spent in Barnes and it was in Barnes that he was educated. His Great Uncle Tom, whom his great-nephew described as the 'black sheep of the family', owned an antique shop at 237 High Street, Watford. Jimmy's father was proprietor of a fine art shop in the Brompton Road, opposite Harrods. Shortly after the outbreak of World War II Jimmy's mother persuaded her uncle to close his shop and the Perry family moved, together with the stock from the London shop, into the premises. It was rumoured that Great-Uncle Tom had had an affair with Marie Lloyd. His family also claimed that he could 'bore for England'.

Much of Jimmy's war service, and while he was waiting to be demobilised, was spent in India. After military service Jimmy returned to Watford and enrolled for a course at the Royal Academy of Dramatic Art (RADA). For a while he worked as a Red Coat at Butlin's which was later to provide him with material for the successful television series *Hi De Hi!*

James and his wife, Gilda, took over the running of the Palace Theatre in 1956 and on the 3rd September they presented their first play, *See How They Run* by Philip King. Ivan Butler remained as director with the same company of players. The repertory company had a strong nucleus of actors which was augmented with others when required.

One of the earliest plays the new management presented was *My Wife's Family* by Fred Duprez. This was during the week beginning the 8th October 1956. Fred Duprez was an American stand-up comedian who lived immediately opposite the Perry family in Nassau Road, Barnes when Jimmy was a child.

The Perrys' years at the Palace were not to be easy and they endured a

The Perrys' first night

great deal of anxiety but during those years a number of actors who were later to make names for themselves were members of the repertory company. These included Glenda Jackson, Tom Bell, Ruth Madoc, Judy Parfitt, Julia Foster, Mavis Pugh, John Clegg, Bob Grant and Michael Knowles amongst others.

When they were not appearing in a play, Jimmy and Gilda made a practice of standing in the entrance foyer to welcome the audience. The proprietors of the theatre were still the Watford Theatre Co., Ltd. but the lessees were now James Perry Productions Limited of which company the directors were, initially, James and his wife, Gilda.

The Perrys continued the repertory tradition very much in the style of their predecessors with a different play every week but it was noticeable that the design of the theatre programme changed and on the front cover Jimmy wrote a weekly letter to the patrons, informing them of events to come and a little about the play being presented in the relevant week. Some of those letters in the years ahead were not always encouraging but they invariably contained a note of optimism.

It was in 1957, the year after the Perrys assumed management of the theatre, that Edna Pool joined the staff as Box Office Manager. She was another long-serving member of staff of the theatre, her work at the Palace continuing until 1985 when she retired. When she joined the staff, the Box Office was situated at the back of the Foyer but shortly after the theatre became a civic theatre it was re-sited nearer to the main entrance doors. It has been said that at one time the Box Office was outside the theatre. This is not so. Today when you enter the theatre through the main entrance doors you are faced with three rising steps to the level of the Foyer. At one time the three steps were outside the main doors. At some time the doors were moved forward towards the road and later the Box Office, which resembled a kiosk, was installed on the left-hand side of the doors but just inside the theatre. In the photograph taken in April 1969 what appears to be the 'kiosk' is shown on the right-hand side. This was, in fact a 'balancing' feature included to maintain the symmetry of the entrance foyer but used for storage purposes. This was never a satisfactory location for the Box Office and in 1981 it returned to its previous position in the centre of the back wall of the Foyer. There it was to remain until 2002.

1958 was to prove a memorable and active year.

That was the year that T. Rigby Taylor joined the Board of James Perry Productions Ltd and immediately his enthusiasm for and generosity towards the Palace Theatre became apparent. During the week commencing the 14th

Edna Pool

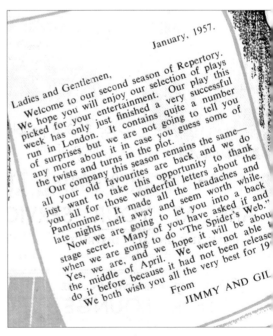

Letter on the programme cover

After the redecoration in 1958

July 1958 the theatre was closed for redecoration and new seating. During the re-seating 50 seats were removed to give patrons increased leg-room. The theatre re-opened on the 21st July 1958 with a production of *Teahouse of the August Moon.* Anna Neagle was amongst the celebrities in the audience which also included the Mayor and Watford Council lors and officials. In the programme of that production James and Gilda Perry said:

'May we welcome you to the "new" Palace Theatre. To all our regular patrons, may we hope that you will enjoy the added comfort of the new seating, as well as the beauty of the new colour scheme. And we hope that you will continue to enjoy the high standard of our plays each week.'

Another page of the same programme contained a tribute to Rigby Taylor, in the following manner:

'The fact that this week marks the turning point in the history of the

T. Rigby Taylor

Palace Theatre is due in no small measure to the help, interest and enthusiasm of Mr. T. Rigby Taylor, whose great love of the theatre has enabled the "Palace" to rank with the most beautiful in the country.'

Rigby Taylor was the proprietor of W.J. Elliott Ltd., the music shop which stood at the corner of Watford High Street and Upton Road. The building which it occupied is still named Rigby House. Elliott's was a high-class music shop selling pianos and other musical instruments as well as sheet music. Rigby Taylor himself was a prominent citizen of Watford. He was a Council lor, a J.P. and had been Mayor of Watford. In fact, it was Mr. Rigby Taylor who, during his year as Mayor, laid the foundation stone for the present Town Hall in 1937. It can be said that but for the timely intervention and substantial donations from his personal pocket the theatre would have disappeared long ago.

Another example of his generosity to the town was demonstrated, at about this time, when he saved Watford Football Club from bankruptcy.

The new décor in the theatre was celebrated by a change of colour of the programme which was now yellow and also, on the cover, displayed cartoons of theatrical characters by Osbert Lancaster.

The February 1959 edition of the magazine Theatre World in its series 'Repertory in Transition' under the title 'The Sense of Occasion' included interesting comment on the redecorated and re-seated Palace Theatre and comments by James Perry. It recorded that James and Gilda Perry had met in the Anna Neagle musical *The Glorious Days* and confirmed that it was not until Rigby Taylor joined them that they were able to finance the 1958 renovations of the theatre. The article stated that the new decoration, 'cushy' seats and thick pile carpet gave members of the audience an 'opulent sense of satisfaction'. That 'sense of satisfaction', it claimed, had increased audience attendance at the theatre by 60 per cent and that the 'luxurious atmosphere of the Palace is far in advance of the dingy surroundings of many of our local cinemas. It is, I believe, inducement enough to make the most ardent viewer leave his TV chair.'

The article went on to describe Mr. Perry's play policy as 'instructive and constructive. He will take risks to experiment. Despite the 12 new plays presented at Watford which were virtual flops, he is not discouraged. He is continuously reading new works and will try again once he considers he has found the one with the right appeal.' This is a statement which reinforces the view taken that there is nothing wrong with new works as long as they are *good* new works. Nevertheless, it calls to mind the sage words of the late, great British conductor, Sir Malcolm Sargent, when he said, 'When people say "I know what I like" they really mean "I like what I know".'

August 1958 saw the appointment of a new manager in Frank Godfrey. The character of Private Godfrey in *Dad's Army*, played by Arnold Ridley, was said to have been modelled on him.

Some time in 1958 a young man joined the company as Assistant Stage Manager. In the programme, following his appointment, he was listed as 'Rooney Bewes', the next week he appeared as 'Roney Bewes' but the following week (third time lucky!) he was correctly listed as 'Rodney Bewes'. This was the man who was to achieve fame in the long-running television sitcom *The Likely Lads* in which he starred with James Bolam. The no less successful sequel in the 1970s was *Whatever Happened to the Likely Lads*. The third member of the cast of that series as 'Thelma', the fiancée of Bob Ferris, played by Rodney Bewes, was Brigit Forsyth, who made several appearances on the stage of the Palace Theatre.

When the theatre was first built there was no provision for a bar, so the audiences used to adjourn to the Coach and Horses or other hostelries in the High Street for interval refreshment. Another event to mark 1958 as an exceptional year was that application was made for a bar licence and this was granted in March. The first bar was situated between and halfway up the two staircases from the Foyer to the Circle. There was room for no more than twenty patrons at a time in the bar. The practice was that as soon as the Interval curtain came down patrons made a dive toward the bar and having secured their refreshment they vacated the bar area, thus making way for the next wave of bar patrons, and consumed their drinks standing on the staircases outside.

Also in 1958, Gwen Watford, a regular member of the Palace repertory company, was named Television Actress of the Year, an award she received twice during her career.

In October the theatre was used to film scenes for *39 Steps*, the adaptation of the John Buchan novel starring Kenneth Moore.

The tradition of the Christmas pantomime continued and opening on Boxing Day 1958, *Robinson Crusoe*, was presented and written by James and Gilda Perry. The photograph is of Joan Lilley (left) as Polly Perkins and Helen Hurst as Robinson Crusoe. The back of the photograph is inscribed in Helen Hurst's hand 'To Nancy With my Fondest Love, from Helen'. It is probable that the autographed photograph was given, fifty years ago, to a young admirer in the audience.

In 1959 a young Judy Parfitt joined the Perry company at the theatre. She was in the cast of Noël Coward's *Present Laughter* for the week of the 2nd November 1959 and again in *Murder on Arrival* on the 23rd of the same month. She was in a number of plays at the Palace. Otherwise 1959 proved to be a difficult year. Maybe the curiosity to view the new decoration of the auditorium had been satisfied but audience attendance declined. However, the tide turned again in 1960. Audience sizes recovered and by 1960 Jimmy Perry was able to report a turn-round. Even so the theatre was in debt and further economies were unavoidable. In April the Theatre Trio left but Billy Durrant, the pianist, returned on his own in May. To pay off some of the theatre's debts a fund-raising Midnight Matinee was organised at the Town Hall. It was a star-studied cast including Jon Pertwee, Beryl Reid, Terry Scott, Jessie Matthews and Frank Williams. Tickets for the event were priced at today's equivalent of 25p to £2.10p. The financial result, however, was disappointing.

Alderman E.C. Amey and Alderman L.C. Johnson joined the Board of the company in June 1960.

In 1961 a play entitled *The Substitute* by Frank Williams was given. Frank Williams had been a regular member of the audience for some fifteen years as well as frequently taking part in Palace Theatre productions. The theme of this play was the crucifixion but the character of Jesus was not included. Gilda Perry played Mary Magdalene. It may seem appropriate that a few years later Frank Williams was to play the part of the vicar in *Dad's Army*.

Left: *Robinson Crusoe 1958*

Above: *Jimmy Perry and Judy Parfitt*

During the time in which the theatre was under the management of the Perrys the audience revealed a taste for thrillers and their appetite was satisfied by many such plays by Agatha Christie and others providing a generous helping of murder mystery plays.

Billy Durrant finally vacated the pit at the theatre in March 1962 and his place was taken by Sidney Cooke. He was a frequent broadcaster, for three years he had played with the celebrated violinist Alfredo Campoli, who combined jazz music with the more serious variety. Sidney Cooke was also a soloist to be heard at both the Royal Albert Hall and at the Royal Festival Hall.

A small fire broke out in one of the dressing rooms in May of that year. There were no casualties, the theatre at the time was not occupied by an audience and no great damage was caused but the audience, when it arrived for the performance that evening, was assailed by a smell of burning.

Beatrix Carter joined the company in 1962. She was the daughter of William Carter who from 1884 to 1914 was Headmaster of Watford Boys' Endowed School which has today evolved into Watford Grammar School for

Boys. She was to remain a member of the company for some years.

Another actress to join the Perrys' repertory company in 1962 was Glenda Jackson. Her stage debut had been in 1957. At the time she joined the Palace Theatre company she was married to Roy Hodges who was assistant stage manager at the Palace. Glenda Jackson was born in Birkenhead and trained at the Royal Academy of Dramatic Art. She started her film career in 1963 as a member of the cast of *This Sporting Life*. In 1969 she won an Oscar for her part in *Women in Love* and a second Oscar followed four years later for *A Touch of Class*. She was awarded the C.B.E. in 1978. Her acting career came to an end when in 1992 she was elected to Parliament as Labour M.P. for Hampstead and Highgate. After the 1997 General Election she was appointed a junior minister with responsibility for transport in London. Some years later Jimmy Perry was to say 'Little did I know I was performing love scenes with the future Minister of Transport.'

Diane Holland was also in the repertory company at the Palace Theatre

Poster from 1961

in 1962 and found herself subsequently cast in *Hi-De-Hi!*, another of the Jimmy Perry television series, as Yvonne Stuart-Hargreaves, the upper-crust, in her opinion, dancing instructor at the holiday camp. Diane Holland was the sister of Gilda Perry and so was Jimmy's sister-in-law.

Financial pressures called for the necessity to hold bingo sessions in the theatre, on Wednesday afternoons at 3.00 p.m. and on Sunday evenings at 7.00 p.m. These sessions ran from the 14th May until the 8th October 1962.

1963 was another bad year from a financial aspect. Bingo sessions were revived and on alternate Monday evenings wrestling took place. Eventually it became necessary to close the theatre for six weeks. In the programme for *Policy for Murder* which played during the week commencing 10th June, James and Gilda Perry wrote:

'Dear Patrons,

As you will all have read in the papers, it is with regret that we have to close down for six weeks from Monday June 14th. Our losses have been so heavy during the past three months that we find it just impossible to continue. We would like to point out that this is only a temporary measure, and we shall be REOPENING ON AUGUST BANK HOLIDAY, AUGUST 5th. We would like to thank all our patrons for being so loyal in their support, and we hope you will enjoy our last two plays, and we look forward to seeing you all from August onwards in force.

Sincerely yours, Jimmy and Gilda.'

This somewhat draconian decision seems to have had an effect because Richard Dare was able to refer in the programme for *Semi-detached* on the 3rd September to the 'so much enlarged audience since re-opening'. The people of Watford and surrounding district had received a shock in the form of a realisation that the theatre's future was by no means secure. People liked to know that the theatre was there but were hesitant to support it by attending.

The improved situation did not last and, despite the repertoire on offer, audiences declined once again in 1964. The events of that fateful year were recalled by John How. In an article written in October 1987 in the *West Herts and Watford Observer*, he wrote that there existed, in 1964, a very real fear that the theatre would close. Strenuous efforts to preserve the theatre were made by actors who had appeared on its stage. Another distinguished actress to lend her support was Margaret Rutherford, who lived nearby at Chalfont St. Peter in Buckinghamshire and who had just completed the filming of scenes at the theatre for the Agatha Christie film *Murder Most Foul*. On the 17th January, three directors of the theatre, James and Gilda Perry and T. Rigby Taylor attended a private meeting with a sub-committee of Watford Borough Council, chaired by Alderman E.C. (Ted) Amey. This was an exploratory meeting to discuss the possibility of the lease of the Palace Theatre being taken over by the Council which would run it as a civic theatre.

Regular discussions took place over a period of four months and then on Monday the 27th April 1964 the matter was debated by the full Council. Alderman Amey, as chairman of the Council's Finance Committee, recommended that the Council should take over the responsibility of running the theatre. Terms offered by the Council to James Perry Productions Ltd. were: £4,500 for the unexpired portion of their lease and a refund of the money James and Gilda had spent renovating the flat in which they lived, provided they vacated it within eighteen months. An amendment to the proposal, that no further action be taken in the matter, was proposed by Councillor W.T. Osgathorp. The basis of his argument was that by not attending the theatre, the people of Watford had indicated that they did not want a live theatre. He was emphatic that he was not against a civic theatre in principle but that it had to come at the right time and in the right place which, he contended, was with the central area redevelopment. Later he said that the Council had committed itself to provide the town with a swimming pool at Woodside and added: 'That will give a lot more pleasure and entertainment to a lot more people than that shack down there will.' He was dismissive that the Palace Theatre would simply become a white elephant. In contrary vein, a letter from Margaret Rutherford was read by Alderman Amey, pleading for the survival of 'this darling little theatre', a distinct contrast to the wording used by Councillor Osgathorp during the same debate. Councillor R.S. Horner spoke against the amendment and added that he did not support the sub-committee's report because he considered that the proposals put forward were going to react very unfavourably against the Perrys and he urged that they be reconsidered. He disagreed that the Palace had been mismanaged, as had been suggested by Councillor Osgathorp but thought that the Perrys had done 'a very good job'. Defending the Perrys further he said, 'It does appear that the Perrys haven't been properly consulted on this matter. Their co-operation hasn't been sought by the sub-committee. Right from the start the sub-committee have had it in mind that all we have to do is chuck the

Perrys out and run the theatre ourselves.'

Councillor Miss Doris Scawen suggested that 'live' theatre was more 'human' than television or radio and her following remarks turned out to be a portent of what was to happen some forty years later when she said that the facilities at the Palace Theatre did not measure up to what was expected by the artistes who appeared in it. She went on to say that what was needed was a smaller more modernly-equipped theatre and that support for the Palace was just a matter of throwing money away, adding that 'it in no way lived up to modern standards required for a theatre.'

Alderman Lodder maintained that although he would like to see live theatre continuing in Watford there was no possibility of that happening without the support of Watford and its environs. He went on to predict that as well as the £4,500 payable to James Perry Productions Ltd. a lot more money would be needed for decoration and a full year's running costs. He estimated a total cost of £15,000. Because many people from Watford travelled to London for their theatrical entertainment, he anticipated that the Palace Theatre would stand empty until September 1965, except for the annual pantomime. This would mean a deficit of £175,000. Alderman Lodder asked whether the Council was prepared to saddle the ratepayers with that sort of liability.

In his turn Alderman Buckingham pleaded, 'Not too much about the Perrys.' He said that critical observations about the Perrys could be made, for example, were they trying to force down the throats of people things they did not want? Even so, there should be room in the town for a live theatre and there was no reason why it should not be continued. He believed that a new theatre should be 'part and parcel' of the town centre. He was sure that the time would come when people would be pleased to see live actors but not the same things and the same faces. In other words he was forecasting the demise of repertory.

His words were to prove prophetic. Television was affecting live theatre in the mid-1960s to a serious degree.

This had been building for some years. Television transmission from Alexandra Palace had recommenced in 1946 for the London Victory Parade. Reception was almost exclusively restricted to the London area and Home Counties but it expanded to other parts of the country with the opening of additional transmitters. Television sets at this time were relatively expensive. Not every household possessed one. Even so, by the time of the Coronation in 1953 they were more widely owned and had become almost a necessity when commercial television was introduced in 1955. Cinemas were the first to suffer from the increasing popularity of television and it is estimated that around 2,000 closed between the years 1950 and 1963, most of them being demolished, but many provincial theatres, too, went out of existence. The public when seeking entertainment preferred the 'box' in the corner of the room rather than endure the inconvenience, particular when the weather was inclement, of making the journey to a cinema or theatre and then home again after the performance.

Theatres were able to withstand the onslaught of television but even they suffered and it is said that in 1963 only about 3 per cent of the population ever attended a professional theatre. Television had arrived as the mass form of visual entertainment. With the advent of colour television and the proliferation of channels the problem did not become easier. It is perhaps ironic that television was to make Jimmy Perry's fame and fortune in the years to come as a comedy writer of series such as *It Ain't Half Hot Mum*, *You Rang M'Lord?*, *Hi-De-Hi!* and, of course, *Dad's Army* amongst others.

At this point in the debate Alderman Haines came to the rescue saying that the Council spent very little on music, drama and the arts but no one seemed to mind spending a lot on sport. Whilst he would support the building of a civic theatre, he believed that a cheaper alternative was to take over the Palace.

One Councillor who was a life-time supporter of the theatre and who over the ensuing years was to play a significant role in its progress, survival and, forty years later, in its reconstruction, a youthful Councillor Norman Tyrwhitt proclaimed that 'It would be a tragedy for Watford and Hertfordshire' not to have a live theatre, making the further point that use of the Town Hall, the Park and Woodside Tavern was not stopped because they were not 100 per cent utilised.

Alderman L.C. Johnson contributed to the debate by drawing attention to the fact that the Council already subsidised unprofitable enterprises, mostly in the realms of sport, adding the telling point that over twelve months the theatre catered for more people than did the Council's lawn tennis courts, bowling greens etc.

'Why' he asked, 'do we want to bring a sledgehammer down on the Palace Theatre and its work for the community? Why must it be singled out for death?' Warming to his theme he continued, 'The place to continue a live theatre is in the Palace Theatre, for a period. If you do want a theatre, support this as the best possible in all the circumstances.'

Councillor W.G. Greer took a different view, saying, 'We must make the best use of our shortage of land.' He advocated the building of a new school of music alongside a small concert hall seating 200 to 300 people accessible to all societies and available for pantomime.

To warm applause Alderman H. Horwood rose to deliver his 'swan song'. He insisted that Watford people *did* want a live theatre. TV, he maintained, could not compete with a civic theatre and he firmly believed that live theatre would come back into its own. How correct he was to prove.

Winding up the debate, Alderman Amey informed members that Chelmsford civic theatre with a marginally greater audience capacity made a profit each year. It did not rely on bingo or wrestling to achieve this and catered for amateur operatic and dramatic societies. Land and building costs of a new theatre in the centre of the town would be expensive.

What the Council had to decide, said Alderman Amey, was whether to get a theatre on the cheap for £4,500 and carry on with the Palace for seven years. He acknowledged that the stage was too small and amenities lacking. Echoing the words of Alderman Johnson he repeated that far more people went to the Palace Theatre each year than went to local sporting events, 'Yet we don't complain about keeping sporting facilities for a very small minority.' Alderman Amey, as the finance chairman, concluded by saying, in ringing tones, 'We feel that this is something which is vital to the life of this town. We said there should be a break clause to enable us to build a civic theatre but that is not now.'

The amendment was defeated by 26 votes to 9.

At this time the Perrys were living in a flat over the store in Watford House Lane, just opposite the theatre on the other side of Clarendon Road. At a Press Conference called by Jimmy 24 hours after the announcement of the terms, he said that he and his wife had incurred considerable loss in running the theatre for Watford. He emphasised that they both had a considerable interest in the theatre and wanted to see repertory continue. They had not asked for repayment of all their expenses, they had not pressed for £1,000 to which they felt they were entitled, instead, they had asked for two concessions. One was to be permitted to run bingo sessions once a week for two years and the other that they should be allowed to run the annual pantomime for five years. The Council refused to grant these two concessions. In justification for what they asked, Jimmy said that they had invested their own capital in the theatre and this amounted to some £7,500 and that rising costs were crippling them. He declared that they could not, therefore, accept the Council's offer. This at the time appeared to be a 'sentence of execution'. It seemed that the Palace Theatre, the only 'live' theatre in Hertfordshire was doomed. The outlook was bleak.

A month later, on Monday the 29th May, the Council met again to consider the fate of the theatre. Fresh terms were offered to James Perry Productions Ltd. These were:

- A sum of £4,500 to be paid to James Perry Productions Ltd. in consideration of the transfer to the corporation of the theatre and stores together with all fixtures and fittings, scenery, tools and other equipment;
- It was also agreed to pay £500 to Mr. and Mrs. Perry on their vacating the flat above the store which they would be permitted to occupy as tenants for not more than twelve months after the take-over;
- In consideration of James Perry Productions Ltd. continuing to operate the theatre until 28th February next the corporation would pay £1,760, this representing the loss likely to be incurred by repertory between 3rd August and 21st November of that year;
- The agreement also stipulated that James Perry Productions Ltd. should be engaged to present the Christmas 1965 pantomime, if they so desired;
- Implementation of the terms was subject to agreement between the Council and the freeholders of the theatre in regard to the terms of a new lease of the theatre.

Councillor B.G. Yorke made a last ditch stand in an effort to persuade the majority that the terms were not in the best interests of the town from a financial point of view. He re-affirmed that he was not opposed to a civic theatre in the town but that he did object to it being housed in the existing building. His requirement was for a smaller, more modern building and a new one designed for the purpose would, in his view, be ideal. He sounded the warning that taking into account possible losses, repairs and maintenance and salaries and amounts to be paid over to James Perry Productions Ltd. the theatre would by 1980 have cost the Council £200,000.

'From every aspect of good government,' said Councillor Yorke, 'it is our duty to let this opportunity go by and plan something of substance and modern for the young people interested in the live theatre.' He then moved that the recommendation be not approved.

Councillor J.S. Horner said that it was 'Nonsense' to suggest that a smaller theatre was needed. The amateur operatic societies would be unable to stage their more lavish productions in a smaller theatre.

Alderman Amey did not agree with the figure for a deficit which had been quoted and contended that if the theatre was run properly a loss was not inevitable and he pointed out that a civic theatre with a smaller seating capacity would be more difficult to run profitably. He concluded by saying,

'I said at the last Council meeting I thought we were getting a civic theatre on the cheap – and we are,' adding 'I don't think we shall make a profit but I think any loss can be kept much smaller than we are told tonight.'

Put to the vote, Councillor Yorke's amendment was defeated, only four voting in favour.

Councillor Horner's remark that the amateur societies would not be able to present their shows in a smaller theatre was to come to mind when the last production at the Palace Theatre before it became a civic theatre on the 1st March 1965 was a week of performances of Ivor Novello's *King's Rhapsody* by Watford Operatic Society.

The theatre had been saved for the enjoyment of future generations.

Besides Norman Tyrwhitt, mentioned above, Ted Amey earned the respect and gratitude of the town and district for the fact that we still have a live and flourishing theatre in Watford today. Indeed still the only live theatre in the whole of Hertfordshire.

The story of its eventual reconstruction will be told in a later chapter.

The news was broken to the audience at the theatre on the very evening that the momentous decision was made in the Council Chamber at the Town Hall. Jimmy Perry stepped onto the stage as the cast were taking their fourth curtain call at the end of *Mary, Mary*. Understandably, his voice was shaking with emotion, as he said, 'This was to have been a sad occasion, but I am glad to be able to tell you that the Council met tonight and have decided to take over the theatre.'

A sigh of relief is said to have swept through the theatre and the audience burst into applause. The Palace Theatre was reprieved, at least for the time being.

Jimmy added, 'This is wonderful for the theatre, if a little sad for Gilda and I. But we would like to thank you for your letters and good wishes.'

Another sadness marked 1964. It was on 31st January 1964 that Richard Dare, a member of the repertory company and deputy producer, who had been suffering from pneumonia for some eighteen days, collapsed and died at his home in Chalfont St. Giles. He was only 41. He had been at the Palace for four years but had made appearances in films and on television during his time at the theatre.

Although he had been involved with the activities of the Palace Theatre for only a comparatively short time, Richard Dare had been a much admired member of the Perrys' company and on several occasions had stood in for Ivan Butler as producer. His sudden death, at such an early age, affected many people and it was decided to erect a plaque as a tribute to his memory. It read:

A TRIBUTE TO
RICHARD DARE
WHO ACTED AND PRODUCED
IN THIS THEATRE
1959-1963
GREATLY MISSED BY HIS FELLOW ARTISTES
AND THE PUBLIC

Mary, Mary ended its run on Saturday 31ˢᵗ May and it was announced that Jimmy Jacobs, proprietor of the Gargoyle Night Club in London was to rent the theatre for four weeks in June (Thursdays and Fridays only) to present programmes of Variety. The Saturday evenings were given over to wrestling and the theatre remained 'dark' for the rest of the week. In fact Mr. Jacobs stayed at the theatre for only two weeks and during that time the Palace set a record of which no theatre would be proud. During the second week, one of the 'turns' was a belly-dancer by the name of Zhalita, at least that was her 'stage-name'. In the programme she was listed as Lhalita. She hailed from Mauritius. There were two 'houses', at 6.45 and again at 7.30. At the first 'house' on the Friday night she declined to leave her dressing room and refused to appear on stage because her name had been spelt incorrectly in the programme and also she felt that her act had not been presented as she wished. On that Friday evening the audience consisted of two paying patrons. It seems that the performance was abandoned and the second 'house' cancelled. The title of the show was *Soho Comes to Town*.

The unfortunate Mr. Jacobs decided to cut his losses, *Soho* returned to London and the theatre remained 'dark' until the official re-opening on the

3rd August. His parting shot was that his losses meant that he had invested over £1,000 pounds in Watford, a town which, in his words, did not appreciate 'culture'.

The Perrys maintained their custom of including on the front of each programme a letter addressed to patrons. The letter on the cover of the programme for *Black Coffee* which played in the week commencing 16th November 1964 was especially poignant as it was in effect their farewell to Watford.

'Dear Patrons,

This is a very sad week for us as it is our last Repertory production here at the Palace, during the past eight and a half years we have produced over three hundred plays, eight pantomimes, eight musical productions, and various odd shows. We would like to thank all our friends, you the Patrons for all your support over the years. It has been a hard struggle at times to keep going and as you know several times during the past few years the theatre has been in danger of closing, however we can now safely say that the theatre is no longer in any danger of closing. One person to whom we owe a great deal is Mr. T. Rigby Taylor, whose timely intervention saved the theatre on two occasions.

To all those of you who gave towards the Richard Dare memorial plaque [we] hope to have it erected very soon, so watch for the date in Jack Point's column in the *Watford Observer*.

Finally we should like to wish the new civic theatre every success, and we hope that the future will prove that Watford does really want a live theatre.

Yours sincerely,
GILDA and JIMMY PERRY'

Within three years after leaving the theatre Jimmy Perry was carving out for himself a new career, one which was to establish his reputation as a comedy script writer and secure his future. The television programme with which he will always be associated as a highly successful and ever popular series was *Dad's Army*, the subject of which was the Home Guard during the Second World War, at the fictitious town on the south coast named Walmington-on-Sea. In the feature film of *Dad's Army* the external shots of Walmington-on-Sea were actually filmed at Watford's neighbouring village of Chalfont St. Giles, by strange coincidence the home of Richard Dare, or *was*

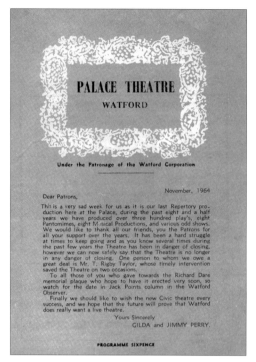

Programme of the last rep play

it a coincidence? For the television series Walmingon-on-Sea was actually Thetford in Norfolk. Jimmy Perry has said that the whole series was based on fact. He had himself been a member of the Home Guard in Watford before he was called up for military service in the Second World War. Many of the characters were based around personalities in Watford or at least were named after them. As already mentioned, Private Godfrey, played by Arnold Ridley was based on Mr. Godfrey, the secretary and bookkeeper at the Palace Theatre. The town clerk of Walmington-on-Sea was named Mr. Gordon. He was named after Gordon Hall who was in reality town clerk of Watford but there was no resemblance between the fictitious and the real town clerk. Another significant inclusion was the recognition of the part played by T. Rigby Taylor in preserving the theatre in Watford and as stated earlier, the proprietor of Elliotts the music shop in Watford High Street. In one episode of *Dad's Army* when Captain Mainwaring wants a radio set he says, 'Go down to Elliott's in the High Street'.

The theatre ended its life under private management on Saturday, 27th February 1965. It was to spend the next thirty-one years as a civic theatre before re-emerging under private management once again in 1996.

CHAPTER 5

Watford Civic Theatre Trust

The Watford Civic Theatre Trust Ltd was incorporated on the 4th January 1965 and took over the management of the theatre on the 1st March 1965. It was a company limited by guarantee and not having a share capital. The members of the first Council of Management, as it was styled, were Alderman E.C. Amey (chairman), Aldermen A.G. Dillingham and H.W.C. Lodder, Councillors R.J. Caton, R.S. Horner, J.S. Oliver, P.W. Roe, N.H. Tyrwhitt and P.A. Wilson with Michael Codron, Pieter Rogers and Dr. C.M.H. Rotman. The secretary was Gordon Hall, as Town Clerk of Watford.

The theatre remained closed for a month and re-opened on the 30th March with a presentation of the Jules Verne masterpiece *Around the World in 80 Days*.

Regular members of the company, who had been members of the repertory company run by James and Gilda Perry, when the theatre became a civic theatre included Jane Lowe, Ian White, Marina McConnell, Norah Nimmo, Jeremy Van Bunnens, Alan Knight, Frances Colyer, Heather Canning, Ray Lonnen, William Simons, Kevin Lindsay, Elizabeth Alys and others who made less regular appearances.

The first artistic director for the civic theatre was Giles Havergal. His actual title was 'General Manager and Director of Productions'. His successors were given various titles until the position became generally known as 'Artistic Director'. One of the first noticeable changes to take place was that plays ran for two weeks instead of just one week as previously. Until August 1966, Giles Havergal continued the Perrys' practice of including in the programme a letter to the patrons. This invariably contained a snippet about the play or the actors taking part. Sometimes there were items of interest about what was going on or planned at the theatre. One welcome piece of news was that audience sizes were on the increase.

In the programme for *Reluctant Debutante* by William Douglas-Home in June 1965, he wrote 'This week's sophisticated comedy is, I hope, a happy example of good plays which stand revival many times. Many people who come to the theatre, like to be assured of the sort of entertainment they will get and nothing gives this assurance like a well-known title.'

For two weeks starting on the 11th May 1965, caution was thrown to the wind and the Shakespearean play which is referred to in the theatre as the 'Scottish Play', for reasons of superstition but which, as the superstition does not apply to the written word, can be revealed as *Macbeth*, was produced. This was a memorable production for two reasons. The first is that it was the first time the theatre had produced its own Shakespearean play. All previous performances of Shakespeare had been by visiting companies. The second reason was that the performance on Wednesday 19th May 1965 was attended by H.R.H. The Princess Margaret and the Earl of Snowdon in an informal capacity. This was the only occasion, to date, that royalty has visited the theatre.

In 1966 an extension of the stage, in the form of an 'apron', was constructed over the orchestra pit. For productions which required use of the pit, part, or all, of the apron could be removed. When the pit was not required the size of the stage was increased by the apron.

A considerable coup was achieved in 1966. In July of that year Tennessee Williams's great play *The Glass Menagerie* was presented and to play the part of Amanda Wingfield, the irritating and oppressive mother, Giles Havergal secured Bessie Love, one of the Hollywood legends dating from the era of silent movies. She was a Texan by birth and her original name was Juanita Horton. Bessie Love had not intended making a career of acting but she met the Movie Director D.W. Griffiths, for whom Chaplin had also worked, and he, struck by her prettiness, in 1915 offered her a part in *The Birth of a Nation*, the film on which he was currently working, and she accepted. This led to a long and successful career. She was diminutive, being only five feet tall and of a slight build. In 1935 she left Hollywood and moved to the United Kingdom where she maintained her main residence until the end of her life apart from a return to the United States during World War II where she worked for the Red Cross. She died in London in 1986 at the age of 87.

1966 also was the year in which John Savident made the first of several visits to the theatre. One of the most well-known faces on British television, he became famous for his portrayal of the butcher, Fred Elliott, in *Coronation Street* which he played for thirteen years. Prior to becoming a full-time professional actor, John Savident had been a policeman. His first appearance in Watford was in the cast of *Entertaining Mr. Sloane* by Joe Orton in September of that year. He returned on a further six separate occasions: *Sweet Bird of Youth* by Tennessee Williams in November 1968; *The Homecoming* in February 1969; *Romeo and Juliet* in March 1972; *The Erpingham Camp* in April 1972; *A Patriot for Me* in December 1973 and *The Merchant of Venice* in February 1976.

1967 was an eventful year in the story of the Palace Theatre. On the 4th April Patricia Burke was a member of the cast of *The Killing of Sister George*. The play which followed included Brigit Forsyth, who played Jane Eyre, the narrator, in an adaptation of Charlotte Bronte's novel *Jane Eyre*. She was required, for much of the action, to sit at the side of the stage. She encountered great difficulty suppressing her giggles and only succeeded by pressing the fingernails of one hand into the back of the other. This was Brigit's first appearance at the theatre. More were to follow. Also in the cast of *Jane Eyre* was a young Liz Gebhardt who was to go on to play Maureen Bullock in *Please, Sir*.

The following month a newly graduated Maureen Lipman made her stage debut in a play entitled *The Knack* at the Palace Theatre. In September she returned as a member of the cast of *Wuthering Heights*. From here it took her little time to gain recognition for the talents she possessed. She was to appear in several of the theatre's subsequent productions, including *Aladdin*, the pantomime selected for 1967 the cast of which also included Amanda Barrie. Even today Maureen Lipman maintains a close interest in the Palace Theatre.

Bessie Love   *John Savident*

Brigit Forsyth   *Mareen Lipman*

Later in 1967 the theatre closed again, this time from 12th June for six weeks, for redecoration. At the same time a new lighting board was installed, paid for by a grant from the Arts Council of Great Britain. The style of redecoration was more in the Regency style than Edwardian but fifteen years later a further redecoration restored the authenticity of the theatre's age. The theatre re-opened on the 25th July with a production of *A Country Wife* by William Wycherley. In the cast was Anthony Booth, the father of Cherie Blair, wife of the former Prime Minister. By coincidence the theatre re-opened after the major re-building programme in 2004 with a modern adaptation of the same play.

Irma la Douce, which opened at the Palace on the 22nd August 1967, had Lynda Baron in the cast, who is probably best known for her role as Nurse Gladys Emanuel in the Ronnie Barker television series *Open All Hours*.

Giles Havergal, in addition to having the apparent ability to recognise talent in young aspiring actresses, seems to have developed a knack for attracting to the Palace celebrated American actresses who had taken up residence in England. In 1967 it was the turn of Constance Cummings. The play was *Dance with a Dolly* and it played from the 10th to the 21st October. Constance Cummings was born in 1910 in Seattle, Washington. She made a number of films in Hollywood but was never entirely satisfied with the roles she was offered or her performances in them. Her beauty stood in the way of her playing many of the roles she would have enjoyed. In 1933 she married the English playwright, Benn W. Levy who was to be elected Labour M.P. for Eton and Slough in the Attlee government of post-war Britain. Their marriage lasted until Levy's death in 1973. It was reported that Constance Cummings was offered a life-peerage but although she had lived in the United Kingdom for most of her life she never renounced her American citizenship and so was not eligible to accept the honour. Constance Cummings established herself as a theatrical actress, appearing in many West End productions but if she was not playing in London she was happy to go out into the provinces and did so on many occasions.

Another event of note, in 1967, was an 'in-house' production of *Merchant of Venice* in which Celia Bannerman played Portia. This play was succeeded, on the 21ˢᵗ November, by *The Waiters* which included in its cast Patricia Burke and Frank Williams.

While at the Palace, in November 1968 Giles Havergal directed the British professional premiere of Tennessee Williams's play *Sweet Bird of Youth*. The play had been produced previously in Manchester by an amateur group – The Experimental Theatre Club. Bessie Love made a welcome return to the Palace playing the part of Aunt Nonnie.

Giles Havergal left the Palace Theatre in 1969 to take up an appointment as Artistic Director of the Citizens Theatre, Glasgow. Rumours were circulating, once again, that the Palace Theatre was on the point of closure. At what he described as his 'farewell performance' Giles Havergal roundly dismissed these rumours as 'just not true' but he suggested that the Palace patrons' club should press for a new theatre for the town. He warned that the lease of the Palace was approaching its end and that the freeholders would want to use the site for alternative purposes. 'You are going to be thrown out of this theatre,' he warned, 'because it doesn't belong to you.' He urged the public to join in the spearhead moves for a new theatre.

Perhaps his words were taken to heart because shortly afterwards in the 1970s the proposition was considered to demolish the existing theatre and build a new one on a vacant site at the top of the town behind Monmouth House. This site was given the 'code name' of the Monmouth Arms. Although this name seems to imply that it was occupied by a hostelry, this is not so. This proposal was speedily abandoned because the demolition of the Edwardian theatre would not have been popular; particularly, it was felt, with the people of Watford, especially those who regularly attended performances. Eventually the Monmouth Arms site was acquired by J. Sainsbury and the present Sainsbury's supermarket was built.

Happily for the theatre, events, which were not predictable at that time, moved on, so that by 1982 the theatre did belong to 'us'; moreover, it had become a Grade II Listed building and by 2004 it became a 'new' theatre, or at least a substantially rebuilt one.

A replacement for Giles Havergal as Artistic Director took a little time finding and for most of 1970 Kay Gardner, with the title either of 'Theatre Director' or 'General Manager', held the fort. Kay resigned in July 1971 after a disagreement over a matter of policy with the Council of Management of the civic theatre Trust.

It was during Kay Gardner's time at the helm that a play by Charles Dyer with the title *Staircase* was produced. Playing the part of Charles was James Beck who was making a name for himself on television as Private Joe Walker, the spiv character in *Dad's Army*. This was in September 1969.

The vacant post of Artistic Director was advertised in 1971 and Stephen Hollis was appointed. He was a former advertising agency man who had worked as Assistant Director with Giles Havergal. It was a gamble appointing a man without experience but it worked. Stephen Hollis remained in post for eight years.

Financial troubles continued to plague the theatre and following a change of political control at the Town Hall, the theatre was closed for twenty-one weeks from early June and the planned programme of plays during the autumn of 1971 was abandoned. It re-opened on the 8th November with *Paint Your* Wagon presented by Cassio Operatic Society.

The 1972 programme of plays commenced with an uproarious 'bang' in more senses than one. First, Stephen Hollis announced that in future plays would run for three weeks instead of two, as previously. This was to prove highly successful because the extra week gave time for word to get around and, consequently, as the run proceeded the size of the audience increased.

Another announcement concerned the personalities appearing on stage. With a new season came a new company. As the programme note said, 'nine young actors and actresses at various stages in their careers who all welcome the challenge and excitement of working together through a series of plays.'

The play chosen to begin the new season was *Don Juan*. Even the occasionally somewhat dour Stephen Pratt, who reviewed stage productions for the *Watford Observer*, ran short of superlatives. The opening remarks in his review read: 'To be brief, Stephen Hollis's opening production of the new 'rep' season is a smasheroo! A swinging, zinging, ring-a-ding-dinging show which is fun with a capital F.' He went on to say 'No one could have expected the new Palace team to have hit the nail so fairly and squarely on the head first go – but they have. They have taken Molière's rarely performed wordy comedy about the immoral exploits of Don Juan and turned it into a sparkling display of saucy fun and games with an inventiveness which rarely flags.'

In 1972 there were two visits by another star of *Coronation Street*, Thelma Barlow, famous for her portrayal of Mavis Wilton in that 'soap'. The first was in June when she was in the cast of *Orpheus Descending* and she was back the following month for *Ladies in Retirement*.

Cheryl Campbell, another local actress, she was born and brought up in St. Albans, spent time at the Palace Theatre from September 1972 until the end of the year. She was in several plays including *Ballad of the False Barman*, *Saved*, *Mother Courage and Her Children* and *Charley's Aunt*. She went on to carve out for herself a career which displayed her versatility on stage, screen and television. She was twice a member of the Royal Shakespeare Company and received various awards.

The list of celebrity actors who appeared on stage at the Palace Theatre in the 1970s is impressive by any standards. In 1973 there were visits by Sian Phillips and Daniel Massey in *Alpha Beta*. In February *The Provoked Wife* by Sir John Vanbrugh attracted Prunella Scales, Trevor Peacock, and Zoe Wanamaker. A production of *Glasstown* in June included Robert Powell and Anne Stallybrass in the cast, while the following play, *The Letter* by Somerset Maugham, starred Jill Bennett. The penultimate play that year was *A Patriot for Me* by John Osborne, and in the cast were Marianne Faithfull and John Savident but in October there had been a production of Shakespeare's *The Tempest* which included rock music. In the cast was Philip Jackson who was to appear in many television series including *Last of the Summer Wine* as Compo's nephew, Gordon and in stark contrast and more famously as Chief Inspector Japp in the television series of Agatha Christie's *Poirot* which starred David Suchet in the name part.

The following year, 1974, another character from *Poirot* paid two visits to the Palace. This was Pauline Moran (Miss Lemon in *Poirot*). She was in the cast of *Three Sisters* in September and *The Threepenny Opera* in October.

Also in 1974, a production of Noël Coward's play *Fallen Angels* was given in February and the cast included Fenella Fielding, Rose Hill and Penelope Keith. Gwen Watford returned for a production of *The Corn is Green* by Emlyn Williams. September 1975 featured a performance of *Irma la Douce* with Una Stubbs which was followed by a new play, *Out on the Lawn* by Don Taylor. In the cast of this play we saw Dinah Sheridan, T.P. McKenna,

Rosemary Leach and Frank Middlemass.

March 1975 saw the premiere of *Happy as a Sandbag* which later transferred to the Ambassadors Theatre, in London. Anita Dobson (Angie in *EastEnders*) was in the cast. This was her second visit to the Palace, her first being three months earlier in the pantomime *Babes in the Wood*. In the space of four months she was in four productions at the theatre. On the 29th January 1975 she was in the cast of *Tonight at 8.30* and on the 17th April that same year she appeared in *Hello, Hollywood, Hello*.

In 1975, from the 8th September to the 1st December, a season of Lunchtime Theatre was presented. These entertainments were mostly on Fridays and Saturdays. On the 16th, 17th and 18th of November, for example, the audience was treated to *Dan Dan the Comedy Man* advertised as 'Half an hour's laughing based on Dan Leno with Raymond Platt'. The duration of these performances was approximately 30 minutes and admission was 20p.

Rather surprisingly there is on record only one visit to the theatre by Patricia Hodge, who was educated locally. At the start of a glittering career in which she played Phyllida Erskine-Brown in *Rumpole of the Bailey* and Margaret Thatcher in *The Falklands Play*, both on television, as well as many other roles on stage and screen. Her visit to the Palace was in *Dick Whittington* at Christmas 1975. She played the part of Alice.

1976 had a great start with two in-house productions which embarked on an international tour. The first was a production of Shaw's *Pygmalion*. This play had in its cast Jan Waters as Eliza and Margaretta Scott playing Mrs. Higgins. Margaretta Scott was famous for playing imperious females; she was predominantly a classical actress but excelled in many other roles.

In February 1976 there was a presentation of Shakespeare's *Merchant of Venice* with a return to the Palace by Jan Waters as Portia, John Savident as Shylock and Donald Pickering playing Antonio. These two productions went on tour to India, Malaysia, Indonesia, Hong Kong and Thailand, sponsored by the British Council.

Rupert Davies, famous for his portrayal of *Maigret* on television, appeared in *Family Matters* by Noel Robinson and in May, Fenella Fielding returned in her one-woman show. In June Hugh Lloyd and Trevor Bannister were in the cast of *A Bit Between the Teeth*. A week of *Olde Tyme Musical Hall* included Sandy Powell and Kim Cordell. On the 8th September the theatre presented *Guys and Dolls* which included Bennie Lee in the cast. The final play that year before the pantomime was Alan Bennett's *Getting On* with Paul Eddington, famous for his roles in *The Good Life* and later in *Yes, Minister*, and

Barbara Lott.

David Kossoff, Ron Moody and Dennis Waterman played on separate Sunday evenings during 1977 and in February that year Shaw's *Mrs. Warren's Profession* was produced, the cast of which included Selina Cadell and Valentine Dyall (the Man in Black). Bernard Bresslaw appeared in *Foxy*, a new musical, in April and a British premiere of a play with the title *Molly* by Simon Gray had Mary Miller and Raymond Francis in the cast.

September 1977 saw the sixth presentation at the theatre of the evergreen Noël Coward play *Blithe Spirit*. Playing the part of Madame Arcati was Irene Handl. She had previously played the same part in the film version of the play. Unaccountably at one performance she 'dried'. She could not remember her lines and became disorientated. Murmuring an apology she left the stage and the curtain descended. After a brief interval an announcement was made that she had recovered her composure and that the play would be resumed with the same scene starting again from the beginning. Whether it was designed to give this popular and well-loved comedy character actor encouragement or just delight that the play was to continue is uncertain, but the audience burst into deafening applause as the curtain rose again to reveal Irene Handl on stage.

1978 opened with Miriam Karlin in her one woman show.

From the 7th June until the 1st July 1978 the play was *Rain*, adapted from the Somerset Maugham short story *Miss Thompson*. When it became known

Robert Powell

Irene Handl

Gloria Grahame

Alan Bennett

that Gloria Grahame was to play the part of Sadie Thompson, the part played previously in the film by Rita Hayworth, many a Watford male heart missed a beat. This was to be Gloria Grahame's debut on the British stage. Gloria was a screen siren. Originally she was under contract to MGM but it was decided that because she was 'incredibly sexy' she did not fit into their rigid assessment of star quality, so the contract was sold on to RKO. She was born in 1923 as Gloria Hallward but took the name of her maternal grandmother. In 1953 she won an Oscar as best supporting actress in a film *The Bad and the Beautiful*. She was descended from royalty, on her father's side, from King Edward III, through John of Gaunt. She married and divorced four times. Her second husband was Nicholas Ray and her fourth husband was Anthony Ray the son of husband No. 2 and therefore her step-son. She played Ado Annie (I'm Just a Girl Who Cain't Say No) in the 1955 film of *Oklahoma* but because she was tone deaf, her songs were edited almost note by note. While rehearsing in Liverpool she collapsed and was diagnosed with cancer and peritonitis. Arrangements were made immediately to fly her back to New York where she died on the 5th October 1981, within a few hours of arriving.

Between the middle to late 1970s through to the middle 1990s a number of plays by established contemporary playwrights were performed at the theatre. Four works by Noël Coward: *Design for Living; Suite in Two Keys; Bitter Sweet* and *Blithe Spirit*. From Alan Ayckbourn we had *Relatively Speaking; Season's Greetings; How the Other Half Loves; Woman in Mind; Absurd Person Singular* and *Bedroom Farce*. Then four of Alan Bennett's plays: *Getting On; The Old Country; Single Spies* and *Habeas Corpus*. Plays such as these ensured that Box Office receipts, at that time, were excellent. More were to follow from each of these playwrights.

Stephen Hollis left in 1980.

Fifty-six applicants sought to replace him and Michael Attenborough was selected. He was the son of Lord Attenborough (formerly Sir Richard) and steeped in the theatre. His period of tenure was to witness many changes at the Palace. In 1980 audience attendance averaged around 50 per cent of capacity. A deficit of £26,000 had accumulated and the theatre's future was once again under threat. Both the Arts Council and Watford Borough Council were considering withdrawal of subsidy and the theatre no longer conformed to current licensing laws.

Within a year Michael Attenborough had increased audience attendances to an average in excess of 90 per cent and the deficit had been paid off. Fears of the withdrawal of subsidies evaporated. Nevertheless the building was in need of restoration. It had been known for some time that a programme of electrical re-wiring was necessary and, in addition to problems associated with licensing laws, the auditorium was badly in need of new seats. To complete the project it would be essential to redecorate the auditorium. An appeal was launched in September 1980 to raise £200,000.

President of the appeal was Councillor S.G. (Ray) Reynolds, the then Mayor of Watford, and the Appeal Committee consisted of Councillor E.C. (Ted) Amey (chairman), Councillor Arthur Reynolds, Philip Case, V. Saxby Hart, Michael Attenborough, Christopher Barron (General Manager of the theatre), Pamela Pullen (Appeal Director) and Shirley Garrett (Appeal Secretary).

The sponsors of the appeal were Trewin Brothers, Barclays Bank (UK) Limited, Midland Bank Limited, National Westminster Bank Limited, Lloyds Bank Limited, Clements (Watford) Limited, Silver-Reed (UK) Ltd, Watford Operatic Society, The Post Office, Centurion Press, Fir Tree Studios, Watford Palace Theatre Patrons Club and Metalcraft (Watford) Limited.

Watford Borough Council donated £75,000; the Arts Council made a grant of £40,000 and the Watford Civic Theatre Trust donated £10,000. The balance was raised from the general public.

The appeal was accompanied by a collection of recipes under the title of 'Something Appealing', no doubt a reference to the Sondheim song from *A Funny Thing Happened on the Way to the Forum*. Each recipe in the booklet was given the name of a play recently performed at the theatre, including 'A Day in the Death of Joe Egg', the ingredients for which relied upon six hardboiled eggs, 'A Taste of Honey', 'French Without Tears' 'A Man for All Seasons' and several others.

Clare Ferraby, a leading expert of theatre decoration was commissioned to design the new décor for the auditorium. She had previously undertaken similar work for the Theatre Royal, Nottingham, the Duke of York's, London and the Palace Theatre, Manchester. New seats were acquired, second-hand but in good condition, from a London cinema which was being demolished. Externally, particularly the main entrance, the theatre was repainted in brown and red. It was also decided to move the Box Office from its little cramped 'kiosk' just inside the street doors on the left-hand side of the foyer to a new position in the back wall of the Stalls.

The theatre was closed for six months for the work to be done and re-opened on the 18th November 1981 with a production of *The Importance of Being Earnest*. It had a cast of leading actors, including Dame Wendy Hiller as Lady Bracknell, Gabrielle Drake and Gary Bond. The programme contained a list of more than five hundred private individuals, including well-known personalities from the world of entertainment, companies and other institutions who had donated to the appeal. Many had purchased a seat and their names were recorded on a brass plaque affixed to the back of the donated seat. This production was subsequently filmed, although in a television studio rather than at the theatre, and shown on television in America as well as in the UK.

Gabrielle Drake was to return to the theatre on 29th June 2007 with Sir John Mortimer in a single performance of *Mortimer's Miscellany*.

The formal re-opening by Sir John Mills and Councillor Ted Amey, as chairman of the Civic Theatre Trust, took place at a Gala performance on Wednesday the 25th November 1981. Two days later thieves broke into the theatre and stole £1,000 worth of sound equipment including tapes of the background noises which were essential to the production. Messrs. Hammonds, then in Queen's Road, Watford, lent the theatre the equipment needed to re-record. No evidence exists to suggest that the thieves were ever

Gabrielle Drake

apprehended.

The auditorium had been restored to its Edwardian elegance. Even the new lighting on the balustrades around the front of the Circle and Gallery and at other strategic positions was made to resemble gas lighting. Suspended from the ceiling was a new chandelier. The decoration was in shades of russet darkening in tone as it neared the proscenium. All of this was so well captured on film by Bob Nunn from one of the boxes, using a wide angle lens.

The Palace Theatre was, by this time, firmly established as a 'producing theatre', one which created its own productions from scratch, usually constructing its own scenery, in its own workshops, and making costumes for the chosen play. Sometimes new plays were commissioned. There was no longer a repertory company, so each play was cast at auditions. It had achieved a national reputation and was, and is, one of only three producing theatres in the Arts Council Eastern Region and, furthermore, remained, and still remains, the only 'live' theatre in Hertfordshire.

It is worth recording that 85 per cent of the theatres which had been in existence in 1914 had, by 1982, been demolished. In this context it is astonishing that the Palace Theatre had survived. Such was the devastating rate at which theatres were disappearing throughout the United Kingdom that in 1976 the Theatres Trust was brought into being by Parliament, with all-party support. The Trust was charge with 'the better protection of theatres for the benefit of the nation'. Some theatres were already designated Listed

Buildings and many more were added to the lists. This brought about a halt to the destruction of theatres.

In September 1982 the theatre was bought by Watford Borough Council from a Midlands-based company – Blackburn Development Group – for £180,000. Blackburn had purchased the theatre and the Carlton Cinema next door from the London owners and had offered to sell the theatre to the town if permission was forthcoming to build an office block on the Carlton site.

The Section 106 Agreement, which is a levy imposed as a condition for the granting of planning consent, provided that Blackburn would donate a part of the new building to the theatre. This part of the enlarged theatre building was often referred to as the 1980s building and served as an annexe to the theatre. It housed on the ground floor the administrative offices, above them on the first floor the Bar and Café, The second floor was occupied by the Rehearsal Room and the Wardrobe Department was on the top floor.

The deal was held up and the planning application had to be re-submitted because the Department of the Environment's Directorate of Ancient Monuments and Historic Buildings, which in 1984 became English Heritage, made the auditorium of the theatre and its façade, Grade II Listed. This single fact was a major contribution to the preservation of the theatre for the foreseeable future.

Blackburn also contributed £255,000 towards the cost of the construction of the Palace Car Park. The development was completed in 1984. The main part of the new development was named 'Arliss Court' after the celebrated actor, with local connections, George Arliss, his full name being George Arliss Andrews.

It was at this time that Sir John Mills, who lived close by at Denham, accepted an invitation to fill the honorary post of President of the Palace Theatre.

In February 1985 the theatre presented a comedy entitled *Natural Causes*. It brought together two established comedy actors who had both made their names in long-running television series. One was Ian Lavender, famous as Private Frank Pike ('You stupid boy') in *Dad's Army* and the other, Michael Robbins, well known for his performances as Arthur Rudge, the sarcastic husband in *On the Buses*. Ian Lavender was no stranger to the Palace having taken part in several of the Jimmy Perry pantomimes.

The 1980s were a period of success for the theatre. It was doing good business. The theatre itself constituted a 'draw' to acknowledged actors. Then with the arrival of Michael Attenborough, the 'draw' became an 'avalanche'.

Sir John Mills   *Michael Robbins and Ian Lavender*

Actors and actresses of distinction flocked to take part in the casts of presented plays. The list resembles a 'Who's Who' of the theatre. Such personalities as Frank Finlay, Susan Penhaligon, Renee Asherson, Marion Montgomery, Roy Castle, Robert Powell, Stephanie Beacham, Acker Bilk, Prunella Scales, Ian McShane, Terence Longdon, George Chisholm, Wendy Hiller, Gabrielle Drake, Gary Bond, Margaret Tyzack, David Kossoff, Simon Callow, Pauline Collins, Humphrey Lyttelton, Sir John Mills, Connie Booth, Paul Hardwick, Warren Mitchell, Tony Britton, Rosemary Leach, Hugh Paddick, Roy Barraclough, Susannah York, Hayley Mills and many, many others were either in the cast of plays or making single Sunday evening appearances.

One memorable production at this time was *Trumpets and Raspberries* by the Italian playwright Dario Fo. This was its British premiere. It contained in its cast Griff Rhys Jones and Gwen Taylor. Dario Fo is arguably the most controversial playwright ever to have a play produced at the Palace Theatre. He has led a colourful life and has been described as a political satirist. Most of his plays contain a political theme. An Italian, he was a strong anti-fascist and has caused heated debate and even attempts on his life for the expression of his views. None the less he was awarded the Nobel Prize for Literature in 1997.

Except for a handful of years the Palace Theatre has always presented a pantomime at Christmas. In the early years, more than one but these were presented by touring companies who stayed for only a week. In 1976 *Jack and the Beanstalk* was written by Peter John and the following eight pantomimes were also written by him and he took part in most of them. Peter John had been a regular member of the repertory company. His last pantomime at the Palace was *Aladdin* in 1984.

In 1985 *Paddington Bear* replaced the more traditional pantomime and this was given as daytime performances only, with *Season's Greetings* by Alan Ayckbourn taking the stage in the evenings. For the ensuing three years a range of entertainment suitable for children was produced. Perhaps Lou Stein, the Artistic Director during that time, and an American by birth, was not imbued with the Christmas pantomime tradition, an essentially British eccentricity. However, Lou's own version of *Pinocchio* was given in 1987 and *The Patchwork Girl of Oz* in 1988. In fact, the idea worked well with a show for children in the afternoon followed by another one suitable for adult tastes in the evening.

Cinderella, however, revived the pantomime tradition in 1989. This was written by John Moffatt and Tudor Davies and was directed by Wendy Toye.

Lou Stein was one of the 'great' Artistic Directors to hold that position at the Palace Theatre. He served a term of nine years, from 1986 to 1995, which was longer than most.

His philosophy was 'You have to keep just ahead of your audiences, not too far ahead but certainly not behind them'. By this he meant that an Artistic

Gwen Taylor   *Lou Stein*

Children queue for a production of Pinocchio *in 1967*

Director should present his audience with a challenge, to lead them gently to experiment with new plays but those plays should not be so outrageous that the audience is frightened away.

During one year of his tenure he decided to concentrate on a programme of new works. Not all of them were to the liking of the public and he reckons that 20 per cent of the regular audience defected to other theatres and it took about eighteen months to restore their confidence. Audiences can be fickle but in the main they have a strong desire to show loyalty and they will return if given sufficient encouragement.

Lou Stein claimed that his greatest achievement while at Watford was to open the theatre up to all sections of the community. He introduced a series of ventures. On the one hand, programmes suitable for the taste of the Afro-Caribbean community and, on the other, programmes and activities for the young. He encouraged productions by the local amateur operatic societies and initiated a Young Playwrights competition. He is thrilled when he meets playwrights whom he introduced to the art and who have succeeded in the profession. Frequently he enquired from the minority groups what they wanted of the theatre and the reply invariably came, 'We want to be part of it'.

He was to say later in his career, 'I never considered Watford as an out-of-town repertory theatre but as a competitor to the National Theatre.'

There had been in existence a supporters club known as the 'Friends of the Palace'. This was a voluntary group which raised money for the theatre and arranged social functions for its members but was in decline, so on 23rd November 1986 a club was revived with the title 'Palace People'. This was shortly before Lou Stein arrived to take up the post of Artistic Director. Unlike its predecessor, Palace People was run by the theatre.

Members were offered a range of benefits. The theatre at that time was doing good business playing, for most of the time, to near capacity audiences. The attraction of becoming one of the Palace People was that members received the brochure detailing forthcoming productions one week before others on the mailing list, giving them the advantage of being able to book tickets ahead of those who were not members.

Members of Palace People were given the opportunity to mingle with the cast and staff of the theatre after the show, with a glass of wine. Visits were organised to other theatres, talks were given by some of the 'star' performers, visiting directors, make-up artists and others such as accent coaches. A periodic Newsletter was published with details of each production, forthcoming events and articles by the directors of plays. Group membership was also available and companies were encouraged to enrol, giving their staff the opportunity to benefit from the facilities on offer.

The annual subscription for individuals was £10, or £8 to those members resident in the Borough of Watford. There was also a Palace People Youth Wing. They enjoyed all the benefits and received their own Newsletter.

Palace People was an outstanding success and exceeded all expectations. A membership of 300 was anticipated but 1,500 people enrolled. This, however, produced its own unique problem. A membership of 300 could quite easily be handled by the existing administrative staff at the theatre but 1,500 was quite another matter and it became necessary to appoint a full-time co-ordinator. In the ranks of Palace People was Clare Burns who had worked in theatre and was ideally suited to take on the role. She worked tirelessly promoting the scheme. It could be said that the success of the scheme was its own undoing. Incentives had to be offered to encourage people to join. These incentives included a reduction in the price of a ticket but the resulting reduction in revenue at the Box Office when added to the cost of employing a co-ordinator eventually proved uneconomic and the scheme fell into abeyance.

During Lou Stein's reign at the theatre its reputation, by now firmly established, increased further and consequently the parade continued of well-known actors and actresses who accepted invitations to perform in the casts of a succession of plays. In fact, the years 1986 to 1988, inclusive, witnessed return performances by some of those already mentioned and also saw the first appearance of a number of others. One of those who came was once asked what it was that induced actors of their standing to come and endure the privations of dingy dressing rooms and back-stage facilities that left a lot to be desired. The answer came, 'Firstly, it is the play which attracts us and also to play in this beautiful theatre,' by which she undoubtedly referred to the beauty of the auditorium as well as to the quality of productions.

In January 1986 Paula Wilcox made the first of several appearances at the Palace Theatre. She and Christopher Timothy were in the cast of *The Real Thing*. Apart from the regular artistes during the repertory years, very few actresses have made more 'guest' appearances at the theatre than Paula Wilcox. She came to the public's notice in the television comedy series *Man About the House* with Richard O'Sullivan. After *The Real Thing* she made return visits in *Spotted Dick* December 1986; *Everything in the Garden* September 1987; *On Approval* March 1992 and *Blithe Spirit* June 2000.

Paula Wilcox, with Michael Frayn, the playwright and novelist, headed the panel of judges for the Young Playwright's Competition, mentioned earlier, initiated in 1989. Paula was also present at the announcement that the theatre had been successful in securing Lottery funding for the 2002/2004 refurbishment. She has been a good friend of the Palace Theatre.

The play which followed *The Real Thing* saw Dorothy Tutin and Paul Daneman in *Are You Sitting Comfortably*. In March Annette Crosbie and Caroline Langrishe played in *Talk of the Devil*.

April saw a return of Maureen Lipman in *Wonderful Town*, the music of which was composed by Leonard Bernstein. Lesley Joseph was also in the cast. The first 'run' of this show was in New York in 1953 and this was to be the first presentation in the United Kingdom. This was a pre-run before it transferred to the West End. Bernstein himself came to Watford to see a performance and was fulsome in his praise.

Double, Double the following month included Jane Lapotaire in the cast and after the summer break, another American actress who had made her home in England, Gayle Hunnicutt, joined the cast of *So Long on Lonely Street*. This was followed by Chekhov's *The Seagull* with a return visit of Prunella Scales.

Then in 1987, the year started with an excitedly anticipated production of a dramatisation by the Irish writer Edna O'Brien of Gustave Flaubert's masterpiece *Madame Bovary* with Helen M̶ ̶ ̶en (now Dame Helen) playing the name part. This was a world premier̶ ̶ceiving much advance publicity including a slot on *Channel 4 News* and an interview by Terry Wogan with Helen Mirren. Sadly the critics did not receive it with unrestrained praise. Like the film which followed in 1991 it was considered that the novel did not transfer readily to the stage or screen.

During the run of *Madame Bovary* did 'Aggie' play a part?

Who, the reader might ask, was 'Aggie'?

Every self-respecting theatre, especially the older ones, boasts a 'ghost'. The ghost at the Palace Theatre has become known as 'Aggie' and it is believed that, in life, she was a 'lime operator' at the Palace. The limes were the 'follow-spots' mounted at the front of the Gallery, The story goes that this particular lime operator lost her footing and fell headlong from the Gallery to her death in the Circle below.

'Aggie' has been seen regularly over the years. She only appears during a 'get in', that is during the time when the scenery for the next production is being installed in the theatre. She is reported to appear in the early hours of the morning and in the Gallery. In times gone by, members of staff at the theatre were reluctant to go up to the Gallery on their own and some refused. One former staff member, herself a lime operator, recalled an occasion when she slept over-night in a Box in the theatre rather than go back to her home in Hemel Hempstead. This was because of an early start the following morning to bring in the scenery required for the new production. During the night her sleep was disturbed and she witnessed a door in the Gallery opening and closing. There was no rational explanation for this. There were no other doors or windows in the vicinity to be the source of sufficient draught to open the door. The door no longer exists in the rebuilt theatre. Has 'Aggie' at last found peace? Time will tell.

But to return to *Madame Bovary*. In one scene a carriage was lowered to the stage from the 'flies'. The carriage was suspended on ropes. When scenery is installed and is 'flown' a knot is tied in the rope so that when the scenery is lowered to the stage the rope fouls a pulley in the fly tower and that is as far as the rope needs to unwind so that the scenery reaches the floor of the stage. This is a process described, in theatrical terminology, as 'tying off'. During one of the performances of *Madame Bovary* the carriage descended and hit the stage with a resounding 'thump'. On inspection it was found that the knot in the rope had moved. None of the stage crew admitted to untying the knot and retying it in a different position. It would be impossible for the knot to move itself. Could this have been a mischievous act by 'Aggie'?

As well as the established actors and actresses who have been attracted to perform at the Palace Theatre, many members of the theatrical profession have performed at the theatre early in their careers, before they had established their reputations. An example of this occurred in March 1987 when a new musical was staged called *Spin of the Wheel*. In the cast was a little-known, young, Maria Friedman. The show transferred to the West End but closed after only four weeks. On the other hand, in her time, the multi-talented Maria Friedman went on to be regarded as 'the first lady of the British musical stage', winning three Olivier Awards and being nominated for seven others. She also achieved popularity on Broadway, especially in the musical shows of Stephen Sondheim.

In April 1987, Patsy Byrne, Trevor Peacock, Donald Douglas and Julian Fellowes were in the cast of *Laburnum Grove*. Trevor Peacock achieved considerable success and popularity as Jim Trott ('No, no, no, no —Yes') in the television series *The Vicar of Dibley*.

In September that same year, Paula Wilcox was back to lead the cast in *Everything in the Garden* with Daniel Hill. This was followed by the J.M. Barrie play *Mary Rose* with Anna Cropper and, in the name part, Amanda Waring (daughter of the late, great, Dame Dorothy Tutin, who, as mentioned above, had appeared at the theatre, with Paul Daneman the previous year). Also in the cast was Michael Burrell playing opposite Anna Cropper. In October Susan Penhaligon, Charlotte Cornwall and John Fortune played in *A Doll's House* by Henrik Ibsen. The following month saw visits by Tony Slattery and Natalie

Spotted Dick

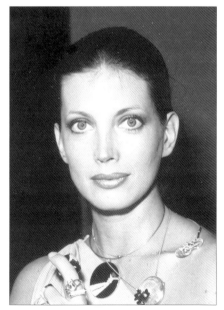

Gayle Hunnicutt

Forbes in *The Cat and the Canary*.

A sad event happened in October 1987 when Arthur King, a long-serving member of staff, died. He had been ill for some time and was a mere 64 years of age. He had originally joined the staff as carpenter and helped to build many a set for the theatre. He doubled as fireman (having been for some years a fire officer at Rickmansworth and Watford Fire Stations, retiring from the fire service in 1975 for health reasons) and latterly had been cellar-man for the Green Room. He had worked at the theatre for 30 years.

1988 opened with *Suite in Two Keys* and in that cast were Francis Matthews, Isla Blair and Caroline Blakiston.

The cast of *The Common Pursuit* in March included John Sessions, Stephen Fry, Rik Mayall, John Gordon Sinclair and Sarah Berger playing lead roles. This play was one of those outstanding successes for the theatre which do not occur with predictable regularity. It went on to the Phoenix Theatre in the West End. At Watford it was a sell-out, probably because of its cast. It was not the policy of the theatre to sell Gallery tickets ahead of the opening performance but because the demand was so great an exception was made and even half of the Gallery tickets were sold before opening night.

In the autumn the theatre welcomed Sheila Steafel and Sandra Dickinson in *The Gingerbread Lady*. There was a break in the flow of plays in November for a week when the programme was presented by the sophisticated duo, Peter Skellern and Richard Stilgoe who sang humorous songs at the piano, in concert.

Another production in 1988 which ran from the 8th to 25th June was a specially commissioned play with the title *Exclusive Yarns*. It was memorable not so much for its content but for the reaction from the critics. On one hand it received rave reviews evoking such comments from the critics as 'Fabulous production', 'You're guaranteed an evening of giggles' and 'Side-splitting comedy'. One critic excelled himself with the words '…the ultimate comedy – a soap opera spoof, with superb actors and a wonderful script… non stop hilarity'. The play transferred to the Comedy Theatre, in the West End where it received less favourable comment. One critic described it as a 'Dire concoction', with 'Not a witty line' and another referred to 'Lamentable proceedings'. It included in its cast Susie Blake, Pam Ferris, Lesley Joseph and others. Can these critics have been witnessing the same play?

1988 was not the happiest year for the Palace Theatre. In December there was a production of *Woman Overboard*. This ran at the theatre from the 11th November to the 10th December. It was a modern musical adaptation of the seventeenth-century play *The Dog in the Manger* by a Spanish playwright named Lope de Vega. The adaptation was set on a luxury yacht in 1932 in the

Anna Cropper and Michael Burrel in Mary Rose *in 1987*

Bay of Naples. The play was advertised as the third play in the Palace's 80th birthday season of 'special treats' and had been commissioned by Lou Stein. It was the world (and probably only) performance. The music was by Monty Norman. It also received mixed reviews from the critics. The advance publicity hailed it as a 'Sparkling new musical', to which one critic responded, 'There is as much sparkle in this dud show as on a dead squid sinking in the Bay of Naples'. Another said of the music that 'Limited to two key boards the music is monotonous'. The *Financial Times* declared, 'There are some evenings in the theatre so magnificently dire that a critic's responsibility to record the event becomes confused with a gleefully manic urge to spread bad news.' The Review liked it! Even Grelle White writing in the *Watford Observer*, clearly unimpressed, described it as a 'Slowboat to Pantoland', appropriately enough, except that that year there was no pantomime. The Christmas season show in 1988 was *The Patchwork Girl of Oz*. This was based on a novel by Adrian

Isla Blair   *Stephen Fry*

Mitchell, which was a sequel to his *Wizard of Oz*.

Famous names continued to appear at the Palace. For three weeks from the 25th January 1990, Jerry Hall appeared in *Bus Stop* in the part played by Marilyn Monroe in the 1956 film. A matinee performance was attended by Mick Jagger, then husband of Jerry Hall, and their children.

Further names to conjure with who appeared at the Palace during this period include: Ronnie Corbett, Tim Brooke-Taylor, Brian Murphy, Don Warrington, Sue Pollard, Lenny Henry, Eleanor Summerfield, Ruby Wax, Roy Hudd and this is not an exhaustive list.

One actress deserves separate and special mention. From the 6th to the 28th March 1992 the renowned actress Helena Bonham Carter appeared in the world premiere of a new translation by Ranjit Bolt of *The Barber of Seville* by Beaumarchais. At least three actresses from titled families have appeared in Palace productions. Helena was the great-granddaughter of H.H. Asquith, who had been Liberal Prime Minister and became the Earl of Oxford, another was Caroline Langrishe whose father was a baronet and thirdly, in 1994, Marsha Fitzalan, daughter of the Duke of Norfolk.

For many years the Palace Theatre has had a reputation for the quality of its Christmas pantomimes but connoisseurs of that form of family entertainment maintain that the quality was excelled during the years 1990 to 2002 by the pantomimes written especially for the Palace by Roy Hudd.

Roy Hudd adhered rigidly to the traditional form, bags of audience participation, songs perfectly complementing the studiously adhered to plot, lots of slapstick comedy and plenty of topical 'clean' gags.

Pantomimes produce a sizeable proportion of the theatre's annual income. Ten of the twelve 'Roy Hudd' pantomimes were designed by Mark Hinton and built in the theatre's own workshop mostly by Tip Pargeter's team. Some of the sets were sold on to other theatres who intended to produce the same pantomime the following year.

Jack and the Beanstalk was the first of the Roy Hudd series of pantos. The following year he persuaded Chris Emmett to play the part of the 'Dame' in *Dick Whittington*. Initially, Chris was a little reticent about doing this but he succumbed to Roy Hudd's blandishments and was an instant success with Watford audiences who took him to their hearts. It was the first of nine successive Dames he was to play at the Palace Theatre. He also directed the last four of the Roy Hudd pantomimes, alongside choreographer Debbie Flitcroft (Mrs. Roy Hudd). In the last two he was not a member of the cast.

Chris Emmett was an established radio and television performer. Since 1975 he has been a regular artiste, along with Roy Hudd and June Whitfield in the cast of *The News Huddlines*, the world's longest running scripted comedy show recorded before a live audience. An actor (including Shakespeare), impersonator and comedian, Chris was part of the team on *3-2-1* with Ted Rogers which ran on television on Saturday evenings from 1978 until 1987.

Pamela Cundell, famous for her role as Mrs Fox in *Dad's Army* was in several of the Roy Hudd pantos invariably playing, and ideally cast as, the Fairy Godmother or the Good Fairy.

There is a story that during one of the pantomimes Chris Emmett flung down the gauntlet saying that unless he was provided with an adequate supply of hot water with which to remove his make-up after the show, he was not going on stage that night. His threat was taken seriously and an urn was procured to satisfy his needs. The truth behind the story was that as the Dame, wearing several layers of clothing, which made him very hot and causing him to perspire, it was necessary for him to use wax make-up and this could only be removed with the aid of soap and hot water. Other members of the cast, playing less strenuous roles, could use cosmetic make up which could be wiped off.

Another story involving Chris Emmett was when, in one pantomime, he appeared on stage in a nurse's uniform, with a red cross on the apron and hat. A member of the audience, singularly lacking, it would seem, in a sense of humour, protested that this was disrespectful to the Red Cross organisation. In spite of Chris's protestations that no disrespect was intended by himself or the designer the red crosses were removed.

Away from what had become his annual performance in the pantomimes, Chris Emmett was in the cast of *Black Comedy* and *The Public Eye* which played at the theatre from the 1st to 23rd September 1995.

Chris Emmett has said that the Palace Theatre was unique in his experience. He praised it for its intimacy and warmth, for the beauty of the auditorium and the contact he felt with the audience. He could see from the stage just the first two or three rows of the audience in the stalls but felt the presence of the rest of the 'house'. In his feelings towards the Palace Theatre he echoed those of Roy Hudd himself who described it as 'my very favourite theatre'.

Another memorable performance which is remembered was the August 1991 guest visit of the Novgorod Regional Theatre. This was during the very week that communism collapsed in the Soviet Union. They presented *The Devils* by Fyodor Dostoevsky, in Russian. Whether or not this was an unconscious comment on their political masters at that time one can only speculate but the political upheaval caused some concern as to whether the Russian visitors would be allowed to return to their home country. In the event any diplomatic difficulty was resolved.

Lou Stein tells an interesting sub-plot to the Russian visit. The actors were paid little more than an honorarium to finance their living expenses while in Watford and a number of Watford residents provided accommodation. So it was surprising to find the Russian actors coming into the theatre carrying brand new microwave ovens and other electrical items. How were they paying for them? They would not have been permitted by the Soviet authorities to bring currency out of Russia. One day towards the end of the week Mr. Stein found himself in an electrical shop in the town and saw on the counter an unopened bottle of vodka and a tin of caviar. On enquiry he discovered that the Russians had brought vodka and caviar with them which they used to barter for electrical goods which were not available in Russia.

The pantomime in 1991 was *Dick Whittington* and in the cast was Dr. Evadne Hinge, one half of the popular 'Hinge and Bracket' duo, played by George Logan and Patrick Fyffe. They portrayed two eccentric upper class ladies. Dame Hilda Bracket was a soprano and Dr. Hinge the accompanist. It was a comedy act and had a large following.

In 1995 Lou Stein left the theatre, to take up a position with the Arts Council.

Roy Hudd   *Chris Emmett*

He had made a major contribution to the theatrical life of Watford and his report in 1987 on the health of the Palace was to feature in the development of the theatre. Details of this report and of its significance appear in the next chapter.

Lou Stein was succeeded by Giles Croft who came to the Palace from the National Theatre where he had been Literary Director.

The theatre celebrated its ninetieth birthday during the run of the 1998 pantomime *Jack and the Beanstalk* and at the end of the performance on the 9th December Chris Emmett, in his familiar role as the Dame, stepped forward and said to the audience that an actor he had admired all his life was in the audience. He went on to say that he had never before met him, 'but tonight I am going to. Please welcome to the stage Sir John Mills'. It was an emotional moment. Sir John's sight was failing him but he was guided on to the stage and met by Chris. In his remarks Sir John said that this was one performance at his 'local theatre' he was not going to miss. 'You all know that the dear old Palace Theatre is now ninety years old. And so am I.'

It set the tone for Christmas 1999.

CHAPTER 6

Time to Rebuild

In the early 1990s Watford Borough Council decided to return the theatre to private management. The reason for this has never been totally clear. There may have been several factors influencing the decision. Central Government legislation had enacted that Local Authorities should not hold controlling interests in commercial enterprises. The Palace Theatre certainly fell into this category and this fact was certainly a consideration.

It may also have had some bearing on the decision that it was becoming increasing clear that the fabric of the building was showing its age and rapidly approaching the time when it would be in need of drastic remedial attention.

After a period of some thirty years the theatre was poised to surrender its role as a civic theatre and return to 'private' management.

In June1987 the Council of Management had called for a report dealing with the rear extension of the building and the longer term view under the heading of a 'Three Year Plan'. The report was also intended to outline the theatre's proposed development into the 1990s.

The report was duly prepared by Lou Stein who was in his first year as Artistic Director and Meryl Faiers, who had been General Manager for five years. It took four months to prepare. The chairman of the Council of Management at that time was Councillor Veronica Conlon.

Their report contained some uncomfortable truths. Outwardly the theatre showed evidence of being successful but it was unquestionably in a precarious financial situation. The autumn of 1980 had marked a significant point in the theatre's fortunes. That year had witnessed a dramatic upswing in audience attendance.

Then the theatre had closed for the 1981 refurbishment and restoration to its Edwardian beauty but after the six months' closure there was a great fear that audience loyalty would have been lost to other theatres including the West End.

The report recalled that the theatre's subsidy in 1981/82 was £142,700 from Watford Borough Council and £58,300 from the Arts Council. The theatre was about to receive a 20 per cent increase from The Arts Council and an increase of 4.2 per cent in the grant from Watford Borough Council.

In the event, audience loyalty had not diminished and at the date of the report, productions were playing to near capacity houses which meant that there was little, if any, scope to increase box office revenue. The current repertoire concentrated on comedies and plays with 'big names' in the cast. Any diminution in box office receipts resulting from the presentation of new writings or plays of a more challenging nature could spell disaster. A fall in the level of attendance to 65 per cent of capacity, an enviable level for many repertory theatres, would be serious at the box office.

In short, the theatre could not undertake any risky business although there was an apparent need for an element of innovative work. The continuous pressure for unrealistically high box office achievement constituted a serious stranglehold on the future of the theatre. On top of all this it was felt that the theatre needed to play a larger part in the life of the community.

The theatre was seriously underfunded; the staff were underpaid and were being worked to near exhaustion in cramped conditions.

The obvious solution was to pressure the funding bodies, particularly the Arts Council, for greater support.

By February 1987 the grant from Watford Borough Council had risen in the previous five years by only £6,000, to £148,700 and it was about to be increased by £4,461. Councillor Alistair Allen, who was also a member of the Council of Management, had proposed an increase of 5 per cent but that proposal was unsuccessful. This was the first increase for four years. The Arts Council grant by this time had risen to £105,500.

The report went on to say that since 1965, the year in which it became a civic theatre, plays had been interesting and often challenging to its audience and usually widely, if not always favourably, reviewed. In the late 1970s there had been a slump in attendances which led to a tendency to mix the safe with the bold. By 1987 the theatre was beginning to escape from this scenario. The Palace Theatre was now being perceived in a different light, as a producing theatre which tended to lead rather than follow the West End.

Now, in 1987, the theatre was seen as a larger building which, since it now occupied part of the block constructed on the site formerly occupied by the Carlton Cinema, it was.

The report envisaged the addition of a 'studio' theatre as a long-term goal. It was suggested that the workshop space in Watford House Lane be converted for the purpose and to include a gallery/art workshop space and bistro. This would facilitate a stronger and more accessible presence in the community for young people, minority groups and schools.

It also recommended that the stage of the main theatre be squared up and extended by 10 feet so that the greater depth would avoid the feeling of the action being 'cramped' and the actors could be 'backlit'. Also, it was suggested that the Gallery should be equipped with comfortable seating in place of the wooden forms without back rests. A climb up sixty concrete steps to the Gallery added further discouragement to the public to utilise that part of the theatre. The Stalls and Circle were occupied at capacity but because of its discomfort, the Gallery was not being used.

The report was ambitious and far-seeing, but none of the plans materialised at the time. They would have been costly and although a public appeal was suggested it did not happen, probably because the 1981 appeal was comparatively recent. The workshop space in Watford House Lane was

Left: *Steps to the gallery*

Below: *Wooden seats in the gallery*

unsuitable for conversion because of its condition. Much of what the report called for, and more, was to be accomplished fifteen years later.

At the same time that the report was in preparation, a Watford schoolgirl, Jane Parker, was preparing a detailed study of the theatre for her 'AO' Level General Studies examination. As part of her project she interviewed every head of department at the theatre and in many cases the assistant or deputy in that department. It is a workman-like project and underlines much of what the official report was to say. What the staff told her is illuminating. Clearly all the staff enjoyed working at the theatre. Some had worked in other theatres before coming to Watford. All were aware of its shortcomings but all praised its 'cosiness' and the beauty of the auditorium. Most of them were critical of the lack of space for working and for storage. The stage crew and those actively involved with the staging of plays commented on the need for an enlarged stage and referred to the strenuous effort needed to haul the scenery manually, on hemp ropes, up into the fly tower. It is noticeable in Jane's project that no one in the Wardrobe Department, which was housed at the top of the building, mentioned the fatigue caused by having to climb to the third floor several times a day, especially in warm weather. The incorporation of a lift in 2004 was to bring relief from that.

The cost of the improvements mentioned in Lou Stein's report amounted to an estimated £300,000 which was unlikely to be raised by an appeal to the public.

It is, therefore, reasonable to suppose that another consideration in the minds of Watford Borough Council through the Council of Management of the Watford Civic Theatre Trust Ltd. was that a public appeal would stand a greater chance of success if the management of the theatre was in private hands, even if the freehold of the theatre remained in the ownership of Watford Borough Council. If the ownership and active management of the theatre, in effect, remained with the Borough Council it would have invited the comment 'It's your theatre, you pay for it.'

Yet another reason for the change of management may have been that there was a problem regarding productions going on from Watford to other theatres. Lou Stein considered that the theatre should in some way benefit financially but some Borough Councillors were concerned that the Registered Charity status of the theatre might be compromised if it was thought that the theatre was 'trading'. One way in which this problem might be resolved would be to establish a separate 'trading company' as a wholly-owned subsidiary.

It is probable that the sum total of all these factors influenced the

Borough Council and resulted in their decision to return the theatre to the private sector.

To 'Bubble' Lodge, the Administrative Manager of the theatre, was entrusted the task of recruiting a board of responsible local residents, who between them possessed a range of skills which would enable them to manage the theatre efficiently and effectively on a business, as well as an artistic, footing.

Various local organisations and institutions such as Rotary, Women's Institutes and of course the three amateur operatic societies who regularly performed at the theatre were invited to nominate candidates for consideration by the Council   to be appointed members of the board of directors in place of the Council of Management. In addition people interested in the theatre, who were professional in the fields of accountancy and the law, and others experienced in theatre management, were approached.

Eventually the list of those nominated was whittled down to a list of twelve and they assumed management of the theatre from 1994. But there were legal difficulties to be resolved. The theatre had debts amounting to some £160,000 almost all of which consisted of arrears of rent due to the freeholders, Watford Borough Council. The new board was reluctant to assume responsibility for these debts. The Council agreed to write-off the rent arrears but even so it was decided to form an entirely new company in order to ensure that if there were any undisclosed debts, they would not become the liability of the new company.

The Council of Management of the Watford Civic Theatre Trust remained, for the time being, the *de facto* managers but its members were content to 'rubber stamp' the decisions of the nominated Board of Directors of the new company until such time as they achieved legal status.

Lou Stein left Watford when he was offered the post of chairman of the Arts Council Eastern Region on terms he could not refuse. This was about the time when moves were being made to refurbish the Palace Theatre. At a meeting of the Board of Directors of the 'privatised' theatre a remark was made that 'we must not expect favouritism from Lou', but the theatre did not suffer from having Lou as chairman of that part of the Arts Council within which the Palace was situated. He remained with the Arts Council for three years.

The Palace Theatre Watford Limited was incorporated on 1st July 1996, as successor to The Watford Civic Theatre Trust Ltd. which was put into voluntary liquidation. So, on the 1st July 1996 the Board of Directors of the new company assumed total control and management of the Palace Theatre.

Watford Borough Council, as freeholders of the theatre, were entitled to representation on the board but the Memorandum and Articles of Association of the new company stipulated that the voting strength of Watford Borough Council was not to exceed 20 per cent of the total. The first list of directors of the new company were Bill Aldridge, Ian Avent, Mrs. Jennifer Cooper, Ian Griffiths, M.B.E., Nicola Pallot, Mrs. Julia Price, April Read, Ian Scleater, C.V.O., Prabkirt Singh Seyan, Brian Swabey, Albert Tucker, and Don Warrington, together with Norman Tyrwhitt and Mike Jackson as the two representatives of the Borough Council. Smooth transition from civic theatre to an independent institution was facilitated by virtue of Councillor Norman Tyrwhitt continuing in the position of chairman.

There was already in place a Finance Sub-committee consisting of Norman Tyrwhitt, Ian Avent, Brian Swabey and Ian Scleater, by strange coincidence all former pupils of Watford Grammar School for Boys. Membership of this committee was not a sinecure.

There were worrying times but comfort was invariably forthcoming in the substantial and imposing form of Harry Holt the Finance Officer of the theatre, who displayed great skill in keeping the fledgling company solvent, assuring the Finance Committee, and through them the rest of the Board, that the company was not trading fraudulently, and resorting on occasions to persuading the two principal funding bodies to provide an advance of the quarterly grant and, by various means, finding a source of cash to cover eventualities and all contractual obligations.

The Artistic Director and the Administrative Director at that time were Giles Croft and Alastair Moir respectively and both were to play key roles at the Palace Theatre preparing for the rebuilding programme. The theatre was by now a fully-fledged producing theatre, one of only three in the Eastern region of the Arts Council of England. As such it created plays from scratch; it selected the cast, the play was directed either by its own artistic director or by a guest director engaged by the artistic director. The scenery for each play was constructed by the theatre's own team of scenery builders at the workshop in Watford Fields, having been designed by someone engaged for the task. In some instances the costumes were made by the theatre's own wardrobe department. Only on infrequent occasions was a production imported from another theatre. Some plays were joint productions with other theatres and some went on to production at other venues including the West End of London.

Many well-known and distinguished actors were cast and the theatre's reputation continued to increase. It was attracting reviews of its plays by the national press. Although not always playing to capacity audiences the average

Giles Croft

attendance was in the region of 70 per cent

Some new plays were commissioned with the encouragement of the Arts Council, which was a substantial contributor to the annual grants received. Many new plays were produced.

The surveyor to the theatre had warned the directors that there was reason to be concerned about the stability of the fly tower, the vacant area above the stage into which scenery is hoisted when not required on stage. He advised that, in his estimation, its useful life was not more than ten years.

This information, although later to be proved ultra-cautious, concentrated the minds of the theatre Board and they came to think in terms of modernising the theatre which was almost ninety years old, as well as concentrating upon the day-to-day operations of presenting entertainment for its audiences. Perhaps now was the time, if the circumstances were opportune, to fulfil the required measures suggested in Lou Stein's 1987 report, to secure the future of the Palace Theatre.

What were the chances of securing Lottery funding for a project to modernise the theatre? A tentative approach was made to the Arts Council which confirmed that if the theatre fitted all the criteria, money might be made available but there were conditions attached, one of which was that the theatre would have to contribute what is termed Partnership Funding. This amount is equivalent to one-third of the sum granted by the Lottery.

Entertainment was being well received and, despite the uncongenial dressing rooms, the theatre continued to attract well-known actors and actresses. Many of whom commented on the beauty of the auditorium and the quality of its acoustics.

In March 1994, a production of Noël Coward's *Private Lives* saw Caroline Langrishe making her second visit to the Palace Theatre. She was known to a wider audience for her part in two long-running television series, *Lovejoy* and later, *Judge John Deed*.

In June of that year Don Warrington from the cast of *Rising Damp* and also at that time a member of the Board of Directors of the theatre, was in the cast of *Middle-Age Spread*.

Alan Ayckbourn's play *Woman in Mind* included, in the cast, Marsha Fitzalan, otherwise known, in private life, as The Lady Marcia Fitzalan-Howard, actress daughter of the 17th Duke of Norfolk.

In 1995, in February, Alan Bennett's celebrated double bill *Single Spies* was given with Edward de Souza playing Guy Burgess and Meg Davies as Coral Browne in the first play, *An Englishman Abroad*. In the companion play, *A Question of Attribution*, Anthony Blunt was played by Shaughan Seymour and Her Majesty The Queen (in the programme the part was listed as 'HMQ') was portrayed by Meg Davies.

In September, Chris Emmett was in the cast of *Black Comedy* and *The Public Eye*. Chris was to return at Christmas to play one of the Ugly Sisters in *Cinderella*. Also in the cast of *Cinderella* were Nick Staverson and Pamela Cundell. Before the pantomime, in November Sara Crowe came to the Palace in the cast of *French Without Tears*.

Early in 1996 there was a revival of the ever-popular *Charley's Aunt* which was followed by *FACE The Musical with Bottle*. This was produced in association with Queen's Theatre, Hornchurch, the Nuffield Theatre, Southampton and the Belgrade Theatre, Coventry.

Then in May came *Kindertransport* by Diane Samuels, with Jean Boht and Diana Quick in the cast. From Watford this play transferred to the Vaudeville Theatre in the West End. It was a moving play, the theme of which was the bringing of Jewish children to Britain from Germany during the last nine months before the outbreak of World War II.

Caroline Langrishe and Christopher Bowen 'Private Lives' 1994

Immediately after *Kindertransport* the atmosphere changed dramatically with a performance of Sir Peter Ustinov's play *Beethoven's Tenth* starring Philip Bretherton, who played Alistair in the television series *As Time Goes By*, in which the lead parts were played by Dame Judy Dench and Geoffrey Palmer.

During this time, behind the scenes, enquiries were being made regarding ownership of the land directly behind the stage of the theatre. It transpired that the owners were the Prudential Corporation but they were in course of selling it together with a much larger plot which included three shops fronting onto Watford High Street, but because negotiations had reached a delicate stage the Prudential were reluctant to disclose the name of the prospective purchaser.

The Board was considering a fund-raising feasibility target figure for a two-year capital campaign. This would indicate the level of Lottery funding for which the theatre should aim.

Burrell Foley Fischer, who were acknowledged experts as architects in the field of cinema and theatre design had been engaged to undertake a feasibility study of what needed doing and at the same time it was agreed that members of the Board would tour the theatre and discuss with key members of staff the order of priority of what was required to bring the building up to standard.

As well as all of this, David Dixon Associates were invited to prepare a fund raising feasibility study. They were also being considered to implement a telephone fund raising campaign aimed at securing a four year programme of covenanted donations. The theatre, as a Registered Charity, would be entitled to reclaim tax if the donations were made under Deed of Covenant. This scheme was the forerunner of today's Gift Aid. The study would give a realistic indication of what public support might be expected for the project.

At a Board meeting in October 1996 the general feeling was that the appropriate target figure to be raised was in the region of £500,000–750,000 with a project cost for the refurbishment of £4 million.

At this juncture, a discussion took place as to whether or not the names of the directors of The Palace Theatre Watford Limited should be included in the programme where the names of the Council of Management of the Watford Civic Theatre Trust Limited had previously been printed. Modesty and reticence pervaded the atmosphere until Ian Griffiths said that including the names of the new Board would clarify in the minds of the audience and the public at large, the independence of the new Board from the Borough Council and would facilitate fund raising.

At the last Board meeting for that year the David Dixon report disclosed that if the theatre raised £375,000-450,000 in cash after fund raising expenses, it would be doing well. This was not encouraging news. A sum of £450,000 would unlock, at most £1.35 million from the National Lottery, resulting in a total sum available for the project of £1.8 million. The Directors had more ambitious targets and it was becoming increasingly obvious that a major scheme to reconstruct the theatre was needed rather than an attempt to remedy faults in the fabric of the eighty-eight-year-old building. This would only postpone the inevitable but could a comprehensive modernisation plan be afforded?

After professional and other costs the stark reality was that of £1.8 million only about £1.2 million would be available to spend on the refurbishment. It was considered that this sum would be unlikely to enable the theatre to carry out a satisfactory refurbishment plan which would seem worthwhile either to the public or to the staff.

It was clear that a general fund-raising exercise was essential, not only to provide 'partnership funding' to qualify for a Lottery grant but also to provide a reserve behind the theatre's operations. The notional timetable for the refurbishment programme provided for submission of a Lottery bid in May

1997, with a view to the theatre closing in the autumn of 1999 and re-opening twelve months later. Such a time-scale was to prove unrealistically optimistic.

The refurbishment of the 1980s had concentrated on improvements which were most likely to be appreciated by the public and had been forced to abandon plans to improve the working conditions for artistic and backstage staff. This time every possible effort should be made to achieve improvements on both sides of the proscenium arch. The following list of criteria was compiled:

Public benefit including access for the disabled

Financial viability

Partnership Funding

Quality of design and construction

Quality of artistic plan

Regional and national significance

Involvement of artists

Quality of plans for education and marketing.

The Board meeting held on the 13th February 1997 was the last to be attended by Mrs. Jennifer Cooper who was leaving the district. Jenny Cooper had been a member of the Council of Management of the Watford Civic Theatre Trust and she had transferred her responsibilities to becoming a member of the Board of the privatised theatre. She was thanked for her contribution to the management of the theatre in both of these manifestations. Jenny was a prominent member of Watford Operatic Society and Stage Manager of the society. Staging was more elaborate in former years and it is only within the last decade that it has become simpler, yet no less evocative. Because some sets were cumbersome and the 'wings' of the theatre are not large, changing a scene could be a complicated business, particularly if it had to be accomplished within limited a time as dictated by the amount of covering music the orchestra had to play. Jenny conceived the idea of training a stage crew so that every member of that crew knew precisely what he or she had to do to change the scene and accompanying props. She would rehearse the stage crew for each scene change. Descendants of Jenny's crew are still active today and the amateur societies continue to benefit from her ideas. The team today is led by Chris Swallow who follows the tenets established by Jenny Cooper and the services of Chris and his team are enjoyed by all three of the amateur operatic societies who regularly perform at the theatre.

Consideration by the Board of what measures should or could be

undertaken to ensure the future of the theatre inevitably led to a period of
uncertainty but the theatre continued with its core business of entertainment.
It was a period of some financial volatility including one play which proved
not to be to the public's taste. This was a play by Gary Lyons entitled *Frankie
& Tommy*, presented from the 18th April to 10th May 1997. It told the story of
the late Tommy Cooper and his wartime association with Frankie Lyons the
father of Gary Lyons, as a comedy duo. The audience stayed away in droves.
Perhaps some patrons were not fans of Tommy Cooper and so had no burning
desire to see him portrayed on stage. Others, perhaps, who *were* his fans were
fearful that their hero, the fez wearing conjuror whose tricks invariably went
wrong, might be portrayed unsympathetically. The play did show that there
was no love lost between the stage partners who entertained the troops in the
Middle East theatre of war with ENSA. Eventually their relationship
descended into bitterness and the two were persuaded to break up the
association.

Planning for improvements to the ageing theatre continued and in August
1997 the five yearly electrical inspection took place. This was a very important
requirement for the renewal of the entertainment licence. No deficiencies of
major importance were found.

The Lottery fund had to be assured that after completion of the proposed
project the lease would have at least 49 years left to run. The current lease, from
Watford Borough Council as freeholders of the premises, to The Palace Theatre
Watford Limited had only 18 years to run. The then leader of the Borough
Council, Councillor Vince Muspratt said that he thought that a fresh lease to
conform to the Lottery requirements could be arranged. As indeed it was.

Another hurdle to be overcome was the requirement from the Arts
Council of England that during the closure period the theatre would be
required to operate at 50 per cent of capacity in order to qualify for its annual
grant. It was not clear whether this figure related to performances or seats.

Various alternative venues were considered. A tent in the town centre to
act as a temporary theatre for two short seasons of two or three months each.
One season in the Spring and another in the Autumn. Another alternative
venue might be in Cassiobury Park, perhaps a performance of a play by
Shakespeare.

By this time the theatre had been provisionally promised the strip of land
behind the theatre which would facilitate the enlargement and 'squaring up'
of the stage. The freeholders of the land were by now Chartwell, a subsidiary
company of Kingfisher who also owned Woolworths, having concluded the
purchase from Prudential Corporation. It had emerged that Chartwell had

plans to build a new store for Woolworths fronting on to the High Street. The Planning Department at the Town Hall had suggested that as part of the Section 106* agreement, Kingfisher would be asked to donate this strip of land. Kingfisher declared themselves sympathetic to the proposal. Chartwell indicated that it was unlikely that they would require the piece of land and eventually, in 1999, acceded to the request.

In October 1997 the theatre was half way through Stage I of the Lottery bid for funding but there were still no definite ideas of what could be achieved. The Board were still investigating three options:

1.   Do nothing beyond essential repairs;
2.   Undertake a limited modernisation with a contract price of not more than £2.5 million; and
3.   Undertake a modernisation project with a contract price of £4.5 million.

Giles Croft stressed the importance of taking artistic risks in the selection of plays, to please the Eastern Arts Board, especially in view of the Lottery application.

The Stage I application was lodged and the response was eagerly awaited. The Arts Council was undergoing internal reorganisation and this delayed their response.

Meanwhile the architects advised that the theatre should think in terms of delaying the starting of work until 2001. Several reasons were given. Work could not commence until it was certain that the Lottery funding would be forthcoming; secondly, it would give the theatre longer to raise its share of the cost and, thirdly, there was a better chance that the theatre would 'get it right'. Burrell Foley Fischer asked for adequate time to complete detailed plans which would be final, so that there would be no requirement for any modification which could result in an expensive delay during construction. The Board expressed its reservations about the effects of building inflation and the danger of the industry being active enough to endanger the chances of receiving tenders for the work within the projected budget. But they also had in mind the importance of securing the land behind the theatre which, at that time, had not been confirmed. On the other hand they knew by this time that the Borough Council were prepared to give a lease with a life long enough to satisfy the Arts Council.

Eventually the anticipated response to the Stage I application was

* see Chapter 6, Page 124

received and it was positive. The Arts Council Lottery Fund had ear-marked up to £5 million for the modernisation of the theatre but, of course, this depended upon the ability of the theatre to raise £1.7 million in partnership funding. The figure of £1.7 million would unlock the Lottery grant but if the total cost of the work, including professional fees, exceeded £6.7 million, there would be cash additional to the £1.7 million to be raised. Still, it was a big step forward.

Little by little the theatre building continued to reveal what needed to be done. A piece-meal approach to the problems would be expensive. It was preferable, therefore, that the entire project should be undertaken and completed during the period when the theatre was closed. It was also felt that the audience would take a dim view if the theatre had to be closed a second time. It was now quite clear that much needed to be done if the building was to be preserved. Little, if anything, had been done to the dressing rooms apart from periodic redecoration since 1911. The fly tower was wearing out and there had only ever been two toilets backstage. Most of the dressing rooms had no facilities for washing. The ideal solution might have been to demolish the entire edifice and construct a new theatre on the site. Such a course would have been both quicker and cheaper. That was not possible and was never an option. For one thing the Edwardian auditorium and the façade onto Clarendon Road were Grade II Listed. For another, even if it was legally possible to demolish the theatre it was recognised that the people of Watford would not tolerate a demolition of the auditorium.

It became obvious that the whole of the 'stage house', that is, that part of the theatre behind the proscenium arch, consisting of the stage, scenery dock, fly tower and dressing rooms, would have to come down and be replaced. That was the area where most of the money would have to be spent and where previously it had been starved of modernisation. How would the public react? They would not see and enjoy the improvements, apart from the benefits accruing from a larger stage and the consequent ability to stage more lavish productions.

Two other features of the project would help. One was to move the control box, which was at that time situated behind the Stalls on the right-hand side of the theatre, that is the side nearer to the High Street, up to behind the Gallery. At the same time the Box Office would be moved away down to the right-hand side of the enlarged entrance foyer, into an area which was, at that time, an alleyway between the theatre and the kebab shop next door on the High Street side of the building. This was no longer needed as a route for bringing scenery into and out of the theatre. Access would be at the rear of

Back stage

the theatre, obviating the need for lorries to park outside the theatre in Clarendon Road while unloading. Moving the Box Office would provide additional space for a fully computerised ticket selling system and additional working space.

Furthermore, removal of the Box Office and Control Box would make room for an additional row of seats in the Stalls and also provide space to give the audience more leg room.

Audiences had long complained about inadequate toilet facilities. It was determined to rectify this short-coming.

With the Control Box moved up to the Gallery, the hard wooden forms, used for seating but only rarely occupied could be removed and replaced by three rows of comfortable tip-up seats complete with backrests. The Gallery would be renamed the Upper Circle.

Steps would also be taken to integrate fully the 1980s building into the theatre and to install a lift up to the Circle, the new Upper Circle and the offices relocated to the top floor. A lift would also be a feature to improve accessibility for the handicapped.

The net effect on the comfortable seating capacity of the theatre would be an increase of some 90 seats.

It was also confirmed that because of the materials used in the reconstruction of the stage house a safety curtain could be dispensed with.

Work immediately started on preparation of Stage II of the application to the Arts Council Lottery Fund. This involved submission of outline plans for what was intended, including architects' plans. The Arts Council released a sum of money from the £5 million so that the architects could be paid for the work needed to formulate the plans.

The Phone Room campaign was started, although some members of the Board had reservations about the reaction of the theatre's patrons to receiving 'cold-calling' telephone calls asking for donations to the campaign. By December the campaign was regarded as 'moderately successful' and it was anticipated to net about £25,000.

The Stage II, feasibility study, was lodged with the Arts Council in August 1998 and much credit goes to the Administrative Director of the theatre, Alastair Moir, for completing this monumental task on time. A favourable response was received in December. Another hurdle had been cleared.

Matters were gathering momentum. But the project was becoming larger by the hour. The complexity of drawing all the strands together was intimidating and the prospect of arranging the required finance seemed, at times, overwhelming. The prospect of Watford, for ever, losing its theatre drove the management team onwards.

Helen Mirren and the Member of Parliament for Watford, Claire Ward, accepted invitations to become Vice-Presidents of the Palace Theatre, joining Sir John Mills (President) and Elton John (now Sir Elton), already a Vice-President.

The pantomime at Christmas 1998 was *Jack and the Beanstalk* and the Harlequin Shopping Centre sponsored it to the tune of £10,000. This was another panto written for the Palace by Roy Hudd and the cast contained three of the audience's favourites, Chris Emmett, Pamela Cundell and Nick Staverson.

Daphne Boskey was working three days a week fund raising with Anna Quinllin contributing thirty days consultancy over a six-month period. The Finance Committee were then asked whether the theatre's budget would support a full time fund raiser. The reply was that it was a risk that had to be taken.

The new Woolworths store would require a new electricity sub-station and the theatre was invited to share in its facilities for a cost of between £3,000 and £7,000. Advice given was that if the theatre had to install its own sub-station at a later date the cost would be £35,000. The invitation was accepted.

In April Jane Steele was appointed full-time Development Director with special responsibility for fund raising.

Although he was enthusiastic to see the theatre modernised, the prospect of the actual rebuilding process was not a project that Giles Croft relished and so when the position of Artistic Director at the Nottingham Playhouse became vacant early in 1999 he applied for and secured the post. In June of the same year Lawrence Till replaced him as Artistic Director.

Also in June it was suggested that the rear wall of the new Woolworths store would be extended backwards by one metre. This came as a serious set-back for the theatre because, if true, it would prejudice the possibility of extending the stage house. Happily it did not happen and, at last, the theatre was informed by the Town Hall that the strip of land necessary for the extension was secure.

The timetable continued to slip and by the middle of 1999 it was obvious that preparations would not be sufficiently advanced to allow for building work to take place in 2001. In fact the timetable now dictated that the application for design costs would not be lodged until December 1999 and that the response from the Arts Council was unlikely to be received before June 2000. It was anticipated that the design stage would be completed by December so that the application for building costs could be submitted in January 2001. It was hoped that the response to this application would be received by July in which case the actual work on the theatre would finally start in January 2002. It was, at that time, still hoped that the actual construction work would be completed in a year and that the theatre would re-open in time for the pantomime in December 2002.

Once again hopes were to be frustrated.

The core work of the theatre went on as usual, although an uncertain situation regarding timing complicated forward planning.

February 1999 saw a return of Philip Bretherton in Jonathan Holloway's play *Darkness Falls* and in March a new play, *The Late Middle Classes* by Simon Gray, was produced. It had in its cast Harriet Walter, Angela Pleasence and James Fleet (Hugo Horton in *The Vicar of Dibley*). *The Late Middle Classes* was directed by Harold Pinter and was well received. It was expected to go into the West End but at the last moment a different play went into the selected theatre only to close after ten days. *The Late Middle Classes* went on to be voted Best New Play in the 1999 Theatrical Management Association Awards. The proprietors of the West End theatre that turned it down must still be rueing the fact. On the other hand, they were not alone. Before it received its premiere at Watford it had been offered to The Royal National Theatre, who had also turned it down.

To the consternation of all concerned the submission of the application for funding of the design costs was postponed from December 1999 to May 2000. It had been intended that the theatre closure for rebuilding works would be between two pantomimes, the annual money-spinner but the architects advised against a precise timing of the period of closure. They felt that if the contractors knew that a re-opening in time for the pantomime was essential there would be opportunities for over-time working which would increase costs.

Not every play during the twelve month period ending on 31st March 2000 made a profit; they were not expected to, but right at the end of the financial year, *Three Steps to Heaven* was produced. This play had as its subject the aeroplane accident in which Buddy Holly and others lost their lives in 1957. Included in the cast was Jane Milligan, the daughter of the great 'Goons' comedian Spike Milligan. *Three Steps to Heaven* caught the attention of the public and played to full houses. The theatre's finances for that year were transformed.

During the year 2000 there were two visits from Gemma Craven. The first was in January when she starred in *The Shakespeare Revue* and she returned in November to appear in the Shelagh Delaney play *A Taste of Honey*. Dora Bryan, Nichola McAuliffe and Zena Walker were at the Palace Theatre for three weeks in May/June in Alan Bennett's *Talking Heads*. The following month saw a production of Noël Coward's *Blithe Spirit* with an exceptional cast which included Paula Wilcox, Anne Reid *(Dinnerladies)*, Debra Penny and the celebrated Russian ballerina, famous, probably, for her defection to the West, Natalia Makarova.

It is interesting to note that, including the production which was to take place in 2007, *Blithe Spirit* has been performed eight times at the Palace. The only other play to rival that number of performances was a play entitled *While Parents Sleep* by Anthony Kimmins. Between 1933 and 1957 it, too, was performed eight times. Kimmins was a professional sailor. He rose to the rank of Commander in the Royal Navy. He was born in 1901 in Harrow, Middlesex.

After leaving the Navy he became an actor and playwright. Another of his plays *The Amorous Prawn* was presented at the Palace in 1962. He also wrote and directed several of George Formby's best films. He died in 1964.

The last two plays produced in 2000 were *Rough Crossing* in which Matthew Kelly played the lead and *A Taste of Honey*.

By this time, such was the condition of the building that the Entertainment Licence had to be renewed every three months, instead of annually. Matters were becoming serious.

The Stage II application for design costs was duly submitted in May 2000 and the Arts Council promised a response in September.

In the meantime the Arts Council published the Boyden Report. It expounded on debt and reasons for poor attendance at theatres but offered no solutions. Its strategic intention was believed by many to be a document to lobby the Government for more money for regional theatres. The second stage of the report suggested reducing the number of producing theatres in Britain from 49 to 30 and for theatres to undertake a greater number of collaborations and co-productions.

Another indication of the condition of the building occurred in 2000 when two performances were lost as a result of plaster falling from the ceiling above the Gallery. This was repaired on a temporary basis but during the summer break, work was carried out by an expert in fibrous plastic on the maintenance of the auditorium ceiling. There were no safety implications but the loose plaster above the Gallery and moulded plaster around the chandelier needed to be secured.

Bucket collections were organised at the end of performances in the theatre and this, too, was to prove successful. The amateur operatic societies made successful appeals from the stage for contributions to which the audiences responded generously.

To conform to European Union regulations it was necessary to advertise for a firm of Quantity Surveyors and Architects in the European Journal OJEC. In response to the advertisement six firms of architects were invited to tender for the position and Burrell Foley Fischer, who had undertaken the preliminary studies, were appointed.

Seating capacity at this stage was running at 65–75 per cent, which was above the national average. Realistically 'new writing' can be targeted at only 51 per cent of the theatre-going public. Lawrence Till explained to the Board that high targets and new writing tended not to be compatible.

As so often has occurred, one play during the year 1st April 2000 to 31st

March 2001, made a substantial loss. This was a play presented in September 2000 with the title *Cor Blimey!* which was about the relationship between Sid James and Barbara Windsor during the making of the *Carry On* films. Whether this play held little interest for Watford audiences or whether it was because it had, in the recent past, been produced on television under a different title is not known but audience attendance was disappointing. The Board was facing a sizeable deficit for the year. However, this was not the end of the story. The production in November 2000 of *A Taste of Honey* did not achieve its target. It was a roller coaster of a financial year. To the rescue came *Martha, Josie and the Chinese Elvis* the cast of which included Belinda Lang and Debra Penny. It was an extremely funny play. Not only did it do well at the Box Office but the bucket collection, from full houses, was well supported. Belinda Lang, a popular actress, was to return in February 2005 in one of the first plays after the re-opening, *Sitting Pretty*, by Amy Rosenthal, another artistic and financial success.

Artistic Directors and Administrative Directors seem to work in pairs and in October 2000 the Board received with regret, notice of Alastair Moir's resignation as Administrative Director. This was viewed by the Board as a serious matter. Alastair had rendered exceptional service dealing with the copious amount of paper work needed in support of the various stages of the application for Lottery funding. He was asked to reconsider but he declined. He had been offered another post to which he was eminently suited. It was recognised as inevitable that, as promotion was limited at the Palace Theatre, members of staff, particularly the younger members, viewed the theatre as a stepping stone towards ambitious achievement. Alastair's eventual replacement was Mary Caws. For health reasons, Mary was not able, immediately, to take up the post but in the interim, Andrew Leigh, a former General Manager of the Old Vic stood in.

At around this time it emerged that the Boyden Report had found its mark. Chris Smith, the Secretary of State for Culture, Media and Sport persuaded the Treasury to recognise that the grant from central government funds to 'theatre' had been in decline, in real terms, since 1980.

This was to have a dramatic effect on the finances at the Palace Theatre. In the year 2001/2002 the East England Arts grant to the Palace Theatre was £262,370. It was announced that it was to increase, in stages, to £645,997 in the year 2003/2004; an increase of £384,627 or 146 per cent. This was one of the largest increases awarded to any theatre in the country and brought the funding up to the level it would have been at, had the grant been increased each year in line with inflation.

Belinda Lang

The Press release issued by East England Arts stated: 'The Palace is a producing theatre with a successful track record of new writing and commercial transfers. It has strong links with the formal education sector and its education programme reflects cultural diversity and social inclusion. The new investment will enable it to play a regional leadership role in promoting new writing for the benefit of other companies in the region.'

Eventually, on the 18th April 2001, Mary Caws took up the task of Administrative Director, a post she was to hold until July 2006.

Together Lawrence and Mary saw the rebuild through to completion. There were opportunities in plenty for them to move on, during what were, on occasions, worrying times, but unknown to the Board they had made a mutual agreement that they would see the project through. Watford owes much to both of them.

Andrew Thomas of Charity Consultants Limited visited the theatre and gave a morning's workshop to members of the Fund Raising Committee. The main thrust of what he had to say was that time was being wasted encouraging small donations whereas those involved with fund raising should be looking for the larger sums. He emphasised the 'pyramid principle', which was to secure one large donation and then two smaller ones and so forth until when the base of the pyramid was reached a large number of small donations completed the pyramid.

Acceptance of Stage II of the Lottery bid was further delayed because of an internal reorganisation of the Arts Council. No officer had been allocated to the Palace project.

The architects introduced another requirement, which was, to include air conditioning in the auditorium. This would greatly improve audience comfort especially in hot weather and enable the theatre, if it so wished, to remain open and active during the hot summer months.

A comprehensive plan was put together to ensure that partnership funding was in place within eighteen months. It was suggested that there were a surprising number of wealthy people living in Hertfordshire, the problem was, where were they, who were they and how were we to reach them? It was also recognised that if the pyramid principle was to work and be effective, the campaign would benefit from two donations of £250,000 each to add to the £500,000 which had already been promised by Watford Borough Council. The Borough Council had always maintained that the theatre was very much part of the Council's Leisure Strategy.

Charity Consultants Limited produced a list of wealthy residents in the area and some were approached, particularly those who were known to attend performances at the theatre. Unfortunately, the results of these approaches were disappointing.

The theatre was required to complete a 'Business Plan'. This would include forecasts of future profitability, not an easy matter given the fluctuating support of theatre audiences. In any case the Business Plan could change after the Evaluation Day which was another hurdle introduced by the Arts Council. This was intended to assess progress made to date.

Another two important staff changes occurred in April 2001. Hassina Khan, who had been Education Officer at the theatre left to take up a new post at the Arts Council and Craig Titley was appointed marketing manager, a post he had previously held at the Theatre Royal, Windsor.

The financial turbulence of the year continued. The projected deficit for the year had grown again. It was now in the region of £100,000. The view was expressed that 'If the theatre is not careful it will go into closure with a deficit, which will not encourage people to contribute to the appeal fund.' Emergency measures were considered – avoid unpopular single presentations and schedule in money-spinners for the coming season. Then it was discovered that the maintenance of the building had been financed out of the theatre's own budget and that the grant from the freeholders to maintain the fabric of their building had not been claimed for four years and this covered the anticipated deficit.

In July of 2001 it was reported that the Arts Council required the theatre to appoint a project manager. The architects did not consider this necessary.

More staff changes happened, Jane Steele, the Development Director resigned for health reasons and Kirstie Davis joined the staff as Acting Education Officer, as replacement for Hassina Khan. She was soon to drop the 'Acting' part of her title and proved to be, over the ensuing years, a most efficient and enthusiastic member of staff.

During a period of some turmoil, uncertainty and at times pessimism and worry, Divine Providence stepped in and the most amazing event turned aspirations for the preservation of the Palace Theatre, overnight, into reality. The theatre was making only modest headway in securing the money needed to unlock the Arts Council Lottery grant of £5 million. Small donations were being gratefully received and the promise of £500,000 from the Council was encouraging; nevertheless the theatre was a long way short of the £1.7 million partnership funding.

A member of the Board secured an introduction to a possible donor. The result of this introduction was that, conditional upon the successful outcome of the application for a Lottery grant, a donation would be made of £1 million. This was a donation which exceeded everyone's wildest and most optimistic expectations. In an instant it became clear that the way was open to save the theatre, that the ambitious plans to modernise the building and make it fit for the twenty-first Century were no longer a 'pipe dream' bordering on the unrealistic. More than that, it was an encouragement to others to donate. It was going to happen. The only other condition was that the identity of the donor was to remain a secret. One day the name of that anonymous donor will be known and the full amazing story will be told but for now the condition of anonymity will be respected. It is no exaggeration, however, to state that without the generosity of a Watford resident it is improbable that Watford would still possess a live theatre.

In effect the two largest prospective donors were now conditional on each other and therefore both sums were secure. Nevertheless the theatre and its Board of Directors still had some way to go to raise the balance of the cash needed.

In September 2001 it was brought to the attention of the Board that in the interests of the Health and Safety regulations it would be necessary to raise the height of the balustrade around the front of the Circle. This in turn would mean that to maintain the 'sight lines' and not obscure the view of the stage from some of the rows in the Circle the 'rake' would have to be increased. More expense. It was also decided to omit the central aisle in the

Circle and open two extra doorways at the lower level of the Circle adjacent to the Boxes, thus increasing the safety of the audience if at any time a hurried evacuation was necessary. It was decided that the existing two doors, one either side at the top level of the Circle, could present a hazard in an emergency if an elderly person or someone with reduced mobility was blocking the stairs up to these doors. In such a situation the safety of many of the audience could be in jeopardy. Furthermore a fire on either of the existing staircases from the Circle down to the foyer could have had disastrous consequences. The proposed doors at the lower level of the Circle would take people almost directly to the foyer on the ground floor. The aisle behind the last row of seats in the Circle now became superfluous and could be dispensed with. This made room for an extra row of seats. The centre aisle in the Stalls had been done away with in the refurbishment of the early 1980s and now the centre aisle in the Circle which was added in 1912 was also to be removed.

Access to the theatre for wheel-chairs remained a priority. This involved raising the pavement outside the theatre in Clarendon Road and installing a ramp inside the building up to the foyer level. The Borough Council undertook to raise the height of the pavement.

In November it was announced that Mike Terry had been appointed Project Manager. Mike was highly experienced in the construction and restoration processes of cinemas and theatres and he was to prove a valuable addition to the design team.

A review of the funding progress revealed that even after economies had been made the appeal still had to raise a further £600,000 to complete the project. It was reported that a Gala Dinner held at Shendish Manor, Apsley, with Ronnie Corbett as guest speaker, had contributed £5,300 to the fund.

A massive total of £25,000 had been collected in the buckets at the theatre from audiences emptying their loose change into these buckets at the end of performances.

The timetable provided that the final 'go-ahead' would be expected from the Arts Council by the end of March 2002 and that the invitations to tender would go out to prospective contractors shortly afterwards.

While all the drama of the prospective rebuilding of the theatre was being played out productions continued in the customary fashion.

Described as 'A bittersweet romantic comedy', a play entitled *Perfect Days* was presented from the 31st October until the 24th November 2001 and the cast included Janet Henfrey, an actress with wide experience not only in the theatre but in films and television. Her most famous television role was as the housekeeper, Mrs. Bale, in *As Time Goes By*. The lead part in *Perfect Days* was played by Race Davies, a member of the cast of *EastEnders* and who had previously worked at the Palace Theatre as a props maker and on occasions playing small parts. This was a sensitive play centring around the dual themes of an adult who had been adopted at birth and was searching for his natural mother and of a woman desperate to have a baby and for whom the biological clock was ticking.

A number of actors who have appeared at the theatre made reputations for themselves by way of television 'soaps'.

In an earlier chapter mention was made of the performance of John Savident and that he had been a regular cast member of *Coronation Street*. In October 2001 another *Coronation Street* regular appeared at the Palace Theatre. This was Roy Barraclough who played the roles of a brother in the first act and his sister in the second act of a play named *A Different Way Home*. Previously in October 1983 he had been in the cast of *Some of My Best Friends Are Husbands* along with Tony Britton and Hugh Paddick. During the run of *A Different Way Home* Roy made a contribution to the work of fund raising for the theatre by attending a lunch at which the aims of the project were outlined to a group of Watford business and professional people. He will long be remembered in the comedy act with Les Dawson in which they played two elderly women in curlers (Cissie and Ada, respectively) gossiping at the launderette.

One play at this time caused particular interest. *The True Life Fiction of Mata Hari*. Excitement reached fever pitch when it became known that the name part would be played by the film and stage star Greta Scacchi.

Productions during the first half of the financial year had been in balance.

In the spring of the same year new terms were agreed with Hertfordshire County Council under which the County Council agreed to pay £106,000 a year for three years to fund the Theatre in Education programme. The Palace Theatre was obligated to pay the salary of the Education Officer out of this sum.

At the same time, from the Arts Council final confirmation was received that the sum of £5 million would be available to the theatre for the rebuilding project. Furthermore, the Arts Council praised the project plans and understanding of the Board. They said that the risks had been well examined and that there had been a sensible approach to the entire process. Well deserved praise for Dr. David Fisk, as chairman of the Modernisation Committee, the members of that committee, the two Executive Directors

Above left: *Roy Barraclough*

Above right: *Lawrence Till makes the announcement that lottery funds had been secured*

Right: *Celebration of the Lottery Award*
Left to Right: Jane Foy, Phillip Madoc, Norman Tyrwhitt, Paula Wilcox Mary Caws, Lawrence Till

and, it might be said, for the entire Board of Directors of The Palace Theatre Watford Limited, who had all, individually and collectively, devoted many hours of discussion, investigation and effort into the viability of the project.

On Wednesday the 10th April 2002 a press conference was called at the Palace Theatre at which Lawrence Till made the announcement, 'with delight and relief' that the Arts Council Lottery grant of £5 million had been confirmed and that, together with the anonymous donation of a further £1 million, had guaranteed the refurbishment of the Palace Theatre. Also present at the press conference were Paula Wilcox and Philip Madoc. Miss Wilcox said, 'I feel that for a long time a lot of care and love has been lavished on the theatre by the people who work here and the people who come here, it is time it had the money for a real face lift. You always see the best theatre here. Now it has become a real centre of excellence.'

The seat naming campaign was about to begin. Contributors of £100 would have their names inscribed on a small plaque to be fixed to the rear of a seat in the Upper Circle. Donors of £500 would be eligible to name a seat in the Stalls or Circle and a donation of £2,000 would secure the naming of an entire Box. Those who made major contributions to the appeal were invited to name a part of the building. One who accepted was the anonymous donor who elected to name the auditorium after a member of her family, hence the word 'Victoria' which is today above the proscenium arch.

Borough Councillor Tim Williams announced that he would be running in the London Marathon in aid of the theatre appeal. With a note of pleasure in his voice he said, 'It's important that Watford keeps such a quality theatre and for a while it looked in jeopardy.'

Philip Madoc, who resides in St. Albans and who had only recently been in the cast of Terence Rattigan's play *The Deep Blue Sea*, at the theatre said that 'there is within this theatre, an extraordinary professionalism. It is a place where people communicate with ease. It is the only theatre I know that deserves this award.' Alan Orme, theatre officer at East England Arts, added 'this theatre is one of the finest jewels in the region's crown.'

After months of negotiations, consideration of reports from the Architects and Quantity Surveyors, listening to the advice of professional fund raisers and, not least, the cautious warnings of the Arts Council, the time had arrived for the final momentous decision to be made. A meeting of the Board of Directors was called.

The agenda consisted of only one item: whether or not to embark on the project which would secure the future of the Palace Theatre, Watford for the twenty-first century.

The chairman called the meeting to order and reminded the members of the serious nature of the proceedings. He said that at the outset and before the discussion started he wanted to know, as a guidance, how each member felt about the magnitude of the decision and of the resulting task which lay ahead. He said that if the members felt that the risk was too great to undertake there would be no shame attached if they decided not to proceed. He warned that there would be worrying times ahead. They still had much fund raising to do. It would be a 'leap into the dark'. The alternative, not to proceed with the rebuilding programme, on the other hand, would signal that the theatre would close, probably never to re-open. He reminded the Board that the theatre was operating on an Entertainment Licence which had to be renewed quarterly. Watford would, inevitably, lose its theatre. He then invited the members present to raise a hand if they were in favour of proceeding with the rebuilding project. A silence descended on the room. A sombre mood took hold.

Slowly every hand was raised.

The chairman broke the seriousness of the occasion by thanking all present for relieving him of the responsibility of using his casting vote.

Metaphorically, at that moment every member of the Board, the Executive Directors and the staff of the theatre, rolled up their collective sleeves. The project at last swung into action. Many sleepless nights lay ahead. There were to be set-backs and disappointments but mostly these were overcome due to the enthusiasm that everyone felt for an inspired project.

Then a strange thought occurred. How was the project to be described? The terms Modernisation, Refurbishment or Rebuilding did not seem to fit the circumstances. The public must not be given the impression that the building was to be demolished and redeveloped. Audiences would not forgive any disturbance to the admired Edwardian auditorium or to the façade on to Clarendon Road which was such a familiar landmark on the Watford scene. It was never the intention to destroy either of these features. The installation of air conditioning in the auditorium would have to be done with the minimum of disruption to the appearance of the auditorium. Indeed, because both the auditorium and the façade are Grade II Listed they had to be preserved. Any significant changes would not have been allowed by English Heritage. It is probable that an accurate term to describe what was to be done was never determined, although it seems now to be referred to as a 'rebuilding' of the theatre.

Redundancy payments had to be agreed and worked out. All staff were to receive full salary up until the end of July 2002. Thirteen members of staff were retained over the closure period. Dot Butcher, the indefatigable Education Assistant, took voluntary redundancy.

Sir Elton John, a long-time Vice-President of the theatre resigned on taking on the chairmanship of the Old Vic, leaving Dame Helen Mirren and Claire Ward, M.P. as the two remaining Vice-Presidents. Sir John Mills continued as President.

Fund raising was now in full swing. On Saturday 8th June 2002 the three amateur operatic societies, Abbots Langley Gilbert & Sullivan Society, Cassio Operatic Society and Watford Operatic Society combined to give a matinee and evening performance at the theatre of music from some of the musical shows the societies have performed at the Palace. The show bore the title *Intervals* and was their way of paying a tribute and saying farewell to the old theatre. Both performances were well attended and the show produced a contribution to the appeal of more than £10,000.

Members of the audience when booking tickets for the remaining plays before closure were adding a donation to the cost of their tickets. The enthusiasm was infectious.

During the late summer of 2002 Norman Tyrwhitt completed his second term of three years as chairman of the Board and so under the terms of the Articles of Association, he retired but remained a member of the Board. Ian Avent was elected chairman in his place and Ian Scleater was elected as his Deputy for as long as Mr. Avent was chairman.

To end the last season before closure, Sandi Toksvig wrote a hilarious play entitled *Big Night Out at the Little Palace Theatre*. The play was actually set in a cinema that was facing permanent closure. The audience at the theatre was well aware that far from facing permanent closure the Palace was embarking on the most comprehensive refurbishment in its history. The Gala Performance was given on Saturday 6th July. At the end and while the audience was still in its seats champagne was served and a toast was drunk, by everyone present, cast and audience, to the future of the theatre.

The cast of *Big Night Out* included Sandi Toksvig herself as well as Dillie Keane, who wrote the music, and Bonny Langford. Also in the cast were Ken Bradshaw, Simon Coulthard, David Ashley and Russell Churney. The play was directed by Lawrence Till and it was said that due to the nature of the play and its subject every mistake in rehearsal which led to hilarity amongst the cast also gave rise to the shout 'Keep it in!' Sandi Toksvig whole heartedly agreed but admitted that by the time the play opened on stage she scarcely recognised it as her work.

The Gala programme contained a message from Sir John Mills which included the following:

'The Palace Theatre Watford is my local theatre, as it is for thousands of people in this area, and as such provides us with a unique and indispensable service. The only producing theatre in Hertfordshire, it is like having the West End on your doorstep, presenting a range of work that you could not see elsewhere.

'I am privileged to be President of this delightful part of Watford's heritage and can stand with many other actors who too have appeared on the Palace Theatre's stage.

'The theatre has undergone various alterations over the past ninety-four years but now has come the time for a substantial face-lift.

'We are so fortunate to have such a beautiful theatre as part of our community, you only have to visit it to appreciate what an utter pleasure it is to watch and listen to a play in that auditorium.'

Sir John had intended to be present at the Gala and give an address before the performance but on the night, with his sight almost extinguished and in frail health he was advised not to come and his daughter, Hayley, spoke his words in his absence.

The Gala Night raised £15,000 for the appeal.

Jane Foy was appointed Development Director in the autumn of 2002 with the responsibility of fund raising. Jane herself had connections with the entertainment world as she was the daughter of Jack Smethurst, the noted comedy character actor. She was to accomplish the task she faced, with great success. At this time the total sum raised by the theatre amounted to £1,848,409.

The cheapest tender for the work to be done came in at £720,000 over budget. This was a set-back but undaunted the Modernisation Committee reviewed the plans to find economies and the Board unanimously approved an overspend on the project of £150,000. The bank agreed an overdraft facility of £200,000 if needed.

Haymills were appointed contractors and Ross Love was appointed by the Arts Council to monitor progress.

Work began on 2nd September 2002.

The Stage House was the first part of the building to be pulled down. The complication of the project was to dismantle most of the building around the auditorium without disturbing either the auditorium itself or the façade onto Clarendon Road.

In November 2002, Grelle White, the noted writer and journalist and regular contributor to the *Watford Observer*, especially on matters pertaining to the Palace Theatre and the arts generally, wrote an article in the *Watford Observer* following a visit to the partially demolished theatre and based on interviews with the contractors.

In the article she wrote:

'It is the biggest disappearing act ever performed at the Palace Theatre Watford.

'Production "Refurbishment" has been plotted and planned for a very long time. Seven years to be precise. We came prepared. Yet, as the doors swing open to what was once the rather gloomy theatre foyer, the sensation is one of shock, bordering on horror.

'In a place so closely associated with a soft shell of plush darkness, occasionally lit by banks and beams of artificial lights and a world of make-believe and fairy tales, the bright daylight is blinding. You can see forever… the sky, the clouds, the YMCA building in Charter Place, a distinctly concrete part of the real world now rather eerily posing as a backdrop for the still perfectly framed Palace stage.

'It is as if the back has dropped off the theatre and a giant broom has swept the entire contents of the building out through a large hole in the wall.

'The demolition crew has been hard at work inside the Edwardian building for just over six weeks but, from the front, the Palace has looked as if still closed for the summer break with no real hint of the dramatic happenings inside.

'"We get lots of calls from people wanting to book tickets for the Christmas pantomime," reveals administration assistant, Val Heyden, from the theatre's temporary office, a smallish space perched high above an industrial unit in Sydney Road.

'Artistic director Lawrence Till and his much reduced staff are gradually coming to terms with the Watford Palace Gap Year and the challenging task of producing and promoting theatre without a permanent building, as well as planning ahead.

'Next week Lawrence will be working in London on the development of a musical interpretation of Bill Naughton's novel *Alfie*. The new musical is planned for a Palace Theatre premiere in 2004.

'At this point it is a little difficult to imagine the grand opening night with people beautifully attired sweeping along the airy foyer for a pre-show drink in the new ground floor bar which will be a lofty and light two-storey atrium with a couple of walkways above.

'Here we are in safety helmets, fluorescent yellow jackets and huge Wellington boots plodding our way through the rubble trying to grasp the vision of the future Palace Theatre with expert help from the

Dismantling

Demolition begins

contractor Haymills' project manager, Scott Dowell.

'Scott has just completed building a new lecture theatre for Haberdashers Askes School for Girls – a much easier task than rebuilding the inside of an old theatre.

'"We have just reached the point where I start to smile." he says quietly, referring to the fact that the demolition task is nearly complete without revealing any nasty surprises.

'They did find a cellar not marked on the plans, all full of concrete, which needs to be broken up and removed before construction of a lift-shaft can start – but an empty basement could have been less pleasant to deal with.

'A few remnants from the past still linger: a wooden board commemorating the fact that Sir John Mills performed the official opening following the last major refurbishment, on November 25, 1981, and the spiral staircase in the John Mills Room. The banister has been welded in such a way, the staircase cannot be taken apart for removal, which is rather a pity as no doubt it could have raised a tidy sum towards the Palace Theatre Appeal.

'The enormous chandelier in the auditorium, from the 1981 revamp, is not part of the new scheme of things, but still hangs there like a huge prop on a set for a horror film.

'"If anyone would like to remove that I will personally make a contribution to the appeal," Scott smiles.

'He is sensitive in his enthusiasm for the changes, but once he realises that our sentimental feelings for the building are concerned with keeping the auditorium in its original period dress, he relaxes and points out that the old lay-out involved a tremendous waste of space with corridors, nooks and crannies which will now be put to better use.

'It is very outdated. The building will be much more user-friendly and comfortable and we are not touching anything of historic value,' Scott points out.

'The box office will move to the side of the foyer – or rather concourse – which releases space for more seating inside the auditorium. Brand new this time. For the last refurbishment old seats were replaced with not so old ones from another theatre. The alleyway between the theatre and the kebab shop will be included in the building.

'The stage will be extended. No longer will actors have to dash round the outside to exit stage one side and re-enter the other and the original flytower from 1908 is being replaced.

'Diggers are clanking away outside the half-raised safety curtain, which can usefully be lowered at night to help secure the building.

'Lawrence Till has found his bearings and reference points between old and new.

'"I find it very exciting to see the drawings coming to life and how the building is going to work," he says.

'Administrative director Mary Caws admits her first visit to the theatre after a month long holiday filled her with a strange mixture of excitement and terror.

'"I just looked at it and thought: 'Oh, my God, it is finally happening'. It was very emotional going round a building you think you know with no clear idea of where you are, like a building you don't know at all.

'"Now I am feeling very excited about it all happening after all the time and agonising over plans and budgets. It's upwards and onwards." She smiles with an appreciative glance around the auditorium with its prominent proscenium arch, the boxes, the balconies and the Edwardian décor still in place.

'Soon the safety curtain will come down and darkness will fall. Has Aggie, the resident ghost, been spotted during all the upheaval?

'"Ghost! Haven't seen one. But we did find doors mysteriously unlocked in the morning until we changed the locks," Scott recalls.

'Could be that Aggie approves of the Palace Theatre make-over.'

This account eloquently reflected the impressions of others who visited the theatre during the rebuilding programme.

The contractors had drilled bore holes where the extension behind the theatre would be. Nothing untoward was found until the earth was removed to put down the foundations. It was at this point that two brick culverts were uncovered, which the bore holes had not detected. What could they be? Progress was halted while enquiries were made. No one had any inkling. It was concluded that they were relics of an old drainage system and the *Watford Observer* in its issue of the 11th April 2003 reported that 'two large underground culverts' had been discovered. After the most careful consideration it was decided to inject concrete into them.

It was not until four years later that it was discovered that these culverts were all that remained of the roof of the second chamber and the roof of the Ice House of 1781 attached to Mr. Meadows's Pyramid Mausoleum. So the strange, irregular shape of the old stage was finally explained. The rear wall of the 1908 theatre had to be constructed so as to avoid the consecrated mausoleum.

The discovery of the culverts at the beginning of the refurbishment had delayed the project by some two or three weeks and this had a 'knock-on effect' adding a considerable sum to the cost.

It had been the plan to build the new fly tower with blocks but a suggestion was made that some of the lost time could be made up if the fly tower was constructed using continuous pouring concrete. This was agreed upon, even although it would increase the cost by another £40,000.

Lawrence Till and Mary Caws were in constant touch with the Arts Council throughout the tender process and were still keeping them up-to-date with progress on the project. Consequently the Arts Council were only too well aware that although every opportunity was being taken to bring the project within budget, a deficit of £137,000 still remained. At the time of approving the grant of £5 million from the Lottery Fund the Arts Council had made it very clear that there would be no further money available. It was a pleasant surprise therefore when they advised that the theatre should make an application for a supplementary grant to cover the overspend. Advice with which, naturally, it was not difficult to comply. In very swift response, Mary Caws was about to board a train to Watford at Birmingham when her mobile telephone rang and the caller told her that the application for the supplementary grant had been approved.

As the theatre was now closed it seemed appropriate to merge the Modernisation and Finance Committees into one entity under the chairmanship of Professor David Fisk.

At the time of closure the annual grant from Watford Borough Council was £310,000 and the Council suggested that as the theatre was closed and therefore not producing any work, the grant would be reduced by £100,000 a year. This caused a degree of consternation because in broad terms the productions at the theatre paid for themselves at the Box Office but made no contribution to the salaries of the administrative staff. If more staff had to be laid off there would be little chance of a pantomime at Christmas 2003 in the theatre or at any other location. It was considered that if the Palace Theatre missed two annual pantomimes the speed at which audiences returned to the theatre could be affected.

The Arts Council offered to talk to the Borough Council, as a result of which the grant remained intact.

The Education Department continued to function even though the theatre was closed. Its base was moved to the Newton Price Centre, in

Grosvenor Road, Watford. *The Caucasian Chalk Circle* was in rehearsal, directed by Kirstie Davis and was set to tour thirty schools in the county and nine small theatres in Hertfordshire.

Even as early as April 2003 possible colour combinations for the auditorium and the public areas were being considered. One idea being canvassed was for the new seats to be in different shades of plum. Each seat to be free standing so that should a seat need replacing it could be removed and replaced without disturbing the rest of the row and, if there was more than one shade of colour the replacement would not be so obvious. The colouring eventually decided upon, however, was for a uniform shade of bright red.

The chandelier presented a problem. Many of the theatre's patrons were under the impression that it was the original and had hung from the ceiling since 1908. This was not so. It was installed as part of the 1981 refurbishment which restored the theatre to its Edwardian elegance. Surprisingly, when it was taken down it was found to be not worth cleaning and in any case with the increased 'rake' of the upper floors it would have obscured the view of the stage from some seats as well as from the new control box at the back of the Gallery, or, as it was to be re-named, the Upper Circle.

As a supplementary condition of the Arts Council Lottery Grant, a sum

Construction of the flytower

Professor David Fisk

of money was required to be spent on 'art'. It is not clear what form the 'art' should take but the idea of a lighting 'sculpture' in the auditorium, in the Entrance Foyer and on the landing behind the Circle, where the Mills Room had previously been positioned, was decided upon. It seemed to fit the bill, being utilitarian as well as artistic.

Bill Culbert was recommended to the Board as an expert, described as the world's leading exponent of tubular lighting. His proposals were considered by the Board in some depth and it was realised that his ideas were controversial and likely to provoke comment from the theatre's traditional audience. In the event the cost of art work in three areas proved to be too costly, exceeding the budget for them and so it was decided to omit the piece intended for the Circle foyer.

The lighting sculpture in the ceiling of the auditorium proved to be the most controversial item in the refurbishment programme.

At this stage of the rebuilding the project was thirty-five days behind schedule. This was largely due to the discovery of the two large brick culverts.

In May 2003 Norman Tyrwhitt lost his seat in the Local Council elections and so was disqualified from membership of the Board of Directors bringing to an end some thirty-eight years of 'hands on' involvement in the management of the theatre, apart from a brief period during the late 1960s. He had been a member of the original Council of Management while the theatre was a civic theatre and following 'privatisation', as a member of the Board of Directors. His personal interest in the activities and success of the theatre remains undiminished. The Board of Directors and the Executive Directors paid handsome tribute to

Mr. Tyrwhitt for his devoted, voluntary service to the local theatre.

Norman Tyrwhitt's replacement as a Watford Borough Council representative was Councillor Sheila Smillie.

Although the theatre was now closed, a programme of plays continued, although in a reduced quantity. One innovative and highly successful play was *News from the Seventh Floor*. This play was a co-production with Wilson & Wilson and presented in Clements store, after the store had closed in the evening and the audience of twenty five, at a time, was led to different parts of the shop for different scenes, starting in the boiler room downstairs finishing up on the roof of the building in the roof car park. Some thought this was an appropriate venue for this play given that the popular television comedy series *Are You Being Served* is said to have been inspired by the family-owned store in the High Street and on the site formerly occupied by Watford House, mentioned in Chapter 1 of this book.

Meanwhile the Youth Theatre was selected to give a performance of *Brokenville* by Philip Ridley, at the Royal National Theatre before a packed audience.

Circle 'rake'

By September 2003 the sum needed to complete the capital project had grown to £800,000. The Arts Council East advised that a further application to the Arts Council of England Lottery Fund for additional funding would not be successful. However, the Arts Council East intimated that they would in all probability look favourably on making a grant and confirmed that they were agreeable to a transfer of a part of the accumulated revenue income surplus to capital.

Watford Borough Council similarly agreed to a transfer of surplus revenue to capital and said that they would consider a loan of £200,000 to the theatre, repayable over five years. Initially the Borough Council suggested that the loan would be repaid by a reduction of £50,000 from the annual grant. The Executive Directors and a representative of the Arts Council East expressed strong reservations at this suggested method of repayment because they felt that such a reduction would have a serious adverse effect upon the quality of the work produced at the theatre and feared that the Arts Council strategy could not be delivered. The Board, however, overruled these

Lighting sculpture in the ceiling

reservations, taking the view that completion of the rebuilding was top priority. Nevertheless, the Board also took the view that with the transfers of surplus income to capital, the further grant and a renewed fund raising effort the shortfall could be covered without recourse to a loan from the Borough Council.

It was at this time that it was agreed to look for an outside caterer to manage the in-house bar and coffee shop. This would have to be put out to tender in accordance with Arts Council Lottery regulations. At the same time closure of Clements, the department store was imminent. Those who ran the Sheraton Restaurant at the store were looking for new premises for their business. The fit seemed perfect. The theatre could provide the venue and the Sheraton would bring with them their displaced customers. The new coffee shop was to be named the Purple Café. The new tenants were prepared to finance the fittings in their new venue and in compensation the theatre agreed to waive rent until the cost of the fittings had been recouped. Thereafter rent would be based on a proportion of the Purple Café profits.

Completion date, in March 2004, was approaching but difficulty was experienced in tying the contractors down to a definite date. It was expected to be mid-May but since the project was already running late as well as over budget, a more realistic date of completion was expected to be late June. This uncertainty was causing problems in making plans for the re-opening and recruiting a staff to run the renovated theatre, additionally a programme of plays needed to be decided upon. Both of the theatre's funders, Watford Borough Council and the Arts Council of England, East, were keen that the re-opening should not be delayed longer than was absolutely unavoidable. In practical terms it looked as though, taking the re-commissioning time needed, it might not be possible to re-open before the pantomime. This latter consideration had a bearing on the fact that the appeal fund was still short of funds to meet all the remaining costs. It was decided to approach the Council with a request for a loan of £500,000 to ensure that all the contractor's costs could be paid on schedule. The response was that such a loan would have to be authorised by the District Auditor.

Indication received from the Council was that they were inclined to grant a loan but that it would have to have Council Cabinet approval and it was not due to meet until the 19th April.

A formal request was made for a loan of £500,000, later to be shaved to £450,000 because of the transfer to capital of a further tranche of unspent income.

An application was also made to the East England Development Agency for a grant but this was refused.

On the 27th April 2004 it was reported that the Borough Council Cabinet had referred the application to a full Council meeting due to take place on Wednesday the 5th May.

The Arts Council East said that there was no possibility of further finance from them.

Matters were looking increasingly serious.

Then it was realised that on the eve of the re-opening of the theatre, if it was to be in the second half of 2004, no fewer than eight members of the Board of Directors would be due to retire. This would be at the end of June, those members having completed their maximum eight years' term of office as permitted under the Articles of Association of the company, just when their invaluable knowledge of the theatre would be most missed.

The Board retained the offer of overdraft facilities from the bank but would the bank be prepared to honour that commitment if they were not the principal lender?

Reconstruction in progress (2002)

It was agreed at a Board meeting that a request should be made to the Council for a loan for £400,000, repayable over eight years. Councillor Sheila Smillie, representing the theatre as a member of its Board of Directors offered to make a counter proposal at the Council meeting for a reduced loan if the full amount was not agreed.

In the meantime it was accepted that the recruitment of staff could not proceed until the financial situation was secured.

The eventual request was reduced to £350,000, the amount required having fallen because of a further tranche of unspent income which had been transferred to capital. At the Council meeting, Councillor Geoff O'Connell asked what had changed to alter the Cabinet's decision to make a loan, apart from the fact that the amount which the theatre now needed to complete had been reduced by £100,000? The two opposition parties, Labour and Conservative, supported the theatre's case but the Liberal Democrat ruling party felt that there were other institutions in the town in need of financial support, so at its meeting on 5th May the Council agreed a loan of £250,000.*

The news of the £100,000 shortfall on the amount needed reached the ears of the anonymous donor who generously offered a further grant of £100,000.

Finance was now secure for the payment of all outstanding bills but the theatre had incurred a liability to Watford Borough Council of £250,000. Fund raising would have to continue but it was acknowledged that that would not be easy. If the public saw that the theatre was completed and re-opened would they conclude that the need for support was no longer a priority?

In spite of all of this, minds could now be concentrated on preparation for the re-opening.

On 17th May 2004, Peter McInerney was elected to the Board with a view to him succeeding Ian Avent as chairman when the latter retired from the Board at the end of June that year. Mr McInerney was a lawyer by profession specialising in entertainment law. This made him an ideal successor to another lawyer, now a judge, as chairman of the Board.

It was agreed at the same meeting that the theatre would open with a modern adaptation by Tanika Gupta of William Wycherley's period play *The Country Wife* to run from 8th to 30th October and that the pantomime for that year would be *Mother Goose*.

---

* The loan was eventually negotiated at £275,000 repayable over five years at an interest rate of 4.5 per cent

This programme would give a two-week trial period before the first production; a showcasing of educational programmes and for a limited range of one-off events to extend the range of the programmes. It would also allow for 'snagging' time after the first production and events, prior to the pantomime.

The Education Department and Youth Theatre were renamed, most appropriately, 'Active' and gave a production of *Mother Courage & Her Children* by Bertolt Brecht. This toured to small-scale venues and secondary schools throughout Hertfordshire from the end of September to 13th November. The inspiration behind the change of name demonstrated an ambition to be both proactive and reactive.

The 'one-night stands', in September included the *Top Brass Jazz Orchestra* on the 22nd, followed by *Aspires Night of Comedy, Live and Giggin*, with local live bands and *A Vision of Ireland Dance Company* on successive evenings.

Joyce Branagh was appointed to fill a new post, that of Literary Director. She was a sister of the renowned actor/director Kenneth Branagh.

On the conclusion of the three-year funding agreement by Hertfordshire County Council, 'Active' made a fresh application for funding and this was agreed in the sum of £100,000 per annum. This was a 10 per cent reduction on the amount previously received but welcome, none the less.

The Gala re-opening took place on Thursday, 21st October 2004 before an invited audience, largely comprising those who had supported the appeal.

The task was completed. The total cost had exceeded the original budget and the project took rather longer than the anticipated period of closure of one year but the future of the Palace Theatre was assured

Throughout all the vicissitudes, the fortunes of the historic theatre had been guided by Professor David Fisk CB and it is to him primarily and to the members of the Modernisation and Finance Committee that thanks are due. It will never be forgotten that the biggest 'thank you' is owed to the anonymous donor without whose generosity it might never have happened.

Reaction to the re-opened theatre was mixed. Some felt that the entrance concourse was unwelcoming. Comment was also made about sections of unplastered walls. The removal of the centre aisle in the Circle also brought forth comment. The lack of signage was complained about and people said that they could not find the Box Office. Criticism of the lack of signage was acknowledged and speedily rectified.

During the period approaching and during the reconstruction, people were apprehensive about the 'atmosphere' of the theatre, particularly in the auditorium, and whether that atmosphere would be lost. The smell of a century of grease paint *was* dissipated together with the smell of overheating lights but the general ambience of the auditorium was retained.

Most of the adverse comment, it must be admitted, was directed at the lighting sculpture in the ceiling of the auditorium. People felt that it was out of place in an Edwardian setting. It was almost universally disliked. 'Incongruous' was the word most frequently used.

Letters were written to the local newspaper. The severity of the criticism was unexpected and, in some respects, possibly due to misunderstanding. Unless those who passed comment appreciated the necessity for what had been achieved and the availability of funds to pay for it they may not have been in a position to appreciate fully the magnitude of the task and the consequences if nothing had been done. It was noticeable that the severest criticism was expressed by people whose names did not appear on the list of donors, although it is, of course, acknowledged that they may well have contributed by other means such as the bucket collections. Possibly, therefore, they were not aware of the facts concerning the financing of the rebuilding programme.

There is little doubt that had the refurbishment not taken place there would not be a live theatre in Watford today. Had there been unlimited funds available some of the modernisation of the theatre might have been done differently. It is not an understatement to say that many aspects of the task had to be dropped from the scheme because of a need to 'cut our coat according to our cloth'.

The Board of Directors and senior management did not set out to build a museum. It would have been less costly and certainly quicker to have demolished the entire building and started again from scratch. That was never an option. English Heritage would not have permitted such a sacrilegious move and it is doubtful whether the theatre's audiences would have enjoyed the prospect of an entirely new building which lacked the atmosphere and appearance of the old Palace Theatre.

On the other hand most members of the public applauded the extra leg room and an increase in the number of toilets. They also appreciated the ability to obtain a drink in the interval without a seemingly interminable wait for service. Many, perhaps surprisingly, applauded the very features which had engendered criticism from others.

Favourable comment was also received concerning the re-siting of the Box Office and the reduced but comfortable seating in the Gallery, now re-

Left: The new decor 2004

Above: Location of the box office

named the 'Upper Circle'. Comfortable seating had been increased.

Eventually a former member of the Board, and one who was a part of the decision-making process with a knowledge of how those decisions were made, was motivated to write to the *Watford Observer* in an effort to put the matter into context and correct some of the misunderstandings which seemed to be circulating. This letter, which emphasised that Watford had been on the threshold of losing its theatre, brought about a cessation of the criticism.

After some nine years of trials and tribulations, discussions, occasional disappointments and, at times, considerable worry a new theatre for Watford had at last emerged and the town was secure in the knowledge that, for its residents, a theatre had been created for the twenty-first century with an enlarged stage equipped with all the most modern technology and, for the audience, greatly increased comfort.

At the end of 2004, another stalwart of the theatre, its Finance Officer for ten years, Harry Holt retired. He had guided the theatre through the uncharted seas of the rebuilding and kept payments and receipts from the funders on schedule.

CHAPTER 7

Metamorphoses

As we have seen, the Palace Theatre, Watford has undergone various metamorphoses during its first century.

Structurally, in 1908 it was built as a relatively modest building with an uninspiring exterior and a plain, somewhat basic, interior. The audience was seated on only two floors, although the upper floor consisted of a Circle with a Gallery behind. Comfort for the majority had not been a feature.

The decoration of the auditorium did not include the rococo style ornamentation with which we are familiar today.

For the majority seating was on wooden forms without back rests.

In 1911, not the year after the theatre was originally constructed, as some accounts would have us believe, it acquired a new façade, which, at the same time, enabled a third tier to be constructed, to which the wooden forms from the Circle and some from the Stalls were transferred. The spaces vacated on the two original levels enabled additional comfortable seats to be installed.

It remained in this form until the rebuilding programme in 2002/04. Apart, that is, from the '1980s' building which was added in 1982. The floors of the two connected buildings were not on the same level, involving steps up or down. So it was not until the re-building programme that the integration of the two buildings was eventually and satisfactorily completed.

Like a lady changing her clothes to conform to the taste of current fashion, the theatre has been redecorated from time to time and in sharply contrasting styles. No record has been found to show in detail what the original interior decoration was like, apart from the black and white photograph taken from the stage on the opening night in 1908. The ornate decoration was to follow later, possibly, although it cannot be confirmed with certainty, in 1911. Today, although now equipped with air conditioning, the auditorium of the theatre retains its Edwardian elegance. During the recent rebuilding a correspondent expressed the hope that the decorative relief work around the Circle and Gallery balustrades would be picked out in gold leaf. If only the budget could have stretched that far! In 1958, while the lease was in the hands of James and Gilda Perry, the décor was 'Wedgewood' with panels picked out in turquoise within white frames. The redecoration in 1967 was in a Regency style with vertically striped wallpaper. In 1982, under Michael Attenborough's direction, Clare Ferraby restored the Edwardian appearance of the auditorium with shades of deep red darkening the closer it was to the stage. This redecoration included lighting fixtures which had the appearance of gas lights.

The rebuilding in 2002/04 was undoubtedly the most significant period of the theatre's existence. It acquired the technology, the audience capacity and the general ambience of what a twenty-first-century theatre should have: more comfort and accessibility for the audience, a rectangular, deeper stage and more congenial working conditions for the staff, and for the performing artistes modern dressing rooms with improved facilities. In fact a theatre in which the 'big name' personalities of the entertainment world would wish to perform and plays, which a twenty-first-century theatre should be capable of presenting for the enjoyment of its audience.

For those engaged in the musical life of the theatre it may be said that the only disappointment in the reconstruction of the theatre is that the space to accommodate an orchestra has been reduced. In the past there have been occasions when an orchestra of more than thirty players has been accommodated, now it is not possible to use an orchestra of more than twelve players without causing them considerable discomfort. This number is arbitrary; it does, of course, depend on which instruments are required. A flute takes up a lot less space in the pit than does a double bass or a harp. It would be possible to remove another row or two of seats in the Stalls but that would mean some, if not all of the orchestra sitting on ground level and not in a pit. This would put the clock back to 1908 and would undoubtedly cause a considerable amount of work each time a larger orchestra needed to be accommodated. So a smaller orchestra pit does inhibit visits by touring opera or ballet companies and certainly restricts the orchestral accompaniment for performances by the amateur operatic societies, most probably for the Gilbert & Sullivan operettas by the Abbots Langley Gilbert & Sullivan Society. Sir Arthur Sullivan's scores call for relatively large orchestras, well exceeding what the new pit can accommodate.

The Palace Theatre, Watford also underwent a series of metamorphoses in regard to the types of entertainment it produced.

In 1908 the theatre was, like so many of its contemporary structures, no more nor less than a provincial music hall. It remained so, with occasional forays into 'legitimate theatre', involving visits from West End theatre companies presenting musical comedies and plays, visits by opera companies and by ballet companies, up until almost the outbreak of World War II. During the 1930s it had flirted with repertory, with visits for sometimes extended periods by Henry Baynton and his company, the Denville Players, the Edward Nelson Players and the first visit of the Melvilles.

It was not until 1939 that it became, in practical terms, a repertory theatre. This was when Andrew and Winifred Melville acquired the lease and assumed management. As a repertory theatre it continued, in uninterrupted vein, under the management of Jimmy and Gilda Perry. In 1965 it became a civic theatre and under the guidance of a series of accomplished Artistic Directors it prospered, with the inevitable occasional set-back, presenting a varied assortment of plays but cast externally, so that Watford audiences enjoyed the pleasure of seeing visiting artistes on the Palace Theatre stage, many of whom were, or became, prominent in their profession.

Some contemporary accounts of the history of the theatre have spoken of the Melvilles 'selling' the theatre to the Perrys. Neither of them ever 'owned' the theatre. They did, however, 'own' the lease of the building and it was the unexpired portion of this lease which was acquired by the Borough Council from the Perrys when the theatre became a civic theatre in 1965.

From early after the new façade was built in 1911 it was adorned with two large advertising placards. The photograph in Chapter 2 and believed to date from September 1915 shows the placards in position

Towards the end of the Perrys' tenure of the theatre these two large banners proclaimed that the Palace Theatre was 'The Only Live Theatre in Herts'. A photograph opposite shows the banners in position. This photograph dates from February 1965 because the notices outside the theatre advertise a production of Ivor Novello's last musical show *King's Rhapsody*, the only production of that show at the Palace having taken place in that month.

By 1969 the banners had been taken down. We are able to date a photograph of the façade taken from a position opposite the theatre, from what in those days was named 'Watford House Lane', as taken in April 1969. The photograph shows posters advertising a production of Henrik Ibsen's play *A Doll's House*. There were two productions of this classic in the 1960s. The first was during the week commencing the 8th February 1960 and the second was in the week of the 15th April 1969. The photograph referred to clearly shows where the banners were fixed to the façade and so must have been taken after 1965.

1965 work

The theatre in April 1969

At one time the theatre also had its name displayed in red neon lighting on the side wall facing the High Street.

Ballet companies which have visited the theatre have included Ballet Rambert, the City of London Ballet Company and the Royal Ballet.

Gradually the Palace Theatre had become, almost imperceptibly, a Producing theatre. By the time it was handed back by the Borough Council to private management it had acquired a national reputation for the quality of the work it was producing.

In 2008 Watford can boast a modern 'high tech' theatre. Still the only 'live theatre' in Hertfordshire and one with an established national reputation.

It has not entirely forgotten its music hall origins. Today the occasional one night stand takes place on Sunday evenings and memories remain fresh of appearances for single performances from Roy Hudd and his company, Sir John Mortimer and hilarious appearances of Barry Cryer, who lives in Hatch End and who regards the Palace, as do a number of other stage celebrities, as his local theatre.

Considering its history and the several times it came near to closure it is almost a miracle that it still exists. Today the Palace Theatre is widely regarded as one of the most beautiful theatres in the country, indeed, it has even been said that it is the most beautiful Edwardian theatre in the United Kingdom and it is here in Watford.

CHAPTER 8

Amateur Productions at the Theatre

Throughout its history the Palace Theatre has provided a venue for amateur productions. The first recorded performances by an amateur company took place on the 1st and 3rd November 1909, by the Watford Amateur Players when they presented *In the Storm* by W. Strange Hall, the evening performances being given in aid of The Society for Improving the Conditions of the Watford Poor. The matinee performance on the 3rd November was in aid of Watford District Hospital. The author of this play was a Watford doctor. He wrote several plays some of which were performed at London theatres. It would seem that the theme of storms held a fascination for him. Another of his plays, *The Stormy Petrel*, had more than one performance at the Palace, in January 1916 and again in February 1917.

The following year a week of performances of *Lady Huntworth's Experiment* were given by Mr. Russell's Company. We do not know whether this was another amateur company but as it was given in aid of the Watford & District Bureau for the Employment of Women, it would seem likely that they were an amateur group.

In the early part of the 1920s a new craze swept the country, the amateur operatic society. It was prompted perhaps by the fashion of musical comedies, and also perhaps by the popularity of the operettas of Gilbert & Sullivan. In 1899 the National Operatic & Dramatic Association, known by its initials as NODA, was formed. An explosion in the formation of new amateur theatrical societies and companies was taking place and by 1922 when Watford Operatic Society was founded there were just under 400 member societies. At the time of the celebration of NODA's centenary in 1999 there were over 3,000 member societies.

WATFORD OPERATIC SOCIETY

On the afternoon of Saturday the 27th May 1922 there took place at the Palace Theatre a production of Gilbert & Sullivan's operetta *Iolanthe*. So great was the demand for tickets that a repeat was made a week later. It was an *ad hoc* performance given by an opera class organised by the Watford School of Music with the energetic encouragement of Mrs. Saxon-Mills. Several of those who took parts were later to feature in a more permanent society.

The *West Herts and Watford Observer* critic was a trifle patronising in his review of the production and it was clear that in his opinion it was a brave attempt which could have been better. One of those who took part, in the role of the Earl of Mountararat, was J.J. Sterling Hill and Mrs Vera Sterling Hill, his wife, played the part of the Queen of the Fairies. Sterling Hill apparently felt that the event had been worthwhile but that 'something had to be done about it'. Accordingly, as was typical of him, he took control of the venture. Furthermore he wasted no time. The first committee meeting of the newly formed Watford School of Music Operatic Society took place on Wednesday 19th July 1922 at the School of Music then in Queens Road in a building which it shared with the Public Library. Sterling Hill was, at this time a member of the Council of the Watford School of Music and was to become its chairman in 1930.

It was one of the earliest amateur operatic societies in the country. Certainly it was the first in South West Herts.

Sterling Hill, who was by nature a perfectionist, was also possessed of a dynamic personality. He was born and brought up in Cambridge. In his youth he had been a solo-chorister at Worcester Cathedral. He studied music at Oxford University as an organ scholar but eventually diverted his professional talents into the medical profession and duly qualified as a dental surgeon. His surgery was at Ruan Lodge in Clarendon Road, Watford, close to the junction with St. John's Road on the corner diagonally opposite the Magistrates' Court.

Because of his musical training, essentially as a composer and conductor, he knew many prominent musicians and many of them played in his orchestras, amongst others, the two sisters Sidonie and Marie Goossens, members of the celebrated musical family and respectively harpists with the BBC Symphony and London Symphony Orchestras. Marie Goossens also played the harp in the orchestra for *Chu Chin Chow* in 1950, which was the first show by Watford Operatic Society after Allan Baldwin became musical director.

The quality of the orchestra employed by the society has always been a feature of its productions and this was especially so in the early days. It was even said that some people came to their shows, primarily, to listen to the orchestra. Indeed, a professional musician once told the author that in those days it used to be said in the profession that if you were good enough to play in the orchestra for Watford Operatic Society, you were good enough to play anywhere. A slight exaggeration perhaps but complimentary, with more than a hint of truth in it.

In those days the Palace Theatre did not have an orchestra pit. That came later. To accommodate a large orchestra, the first three rows of stalls were removed.

Sterling Hill was the founder, Musical Director and for the early years of the fledgling society its Hon. Secretary.

1922 was also the year in which Watford was granted its charter and so the Watford Urban District Council in that year became the Watford Borough Council. One of its most distinguished residents was the Earl of Clarendon. It was natural that Lord Clarendon should be the Charter Mayor of Watford and it was also natural that he should be the first President of Watford School of Music Operatic Society. The list of personalities who accepted the invitation to be Vice-Presidents is impressive to put it mildly. The list included the Countess of Clarendon, Viscount Hampden (Lord Lieutenant of Hertfordshire), the Hon. A. Holland-Hibbert (later Viscount Knutsford), Sir Henry Wood, the great conductor and Founder of the annual Promenade Concerts, Lady Gilbert (widow of Sir William of Gilbert and Sullivan fame), Sir Arthur O'Neil, who lived in Bushey, Dr. Herbert Hall, Sir Gerald Du Maurier, Sir Johnston Forbes-Robertson, Sir William Waterlow (who was to be Lord Mayor of London 1929-30), Dennis (later Sir Dennis) Herbert, M.P. – (Sir Dennis Herbert eventually became Lord Hemingford), among a galaxy of luminaries.

The society had three 'dynastic' families. At least one member of each of the three families was a founder member and to date each of these families has had three generations active in the society. One is, of course, the Sterling Hill family. The daughters of Mr. and Mrs. Sterling Hill have all played their parts, none more so than Mrs. Myra Currie, their eldest daughter, who was Hon. Secretary of the society from 1965 until 1977.

Donald Scleater was a founder member and his wife-to-be, joined the society for *The Gondoliers* in December 1923. Their son was Hon. Musical Director from 1963 until 1982 and their granddaughters helped either back stage or on stage; Deborah was one of the children in *The Sound of Music* in

1972 and one of the younger of Tevye's daughters in *Fiddler on the Roof* in 1977.

The third of these families descended from Mrs. Gertrude Gilbert, another founder member, who was a member of the Committee for many years, Ticket Secretary and a performer on stage. Her husband Ernest joined the society a few years later. Their son Douglas and his wife Beryl were also prominent members of the society. Nicky Chryssaphes, their daughter, was destined to play many roles in the society's productions and to be the chairman of Watford Operatic Society.

Since 1922 the society has performed at least one show every year at the Palace Theatre apart from a five-year break during World War II and for two years during the recent refurbishment of the theatre.

For five of the first six years of the society's existence they produced two shows a year but this practice was discontinued in 1929 because members decided that there was more to life than 'operatics' and they wanted to use the lighter evenings to follow other pursuits. Also, too many requests to the public (and friends and relations) to support productions with their presence was becoming irksome and affecting ticket sales.

The first production by the society was *The Mikado* in January 1923; the budget for this show was set at £330. The total cost of the orchestra for the

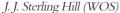

J. J. Sterling Hill (WOS)   *Donald Scleater (WOS)*
                                              aged 26 as King Gamma

first production of *The Mikado*, at full union rates was some £100 and the cost of hiring the theatre for the week had been £150. The society was permitted to sub-let the theatre to the Watford Public Library Students' Association for a production of *The Merchant of Venice* on the Thursday evening, 25th January and the matinee on Saturday 27th January for a performance of *Twelfth Night*.

The Mikado was followed later that year by *The Gondoliers*.

From 31st March until 5th April 1924 the society presented *Trial by Jury* and *Pirates of Penzance*. Later in the year the society changed its name to Watford Operatic Society, the name by which it is known to this day.

In December 1924 Watford Operatic Society presented *Iolanthe* and for that production the leader of the orchestra was Herbert Kinsey (Deputy Leader of the Halle Orchestra) and another violinist was a young Kim Peacock who was to make his name playing the part of Paul Temple in the BBC radio series of that name. He was also a member of the Peacock family, proprietors at that time and for many years thereafter, of the *Watford Observer*.

Fred E. Stone played second horn and he was later to be recognised as the finest English exponent of the French Horn of his day. Messrs. Kinsey and Stone were back for the next production, *Yeomen of the Guard* in March 1925. These two distinguished musicians continued their association with the society for several shows. A copy of the programme of that performance of *Yeomen of the Guard* has a pencil note at the bottom of the orchestra list, reading   'Bell, A.B. Cox'. This note is believed to have been written by Mr. Cox himself and no doubt referred to the tolling of the funeral bell in the finale to Act I. Tony Cox succeeded J.J. Sterling Hill as Hon. Secretary. All this he fitted in while at the same time being a regular contributor to *Punch* magazine and a prolific writer of crime fiction under various names among them 'Anthony Berkeley', his two first names, 'A. Monmouth Platts' doubtless because he lived at Monmouth House situated near the pond at the top of the town, close by Platts Avenue, and also as 'Francis Iles'.

In the early years there was no opportunity for a Dress Rehearsal. The first time the company performed the selected show in full costume, with make-up and scenery was at the first performance on the Monday evening in the presence of the audience. The theatre was needed in the evening for a Sunday evening performance sponsored by the National Sunday League. If they were lucky the society had the opportunity to stand on the stage in the afternoon and sing through the score with the orchestra, often, because of the temperatures prevailing at that time of the year, in their overcoats.

There was no central heating in the theatre until 1925.

The initials 'M.D.' stand for 'Musical Director'. Up until 1982 it could have stood also for 'Managing Director'. The Musical Director was elected to the post and to the Committee by the members of the society at the Annual General Meeting. It was an honorary position in the society. During the first sixty years of its life, Watford Operatic Society had only three Musical Directors: J.J. Sterling Hill 1922-1949; Alan Baldwin 1949-1963 and Ian Scleater 1963-1982. In each case they acted in an honorary capacity. Under this regime it was customary for the M.D. to act in a way similar to that of the Managing Director of a company. Since 1982 it has been the custom for the Committee to appoint a Musical Director for each show. He is no longer an elected member of the committee of the society. The role of Musical Directors of amateur operatic societies has today altered substantially. Over the last twenty to thirty years his or her responsibility has changed so that today, in addition to being responsible for the musical standard achieved by the company, by teaching the music to those playing principal roles and the chorus, the Musical Director recruits the orchestra and conducts the performances. His responsibilities extend no further.

The Producer of the shows, today referred to as the 'Director', of Watford Operatic Society has always been a professional appointed by the Committee or at least someone experienced in stage direction and almost invariably paid for his or her services. The first Producer of the society was Sydney Rendell and he was succeeded a year or two later by his wife, Elsie Rendell, who was Producer for the society for forty years. She was affectionately known by many of the amateur societies for which she acted as producer as 'Auntie'. This title derived from a short member of the Watford Society who was known to the wife of the then Musical Director, because of his stature, or lack of it, as the 'Puppy'; he, in affectionate retaliation, called her 'Mummy'. When Mrs Rendell adopted the name of the 'Puppy' he responded by giving her the name 'Auntie'. Although an affectionate name, members of other amateur societies for whom she was Producer and whose members also called her 'Auntie' did not realise that, in this particular instance, it was, additionally, a mildly derogative name.

For the first few years, the society concentrated on the operettas of Gilbert & Sullivan, except that in February 1926, for a week, performances of *Merrie England* were given. Then in March 1928 the society presented *The Merchant Prince*, music by J.J. Sterling Hill to a libretto by A.B. Cox. *The Merchant Prince* was intentionally, and very much, in the style of Gilbert & Sullivan. The story centred around, in those days, the highly unlikely situation of the employees dictating terms to the employers. Later in the year the operetta was performed at the Scala Theatre in London. Gradually the society's repertoire moved away from Gilbert & Sullivan, except for a production of *The Yeomen of the Guard* in 1949, which was to be Sterling Hill's last show as Musical Director. Today the Abbots Langley Gilbert & Sullivan Society have the exclusive right to perform the operettas of G & S at the Palace Theatre.

Sterling Hill was succeeded as Hon. Musical Director by Allan Baldwin who had previously acted as accompanist at rehearsals. By profession he was a solicitor and senior partner, at that time, of Messrs Matthew Arnold & Baldwin. He had been encouraged to take on the role of accompanist by Mr. Matthew Arnold, himself, one time chairman of the society.

'The Official Guide' of Watford, published in or about 1929, on page 122 under the heading 'Amusements' in referring to the Palace Theatre says 'Watford is well provided for in the matter of amusements. There is the Palace Theatre, a "twice nightly" house providing the usual type of Variety show with an occasional drama or comedy. On several occasions Henry Baynton and his talented company have given a Shakespeare week, while the now well-established and capable Watford Operatic Society take the theatre once or twice a year for performances of the Sullivan Operas etc. These "opera weeks" are always looked forward to and are quite an event in the life of the town.'

Over the years since 1930 Watford Operatic Society has produced a variety of musicals, musical comedies and operettas, including the works

Desirée Faithfull and Douglas Gilbert (W.O.S.)

The Sound of Music *1972 (WOS)*
Carol Creed as Maria (left) with two third generation members of WOS – Debbie Scleater
[Swift] (third child from left) and Nicky Gilbert [Chryssaphes] (centre, standing behind sofa)

of Lerner & Loewe, Ivor Novello, Noël Coward, Rudolf Friml, Sigmund Romberg, Franz Lehar among many others as well as several of those by Rodgers & Hammerstein. In 1972, as well as the usual annual production, which that year was *The Merry Widow*, Watford Operatic Society was invited to perform for two weeks in July to celebrate the Golden Anniversary of the Borough of Watford and the founding of the society. The show chosen was *The Sound of Music* and it was performed in a heatwave.

The society has, over the years, had a succession of members playing leading roles. At the start Wynne Saunders played the female lead and she was followed by Ida Brocklehurst, Desiree Faithfull and, probably the most versatile of them all, Carol Creed. Donovan Cross played the male lead for a number of years and his successors included Stanley Evans, Tony Brockwell and a variety of other members.

In the musical comedies between the wars, such as *Desert Song* and *Rose Marie* the comedy lead was frequently played by Donald Scleater. As a comedy actor, he was popular with the audiences and was often greeted with applause at his first entry. After World War II the society resumed its annual productions at the Palace Theatre. They had been away for five years and many wondered on the first night whether the audience had changed. There had been a large influx of people into the area during the war years, many from the East End of London and also from South Wales.

Donald Scleater was cast as Solomon Hooker in *The Rebel Maid*. Hooker is heard singing off-stage prior to his first entrance and the audience broke into impromptu applause at the sound of his voice. It was an emotional return to the theatre and the society knew at that moment that their old audience was in the theatre to welcome the players' return.

After Mrs. Elsie Rendell, the society enjoyed the services of a number of different directors, some of whom produced only one or two shows but those who directed on several occasions included Olive Hurford-Porter, Sidi Scott and in recent years Alan Cox, who has directed many shows for the society. Musical Directors during this period have come and gone and none has been responsible for more than a couple of shows.

On the evening of Sunday the 26th June 1966 the society made what some regard as its most significant contribution to the history of the theatre when it provided the chorus for the visit that evening of two distinguished international opera stars – Elizabeth Fretwell and the renowned Wagnerian tenor, Alberto Remedios.

Another highlight in the society's history occurred in 2003 when the society won third place at the prestigious Waterford Festival for its production of *Man of La Mancha*.

ABBOTS LANGLEY GILBERT & SULLIVAN SOCIETY

It has been said that the dividing line between those who deliver their lines on stage and those who preach from a pulpit is slim. This was certainly true of the Reverend Raymond Wilkinson. He possessed a passion for the operettas of Gilbert & Sullivan. While vicar of St. Oswald's Church at Croxley Green he formed a company for a production of *The Gondoliers* which was performed in the main assembly hall at Watford Town Hall. Canon Wilkinson, as he was to become, was a man of impressive stature and ambition. When he was appointed vicar of St. Lawrence's Church, Abbots Langley he immediately set about the formation of an amateur operatic company in that village. This became the Abbots Langley Gilbert & Sullivan Society in 1950.

The new society's first production, on 29th January 1951, was *The Mikado*, as it had been for Watford Operatic Society, and it, and the next few shows, were performed in the fine big hall at Leavesden Hospital. Mr. Wilkinson played the part of the Mikado and the comedy part, Ko-Ko, was played by his curate, the Reverend William Peverley. The patients at the Leavesden Hospital were what are described today as those with 'learning difficulties'. During a performance of *The Pirates of Penzance* the pirate king's sword went missing and was eventually retrieved from under a patient's bed.

At the start few of the members of the new society had had any stage experience, one notable exception to this being the late Derrick Phoenix, possessor of a fine tenor voice and an acting ability to match. He it was who, in a newspaper interview, said that 'You could go up and down the High Street in Abbots Langley and find the whole cast'. The enthusiasm was infectious.

A series of productions of the operettas of Gilbert and Sullivan followed, some at Leavesden Hospital and sometimes a second one during the year at the Henderson Memorial Hall, Abbots Langley. During this time in the society's history Christine Jordan played a number of the soprano leads and held various offices on the society's Executive Committee, including that of Hon. Secretary. She went on to direct for several local amateur operatic societies. Sadly, she died in 2006. Others to feature in the society's productions were Anne and Bryan Rycroft and the Crouch sisters and in several of the operettas the contralto part was sung either by Sylvia Park or Brenda Southorn whose daughter Emma established a well-deserved reputation for playing roles with Abbots and other societies, as well as being an accomplished choreographer. Nor should Norman Southorn, husband of Brenda and Emma's father, be omitted from mention as the possessor of an excellent baritone voice.

The society established a good reputation and eventually received the ultimate accolade when in September 1959, James Perry invited them to perform at the Palace Theatre. Much debate took place in committee; it was, after all, a big step to take. It was all of eleven years since the last production of a G&S operetta had been given at the theatre. In 1960 did the audience still have an appetite for G&S? The seating capacity of the theatre was larger than that of the Henderson Memorial Hall and a production at the theatre would be much more expensive. The estimate of the expense of a production at the Palace was between £750 and £1,000. If it all went wrong it could be the end of the society. With great courage and not a little trepidation, the decision was taken to go ahead.

The first production by the Abbots Langley Gilbert & Sullivan Society at the Palace Theatre was *Pirates of Penzance*, directed by J. Edward (Andy) Anderson with the musical direction in the capable hands of Eric McGavin. Raymond Wilkinson was by this time not only Chairman of the society

Derrick Phoenix and Christine Jordan (ALG&SS)   *Derrick Phoenix (ALG&SS)*

but also its President.

Apprehension was unfounded. The first show was a success and enjoyed by the audiences.

A year later *The Gondoliers* was presented.

In 1964, however, it was to be a different story. For the Committee, that year must have been what a later year was to be referred to by the Queen, as an *Annus Horribilis*. The society's finances were under pressure. *Princess Ida*, presented at the theatre in March 1963, had resulted in a loss of some £218.

The Committee authorised the Treasurer to negotiate an overdraft of £50 at the bank, only half of which they hoped would be needed. The situation was aggravated by late payment, by some members, of their subscription. It is to be wondered whether some of the late payers were concerned about the viability of the society. Twelve active members of the society, half of whom were soloists, had resigned from the society for reasons 'beyond their control'.

Early in the year the long-time Musical Director, Eric McGavin, informed the Committee that because of other commitments, including work, he could no longer devote as much time and energy to the society

Pirates 2006 (ALG&SS)

as it required and was, therefore, resigning. The Committee produced a list of possible successors and eventually invited a local and distinguished professional musician to accept the post of Musical Director. This he did in June but after his first rehearsal he indicated that he would be unable to continue. Rehearsals for *HMS Pinafore* had already commenced but in view of the shortage of members and lack of a Musical Director the Committee considered cancelling the production. Eric McGavin came to the rescue and said that he would act as Musical Director until a long-term replacement could be found. In the end he took the show right through to conclusion, including performances.

The Minutes of the Annual General Meeting held on 17th May 1965 referred to the society's 'precarious position'. Under the inspired leadership of Chairman Maurice Staines, for which he was duly thanked at the meeting, the society picked itself up and dealt effectively with its problems. In October that year the society was invited to provide the chorus for a 'Gilbert & Sullivan for All' concert at the theatre. Local resident and a principal tenor with the D'Oyly Carte Opera Company, Thomas Round took part. This provided a substantial morale booster for the members and at the A.G.M. in 1967 the Committee was able to report a greatly improved financial situation.

At the end of the season Mr. Caudle was offered the position of Musical Director to the society, a post he willingly accepted and held until 1971.

The 'Gilbert & Sullivan for All' concerts continued for several years with the society regularly taking part.

In 1969 the Rickmansworth Players approached the society saying that they would like to present *The Gondoliers* at the theatre. Tom Beckford, as Hon. Business Manager, was deputed by the Executive Committee of the Abbots Langley Gilbert & Sullivan Society to discuss the matter with Giles Havergal, Artistic Director at the theatre, and members of the Council of Management of the Civic Theatre Trust and tell them of the problems this would create for the society. The society's chairman wrote to the Civic Theatre Trust and eventually Rickmansworth Players abandoned the idea.

Also in 1969 Frank Jarvis was invited to be producer following the retirement of Mr. Anderson. Frank Jarvis was a professional actor who had appeared many times on television, notably in *Dixon of Dock Green*. He was an experienced Shakespearean actor and played one of the members of Michael Caine's gang in the original version of the feature film *The Italian Job*. He had also played roles, as a professional, in plays at the Palace, most notably *The Odd Couple* in March 1971 and *It's a Two Foot Six Inches Above the Ground World* on the 9th February of the same year.

The show in 1972 was *The Mikado* and it was directed by Frank Jarvis with David Pinchin as Musical Director, a new partnership which was to last for several years. David Pinchin worked in the National Health Service as an administrator and had played many parts with Watford Operatic Society. David established for himself a reputation for playing mature character parts including Fagin in *Oliver!*, Colonel Pickering in *My Fair Lady* and Captain Von Trapp in that society's 1972 production of *The Sound of Music*.

Maurice Staines was followed by a succession of chairmen including Bryan Rycroft, Brian Abell, Les Beckwith and Wendy Morelli. In recent years Brenda Southorn has held the position and currently Lennie Self.

In 1972 Cassio Operatic Society approached the society to ask what their attitude would be if they were to produce *Pirates of Penzance* at the theatre. As this was a similar approach to that made by Rickmansworth Players three years earlier, the then Chairman, Brian Abell, was prompted to write to the theatre requesting, in effect, exclusive rights to present the works of Gilbert & Sullivan at the Palace Theatre. The Watford Civic Theatre Trust responded by saying that it would be unwise of them to dictate to the amateur societies which shows they were to present and suggesting that it was a problem to be sorted out by the amateur societies themselves.

There has never been any formal agreement between the societies but by a 'gentlemen's agreement' Abbots Langley were accorded the exclusivity which they sought and it was probably felt by the other societies that their own position, when choosing a show, was eased by having one society which was content to perform Gilbert & Sullivan and not be in competition with them for selection of show.

In addition to their regular Gilbert & Sullivan production at the Palace Theatre, the society produced another show as an alternative to G&S but at a different venue, frequently the Abbey Theatre at St. Albans. These alternative shows included *Guys and Dolls* and *Carousel*.

Having experienced difficulties during the mid-1960s, the Abbots Langley Gilbert & Sullivan Society is today a well-established and flourishing amateur operatic society.

In 1994 the first Gilbert & Sullivan International Festival took place. Amateur societies were invited to give a performance of one of the operettas in the celebrated Buxton Opera House. In August 1998 the Abbots Langley society gave a performance of *The Gondoliers* in the festival and has returned several times since, winning nominations and awards for the standard of its productions. In 2005 Emma Southorn won the award of Best Actress in a supporting role for the part of Phoebe in *Yeomen of the Guard*.

The society has benefited from the quality of its committee, several members of which have served for a considerable number of years. In addition to those mentioned above, one name stands out, that of Tom Beckford who served as Hon. Business Manager throughout the 1970s and well into the following decade.

CASSIO OPERATIC SOCIETY

Founded in 1949, a year before the Abbots Langley society was formed, the Cassio Operatic Society is the most recent of the three societies to perform regularly at the theatre and has gained over the years an enviable reputation for the quality of its productions.

Mr. C.F. Hedges was the first chairman and his tenure of that office lasted until 1972 when he was succeeded by Alan Nicholson for the first of his two periods as chairman. The secretary at that time was Mrs. Elizabeth Hedges. The Treasurer was Mr. Eric Hart. Although the present society was formed in 1949 it grew out of a society which evolved from the choir at St. Michael's

Left: *Jo Jenkin and Brian Abell (ALG&SS)*

Above: *Iolanthe, 2004 (ALG&SS)*

Church, Watford but its activities were suspended with the outbreak of World War II. The first Musical Director of the Cassio society was the elderly but respected Tommy Gayton White. He was followed by Gladys Money, then Roger Elliott, who, when not wielding the baton was an accomplished exponent of the trumpet, and eventually Ron Cowie. Latterly, in common with the other societies they have had frequent changes of Musical Director, according to the type of show they are producing. Three most notable directors have been Nancy Taylor and Sidi Scott followed by her daughter, Nikki Scott.

Initially, in common with both Watford Operatic Society and Abbots Langley Gilbert & Sullivan Society in their early years, the new society concentrated upon the operettas of Gilbert & Sullivan. This is how many amateur operatic societies started, simply because of expense. These works required, at most, only two sets of scenery. In addition there are not many changes of costume. Today the G&S operettas are out of copyright and so there are no royalties to be paid. It has been said, and with justification, that the operettas of G&S are too difficult for amateurs. Nevertheless, the local societies have each produced praiseworthy interpretations of these evergreen operettas.

The first production in 1949 by the newly formed society was *Trial by Jury*, the one-act operetta by the celebrated duo. This piece is more usually presented with either *Pirates of Penzance* or *H.M.S. Pinafore* but on this occasion it was followed by 'concert items'. Perhaps the society was finding its feet. In the following year *Pirates of Penzance* was produced. These and the following ten productions, all by Gilbert & Sullivan, except for *Merrie England* in 1958, were given in the St. Michael's Hall, Durban Road West, now known and used as the Multi Racial Community Hall.

The debut performance by the Cassio Society at the Palace Theatre was on 3rd December 1962 when *Merrie England* was revived.

If the Watford and Abbots Langley societies had their dynastic families, Cassio was certainly not the exception. One family which played a significant role in the success of Cassio was that of Alan and Vivien Nicholson. Both played many parts during the society's history and Vivien played the female lead in a number of shows, including Anna Glavari in *The Merry Widow*. Their children have followed admirably in their parents' footsteps. Kathryn helped backstage while her siblings Julie and Jeff trod the boards. Jeff eventually turned professional, while Julie played lead roles with Cassio and with both the other amateur societies who habitually perform at the Palace Theatre.

Other local families who have been a part of the Cassio Operatic Society history have been the Hales family, mother Linda and daughter Julie and, of course, the Knight family. Dennis was Hon. Treasurer for no less than twenty-two years. His wife Marlene, a close friend of Viv Nicholson, played many lead roles and their son Martyn, now a professional, featured in what used to be referred to in the days of musical comedy as the juvenile lead. He made a virile Curly in *Oklahoma* in 1994. Today Dennis and Marlene's grandson Chris Wheeler takes part in musicals with the Cassio Operatic Society.

It is sad to record that Vivien and Marlene both died in 1996 at a comparatively early age and at a time when they both had so much more to offer. In their memory the Cassio society established a trophy in their name to be awarded for the best amateur musical production each year in the district, the winner to be selected by the local representative of NODA.

Because the Abbots Langley Gilbert & Sullivan Society had the unofficial 'rights' to G&S at the Palace Theatre, the Cassio Operatic Society broke away from G&S, although they did perform at the St. Michael's hall *The Gondoliers* in 1966 and *Pirates of Penzance* in 1972. More recently *Iolanthe* was performed at the Cassio Hall at Lincolnsfields, Bushey in 1990.

At the theatre, there followed a succession of popular shows. *Merrie*

England was followed by *Rose Marie, Carousel, The Gypsy Princess, The King & I, The Student Prince* and a varied programme of old and not so old favourite musicals and operettas. Today the society is firmly established and playing to large and appreciative audiences.

For many years, Cassio, performed two shows a year. That worked well whilst one of the shows was produced at the Cassio Hall at Lincolnsfields Centre. There were not so many seats to fill as there were at the Palace but from 1996 when a second show was presented at the Palace the situation changed. Risks and costs escalated and when productions were resumed at the theatre in 2004, after the rebuilding it was decided to revert to the practice of just one show a year.

The local amateur societies, particularly Cassio and Watford, today design and construct their own scenery. The prime mover in the design direction is Martin Smith, a graphics designer by profession. He has played parts on stage with the amateurs, he had also acted as Musical Director for a number of shows but he probably reached the pinnacle of success as a designer of scenery. His sets for the Cassio production of *Merry Widow* and the 2005 production of *Fiddler on the Roof* were dazzling examples of his work.

Home-produced scenery moved away from the hired scenery which was

Alan and Vivien Nicholson

Julie Nicholson

Marlene Knight

heavy, incorporating 'flats' which made changing scenery complicated. Added to which the hired scenery had sometimes been stored in the open resulting in unsightly streaks where rain had affected it.

Another designer of scenery for amateur productions was David Windsor. He excelled with his design for *The Hot Mikado* presented by Cassio Operatic Society in 1999. So successful was this set that it was hired by other amateur societies throughout the length and breadth of the United Kingdom.

Unlike the professional productions, which these days tend to run for about three weeks, the amateur societies perform for just one week with a matinee performance on the Saturday afternoon. Whilst the professional productions will enjoy three or four days for the installation of the scenery and rehearsals on stage the amateurs are required to accomplish all of this in one day. The Sunday morning of their allotted week will be spent installing the scenery. Basic lighting will be worked on during the afternoon. The orchestra meets for the first time on the Sunday afternoon and uses the Rehearsal Room on the second floor at the theatre to rehearse the music. At about 6.00 p. m. the dress rehearsal begins, finishing around 9.00 p. m..

This schedule was seriously disrupted during the 1950s when Bingo sessions were held on Sunday evenings in the auditorium, so that on occasions the amateurs were obliged to 'hang around' until Bingo finished and then resume their dress rehearsal.

Amateur productions tended to be 'bunched' together during the first three months of the year, enabling them to rehearse their respective productions during the dark winter evenings, leaving the light evenings of summer free for other pursuits. This, however, had its drawbacks, one of which, inevitably, was the impact it had on ticket sales. During the 1964 season the Abbots Langley production of *The Mikado* was followed by Watford Operatic Society's production of *Kismet*, the scenery for which was delivered to the theatre during the Saturday performances of *The Mikado*. A most unsatisfactory situation.

OTHER AMATEUR PRODUCTIONS

Set for Fiddler on the Roof

Two other amateur operatic societies played at the theatre for limited periods during the 1960s and early 1970s.

Rickmansworth Players presented *Annie Get Your Gun* for a week commencing on 21st January 1961 and over the following thirteen years produced such shows as *Brigadoon, Kiss Me Kate, Show Boat, South Pacific, Oklahoma!, Guys and Dolls, The Desert Song, Tenderloin, Pickwick, Fiddler on the Roof* and finished their time at the theatre with *Hello Dolly*. In 1974 they transferred their productions to the newly completed Watersmeet Theatre in Rickmansworth. Rickmansworth Players still flourish today.

In 1966 the Bushey Operatic and Dramatic Society joined the band of amateurs performing at the theatre with a production of *Chu Chin Chow*. They then performed a series of six ambitious shows more in the operetta genre. These operettas included *The Merry Widow, Orpheus in the Underworld, Song of Norway* (to the music of Grieg), *La Belle Hélène,* and *Die Fledermaus.* Credit must be given to this society for the bravery they displayed in selecting to perform these shows which required singers of a higher calibre than those required for, say, the musicals of Rodgers and Hammerstein. Were they perhaps too ambitious? It is to be regretted that the society does not exist today. It is possible that its demise was due to the fact that there were too many amateur operatic societies in the district and not enough local talent to support them.

The proliferation of amateur productions at the theatre during the early months of the year continued to present problems and in 1966 matters came to a head. There took place four consecutive weeks of shows by amateur operatic societies. On the 14th February that year Rickmansworth Players performed *South Pacific* followed by *Ruddigore* by Abbots Langley Gilbert & Sullivan Society, then *The Most Happy Fella* by Watford Operatic Society and finally *Chu Chin Chow*, the debut show at the Palace by Bushey Operatic & Dramatic Society. Cassio Operatic Society presented their show later in the year. Clearly, in the interests of all parties concerned the amateur shows had to be separated. The initiative not to allow the amateur shows to run together was taken by the management of the theatre.

A meeting of the societies was called and various alternatives to 'spread the dates' were considered. One suggestion was for the societies to be allocated five slots of a week each during the season and for each society to move on by one slot each year, but it was soon realised that this system would lead to a complicated arrangement with practical difficulties. Furthermore, Watford Operatic Society, which regarded itself as the senior society was disinclined to give up its traditional time of the year – March. It had performed in the early spring since 1923 and its audiences were accustomed to that time. It was decided not to pursue the scheme because it was impractical

The problem resolved itself and in the following season *Vagabond King* was given by Watford Operatic Society in March; *Oklahoma!* by Rickmansworth Players in April; *The Merry Widow* by Bushey Operatic & Dramatic Society in May, *King & I* by Cassio Operatic Society in October and *Iolanthe* by Abbots Langley G&S Society in December.

For twenty-five years from 1959 until 1975 the year started immediately after the closure of the pantomime with Ralph Reader's *Gang Show* performed with great aplomb by the South West Herts Boy Scouts Association. The Boy Scouts Association also provided seventy of their members to form the cast in July 1961 of *The Story of Mike*, a musical play written by Ralph Reader.

Today the only regular amateur productions at the theatre are the annual visits by the three operatic societies but in the past there have been various *ad hoc* performances. In addition to those already mentioned the Bushey Grove Dramatic Society in April 1922 produced *Brown Sugar*. On the 18th April 1931 the pupils of local dancing schools gave a display at the theatre in aid of the NSPCC and Dr. Barnardo's Homes. There were two visits by the

Poster from 1966

Aldenham Players, the first on the 4th December 1933, presenting *The Ringer* by Edgar Wallace and on the 9th December 1936 when they presented *The Middle Watch*. Possibly because of the perception of imminent hostilities the pantomime opening in December 1938 was presented, not by the theatre company itself, but by the Star Amateur Musical Comedy and Pantomime Society. This was *Aladdin*.

Chipperfield Womens' Institute Drama Group brought an all-female cast to the theatre on the 6th December 1960 to present *Hamlet* and then on the 3rd August 1968 for one night only at 10.30 p. m. there was presented *Fracas at the Palace*, described as a 'bright new University based revue. Five men and a girl, all former pupils at Watford and Bushey Grammar Schools.' Bushey Grammar School is now named 'Queen's School'.

Mention must also be made of a week of Old Tyme Music Hall when Jimmy Perry returned to the theatre with his *Hi-De-Hi* company on 26th February 1984, supported by the St. Peters Players from Bushey.

Today the three remaining societies who perform regularly at the theatre, maintain close contact and co-operation.

From 2002 until 2004 when the theatre was closed and undergoing reconstruction the three amateur societies went their separate ways with smaller scale productions. Watford Operatic Society presented *Company, Man of La Mancha* and *The Singing Years* at the Pump House, Abbots Langley Gilbert & Sullivan Society gave *The Sorcerer* and *Iolanthe* at the Rudolf Steiner School at Kings Langley and Cassio Operatic Society produced *Cabaret, Sweeney Todd* and *A Chorus Line* at the James Theatre, Watford Grammar School for Boys.

Whereas, in the past, each society had its own members who maintained an almost fanatical loyalty to that society, today they may be members of more than one society and audition for parts with the different societies. This helps to keep standards high.

Artistic Directors at the Palace Theatre have been known to say that as long as the amateur societies achieve satisfactory standards they will always be welcome. Their shows help to provide the local theatregoing public with the variety they require. The theatre's own budgets would not sustain expensive, professional musical productions requiring large casts, a chorus, dancers and an orchestra. The amateur societies with those on stage enjoying participation as a hobby, and with their 'captive' audiences of friends and relations, are in a position to afford the presentation of musicals and operettas.

All three of the amateur societies who still regularly perform at the theatre have won prestigious awards for the standards of their performances.

A problem which existed for the amateur societies and to a degree still

The Sorcerer

does today is the choice of show. During the years when five amateur societies presented shows at the theatre this became a matter of some difficulty, simply because they found themselves competing against each other. Rivalry became particularly intense at times when a show was being released for amateur production, especially if that show had enjoyed a lengthy run in the West End. Memories of the release of *My Fair Lady* and *Fiddler on the Roof*, both of which were eagerly anticipated, come readily to mind.

The selected show needed to have a suitable amount of chorus work as well as a range of parts which the society would be able to cast from its membership. Staging was also significant and hopefully an assured success at the Box Office.

Today a supply of such shows is far from plentiful. Very few suitable shows which fit the criteria have been written in recent years. The outstanding successes of the Lloyd Webber shows, for example, are not easily transferred to the amateur stage. They are costly and in some cases complicated to fit on to a small stage. Frequent revivals of established musicals are inevitable but, fortunately, tend to be welcomed by the audiences. We have a local society specialising in the operettas of Gilbert and Sullivan; perhaps there is a need for another, specialising in, say, the musicals of Rodgers and Hammerstein.

CHAPTER 9

Theatre in Education

In 1965, the same year and at about the same time that the theatre became a civic theatre, Barry Davis came to Watford as part-time teacher of drama in the area, based at Durrants School combining his duties with that of Assistant Director at the theatre. He directed *Alfie* at the Palace. At the end of his first school term in July he was able to write in the programme for *Pygmalion*:

> 'We have not only presented plays but also launched all kinds of activities aimed primarily at interesting young people in the theatre and the work that it is doing. Members of the company have gone into many different schools to teach, demonstrate and present extracts from plays and have also acted as hosts when many young people have visited the theatre for our "workshop" sessions both after school and on Saturday mornings.
>
> In addition we recently presented a reading of *A Man for All Seasons* on the stage for the benefit of children who were studying the play for an examination.'

At the end of 1966 'Theatre-in-Education' had become established under the direction of Mick Jones with Caroline Eves as Assistant Director. They were continuing the practice of taking drama into schools and some plays were given in the theatre during the day time for the benefit of schools. Each Wednesday, in the theatre, at 5.00 p. m. there was a Drama Workshop for teachers and on Thursday evenings, Theatre for Youth sessions.

Children's Workshop sessions were held in the theatre at 10.30 on Saturday mornings

In 1973 the Director of Theatre in Education was Martin Canter. He was succeeded by Hilary Clulow in September 1975. Hilary was a graduate of the Guildhall School of Music and Drama. A native of Southend, she founded and directed the Southend Youth Theatre Company and the Ridley Theatre Workshop, an experimental mime group which worked in this country and abroad. Also at Southend, Hilary directed ten large scale musical productions and three professional operas.

In 1983 Gwenda Hughes took over the position of Director of Theatre in Education with Ian Milton as Associate director and Dorothy Butcher continuing as secretary, a position she held right up until the theatre closed for restoration in 2002.

Gwenda Hughes's reign lasted until 1987. Ian Milton held the fort until Alan Orme took over later in the year. Alan remained in post until 1991, when he joined the staff of the Arts Council Eastern Region. In December of that year Hetty Shand was appointed Education Officer (the post previously called Director of Theatre-in-Education) and was succeeded in October 1995 by Hassina Khan, who later also joined the staff of the Arts Council.

When Hassina Khan came to the post of Education Officer she instituted a number of Youth Theatres: a Junior Youth Theatre for young people aged 11 to 14; Palace Girls for girls of 13 and over (this venture was particularly aimed at the Asian minorities in the area); Palace Youth Theatre for those aged 15 to 19 and the Task Force for young people interested in stage management. The theatre also carried out workshops for GCSE and 'A' Level students linked to productions being shown at the Palace and INSET workshops for teachers.

Every year for some while past the department has run a Summer School in which over a three-week period, young people may choose to be a performer, stage manager, set and costume designer or lighting and sound designer and work towards a production on the stage at the Palace Theatre.

The department was, and remains, available to all young people in Hertfordshire but it also works with people from North London, Bucking-hamshire and Bedfordshire.

The Youth Theatre was seen very much as a facilitator, bringing theatre to young people whilst also assisting with examination texts and providing fun workshops. An example of which was the rock 'n' roll workshops which accompanied the production of *Three Steps to Heaven* in February/March 2000. This play contained some of the rock 'n' roll music of Buddy Holly.

In 2001 Kirstie Davis joined the staff of the Palace Theatre with respon-sibility, originally, for Theatre-in-Education. This responsibility was not enough for someone with her talents and it was not long before she expanded the job to embrace an involvement with the main theatre productions and she directed a number of highly successful plays.

After Lawrence Till vacated the position of Artistic Director early in 2006, Kirstie and Joyce Branagh, the Literary Director, whilst retaining their original responsibilities, also assumed the artistic direction of the theatre and planned the autumn and winter season for that year. Between them they also shared direction of most of the productions. For three years running Joyce directed the pantomime. These were *Cinderella* in 2005/06, *Aladdin* in 2006/07 and in 2007/08 she wrote and directed *Jack and the Beanstalk*.

They made an excellent partnership.

During the rebuilding programme Theatre-in-Education maintained its activities but when the theatre re-opened in 2004 a number of changes took place. For some time the word 'Education' had contained certain connotations which seemed to some to convey the wrong impression. Certainly the education, mostly of young people, was the motive behind the scheme but was it necessary to emphasise it to this degree?

It was decided to change the title to just one word – 'Active'. This word indicated a more adult and acceptable ambition for the project. It was a learning and participation project.

'Active' became the umbrella for three differing programmes but all are associated with live theatre. The programme remained undisturbed but its objects had changed over the years.

The three branches to its work consisted of:

- **The Palace Theatre Young Peoples' Theatre.** This programme is open to young people between the ages of 10 and 21. Apart from producing and performing plays in the theatre, they are also called upon when required to take part in the theatre's main productions.

    On occasions they assist in reading through plays and invariably they take part in the first read=through of the script for the annual pantomime. The theatre is 'open' to them and members of the group are often to be seen around the building.
- **Hertfordshire County Youth Theatre.** Members of this group tend to be the best young talent from across the County. They take part in two big shows each year.
- **Schools work.** Perhaps this is where the education aspect comes into its own. Every year a chosen play tours for some six or seven weeks. The cast are all professional actors. It tours to approximately twenty-six schools in the county and perhaps four other venues such as the Radlett Centre

and the Old Town Hall at Hemel Hempstead. The play is prepared as meticulously as a main 'in-house' production. The scenery is constructed by the theatre's own team of scenery builders. Similarly the costumes are made 'in=house'.

Choice of play is paramount. Naturally it has to be a good play and it is the intention that the young people who see it will learn from it. It is part of their education. Sometimes a play is chosen because of its historical content. Others might be chosen because of the quality of the English spoken. Plays are not chosen because of lessons in morality which the script might contain. Young people are constantly being warned of the danger of drugs, so it is felt that to use the vehicle for this kind of purpose was unnecessary and could be self-defeating.

Children in school learn about theatrical history, acting styles and are encouraged to write about what they have witnessed from a Director's point of view.

The project also arranges workshops and teachers are taught stage-craft in sets.

The name 'Active' did not survive for long and by 2007 the title 'Creative Learning and Participation' was adopted.

CHAPTER 10

A Producing Theatre

As has been noted, contemporaneously with becoming a civic theatre, the Palace Theatre converted to become a 'producing' theatre. This was part of a natural evolution. Prior to this it had been a 'repertory' theatre.

The third main category of theatre is a 'receiving' theatre. The majority of active theatres in this country today are 'receiving' theatres.

A repertory theatre is one which produces a fresh play at frequent intervals, usually weekly. Those plays would, in the main, be revivals of tried and proved successes with audiences. It has a regular company of players and only occasionally employs the services of an actor who is not one of their number.

A receiving theatre, on the other hand, does not produce its own plays or other forms of entertainment. It plays 'host' to any company or institution that wishes to make use of the facilities it offers. In short, it 'receives' previously rehearsed productions by visiting companies. As long as the visiting company does well at the Box Office and is able to pay the rent due to the theatre, which consequently is able to pay its way, the theatre itself takes no financial risk. It may, for example, be used to 'try out' a new play prior to transferring to the West End of London.

The Palace Theatre, Watford is one of only three producing theatres in the geographical area covered by what is today known as the Arts Council of England East, or as it prefers to be known 'ACE East', which covers the counties of Norfolk, Suffolk, Essex, Hertfordshire, Buckinghamshire, Bedfordshire and Cambridgeshire.

The other two producing theatres in the area are the New Wolsey Theatre, Ipswich and the Mercury Theatre, Colchester.

The Palace Theatre is the largest of the three, with seating to

Mercury Theatre, Colchester

accommodate an audience of some 625 patrons. The Mercury Theatre, Colchester is a little smaller with a seating capacity of 500 and the New Wolsey Theatre at Ipswich has seating to accommodate an audience of 400.

The Palace Theatre is also the oldest of the three. The Mercury Theatre dates from 1973 and the Wolsey Theatre was built in the early part of the 1980s.

In 2001 it was found that the Wolsey Theatre was in need of substantial repairs and it re-opened after these repairs had been carried out as the New Wolsey Theatre. Doubts as to its viability were soon dispelled, it having had the misfortune to spend a short time in Receivership and in 2006 it underwent a major refurbishment at a cost of £1.35 million. This work was carried out during the summer months when it would have been closed in any case for its annual maintenance work.

The comprehensive work included correcting a defective roof, the artistes' space was upgraded, air conditioning was installed and the New Wolsey was the first theatre in the U.K. to benefit from the introduction of an ASM Winch Motorised Band Flying System.

There are many similarities between the three theatres. Each of them enjoys charitable status. All of them act as hosts to amateur productions. The Colchester Operatic Society performs at the Mercury along with other local organisations, including the scouts. Like the Palace, being a producing theatre

New Wolsey Theatre, Ipswich

it makes its own scenery in its own workshop but, unlike the Palace, enjoys the advantage of having its workshop within the confines of the theatre itself.

There are, of course differences. For example, both the Mercury Theatre and the New Wolsey Theatre have studio theatres in which are staged smaller productions before smaller audiences, a feature which, unfortunately, is lacking at Watford. Seating capacity at the Mercury Studio is for approximately eighty.

On the other hand the Palace Theatre has an internal rehearsal room. The other two theatres rehearse their productions in halls apart from the theatre.

The theatre at Colchester specialises in productions of the classics and so is not under the same pressure to present new writings as is the case at the Palace.

Unlike the Palace, the Mercury possesses a resident company of actors, not unlike a repertory theatre but guest directors are not excluded from importing actors from outside the company.

All three theatres rely heavily on annual grants from their respective local authority and from ACE East. The level of public funding is approximately the same.

Unlike the Palace Theatre, neither of the other two theatres has ever been a civic theatre, although, certainly at Colchester, as at Watford, the local authority owns the freehold of the building.

The executive officers at the Mercury Theatre consist of the Chief Executive who is also artistic director and the General Manager who doubles as Finance Officer. Because directors of a charitable trust may not benefit financially, neither of the executive officers are members of the Board of Directors.

How does a 'producing' theatre operate?

The planning of a season of plays starts early with a review of what might be on offer.

The Palace Theatre has, for many years, closed during the warmer summer months of July and August. This practice originated in the days before the auditorium was fitted with air conditioning and in a heat wave people did not enjoy the discomfort of watching a play in extreme heat. There are no windows in the auditorium to cool the interior. Although it is still unusual for performances to take place in the summer months, today the emphasis has changed. The auditorium temperature can be reduced but it is an expensive process. Of greater significance are the counter-attractions to be enjoyed during long, light evenings and, of course, people go away on holiday. So, for various reasons, during those months, audience attendance tends to drop.

Even so, on an average year around 120,000 people pass through its doors.

After the summer break, the new season commences in September and the play presented must attract the audiences back into the theatre and re-establish the habit of being 'theatregoers'.

Experience has demonstrated that autumn is the time to present 'meaty' plays, so a classic would be appropriate or a well-known comedy. It is not the time to attempt a 'risky' production such as a new play by an unknown playwright. Most audiences enjoy being 'challenged' but not at this time of the year. Often a revival of a familiar play or comedy, especially by a well-known playwright will attract the audience back after the summer recess.

There are other considerations to be taken into account when choosing plays. Is the stage of suitable size? It used to be said that the stage at the Palace inhibited the choice of plays because it was small and an irregular shape. Today the stage is deeper but no wider and is still too small for some plays. Conversely it is too large for some others.

The theatre strives to present a varied programme. An exclusive diet of the works of any single playwright might prove unacceptable to the audience. The theatre tends to attract audiences, which, in the main, may be defined as 'middle class', 'middle income', 'middle aged' but every effort is made to appeal to audiences of all categories and ages. One of the amateur operatic societies performs a musical in October and this helps to produce a balanced repertoire in the autumn ahead of the annual pantomime.

A finely tuned balance is important so that it caters for the varied tastes of the audience. What might enthral some audiences may be anathema to others. Mistakes can be made; a play which is expected to appeal to a large proportion of the theatre's audience can sometimes be rejected. The political climate can be an influence. Similarly a catastrophe on the national or international scene can conflict with the audience's appreciation of what they may deem to be an inappropriate play.

What about the school curriculum? Is there a play which would help students preparing for exams? Not every school in the county receives the tour by the 'Creative Learning and Participation' team, so would it be more appropriate to produce such a play as part of the main theatre season where it would be available to a far wider audience?

With regard to the younger generation, every effort is made to attract them to the theatre and the 'Creative Learning and Participation' team plays a large part in this process.

ACE East is still keen to see the theatre produce 'new writings' although they are not insistent that revivals and classics should be excluded from the programme. So new work must be included, especially from young, emerging playwrights. This is a delicate path to tread. Too many 'new writings' can drive audiences away.

Clearly cost is a factor in the selection of plays and the production manager keeps a keen eye on this.

A figure is set each season for the amount available to meet actors' fees. This indicates the number of actors who can be employed during that season. So, if one play requires a large cast, there must be another, or others, requiring smaller casts to compensate. Similarly a figure is set to pay the creative team, which consists of the director and those responsible for lighting, designing the scenery and, if the piece requires one, a musical director. An amount is also included for the cost of materials for the construction of the set.

Next a director is appointed. He or she is normally selected and appointed by the theatre's Artistic Director, more often than not the Artistic Director will direct the play him or herself.

The designer will be appointed by the Artistic Director but he will take into consideration the wishes and opinions of the director. Of paramount importance is that the director and designer are able to work together and have respect for each other's contribution to the eventual production. It is a vital relationship. The two will meet and agree the design some weeks before rehearsals commence. This is essential so that, for example, the director knows where the various entrances and exits are positioned on the stage.

Generally, the designer will produce drawings of the sets and make a box so that the workshop staff is able to manufacture the full size set or scenery. In this computer age there is software available to assist the designer in producing the line drawings. The designer will probably be responsible for designing the costumes so that they harmonise with the scenery.

So, at this stage the director and designer will have been appointed and the designs for the scenery and costumes will have been agreed between the two of them. It is time for the lighting designer to become involved and he will read the script and assess what type of lighting is needed for each scene. He will not only decide on the colours to use but also where and when the lighting will change to enhance the dramatic effect. All this will be arranged in collaboration with the director.

Early on in the season a brochure of forthcoming productions will be distributed to those members of the audience on the 'mailing list'. Copies will also be available in the theatre where the public can collect them. The director will have been invited to read what has been said in the brochure about the play he will be directing. He will be anxious to check that there has been no misrepresentation made.

It is time, now, to cast the show. The methods employed are various. In some instances an actor will have heard through the 'grape vine' that a certain play is in the planning stage. If the play appeals he may very well telephone the theatre and enquire whether casting is taking place and indicate that he would like to be considered. More often than not, the director will have a particular actor in mind. Someone with whom he has worked before and who he considers suitable for the part. An approach will be made. Negotiations will ensue. Perhaps the actor is engaged at that time but would be interested in appearing, if the dates of the play can be switched with another play, without inconvenience. Whatever the outcome, the final booking of the actor will be confirmed through his agent.

A more regular occurrence is for the theatre to circularise agents advising them of the parts remaining uncast. There may be as many as 120 agents notified. The agent will notify the theatre of any of their clients who would be suitable, available and interested in taking the part in question.

A meeting at the theatre will take place. Generally but not invariably candidates will be asked to read in the form of an audition. This audition lasts about fifteen minutes. Sometimes they will be asked to read a section from the script of the play being cast. They will have been sent the passage required in advance. This passage in theatrical parlance is referred to as a 'side'.

Casting is all done on a gentlemanly basis.

In due course rehearsals commence. They take about four weeks. At the first rehearsal there will be a 'read through' at which all those in the selected cast will read their parts, seated. Actions will be added later. Very often members of the theatre staff will be present to provide the atmosphere of an audience.

At about this time in the schedule for the next production, work will commence on the physical construction of the scenery. This is carried out at the Workshop in Watford Fields in a premises leased, like the theatre itself, from Watford Borough Council. Head of Construction is Tip Pargeter. He has enjoyed various titles over the years for doing the same job. At one time he was 'Master Carpenter' but today's title aptly describes his responsibilities. Tip joined the staff of the Palace Theatre in 1993. In 2002 when the rebuilding project started, Tip left but was fully employed during the closure period and was welcomed back to resume the task of scenery construction at the reopening. He has a team with him that is augmented at times when a complicated scenery set is being made and time is short. Tip says that the set he most enjoys constructing is the annual Christmas pantomime.

Since 2004 the theatre has been equipped with 'state of the art' technology for scenery changes and Tip Pargeter has enjoyed the challenge of adapting to this greatly improved facility.

Since the rebuilding in 2002-2004 the scenery is brought into the theatre from the workshop, where it has been constructed, through a purpose built doorway at the rear of the theatre. At the end of the run of a production the scenery is removed through the same door. Previously it was unloaded from the lorry which transported it, in Clarendon Road and manhandled up the alleyway to the scenery dock. This alleyway no longer exists.

The theatre then remains 'dark' that is to say, not open to the public because there are no public performances taking place, unless, of course, a single evening performance is scheduled to take place. The scenery is erected or installed on stage and when that is completed the technical and dress rehearsals commence.

The technical rehearsals entail checking that the lighting and sound are correct and balanced. Then come the dress rehearsals. These can be lengthy, they throw up problems which require to be resolved. This means that a particular scene needs to be repeated, sometimes several times.

All of this will usually be accomplished in the first three days of the week, although, depending on the complexity of the set some work may be done on the Sunday at the beginning of the week.

The play will open to the public normally on the Thursday evening. After two or three preview performances comes 'Press Night' when, as the

Tip Pargeter

name implies, the Press are invited and possibly others to whom the theatre owes hospitality. Especially if the play is a new writing, and because Watford is within easy reach of London and close to the mainline station, drama critics from the National Press frequently attend. Those members of the audience who attend on Press Night do well to keep their eyes open very often celebrities from 'stage and screen' are to be spotted in the audience.

Plays usually run for three weeks ending, invariably, on a Saturday evening and at the end of the run the Royalties are payable. The rate has been negotiated in advance but the actual amount payable to the playwright is not known until the Box Office receipts have all been added up. The rate of the royalty varies. An emerging writer who is achieving success at other theatres and especially if he has written a play for premiere presentation at the theatre, may be in a position to command a premium rate but generally the rate is between 10 per cent and 15 per cent of the gross box office receipts.

CHAPTER 11

Celebrities at the Palace

It is an onerous and risky task to attempt to compile a list of the celebrities who have played at the Palace Theatre. Many achieved fame in their day but now are almost, or completely, forgotten. Some who have appeared recently may have yet to establish themselves as celebrities. Others may still be remembered by some but to others their names are unfamiliar. On the other hand many and varied have been those who were well known to the theatre-going public and it might almost be an easier task to make a list of stage personalities who did not or have not graced the stage of the Palace Theatre, Watford.

At the outset of this list the author extends his apologies to those who, through his own ignorance, are not included but should have been. Many famous names have already been mentioned in the text of this book but they are included in this list for the sake of completeness.

The list includes 'stars' of the music hall and vaudeville as well as celebrated actors and actresses of what has been described as the 'legitimate stage'. They are listed in no particular order apart, perhaps, from the date of their first visit to Watford.

As the reader will readily appreciate, especially in the early years of the theatre's existence many of those who played here had not at that time established their reputations. Some who subsequently achieved fame have faded from memory and because today nothing can be discovered about their careers, inevitably, they have not been included.

It has become in recent times the custom in the programme simply to list the 'credits' of previous performances in the various entertainment media. Where and when they took place and in which stage, film or television performance the actor played a part. These somewhat bland statements tell the audience very little about the person behind the performance. Many feel that a glimpse into the private lives of the personalities on stage, which need not be intrusive, would be of interest to the audience.

Some television series have a voracious appetite for actors so that very few of the cast of plays at the Palace cannot state that they have appeared at least in supporting roles in such long-running television series as *The Bill* or *Casualty* to name but two.

In the list of celebrated personalities who have played at the theatre the date of their appearance, unless stated otherwise, indicates the first day of a week or more in which the production was staged.

George Robey. George Robey played at the theatre for one matinee performance on Saturday afternoon, the 12ᵗʰ April 1909. Mention has been made of this appearance in the first chapter of this book.

Harry Tate. Harry Tate was on the bill for a week of Variety starting on the 3ʳᵈ May 1909. He performed a sketch for which he was famous, entitled *Motoring*. This sketch he had performed in the presence of King Edward VII and Queen Alexandra. Harry Tate returned for a second visit on 26ᵗʰ January 1913.

Nellie Wallace. Nellie Wallace was born in 1870 and died in 1948. Her appearance at the Palace was dated the 27ᵗʰ September 1909. She was always styled as 'The Essence of Eccentricity' and portrayed a spinster completely lacking dress sense.

Leo Dryden. He is included not so much for his ability as an entertainer, he has been described as 'a fairly successful London singer', but as the father of Wheeler Dryden who was the younger half-brother of Charlie Chaplin. Hannah Chaplin, Charlie's mother, who performed under the name of Lillie Harley had an affair with Leo Dryden while her husband Charles Chaplin senior was in America. Their marriage was already in trouble but the birth of Wheeler Dryden was most probably the final straw. A few months after the birth of Wheeler his father forcibly removed him from Hannah's care. It has been suggested that this brought on Hannah's mental instability from which she never properly recovered. Years later Wheeler was reunited with his two half-brothers, Charlie and Sydney Chaplin, and worked with, and for, them in movies in America.

Sam Mayo made four visits to Watford. The first was on the 8ᵗʰ October 1910, followed by visits on the 6ᵗʰ March 1911, the 21ˢᵗ October 1912 and again on 30th January 1922. He was always of soulful countenance and referred to as the 'immobile one'. In his day he was a popular artist in any Variety programme and much in demand.

Harry Champion. Harry Champion was born William Crump in 1866 in Shoreditch. His career spanned six decades and his three most famous songs were *Any Old Iron, Boiled Beef and Carrots* and *I'm Henery the Eighth, I am.* His first visit to the Palace was on the 15th October 1910 and he returned to share the bill in another Variety programme with a Fred Karno company which included Sydney Chaplin on the 23rd October 1911. He was back again, such was his popularity, on 12th December 1921 and again on the 11th September 1922

Ted Cowan, a name little remembered today but in his day a popular and well-known artiste. He appeared in a Variety show at the Palace on 9th January 1911. He toured the music halls of Great Britain on his motorcycle with sidecar for some sixty years and used to be billed as the 'Popular Quaint Comedian'. His versatility took him into musical comedy, pantomime, radio and films as well as music halls. He was also the brother of Sam Mayo, see above.

George Leyton was born in America in 1864 but made his name in Britain. In addition to being a music hall artiste he also performed as an actor in several plays, some of which formed part of a Variety programme. These plays included *Bonnie Prince Charlie, Emigrant Ship* and *Duty Calls to Arms* in all of which he received star billing in London theatres including the West End. He took part in a Variety programme at the Palace Theatre on the 23rd January 1911. The critic in the local newspaper observed 'Very good this week. One might be tempted to go three times.' George Leyton died in London in 1948.

Archie Pitt. Archie Pitt described himself as a comedian and during his performance at the theatre during the week of 20th February 1911 he encouraged the audience to sing the chorus of his song about a shop which sold *Short Socks With Spots.* His talent was not excessive but he teamed up with Gracie Fields in the revue *Mr. Tower of London.* They were married in 1923 but the marriage did not last. It is said that it was more of a business partnership rather than one founded in mutual love.

Lottie Lennox played at the theatre on the 5th February 1912. She was a popular music hall artiste but not regarded as an 'A' list performer. She returned to the theatre in a *Grand Star Variety* programme, which included Harry Tate, on the 26th January 1913.

Charles Whittle. On the same bill as Lottie Lennox in February 1912 was Charles Whittle. He was famous for his song *Let's All Go Down the Strand*.

Evie Green. Evie Green was a renowned musical comedy actress and had the good looks to go with it. She played at the Palace on the 4th March 1912.

Harry Lauder. Later Sir Harry Lauder, the great Scots comedian and singer appeared at the theatre on the 1st April 1912. He wrote most of his own songs including *Keep Right on to the End of the Road* and *Roamin' in the Gloamin'*. Possibly the greatest music hall entertainer ever to walk onto the Palace stage. He brought the house down with a rendition of his greatest song *I Love a Lassie*. He was the first artist to entertain the troops in the battlefield. This was in the First World War. He came from humble beginnings and rose to entertain kings and presidents. He was knighted by King George V in 1919.

Marie Kendall appeared at the Palace a week after Harry Lauder in another Variety programme. She was grandmother of Kay Kendall who achieved fame in the film of the London to Brighton veteran motor car rally *Genevieve*. Ten years later on 30th January 1922 she returned to the Palace. She also appeared in a Variety programme during the week of the 10th May 1926.

Charles Coborn played at the Palace on the 22nd April 1912. He was famous for his song *The Man that Broke the Bank at Monte Carlo*.

Gertie Gitana. Born Gertrude Mary Astbury in Stoke-on-Trent in 1887, Gertie Gitana was a firm favourite with music hall audiences. There are very few places of entertainment where she did not perform. She adopted the song *Nellie Dean* as a signature tune and it was said that the song ideally suited her childlike, sweet voice. She made her professional debut at the age of eight. Such was her popularity that her name on the bill would guarantee a full-house. She took part in a Royal Command Performance. Her earnings at the height of her popularity reached £100 a week, a considerable sum a hundred years ago. She played at the Palace on the 6th May 1912, returning on 9th December in the same year. She died in 1957. Her name may not be widely remembered today but it lives on in cockney rhyming slang – Gertie Gitana – banana.

Frank Mayo. Frank Mayo was no relation of the other Mayos who played at the theatre. This one was an American born on 28th June 1886. He achieved success as an actor in the silent movie era, starting his career around 1911. He came to the Palace Theatre in a short play entitled *The Bargain* as part of a Variety programme during the week of the 9th September 1912. The advent of sound affected his career but he continued in films made in Hollywood mainly playing minor roles or 'bit' parts. He was in the cast of more than three hundred films. He died of a heart attack in 1963.

Naughton and Gold. Charlie Naughton and Jimmy Gold came to the Palace Theatre on three occasions: 9th December 1912, 13th September 1926 and 14th May 1928. In 1931, they teamed up with Flanagan and Allen, Nervo and Knox and 'Monsewer' Eddie Grey to form the irrepressible **Crazy Gang**.

Bransby Williams. Born in Hackney in 1870 as Bransby William Pharez, Bransby Williams made his name doing monologues impersonating various characters from Dickens. The most celebrated of these was 'Scrooge' from *A Christmas Carol*. He shared 'top of the bill' with Dan Leno in 1897 at the London Palladium and in 1903, by Royal command, he performed before King Edward VII and Queen Alexandra at Sandringham and this established his reputation. He was a 'quick change artist' and his ability to completely change his character and age in a matter of minutes delighted and amazed his audiences. He first appeared at the theatre on the 30th December 1912.

Minnie Rayner. The name of Minnie Rayner may not spring readily to mind to today's reader. She was born in 1869 and appeared at the Palace on the 9th November 1913 in a production of *The Arcadians*. She had a lengthy career in films but is best known for appearing regularly in the cast of the Ivor Novello musicals between the wars. She was in the original cast of *Glamorous Night* (1935), *Careless Rapture* (1936), *Crest of the Wave* (1937), and *Dancing Years* (1939) all at the Theatre Royal, Drury Lane. She was also in the cast of some of Novello's plays both in London and in New York. She died in London in 1941.

Alfred Drayton. Alfred Drayton was born Alfred Varick in 1880 and came to the theatre as a member of the cast of the comedy *The Glad Eye* on the 30th November 1914. He enjoyed an impressive career in films, most notably in the 1930s and 1940s. He was in several films with other celebrated actors, for example, in 1935 *Look Up and Laugh* with Gracie Fields, *It's a Boy* with Leslie Henson and Heather Thatcher, also in 1935 *First a Girl* with Jessie Matthews. In 1947 he was in the cast of the film *Nicholas Nickleby* together with Cedric Hardwicke, Stanley Holloway, Cyril Fletcher, Bernard (later Lord) Miles, Derek Bond and Sally Ann Howes. In 1948 he made *Things Happen At Night* co-starring with Gordon Harker and Robertson Hare with whom he made a number of other films. He specialised in character parts. He died in 1949.

Louise Hampton was born in Stockport, Cheshire, in 1881. She appeared at the theatre in a production of *The Second Mrs. Tanqueray* on the 1st March 1915. She was primarily a stage actress but did make some films, one of the most notable of which was the 1951 film of *A Christmas Carol*. It contained a 'star-studded cast' which included Alec Guinness, Michael Hordern, Hattie Jacques and Jack Warner. Louise Hampton died in 1954.

Marie Lloyd. Much has been written about Marie Lloyd – the Queen of the Music Hall – in Chapter 2. She is recorded as making two visits to the Palace and was warmly received. Her name is mentioned here to complete the list of personalities who came to Watford. Her first visit was on the 26th April 1915. A subsequent visit was made on the 6th April 1916.

Jack Cock. A sportsman who performed at the Palace was Jack Cock, an international footballer. He had a distinguished career as a footballer and also possessed a good tenor voice and regularly performed in music hall. He was born in Hayle, Cornwall in 1893. During World War I he served in the British Army rising to the rank of Sergeant-major and was awarded the DCM. He visited Watford on the 11th September 1922 and is reported as 'singing with a pleasant, natural voice'.

Fred Emney senior. Fred Emney was especially known for his performances in pantomime. He was born in 1865 and his first pantomime was at Sadlers Wells. He appeared at the Palace Theatre, Watford in a sketch entitled *A Sister to Assist 'er*. Also in the cast was Sydney Fairbrother (see below). This was on the 25th May 1914. At Christmas the following year he played the Baroness in *Cinderella* at the London Opera House and on the Opening Night, during the Whitewashing Scene, he slipped on some soapsuds and fell heavily to the stage. The audience thinking it was part of the act laughed and applauded. He died a week later.

Sydney Fairbrother. Born Sydney Tapping in 1872. She played at the theatre with Fred Emney senior (see above) on 25th May 1914. She went on to become, predominantly, a film actress making her screen debut in 1916. In the 1930s she made several notable films including *Ali Baba Nights* (1934) a film version of the musical *Chu Chin Chow* with George Robey, *King Solomon's Mines* with Paul Robeson and Cedric Hardwicke and *The Private Secretary* with Alistair Sim. She died in 1941.

Montague Love. Born in Portsmouth in 1877 and possessed of an impressive name (his own), Montague Love came to Watford on the 1st June 1913 in a production of *The Importance of Being Earnest*. Later that same year he went to America and established for himself a film career in Hollywood as a character actor. He is widely considered as one of the finest screen villains ever but with the advent of sound he played more likeable characters. Off screen he was courteous and respected. He portrayed many political leaders and historical characters on screen, for example, Henry VIII in *The Prince and the Pauper* (1937), King Philip II of Spain in *The Sea Hawk* (1940), President Thomas Jefferson in *Alexander Hamilton* (1931) and George Washington in *The Remarkable Andrew* (1942). He died in Beverley Hills in 1943.

Robertson Hare. 1891-1979. Came to the theatre on the 3rd March 1916 in the play *Grumpy*. Played parts in many of the Aldwych farces. Like many other comedians he was a short man. He made his television debut in 1966 at the age of 75 in the series *All Gas and Gaiters* with William Mervyn and Derek Nimmo.

Syd Walker. Syd Walker came to the Palace Theatre on the 10th August 1916, sharing the same programme as Fred Karno and his company. He paid a return visit on the 4th February 1924 in a musical comedy revue named *Lights Up*. Syd Walker enjoyed a career in musical comedy but one of his greatest successes was in the radio series *Band Wagon* with Arthur Askey and Richard Murdoch. In the show he had his own 'spot', *Mr. Walker wants to know*, in which he related some recent experience and asked the audience for their advice with the words 'What would you do, chums?' His postbag offering advice reached colossal proportions.

Henry Baynton. Details have been given in Chapter 2 of the visits to the Palace Theatre by Henry Baynton. During his career he played almost every important Shakespearean role. His first stage appearance was in 1910. In 1917 he paid his first visit to the Palace Theatre, when on the 9th August he was in the cast of *The Importance of Being Earnest*. He then joined Henry Irving's company playing Laertes and later the same year he formed his own company which came to Watford for a four weeks' season in 1918. With his company, he returned to the Palace on the 24th March 1930 for a week of different plays. He disbanded the company later in 1930, after which he continued to tour the provinces in Shakespeare.

Ellaline Terriss. Miss Terris was born in 1872 in the Falkland Islands where her father was a sheep farmer. He later returned to England and became an actor. She came to the Palace for one night on the 23rd October 1917 in a new farce written by her husband Seymour (later Sir Seymour) Hicks. In this show she sang several songs. She was described as petite, pretty, demure and talented. She made her name in musical comedy. Lady Hicks, as she had become, died in 1971 at the age of 99.

Richard Hearne. Played in the pantomime *Mother Goose* opening on the 29th December 1919. This Richard Hearne was an acrobat and should not be confused with his more famous son of the same name, who was a popular entertainer as 'Mr. Pastry'.

Gracie Fields. 'Our Gracie' brought her own show *Mr. Tower of London* to the Palace on the 22nd March 1920. She was born Grace Stansfield in 1898 over her grandmother's fish and chip shop in Rochdale, Lancashire. From these humble beginnings she rose to unprecedented popularity on both sides of the Atlantic and further afield. Much has been written about this amazing entertainer. Her most famous song was *The Biggest Aspidistra in the World*. She had a chequered career and because of her marriage to an Italian she was vilified by the Press during the war years. All of this was unfair and untrue as she was assured by Winston Churchill. She re-established herself in the popularity of her multitude of fans. She became Dame Gracie Fields in 1978, the year before her death.

Renee Kelly was a well-known London actress in her day. She was born in 1888 and the stage was her first love although she made several silent 'movies', the first being *All For a Girl* (1915). She made the transition to sound and her last film, made in 1951, was *The Scarlet Thread*. She came to the Palace Theatre on 15th July 1922 starring in *Daddy Long Legs*. The critic

in the *Watford Observer* said that she received a remarkable reception. She
died in 1965.

Dick Ray. The name of Dick Ray presents something of an enigma. On the
1st August 1921, 7th August 1922 and on the 26th February 1923 there was
presented at the theatre a comedy show by the name of *Kick Off*. It was
variously described as 'musical comedy revue' or as a 'sporting revue'. It
featured on each occasion a comedian by the name of Dick Ray. From the
records it is apparent that he was a popular visitor to Watford, but who was
he? In the newspaper review of the 1922 performance it was said that it was
a 'Popular return visit' and that Dick Ray was 'especially funny in his burlesque
of a footballer' and that he made reference to Watford Football Club and to
its new ground. Could he have been the Dick Ray who played for and
subsequently became the Manager of Leeds United Football Club or was this
a comedian, who, like Ted Ray, a comedian of a later generation, adopted the
name of a celebrated sportsman (in Ted Ray's case a golfer)?

Gwen Ffrangcon-Davies. A twenty-year-old Gwen Ffrangcon-Davies
made her stage debut as a singer and actress in 1911. Two years later she was
on the stage of the Palace Theatre in a play entitled *The Glad Eye*. There
followed a distinguished career of 80 years during which she became a legend
of the classical theatre. In 1991, the year in which she attained her centenary,
she was awarded a DBE and became Dame Gwen, which, as in the case of
Dame Gracie Fields, was the year before she died.

Sydney Chaplin. The elder half-brother of Charlie Chaplin who was also
a member of the Fred Karno Company of Comedians. He was in the Karno
company that performed at the Palace Theatre on at least two occasions: 23rd
October 1911 and 16th February 1914.

Ronald Gourley. Ronald Gourley was a pianist in the vein of Russ Conway.
He played light music and was well known in his day. Comparatively little is
remembered of him today apart from his dexterity at the keyboard which
belied the fact that he was blind. He was a regular broadcaster. He took part
in three Sunday concerts at the theatre. The first was on the 11th December
1921 during which he played *When You Come to the End of a Perfect Day*
standing with his back to the keyboard, the second on the 12th February 1922
and the third on the 23rd February 1936.

Nervo and Knox. Two great comedians who appeared at the theatre on the 22nd October 1923. Later they were to join with Flanagan and Allen and Naughton and Gold to form the 'Crazy Gang'. One of the all-time greatest comedy partnerships. The gang played regularly at the Victoria Palace and the Metropolitan, Edgware Road. They were incredibly inventive when it came to original comedy. They would sometimes join the queue outside the theatre and get into a fight, then go into the Stalls and heckle the other acts until they were thrown out, just in time to go on stage themselves for their act.

Talbot O'Farrell. Regarded as a 'music hall great', Talbot O'Farrell was born in 1880 and came to the Palace for the first time on the 10th March 1924. It was noted that his engagement was at the highest salary which at that time had ever been paid to a single performer. He was a member of the Grand Order of Water Rats and was King Rat in 1930 a mark of respect by other members of his profession. He made subsequent appearances at the Palace on the 26th January 1925, 21st June 1926, 1st August 1927 and for a one-night stand on Sunday 8th November 1936. He died in 1952.

Gus Fowler. Gus Fowler 'The Watch King' was an illusionist who perfected an act using watches and clocks. He toured the world with his sensational act for many years. He appeared at the Palace Theatre on the 4th August 1924. He died in a fire in 1960.

Ella Shields. On the 25th August 1924 Ella Shields made her first visit to the Palace. She was, by birth, an American, born in Baltimore in 1879. She was a male impersonator and had a string of well-known songs to her bow, among them *I'm Burlington Bertie from Bow* with which she made her name, *If You Knew Susie* and *Show Me the Way to Go Home*. She returned to the Palace on the 20th June 1927. She performed as a song and dance act in male attire throughout the world. Her final performance, in August 1952, was in northern England. Inevitably, she was required to sing her most famous song but on this occasion she sang 'I *was* Burlington Bertie'. At the end of the song she collapsed and without regaining consciousness, died three days later. It has been suggested that she was the inspiration behind the Julie Andrews film *Victor Victoria*.

Clarkson Rose. Clarkson Rose was a celebrated pantomime 'dame' as well as a Variety artiste. His dames have been described as 'very grand and very posh' and he was probably the most famous panto dame of all. For three years,

1936 to 1938, he played the dame for the Melville Brothers at the Lyceum Theatre in London. He was born in 1890 and made his first stage appearance in 1905. In 1921 he formed his own concert party 'Twinkle' which played at seaside resorts for forty years. He played at the Palace Theatre, Watford on Sunday the 9th November 1924 which was during the 'off-season' for seaside concert parties. Watford audiences had to wait until Sunday the 13th December 1936 for a return visit.

Jack Hylton. Jack Hylton and his band, regular broadcasters between the wars were part of a week of Variety beginning on the 2nd March 1925.

Jimmy James. Almost, it seems, everyone with the name James has become known as 'Jimmy James'. The name has been shared by an eminent journalist on *The Times*, an impersonator of Marilyn Monroe, a blues guitarist, a dog show judge, a former Member of Parliament, a member of the Beastie Boys rap group to mention only a few but the Jimmy James who appeared on the stage of the Palace Theatre on the 9th March 1925 in a sporting revue with title *10 to 1 On* was a north-country comedian who created an act with Roy Castle and Eli Woods.

George Mozart was one of the finest character comedians and pantomime artistes of his day, topping bills at all major halls for nearly 30 years. *The Times* described him as a short, sturdy, dapper, monkey-faced little man bouncing with energy. He came to the Palace on the 1st June 1925.

Florrie Forde. On the 2nd November 1925 Florrie Forde appeared at the Palace in a Variety programme with the title *Here's To You*. Her act was described in the local newspaper as 'very good'. She was known as the 'Grand Lady of Vaudeville'. On stage she wore an assortment of flamboyant costumes and hats and changed for each song in a matter of seconds. She was an Australian by birth, born on 27th August 1876. She had a large repertoire of songs, among them *Has Anybody Here Seen Kelly, Hello! Hello! Who's Your Lady Friend?, It's a Long Way to Tipperary* and *I Do Like to be Beside the Seaside*. She entertained the forces in both World Wars and it was at the end of a performance for the Army in Aberdeen that she collapsed and died in 1940 at the age of 64.

Elsie and Doris Waters. The Waters sisters performed as 'Gert and Daisy', two Cockney Char Ladies or in today's terminology 'Home Helps'. They first appeared at the Palace for a week on the 11th January 1926, returning for two Sunday concerts, the first on Sunday the 12th January 1930 with the Band of the London Fire Brigade and the second on the 14th December 1930. They were immensely popular entertainers in the 1930s and 1940s. They wrote all their own material. Elsie was the elder of the two by nine years and died in 1990 at the age of 95. Doris, the younger sister pre-deceased her sister by twelve years. They were the elder sisters of Jack Warner, born Horace Waters. He was not expected to survive his birth but this he did and after changing his name, so that he did not trade on the fame and success of his sisters, he went on to become Britain's most popular stage policeman as 'Dixon of Dock Green', a part he played for over twenty years.

Houston Sisters. Renee and Billie Houston (real name Gibbin) were two Scots sisters who came to the Palace Theatre on the 25th January 1926 and again on the 16th January 1928. Renee went on to achieve success in films and television and played in many television series and films including *The Saint*, the *Carry On* films, the *Doctor at Sea* films and the *Maigret* series. She died in 1980 aged 77.

Clive Maskelyne. Clive Maskelyne was a member of the world-famous family of illusionists. He visited the Palace Theatre on two occasions the first being on the 1st March 1926 and the second on the 28th May 1928. Another member of the same family, Nevil, was part of the celebrated team of Maskelyne and Devant.

Ethel Revnell and Gracie West. Known as Revnell and West or 'The Long and the Short of it' because of the disparity in their height. Ethel was a little over six feet tall whereas Gracie was only slightly over four feet. In the 1934 pantomime *Cinderella* at Drury Lane in which the pair played the Ugly Sisters, the Baron was renamed Baron Mumm so that Ethel Revnell could be 'Maxi Mumm' and Gracie West 'Mini Mumm'.

Kate Carney. Kate Carney was born in 1869. She started her music hall career singing Irish songs but was more famous for her cockney songs. Kate Carney became known as the Cockney Sweetheart. She took part in a Royal Variety Performance in 1935 and died in 1950. She performed on the stage of the Palace Theatre heading the cast in a revue called *Apple Sauce* in April 1926 and paid a return visit on the 7th March 1927.

Will Hay. Will Hay has been described as a 'comic genius'. He topped the bill in a Variety show during the week commencing 5th July 1926. He is most famous for his role as a bumbling schoolmaster.

Hylda Baker. There is only one recorded visit by Hylda Baker to the Palace and that was in a revue named *What Ho!* on the 28th August 1926. According to the *Watford Observer* she was 'well applauded as a clever comedienne'. She topped the bill in Variety at the age of 10. She was diminutive, standing under five feet tall. She had a distinguished career achieving fame with her silent partner Cynthia and the catchphrase 'She knows, you know'. Sadly she became afflicted by Alzheimer's disease and spent the last years of her life in a nursing home for retired Variety performers almost entirely forgotten, having been at one stage in her life one of Britain's foremost Variety entertainers. She died in 1986 at the age of 81.

Will Fyffe. The great Scots comedian Will Fyffe appeared in a Variety programme at the theatre on the 15th November 1926. Although his most famous song was *I Belong to Glas*gow he was, in fact, born in Dundee in 1885. He was a character actor as well as a comedian. He created many convincing characters having studied them at close hand. His career started in Shakespeare. So popular was he that a Glasgow theatre ran a competition for Will Fyffe impersonations which attracted many contestants. Fyffe himself entered, heavily disguised as himself, and won second prize. He appeared in seven Royal Variety Performances. He died in 1947 by falling from his hotel window while recovering from surgery. He was 62.

Albert Sandler and **Jack Byfield.** This duo played at the Palace on the 30th May 1927. They were famous for their performances of light music with the Palm Court Orchestra which performed variously at the Park Lane Hotel and the Grand Hotel, Eastbourne from where, for many years, they were to be heard on the radio every Sunday evening. They were household names in the 1930s and were renowned for the elegance of their performances. Albert Sandler was a violinist and leader of the orchestra, Jack Byfield was the pianist and arranged many of the works they played.

Lily Morris. Born Lilles Mary Crosby in 1882, Lily Morris was already an established entertainer when she came to the Palace Theatre on the 18th July 1927. In her younger days she had been a principal boy in pantomime. She is remembered today for the songs she sang in the 1920s one of which was

Why Am I Always the Bridesmaid. Like so many music hall stars she was a cockney and she had perfect diction so that every word she sang could be heard and understood. In 1925 she went to America where she was an instant success. She stopped the show at the New York Hippodrome receiving countless encores. She has been variously described as 'a huge star of the music hall' and 'one of the all-time music hall greats'. Lily Morris was as popular in America as she was in Great Britain. Probably her most famous song was *Don't Have Any More Missus Moore.* She performed at the theatre subsequently on the 1st July 1935 in a revue entitled *Crazy Week* and again at a Sunday concert on the 18th October 1936. She died in 1952.

Albert Whelan. Albert Whelan played in a week of Variety from the 9th April 1928 and returned on two subsequent occasions in Sunday evening concerts. These were on the 15th November 1936 and the 4th April 1937. He was born in Melbourne, Australia on the 5th May 1875. He was the first person to use a signature tune which he whistled at the start and finish of his act. He enjoyed a long and successful career up to the end of his life in 1961. He was always immaculately attired on stage in white tie and tails.

Harry Hemsley. Another music hall entertainer to grace the stage of the Palace Theatre, Watford was Harry Hemsley. He came for a Sunday evening concert on the 10th March 1929 and again on Sunday the 19th January 1930. His act, which was ideally suited to radio, or the wireless as it was called in those days, consisted of his impersonations of his imaginary family of four children, Elsie, Winnie, Johnny and the baby Horace whose incoherent babblings had to be translated by one of the older children. His impersonations were so convincing that it is said that some of the radio audience thought that they were listening to real children. He died on the 8th April 1951.

Dolores. Known only by this name, Dolores was the favourite model of Sir Jacob Epstein the American-born sculptor. She appeared at the Palace Theatre during the week commencing 1st July 1929 in a play entitled *By Whose Hand.*

Gladys Cooper. Gladys Cooper was born in 1888. She started her career as a chorus girl at the Gaiety Theatre. Her outstanding beauty soon brought her to the attention of theatre producers, although some thought her acting 'stiff'. During World War I she was the favourite pin-up of the Forces. She came to prominence in 1922 in *The Second Mrs. Tanqueray* by Arthur Wing Pinero. Her appearance at the Palace Theatre, Watford was on the 17th March 1930 in a play entitled *The Sacred Flame*. In 1934 she went to America to appear on Broadway and from there it was a natural step for her to move to Hollywood until 1947. During her time in America she made more than thirty films. She played the part of Mrs. Higgins in the 1964 film of *My Fair Lady*. She was made DBE in 1967. Dame Gladys Cooper died in 1971 at the age of 82.

Joe Boganny. On 31st March 1930, the *West End Variety* bill included Joe Boganny and his College Boys. Boganny was famous for heading a troupe of comedy acrobats.

Hetty King. Hetty King was born Winifred Emms ,the daughter of a famous comedian and one-man-band exponent. She joined him on stage at the age of six. She established her reputation as a male impersonator and comedienne. She came to Watford on the 14th April 1930 in a programme with the title *Rogues and Vagabonds*.

Robb Wilton. Robb Wilton started his stage career playing the villain in melodramas, later graduating to character parts. It was when he realised he was getting laughs that he decided his talents lay in comedy. He specialised in playing incompetent officials. During the Second World War he devised a series of monologues which invariably started with the words, 'The day war broke out…'. His first visit to the Palace was on the 4th August 1930 when he performed a sketch *His Journey*. He returned on the 24th June 1935 in a revue entitled *Honi soi qui Watford Palace*.

Herschel Henlere. Henlere was a composer, music hall artiste as a Variety stage pianist, and actor. His first visit to the theatre was for a Sunday evening concert on the 26th April 1933. He returned to Watford on the 17th June 1935 to feature in the same programme that Robb Wilton was to appear in the following week, *Honi soi qui Watford Palace*. He was in two films in the 1930s. He took part in the *Royal Variety Show* on the 18th November 1957 with David Whitfield. Judy Garland was the main attraction in that show. Herschel Henlere played at the Gaiety Theatre and was regarded in the same category as Turner Layton, Leslie Hutchinson ('Hutch') and Charlie Kunz, all celebrated Variety pianists.

The Western Brothers. Kenneth and George were, in fact, second cousins. They were a brilliant comedy double act. Very similar in appearance and made more so by both sporting a monocle for their act with an 'Old school tie' or more frequently white tie and tails. In the 1920s and 1930s they were much in demand; their material, written by themselves, exuded a cynical view of the world. Their act became dated after the end of the British Empire and this was hastened by the advent of television. They made their first appearance at the theatre on Sunday the 16th November 1930 and returned on Sunday the 10th March 1935 and for a week in *East is East*, a revue starting on the 27th May 1935.

Leonard Henry. Born Leonard H. Ruming in Kensington in 1890, Leonard Henry became a popular cockney comedian. He was master of a range of strange voices with which he illustrated his comedy, He was a regular performer on radio and is said to have been the first entertainer to blow a raspberry on radio. He stood only five feet tall. He was an early performer on television in its experimental days before the Second World War. He died on the 6th January 1973 aged 82.

Flanagan and Allen. The last duo, which made up the Crazy Gang, to perform at the theatre were Bud Flanagan (real name Chaim Reuben Weintrop, son of an émigré Polish/Jewish couple) and Chesney Allen. They combined comedy with song and had a distinctive style which even today is imitated by other performers. Bud Flanagan sang the melody line while Chesney Allen almost spoke his line which provided the harmony. They pursued their individual act concurrently with their performances with the Crazy Gang. Their repertoire of songs was extensive. Probably the song with which they will always be associated was *Underneath the Arches*. In 1968 Flanagan recorded the theme song to *Dad's Army – Who Do You Think You Are Kidding Mr. Hitler?* shortly before his death. They came to the Palace on the 28th September 1931

Phyllis Monkman. Phyllis Monkman came to the Palace with Stanley Holloway on the 26th October 1931 with the *Co-optimists*, of which they were both founder members. She was born in 1892 and at the start of her career she was an actress and dancer. She appeared in a number of revues in the company of many well-known performers of the day including Jack Buchanan, Leslie Henson, Ruby Miller and Jack Hulbert. She had parts written for her by Noël Coward and Ivor Novello. Her beauty attracted the attention of the celebrated portrait photographer Bassano who photographed her several times. She died in 1976.

Stanley Holloway. Stanley Holloway came to the Palace in a *Co-optimists* revue, which included Phyllis Monkman, on 26th October 1931. He was celebrated for his monologues, which included *Sam, Sam pick up thy musket*, but originally had intended to be an opera singer and went to Milan to train. He became famous for his character roles. He was born in 1890 and his first job after leaving school was as a clerk at Billingsgate Fish Market. His most famous role was Alfred P. Doolittle in *My Fair Lady* which he played on Broadway as well as at Drury Lane and in the film version.

Leslie Sarony. At a Sunday concert, with the title *A Modern Entertainment* on the 6th December 1931, at the theatre, Leslie Sarony was top of the bill. He was hugely popular in the 1920s and early 1930s as a solo entertainer. He recorded many songs, some in his own name and some as a nameless vocalist with the Jack Hylton orchestra. Some of his songs were humorous in content, such as *He Played His Ukulele As the Ship Went Down*. In 1935 he teamed up with Leslie Holmes to form the double act 'The Two Leslies'. Leslie Sarony was born in1897 and died in 1985.

Tod Slaughter. Yes, the master of horror and villainy did perform at the Palace Theatre. It was for a week commencing on the 25th April 1932 and typically it was in a production, from the New Theatre, of *The Crimes of Burke and Hare*. In 1948 the play was turned into a film with the title *The Greed of Moore and Hart*. Tod Slaughter's two most famous films, both of which started out as stage plays, were *Murder in the Red Barn* and *The Demon Barber of Fleet Street*. Tod Slaughter was born in Newcastle in 1885 and died in 1956.

Lydia Kyasht. The world-famous Russian Ballerina, who was born in 1885, studied at the St. Petersburg Imperial Ballet School and joined the Maryinski Theatre (known during the Communist era in Russia as the Kirov Theatre) in 1902. She moved to London in 1908. In 1912 she danced with Diaghilev's Ballets Russes. She too was photographed on more than one occasion by Bassano. Lydia Kyasht was part of the programme named *Springtime Cabaret* at the Palace Theatre on the 2nd May 1932. She died in London in 1959.

Alfred Denville. Much has been written about Denville's connection with Watford in Chapter 2 of this book. Here it is recorded that on Friday the 24th March 1933 a single performance of *Jerry the Tramp* was given at the Palace Theatre in which Alfred Denville himself played the name part.

Peter Murray-Hill. Peter Murray-Hill was another local boy who made good. He was born in Bushey, Hertfordshire, in 1908. He starred at the theatre in the play *The Under Dog* with the Denville Players on the 21st November 1932. In private life he was married to Phyllis Calvert who was voted Britain's most popular actress after Margaret Lockwood in 1940. Peter Murray-Hill himself made a number of films in the 1930s and 1940s. He combined acting with that of a well-respected seller of antiquarian books, specialising in eighteenth-century books. Tragically he died in 1957 at the early age of 49.

Tommy Trinder. In contrast to the dancing by Lydia Kyasht, on the same programme in May 1932 Tommy Trinder performed burlesque dances. This was before he achieved national fame. He was born in Streatham, the son of a London tram driver, in 1909. He left school early and at the age of 12 decided to give up his job as an errand boy and take to the stage. He spent many years on the music hall circuit. In 1926 he was the star of the Archie Pitt (first husband of Gracie Fields) touring company but it was not until 1937 that he achieved the success which had so long eluded him. By the outbreak of the Second World War he had become one of the most loved and admired comedians on the British stage. In 1939 he made a film entitled *Sailors Three* co-starring with Claude Hulbert and Michael Wilding, in which the three friends capture a German pocket battleship. He made several more films with Ealing Studios but by this time he had virtually appropriated the London Palladium. He was the first compère of the Sunday evening ITV show *Sunday Night at the London Palladium*. He died in 1989.

Donald Edwards and Betty Nelson. The first recorded appearance of Donald Edwards and Betty Nelson was as members of the Denville Players repertory company which came to the theatre in June 1932 for a 47-week season. They were in a number of plays. Both are listed in the cast of the Oscar Wilde play *A Woman of No Importance* on the 12th September 1932. They were husband and wife having married at Gretna Green within a few weeks of first meeting. They returned to the Palace on the 15th July 1935 with their own company and from the 5th August the company was advertised as the

Edward Nelson Players. A programme from January 1937 lists Donald Edwards as 'Licensee and General Manager'.

Kim Peacock. Kim Peacock was born in Watford in 1901. The Peacock family founded and were proprietors of the local newspaper the *Watford Observer*. He was a talented violinist but became an actor achieving fame as *Paul Temple* in the radio series of that name from 1946 to 1953 on the BBC Light Programme. On the 11th July 1932 he was in the cast of *Spring Cleaning* by Frederick Lonsdale at the Palace Theatre. Kim Peacock died in 1966.

Claude Dampier and Billie Carlyle. Claude Dampier was a popular entertainer in the 1930s through to the 1950s. He was born in Clapham in 1879. His partner, Billie Carlyle, was also his wife. She was born in Adelaide, Australia, in 1901, real name Doris Davy. In their act Dampier played the part of a 'professional idiot'. He had the face to match with a mouth full of teeth. A feature of his act was to address remarks to a fictitious member of the audience known as Mrs. Gibson. The duo came to the Palace on the 8th July 1935. In the same year he made a film *Boys Will Be Boys* with Will Hay. He died in 1955; Billie Carlyle died in 1991 aged 90.

Anton Dolin. Dolin was born in 1904. His name was Sydney Francis Patrick Chippendall Healey-Kay. He came to the Palace Theatre on the 10th December 1934 in the same programme as Wendy Toye (see below). He became a noted ballet dancer appearing with Diaghilev's Ballets Russes. In 1931 he joined the Vic-Wells Ballet which eventually became the Royal Ballet. During a long career he appeared with or choreographed for most of the major ballet companies in the West. He was knighted in 1981 and died in 1983.

Wendy Toye. Wendy Toye was only 17 years old when she appeared at the theatre in a programme of ballet with Anton Dolin. That was on the 10th December 1934. with the West End Vaudeville Company. It was not to be her only visit to Watford. At the age of nine she appeared at the London Palladium in a ballet she had choreographed herself. She was at one time a member of Diaghilev's Ballets Russes. Later in life she turned to directing both for the stage and for films. At the Palace Theatre, Watford she directed *Laburnum Grove* (2nd to 25th April 1987) and *Mrs. Dot* (29th September to 22nd October 1988) and the 1989 pantomime *Cinderella*.

Bertha Wilmot. Bertha Wilmot was born in 1887 and came to the theatre on two occasions, both Sunday concerts. These visits were on the 24th March 1935 and the 25th October 1936. She was a 'big name' Variety artiste in her day but apart from the fact that she was Queen Ratling in the Grand Order of Lady Ratlings in 1953, little is known of her today.

Stainless Stephen. Born in 1892 in Sheffield, real name Arthur Clifford Baynes (or Baines), Stainless Stephen took the name 'Stainless' from the 'stainless steel' for which Sheffield was famous. He even wore, for his act, a stainless steel waistcoat. He started his working life as a schoolmaster but gradually established himself as a radio and Variety comedian. His first stage appearance was at the Palace, Luton. He came to the Palace Theatre, Watford on Sunday the 14th April 1935 and returned on Sunday the 22nd March 1936 and again on Sunday the 1st November 1936. He was an appreciated entertainer and included in the Royal Command Performance in 1945. He died in 1971.

Arthur Askey. 'Big Hearted Arthur' was born in Liverpool and became one of the most popular English comedians of all time. He came to prominence with the radio show *Band Wagon* in which he starred with Richard (Stinker) Murdoch. He had a collection of comic songs the most famous of which was *The Bee Song*. Sadly as he got older his act wound down and because of poor circulation both his legs were amputated. He died in 1982. He came to the Palace Theatre on the 23rd February 1936 and again on the 22nd November 1936 for two Sunday concerts.

Ronald Frankau. Born in 1894, Ronald Frankau developed a unique style of comedy. With his Etonian accent and his slightly risqué songs he has been described as a cross between Max Miller and Noël Coward. Some of his songs were not permitted on radio but sold many records across the counter. His sister was Pamela Frankau, the novelist. As well as achieving fame as an entertainer he wrote books and poems of a humorous nature for children. He came to the theatre for three Sunday concerts, on the 12th April 1936, the 11th October 1936 and the 17th January 1937. He died in 1951.

Tessie O'Shea. An enormously popular entertainer with her ukulele, Tessie O'Shea came to the Palace on Sunday the 7th March 1937. Because of her generous proportions she was known as 'Two Ton Tessie' and adopted as her theme tune *Two Ton Tessie from Tennessee*. She was born in Cardiff on the 13th March 1913. During World War II she toured extensively entertaining the troops. Her big break was in 1963 when she appeared in a Noël Coward musical on Broadway, *The Girl Who Came to Supper*. She continued performing right up until the time of her death, aged 82, in 1995.

Vic Oliver. Born in Vienna on the 8th July 1898, the son of Baron Viktor von Samek, Victor Oliver von Samek, known as Vic Oliver, was an accomplished musician, playing the violin and piano. He started his entertainment career as an accompanist and it is said that at a recital in which he was accompanying a singer he took his seat at the piano when the stool collapsed. He instantly realised that his future lay in comedy. For years he teamed up with Ben Lyon and Bebe Daniels in the radio series *Hi Gang!* He was the first castaway on *Desert Island Discs*. In 1936 he married Sir Winston Churchill's daughter Sarah. They were divorced in 1945. He founded the British Concert Orchestra of which he was the principal conductor. Vic Oliver's first appearance at the theatre was in a Sunday concert on the 21st March 1937. It was not until the 16th March 1964 that he returned in the cast of *Distinguished Gathering*, shortly before his death on the 15th August the same year.

Peggy Cochrane. Peggy Cochrane was born in 1902 and became a celebrated pianist, violinist and singer. She enjoyed a long career touring music halls and broadcasting. She was married to Jack Payne who ran a successful dance band and was for two periods Dance Band Director at the BBC. Peggy Cochrane came to the Palace Theatre on Sunday the 11th April 1937. She died in 1988.

Donald Wolfit. Wolfit was born in Nottinghamshire in 1902. He came to the theatre in a play with the title *The Three Pigeons* on the 13th June 1938. He was not popular with other actors because of apparent vanity and an abrasive personality. He was, however, an outstanding Shakespearean actor playing most of the major roles of Shakespeare during the years 1938 to 1943. He was knighted in 1957 and died in 1968.

John Le Mesurier. He was born in Bedford on the 5th April 1912 with the real name of John Elton Halliley (Le Mesurier was his mother's maiden name). His first wife was June Melville, cousin of Andrew Melville; that marriage was dissolved in 1946. Two years later on the 15th March 1948 he appeared at the Palace in *Message for Margaret*. He appeared in more than a hundred films and was a frequent broadcaster. He was a member of the cast of *Hancock's Half Hour*, being a great friend of Tony Hancock. John Le

Mesurier is most likely to be remembered for his part in *Dad's Army* as Sergeant Arthur Wilson. He died in 1983, or, as in his own words in his obituary, he had 'simply conked out'.

Lupino Lane. Real name Henry William George Lupino. Lupino Lane was born in 1892 into a large theatrical family which could trace its roots back to a seventeenth-century immigrant from Italy. He came to the Palace Theatre on the 18th September 1950 in the play *Twenty to One*. The most famous member of the Lupino family was his niece Ida Lupino (1918-1995) who made a name for herself as an actress, writer and director in Hollywood. Lupino Lane is best remembered for his role of Bill Snibson in *Me and My Girl* in which he made famous the song *Doing the Lambeth Walk*. He returned to the theatre for a non-musical version of *Me and My Girl* on the 17th May 1954.

Jessie Matthews. The daughter of a Soho costermonger, Jessie Matthews had an inauspicious start to life in 1907, as one of ten children. Her break came when, at the age of 17, she took over from Gertrude Lawrence in *Charlot's Revue of 1924*. She was renowned as the possessor of a pure singing voice and for her dancing ability. Her most famous songs were *Over My Shoulder* and *He Dances Overhead*. She broke into films and in the 1930s was the most popular film star in England. She was often temperamental which stemmed from a difficult upbringing. She appeared in two plays at the Palace Theatre, *Larger Than Life* on the 30th July 1951 and *Love In Idleness* on the 5th November 1952. After her film career she concentrated on theatre but in the 1960s she re-established her fame by playing the name part in *Mrs. Dale's Diary* on BBC radio. Jessie Matthews died in 1981.

A.E. Matthews. No relation to Jessie Matthews, Alfred Edward Matthews was born in Yorkshire in 1869 and known to his friends as 'Matty'. In his younger days he played the youthful leading man but later in life he established himself as a character actor playing mostly elderly, titled aristocrats. He made numerous films during his long career and there are many stories illustrating his sense of humour and individuality. In his ninetieth year he sat outside his splendid Georgian house in Bushey Heath for several days and nights to prevent the local authority erecting outside his house, Prospect Cottage, a lamp post, the design of which he did not approve. During rehearsals for *The Manor of Northstead* when he was 84, it was obvious that he was experiencing difficulty memorising his lines. Perceiving the concern of the director he assured him 'Even if we open on Monday, I shall know my lines'; the director replied, 'But Matty, we do'. On another occasion in one scene he was required to answer the telephone on stage. Having picked up the receiver he froze, unable to remember his lines. Eventually he turned to another actor on stage and said, 'It's for you.' He came to the Palace Theatre on three occasions, the first on the 9th July 1951 in a play with the title *But For the Grace of God*. His second visit was on the 3rd September 1951 to play the role of Lord Lister in *The Chiltern Hundreds*, which he had played in the West End, and finally to play the same name part in the sequel, *The Manor of Northstead* on 27th February 1956. He was still performing up to the end of his life and is reported to have said, 'I pick up *The Times* every morning and if I'm not in the obituary list, then I go to work.' He died in 1960 at the age of 91.

Helen Haye. Frequently referred to as 'the magnificent Helen Haye', she was born in Assam, India on the 28th August 1874. Over five decades she made innumerable films. Her last film was *Anastasia* with Ingrid Bergman and Yul Brynner in 1953 in which she played the part of the Dowager Tsarina. For many years she taught at the Royal Academy of Dramatic Art. On the 1st October 1951 she came to the theatre to appear in *Many Happy Returns*. Also in the cast was Irene Handl (see below).

Irene Handl. One of the finest comedy actresses England ever produced, Irene Handl was the daughter of a wealthy Austrian banker and his French aristocrat wife. Her mother died when Irene was quite young and she devoted her early life to looking after her father. At the age of 36 she enrolled at a drama school run by Dame Sybil Thorndike's sister. The first play she was in closed after fourteen days but the second in which she played a maidservant was *George and Margaret*. The success of this play ensured continuous work for her for the next forty years. She concentrated on playing parts totally alien to her own upbringing such as slightly eccentric mothers, grandmothers, landladies and servants. During her career she appeared in more than a hundred films in supporting roles, mostly comedy character parts. She was the author of two best-selling novels *The Sioux* (1965) and *The Gold Tipped Pfizer* (1966). Irene Handl was in the cast of many radio and television series. She came to the Palace on four occasions. These were: *Many Happy Returns* on the 1st October 1951; *The Shop at Sly Corner*, 28th April 1952; *Blithe Spirit*, 7th September 1977 in which she played Madame Arcati (having played the role in the film) and *Local Affairs* on the 2nd April 1981. She never married and died in 1987.

Ralph Lynn. Ralph (pronounced 'Rafe') was born in Manchester in 1882. He was a veteran of the Aldwych Farces written by Ben Travers. Other members of this company included Robertson Hare and Tom Walls. Ralph Lynn sported a monocle and specialised in playing 'silly asses'. He came to Watford to appear in *Rookery Nook* (one of the notable Aldwych Farces) by Ben Travers on the 3rd December 1951 and *Is Your Honeymoon Really Necessary?* on the 24th March 1952.

Derek Oldham. For many the name of Derek Oldham is inextricably linked with Gilbert & Sullivan. He was a member of the D'Oyly Carte Opera Company and played all of the tenor leads. He was also a leading singer/actor at Drury Lane and other West End theatres. He was born in 1887 and was a much-loved man who spread happiness wherever he went, always ready to give help and encouragement when and where it was needed. He came to the Palace Theatre, Watford on the 26th January 1952 to appear in the cast of *The Fifty Mark*. He died on the 20th March 1968.

Gwen Watford. Not because of her name, which was her real name, but because of the length of time she spent at the Palace Theatre, Watford and of her keen interest in its welfare, will Gwen Watford be long remembered. Her first recorded visit was on the 21st April 1952 in *Anna Christie* by Eugene O'Neill. She remained with the Andrew Melville company for some years, whilst at the same time pursuing her career in other directions. Her last appearance at the Palace was in *Abiding Passions* from 23rd May to 15th June 1991. She died in 1994.

Rodney Bewes. Rodney Bewes was born in Bingley, West Yorkshire on the 27th November 1938. He came to the Palace Theatre in 1958 as assistant stage manager. His name in the first programme after his appointment listed him as 'Rooney' Bewes, no doubt due to a misinterpretation of someone's handwriting. In the following programme his name was amended to 'Roney' Bewes. At the third attempt they 'got it right'. He was playing small parts in addition to his other responsibilities but by mid-summer 1958 he was a full member of the resident repertory company. He went on to make a considerable name for himself in the theatre and on television as, mainly but not exclusively, a comedy actor. For a while he was the accompaniment to the puppet Basil Brush but he will be best remembered for playing Bob Ferris in *The Likely Lads*.

Bill Maynard. One of Britain's most-loved comedy actors. He was born Walter Frederick George Williams on 28th October 1928. He has played many characters in a range of comedy series. Most well known as Claude Greengrass, a loveable rogue, and as Selwyn Froggitt. For a time he teamed up with Terry Scott in *Great Scott, It's Maynard.* He came to the Palace Theatre to join the resident repertory company for *You Too Can Have a Body* during the week commencing 6th April 1959 and returned on the 28th September 1970 to appear in *A Face for all Seasons.*

Terry Scott. Another local boy was Terry Scott, born in Watford in 1927. He attended Watford Grammar School for Boys. After school he trained as an accountant. During the Second World War he served in the Royal Navy but after the war he decided to become an actor. He appeared at the theatre on the 1st June 1959 in the play *Man for the Job.* He went on to enjoy success on television and radio, on television in such series as *Great Scott, It's Maynard* with Bill Maynard, *Hugh and I* with Hugh Lloyd and *Terry and June*, one of the longest running sitcoms of all time, with June Whitfield. He made a number of films and appeared in no less than seven of the *Carry On* films. He died after a long battle with cancer on the 26th June 1994.

Bob Grant. It was towards the end of 1959 that Bob Grant joined the Perry's repertory company and he took part in many of their productions. In 1960 he was in the cast of *MacBird* at the Theatre Royal, Stratford. Also in that cast was Jimmy Perry. On the 23rd March 1964 he returned to join the cast of *This Happy Home.* This would seem to have been Bob Grant's last visit to the Palace Theatre. In 1968 he had his big break when he was cast as Jack Harper in the long-running television series *On the Buses*, in which part he achieved world-wide fame and popularity. He was co-writer of several plays and farces. Tragically, he made more than one attempt to end his life and finally succeeded on the 8th November 2003.

Judy Parfitt. Judy Parfittt celebrated her twenty-fourth birthday during the run of Noël Cowards *Present Laughter* at the Palace Theatre, during the week commencing the 2nd November 1959. She was born in Sheffield and trained at RADA. Freshly qualified she came to Watford and was in the cast of a number of plays with the Jimmy and Gilda Perry Company. She came to prominence in the 1960s and has led a distinguished career on the stage and also in films. She is most well known as a classical actress.

Arthur English. Arthur English was born in 1919. He served in the army in World War II and on being demobilised at the end of hostilities he worked as a painter and decorator until auditioning in 1949 for The Windmill Theatre. There, he became resident comedian. Today he is regarded as one of the really great Variety comedians. Arthur English was affectionately known as 'The Prince of Wide Boys' because of his extravagant style of dressing and an enormously wide tie. He would finish his act with the words 'Play the music – open the cage!' He came to the theatre on the 6th June 1960 in the play *Twenty to One*. In 1972 he was cast as the odd-job man, Mr. Harman, in *Are You Being Served?*

Jill Browne. On the 22nd January 1962 *Doctor in the House* was produced at the theatre. It starred Jill Browne and the cast of the television series *Emergency Ward 10* in which she played the part of Nurse Carole Young. This was the first hospital soap, to be followed some years later by *Casualty* and *Holby City*. Jill Browne was a local resident living in Bushey and for six years she was married to John Alderton who was also in the cast of *Emergency Ward 10*. Jill Browne was born in 1937 and, sadly, died of cancer in 1991 at an early age.

Randolph Sutton. Randolph Sutton was born in 1888. On the 9th December 1963 he came to the theatre to appear in an *Old Time Music Hall* with Billy Danvers (see below). He was a popular performer in music hall and Variety, invariably impeccably dressed in white tie and tails. His final performance was at the City Hall in St. Albans on the 26th February 1969 and he died two days later.

Billy Danvers. Full name, William Mikado Danvers. His father was a member of the D'Oyly Carte Opera Company and among the parts he played was the Mikado. He was born in 1889 and became a respected member of the theatrical profession. At one time he was a member of a Fred Karno company. In the 1930s he was engaged in several of Julian Wylie's pantomimes in such theatres as the Theatre Royal, Drury Lane, The Palace Theatre, Manchester and in *Little Old King Cole* with Charlie Drake at the London Palladium. Also in that panto was Pamela Cundell who was later to play the Fairy Godmother in several pantomimes at the Palace Theatre, Watford. He appeared in an *Old Time Music Hall* at the Palace on the same bill as Randolph Sutton (see above) on the 9th December 1963 at the age of 75 and died three months later on the 20th March 1964.

Anna Neagle. Dame Anna Neagle, as she was to become in 1969, was born Florence Marjorie Robertson in 1904. Her first stage appearance was in 1917 as a dancer and chorus member. It was not long before she became noticed and gained popularity. She appeared on stage and screen with Jack Buchanan and Michael Wilding. She made many films portraying in some of them historical characters including Queen Victoria in *Sixty Glorious Years*. She also portrayed Edith Cavell, Florence Nightingale, Amy Johnson and Odette. She did not always find favour with the critics because her films leant towards the romantic but these were so popular with her audiences that for seven years during and immediately after World War II she was Britain's leading Box Office draw. In 1943 she married Herbert Wilcox who had directed many of her films and guided her career. She was a member of the cast of *Person Unknown* at the Palace Theatre on the 23rd November 1964. Anna Neagle was the last celebrity to play at the Palace Theatre, before it ceased to be a repertory theatre. She died in 1986.

Jane Asher. On the 6th July 1965 a nineteen-year-old Jane Asher played the role of Eliza in a production of Shaw's *Pygmalion* at the Palace. It is said that Paul McCartney, with whom at the time she was in a relationship, came to the theatre to see his girlfriend in the play.

Peggy Ashcroft. Dame Peggy Ashcroft visited the Palace Theatre for a *Sunday Night Special* on the 10th October 1965. She was born in 1907. Her career was spent mainly on the stage although she did appear in a few films, winning an Oscar for her part in *A Passage to India* (1984). She was awarded a DBE in 1956 and died in 1991.

Julian Bream. Considered by many as the greatest classical guitarist of the twentieth century, Julian Bream was born in London in 1933. He achieved international recognition at an early age and has performed around the world. Many contemporary composers have written music for him. He came to Watford on Sunday the 10th October 1965 and performed on the same programme as Dame Peggy Ashcroft in a *Sunday Night Special*.

Donald Swann. Donald Swann was one half of the Flanders and Swann double act performing comic songs. Swann was the pianist. Their most famous song was probably *Mud, Mud, Glorious Mud*. Donald Swann was born in Llanelli of Russian parents in 1923. He met Michael Flanders at Westminster School. They were both up at Christ Church, Oxford. Swann was a serious and light composer. He came to the Palace Theatre on Sunday 12th June 1966 for a 'musical evening' under the name of *Set by Swann*. With him on that occasion were Ian Wallace, Marion Studholme and William Elvin. He died in 1994.

Marion Studholme. Marion Studholme came to Watford on Sunday 12th June 1966 in the performance of *Set by Swann* (see above). She was a renowned performer in opera and on the concert platform, especially with Sadlers Wells Opera (later to be named English National Opera). She recorded most of the operas of Benjamin Britten.

Ian Wallace. Ian Wallace, possessor of a fine bass-baritone voice came to the Palace Theatre twice in 1966. The first visit was with Donald Swann (see above) and the second, a month later, on the 19th July in a double bill *Conversation at Night* and *High Fidelity*, described as a new musical by John Gould. He recorded many of the Flanders and Swann songs. A hugely popular entertainer, his career encompassed opera, musicals, plays and films.

Elizabeth Fretwell. Another opera singer (soprano). With Alberto Remedios she came to the Palace two weeks after Donald Swann, on Sunday 26th June 1966 for an evening concert of *Opera Favourites* supported by the chorus of Watford Operatic Society. Elizabeth Fretwell was born in Melbourne, Australia in 1920 and after coming to Britain she was for many years prima donna at Sadlers Wells (today known as English National Opera). Her repertoire was wide taking in Wagner, Puccini, Verdi, Britten and others. She died in Australia on the 5th June 2006, at the age of 86.

Alberto Remedios. In spite of his name Alberto Remedios was born in Liverpool, on the 27th February 1935. He visited the Palace Theatre, Watford on the same occasion as Elizabeth Fretwell with whom he was a colleague at Sadlers Wells. He sang with many of the leading opera houses around the world, including the Metropolitan Opera in New York. He will be especially remembered for his performances in Wagner. He once sang the entire *Ring Cycle* in one week, an immense 'tour de force' for any singer and this achievement established his reputation as the greatest Heldentenor of his generation. He retired to Australia.

Bessie Love. The name of Bessie Love is included here although her appearances are given in more detail in Chapter 5. She was American by birth and was a star of silent films made in the early years of Hollywood. Bessie

Love came to the Palace Theatre as a member of the cast of two plays by Tennessee Williams, *The Glass Menagerie* in July 1966 and *Sweet Bird of Youth* in November 1968. She was born in 1898 and moved to Britain in 1935 where she remained for most of the rest of her life. She died in 1986.

Libby Morris. Libby Morris was born in Manitoba and moved to England in 1955. An outstandingly versatile entertainer, she was known as a singer and comedienne and was famous for her ability to contort her face. She was in the cast of a number of comedy shows on television, including *Two's Company* with Peter Butterworth and Dick Emery. She also played supporting roles in a number of films including *United 93* (2006). She was at the Palace Theatre for the world premiere of a play entitled *As Dorothy Parker Once Said* which opened on the 8th November 1966.

Patricia Burke. Patricia Burke made two visits to the theatre in 1967. The first was in the play *The Killing of Sister George* by Frank Marcus on the 4th April and the second, on the 21st November, in *The Waiters* by Norman Bogner. Also in the cast of that play was Frank Williams. She was the daughter of the singer Marie Burke. She had a long and varied career starting in the musical theatre but progressing to classical roles, including Shakespeare, at the Old Vic. She was a committed pacifist which on one occasion landed her in prison overnight. She led the cast in the wartime film *The Lisbon Story* and was also in the long-running musical *Charlie Girl*. Patricia Burke was born in Milan in 1917, where her father was singing and died in 2003.

Brigit Forsyth. Her most successful television role was as Thelma, the fiancée of Bob Ferris in *Whatever Happened to the Likely Lads*. Her first visit to the Palace Theatre was as Jane Eyre, the narrator, in an adaptation of Charlotte Bronte's novel of the same name. This was on the 25th April 1967. She was also a member of the cast of *You Must be the Husband* by Colin Bostock-Smith on the 1st March 1990 and *Morning Glory* by Diana Samuels on the 20th April 2001.

Liz Gebhardt. Born in Liverpool in 1945, she rose to prominence as the 'love-lorn' Maureen Bullock in television's *Please, Sir!* She also appeared in other television comedy series, including a single performance in *Keeping Up Appearances* and also in *Brookside*. She died at a relatively early age in 1996. She came to the theatre on the 25th April 1967 in a production of *Jane Eyre*, the cast of which also included Brigit Forsyth.

Maureen Lipman. Maureen Lipman made her acting debut on the 9th May 1967 at the Palace Theatre in *The Knack* by Anne Jellicoe after training at the London Academy of Music and Dramatic Art. She returned later in the year in a production of *Wuthering Heights* (26th September to 7th October). She was also in the cast of the 1967 pantomime *Aladdin* and in March 1968 in Joe Orton's play *Loot*. A highly admired and versatile entertainer she has had a crowded career in various genres, including advertising. In a busy schedule she returned to the Palace Theatre again in Noël Coward's *Design for Living* (29th January-21st February 1981) and *Wonderful Town*, the musical by Leonard Bernstein (12th April-10th May 1989). In what was interpreted as a gesture of affection for the Palace she was in the audience on the night it closed for rebuilding in 2002. Indeed, in a note to the author she wrote 'Watford gave me my first break – always grateful!' One of her most recent successes was as 'Aunt Eller' in the Royal National Theatre production of *Oklahoma!* in 1998/9.

David Kossoff. Kossoff gave two Sunday evening performances of his show *A Funny Kind of Evening*. The first on the 4th June 1967 and again, fifteen years later, on the 31st October 1982. He was the son of Russian Jewish parents who had come to Britain to escape persecution and was born in the East End of London on the 24th November 1919. As an actor he played many, although not exclusively, Jewish parts. He came to prominence after playing the Jewish tailor in *The Bespoke Overcoat*. He also played Alf Larkins in *The Larkins* with Peggy Mount. He established for himself a reputation for telling biblical stories. In 1995 his 25-year-old rock musician son died from drug abuse and Kossoff devoted the remainder of his life to campaigning against drugs. He died in March 2005 aged 85.

Anthony Booth. The father of the wife of the former Prime Minister, Anthony Booth came to Watford on the 25th July 1967 in *The Country Wife* by William Wycherley. He has appeared in a number of films and on television. One of the roles for which he is most famous is as the son-in-law of Alf Garnett in the sitcom *Till Death Us Do Part*.

Kevin Lindsay. An Australian by birth, born in 1923, but based in Britain. He was best known for his appearances in the *Doctor Who* television series in secondary roles. He came to the Palace Theatre on the 8th August 1967 in *The Owl and the Pussycat*, on the 19th March 1968 in *Loot*, in *Wise Child* on the 11th March 1969 and again on the 26th August 1969 in *The Hotel in*

Amsterdam by John Osborne with Ann Firbank. Sadly he suffered a heart attack in 1975 and died at the age of 52.

Lynda Baron. Lynda Baron has taken part in more television series and programmes than almost any other actor. She has been seen in *Crossroads, Coronation Street, EastEnders, Doctor Who, Dinnerladies.* The list is endless. One of her earliest television successes was *Not So Much a Programme More a Way of Life* but without question her most famous role was as Nurse Gladys Emanuel in the long running series, *Open All Hours* with Ronnie Barker and David Jason from 1976 to 1985. She visited the Palace Theatre on the 22nd August 1967 in *Irma La Douce.*

Constance Cummings. An American actress who spent most of her life in England. Constance Cummings was born in Seattle on the 15th May 1910. At the age of twenty she was encouraged to go to Hollywood, after achieving success on the stage, but the parts she was offered did not satisfy her. She left the USA in 1934 and moved to England. Her long career was highly successful but on occasions her beauty stood in her way. She came to Watford for *Dance with a Dolly* on the 9th October 1967. She had a string of successes, many of them in plays written by her husband, Benn Levy. Possibly her greatest success, however, for which she received rave notices from the critics, was for her part in *Long Day's Journey Into Night* at the Royal National Theatre opposite Laurence Olivier. She was awarded a CBE in 1974. She died in Oxfordshire, where she ran a dairy farm, on the 23rd November 2005 at the age of 95.

William Lucas. William Lucas was born in Manchester on the 14th April 1925. He is known mostly as a stage and television actor but made a few films. He came to the theatre on the 9th October 1967 in *Dance with a Dolly* by Jack Pulman. As mentioned above, also in the cast of that play was Constance Cummings. He was to return to play in the cast of *The Guardsman* (February 1969) *Beeston Craig* (October 1970), *Candida* (November 1974), and *Variation on a Theme* by Terence Rattigan in November 1975.

Celia Bannerman. Celia Bannerman played Portia in an 'in-house' production of *The Merchant of Venice* in a two week's run starting on the 7th November 1967 and returned on 28th May 1968 in the cast of *The Rehearsal.*

Frank Williams. Frank Williams will forever be known as the eccentric, slightly irritable vicar of Walmington-on-Sea in *Dad's Army.* As well as being a character actor in such television series as *The Army Game* and as the Bishop in *You Rang M'Lord?*, he is a playwright. His play *The Substitute* dealt with an aspect of the Crucifixion and was produced at the Palace Theatre on the 1st May 1961. His ecclesiastical roles and his plays reflect his deep commitment to the Christian faith. He appeared at what he described as his 'local theatre', in *The Waiters* with Patricia Burke on the 21st November 1967.

Amanda Barrie. Real name Shirley Ann Broadbent, Amanda Barrie, as she became, was born in Cheshire on the 14th September 1935. She enjoyed a full career on stage, television and film. In 1967 she married Robin Hunter, the theatre director, who played opposite her when the couple came to the Palace Theatre on the 14th May 1968 in Noël Coward's *Private Lives*. Six months prior to this visit she had been in *Aladdin* at the same theatre. She separated from her husband in the 1980s but the couple remained friends and never divorced. She was in two of the *Carry On* films. *Carry on Cabby* and *Carry on Cleo*. In the latter she played Cleopatra. For twelve years Amanda Barrie played Alma in *Coronation Street*. She also played opposite Paul Eddington *(Yes, Minister!)* in a production of Alan Ayckbourne's play *Absurd Person Singular*.

Anna Dawson. There is only one recorded visit to the theatre by Anna Dawson, this was in *Alladin* the pantomime in 1973 in which she played the name part. Her career started in musicals but she made her name in comedy with such luminaries as Benny Hill, Morecambe and Wise and Charlie Drake for whom she made an ideal partner, being only 5'2' tall. Anna Dawson probably made her name playing Mary Crawford in twenty-three episodes of *Dixon of Dock Green*. She also played Violet (her with a swimming pool, sauna and room for a pony), the sister of Hyacinth as played by Patricia Routledge, in the television series *Keeping Up Appearances*.

Anthony Woodruff. Anthony Woodruff was born in Brighton in 1918 but some sources say that he was born in New Barnet. His was one of the faces that was rarely off television screens. He was a member of the cast of too many series to list but mention of his name may not bring memories of his face immediately to mind. He came to the Palace Theatre in a production of *Sleuth* which played from 25th May to 18th June 1977. He died in 1993.

The list of well-known actors and actresses who have appeared on stage at the Palace Theatre is extensive. Some of them for single performances on Sunday evenings but most of them in plays which ran for at least a week and in many cases for longer. For the sake of brevity just the dates and plays or other entertainment in which they appeared at the Palace Theatre are listed.

John Savident.	*Entertaining Mr. Sloane* 13th September 1966; *Sweet Bird of Youth* 19th November 1968; *The Homecoming* 4th February 1969; *Romeo and Juliet* 8th March 1972; *The Erpingham Camp* 15th April 1972; *A Patriot for Me* 28th November 1973; *The Merchant of Venice* 25th February 1976
Helen Cherry.	*The Rehearsal* 28th May 1968
Elspet Gray.	*The Rehearsal* 28th May 1968
Moira Redmond.	*Candida* 30th July 1968
Charles Tingwell.	*Candida* 30th July 1968
Polly James.	*I am a Camera* 13th August 1968
Steven Murray.	*Inadmissible Evidence* 24th September 1968
Maxine Audley.	*The Spoils* 8th October 1968
Angela Pleasnce.	*The Spoils* 8th October 1968; *The Late Middle Classes* 19th March 1999
Vivien Merchant.	*Sweet Bird of Youth* 10th November 1968
Harold Pinter.	*The Homecoming* 4th February 1969
Larry Noble.	*The Homecoming* 4th February 1969
Maurice Kaufmann.	*The Homecoming* 4th February 1969
Cleo Sylvestre.	*Wise Child* 11th March 1969
Mary Miller.	*Hobson's Choice* 1st April 1969; *Molly* 9th November 1977
Jane Merrow.	*Two for the Seesaw* 29th July 1969
Philip Bond.	*Two for the Seesaw* 29th July 1969
Ann Firbank.	*The Hotel in Amsterdam* 26th August 1969; *The Old Country* 29th January 1993.
Kate O'Mara.	*An Ideal Husband* 6th April 1971
Angharad Rees.	*Romeo and Juliet* 8th March 1972
Rose Hill.	*Ladies in Retirement* 17th May 1972; *Fallen Angels* 6th February 1974
Lesley Joseph.	*Orpheus Descending* 7th June 1972; *Wonderful Town* 12th April 1986; *Winter in the Morning* 31st March 1988; *Exclusive Yarns* 8th June 1988

Cheryl Campbell.	*Ballad of the False Barman* 6th September 1972; *Saved* 27th September 1972; *Mother Courage and Her Children* 1st November 1972 and *Charley's Aunt* 29th November 1972
Miriam Karlin.	*Mother Courage* 1st November 1972; *Liselotte* (a one woman show) 9th January 1978
Sian Phillips.	*Alpha Beta* 31st January 1973
Daniel Massey.	*Alpha Beta* 31st January 1973
Prunella Scales.	*The Provoked Wife* 21st February 1973; *An Evening with Queen Victoria* Sunday 28th March 1982; *The Seagull* 31st October 1986
Trevor Peacock.	*The Provoked Wife* 21st February 1973; *Laburnum Grove* 2nd April 1987
Zoe Wanamaker.	*The Provoked Wife* 21st February 1973
Roger Lloyd Pack.	*The Royal Hunt of the Sun* 9th May 1973
Robert Powell.	*Glasstown* 4th June 1973; *Terra Nova* 28th January 1982
Anne Stallybrass.	*Glasstown* 4th June 1973
Angela Down.	*Glasstown* 4th June 1973; *Ghosts* 16th April 1993; *We That Are Left* 19th April 2007
Jill Bennett.	*The Letter* 20th June 1973
Maxine Audley	*The Milk Train Doesn't Stop Here Any More* 3rd October 1973
Philip Jackson.	*The Tempest* 31st October 1973
Marianne Faithfull.	*A Patriot for Me* 28th November 1973
Anna Dawson.	*Aladdin* 24th December 1973.
Fenella Fielding.	*Fallen Angels* 6th February 1974; *The Fenella Fielding Show* 26th May 1976
Penelope Keith.	*Fallen Angels* 6th February 1974
Joanna van Gyseghem.	*The Corn in Green* 15th May 1974
Pauline Moran.	*Three Sisters* 4th September 1974; *The Threepenny Opera* 2nd October 1974.
Anita Dobson.	*Babes in the Wood* 21st December 1974; *Tonight at 8.30* 29th January 1975; *Happy As a Sandbag* 13th March 1975; *Hello, Hollywood, Hello* 17th April 1975; *Leave Him to Heaven* 1st April 1976
Una Stubbs.	*Irma La Douce* 10th September 1975
Dinah Sheridan.	*Out on the Lawn* 8th October 1975

T. P. McKenna.	*Out on the Lawn* 8th October 1975
Rosemary Leach.	*Out on the Lawn* 8th October 1975; *Some of My Best Friends Are Husbands* 29th September 1983
Frank Middlemass.	*Out on the Lawn* 8th October 1975
Patricia Hodge.	*Dick Whittington* 20th December 1975
Margaretta Scott.	*Pygmalion* 21st January 1976
Jan Waters.	*Pygmalion* 21st January 1976; *Merchant of Venice* 25th February 1976
Brian Protheroe.	*Leave Him to Heaven* 1st April 1976; *So Long on Lonely Street* 2nd October 1986; *I Have Been Here Before* 7th April 1990
Rupert Davies.	*Family Matter* 28th April 1976
Jane Baxter.	*Family Matter* 28th April 1976
Hugh Lloyd.	*A Bit Between the Teeth* 15th June 1976
Trevor Bannister.	*A Bit Between the Teeth* 15th June 1976; *The Real Inspector Hound* 3rd September 1993
Sandy Powell.	*Olde Tyme Musical Hall* 21st June 1976
Kim Cordell.	*Olde Tyme Musical Hall* 21st June 1976
Benny Lee.	*Guys and Dolls* 8th September 1976
Paul Eddington.	*Getting On* 10th November 1976
Barbara Lott.	*Getting On* 10th November 1976
Renee Asherson.	*Hay Fever* 10th January 1977; *The Girl in Melanie Klein* 2nd October 1980
Selina Cadell.	*Mrs. Warren's Profession* 23rd February 1977
Valentine Dyall.	*Mrs. Warren's Profession* 23rd February 1977
Ron Moody.	*Move Along Sideways* Sunday 10th April 1977
Dennis Waterman.	*In Concert* Sunday 8th May 1977
Bernard Bresslaw.	*Foxy* 28th April 1977
Amanda Reiss.	*Blithe Spirit* 7th September 1977; *Bedroom Farce* 3rd May 1979
Ray Woodland.	*So, You Think You Don't Like Opera* Sunday 23rd October 1977
Thomas Round.	*So, You Think You Don't Like Opera* Sunday 23rd October 1977 and *Gilbert & Sullivan for All* on various Sunday evenings
Raymond Francis.	*Molly* 9th November 1977
Lana Morris.	*Relatively Speaking* 25th January 1978
Geoffrey Chater.	*Relatively Speaking* 25th January 1978
Pamela Cundell.	*Cabaret* 6th April 1978; *The Late Christopher Bean*

	9th November 1978; *Cinderella* 8th December 1995; *Jack and the Beanstalk* 5th December 1998; *Robinson Crusoe* 4th December 1999
Alison Fiske.	*The Lady from the Sea* 10th May 1978
Gloria Grahame.	*Rain* 7th June 1978
Diana Fairfax.	*You Never Can Tell* 7th September 1978
Dora Bryan.	*The Late Christopher Bean* 9th November 1978; *Talking Heads* 18th May 2000
Georgie Fame and the Blue Flames.	Sunday 10th December 1978
Mary Peach.	*The Autumn Garden* 5th April 1979
Terence Longdon.	*Bedroom Farce* 3rd May 1979; *How the Other Half Loves* 29th April 1982; *The Real Inspector Hound* 3rd September 1993
Jonathan Miller.	*Talk on directing Shakespeare* Sunday 10th June 1979
George Melly.	Sunday 27th May 1979; Sunday 25th January 1981; Sunday 25th April 1982
Roy Hudd.	*Roy Hudd's Music Hall* Sunday 9th December 1979
Acker Bilk.	Sunday 27th January 1980; Sunday 28th February 1982
Joyce Carey.	*Night Must Fall* 31st January 1980
June Brown.	*Habeas Corpus* 3rd April 1980
Philip Bretherton.	*My Fat Friend* 1st May 1980; *Good Morning Bill* 25th May 1995; *Beethoven's Tenth* 21st June 1996; *Darkness Falls* 29th January 1999.
Imogene Hassell.	*Outside Edge* 26th May 1980
Norman Rossington.	*Outside Edge* 26th May 1980
Amanda Richardson.	*Outside Edge* 26th May 1980
James Ellis.	*Outside Edge* 26th May 1980
Humphrey Lyttelton.	Sunday 26th June 1980
Dillie Keane.	*Crown Matrimonial* 8th September 1980; *Big Night Out at the Little Palace Theatre* 14th June 2002
Victoria Wood.	Sunday 28th September 1980
Geoff Durham.	Sunday 28th September 1980
Frank Finlay.	*The Girl in Melanie Klein* 2nd October 1980
Susan Penhaligon.	*The Girl in Melanie Klein* 2nd October 1980; *A Doll's House* 22nd October 1987; *The Complaisant Lover* 4th October 1991
Robert Flemying.	*The Girl in Melanie Klein* 2nd October 1980

Annie Ross.	Sunday 2nd November 1980
Marion Montgomery.	*Just Good Friends* Sunday 23rd November 1980
Richard Rodney Bennett.	*Just Good Friends* Sunday 23rd November 1980
Jeremy Clyde.	*Design for Living* 29th January 1981
Gwen Taylor.	*Night and Day* 5th March 1981; *The Big Knife* 1st April 1982; *Trumpets and Raspberries* 4th October 1984 and *Conjugal Rites* 24th January 1991
Wendy Hiller.	*The Importance of Being Earnest* 18th November 1981
Gabrielle Drake.	*The Importance of Being Earnest* 18th November 1981; *Mortimer's Miscellany* Friday 29th June 2007
Gary Bond.	*The Importance of Being Earnest* 18th November 1981
Roy Castle.	*An Evening of Victorian Music Hall* Sunday 24th January 1982
Stephanie Beacham.	*Terra Nova* 28th January 1982
Richard Jackson.	*An Evening with Queen Victoria* Sunday 28th March 1982
Ian MacShane.	*The Big Knife* 1st April 1982
Karen Lewis.	*How the Other Half Loves* 29th April 1982
George Chisholm.	*An evening of Louis Armstrong* Sunday 26th September 1982
Margaret Tyzack.	*Veronica's Room* 30th September 1982; *Mornings at Seven* 3rd May 1984
Pauline Collins.	*Romantic Comedy* 27th January 1983
Jan Holden.	*Romantic Comedy* 27th January 1983
Simon Callow.	*Romantic Comedy* 27th January 1983; *On The Spot* 1st March 1984
John Mills.	*Little Lies* 29th April 1983
Anthony Bate.	*Little Lies* 29th April 1983
Connie Booth.	*Little Lies* 29th April 1983
Paul Hardwick.	*Little Lies* 29th April 1983
Warren Mitchell.	*The Beautiful Part of Myself* 31st August 1983
Tony Britton.	*Some of My Best Friends Are Husbands* 29th September 1983
Hugh Paddick.	*Some of My Best Friends Are Husbands* 29th September 1983
Roy Barraclough.	*Some of My Best Friends Are Husbands* 29th

	September 1983; *A Different Way Home* 27th September 2001
Patrick Stewart.	*Body and Soul* 3rd November 1983
Helen Ryan.	*Body and Soul* 3rd November 1983
Faith Brooke.	*Mornings at Seven* 3rd May 1984
Doreen Mantle.	*Mornings at Seven* 3rd May 1984
Andree Melly.	*Mornings at Seven* 3rd May 1984
Peter Jones.	*Mornings at Seven* 3rd May 1984
Simon Cadell.	*Raffles* 6th September 1984
Alan Dobin.	*Raffles* 6th September 1984
Griff Rhys Jones.	*Trumpets and Raspberries* 4th October 1984
Ian Lavender.	*Natural Causes* 31st January 1985
Michael Robbins.	*Natural Causes* 31st January 1985
Robert Eddison.	*A Private Treason* 7th March 1985
Susannah York.	*A Private Treason* 7th March 1985
Hayley Mills.	*Toys in the Attic* 31st October 1985
Lysette Anthony.	*Toys in the Attic* 31st October 1985
Barbara Murray.	*Toys in the Attic* 31st October 1985
Christopher Timothy.	*The Real Thing* 20th 1986
Paula Wilcox.	*The Real Thing* 1986; *Everything in the Garden* 3rd September 1987; *Spotted Dick* 19th December 1987; *On Approval* 12th March; *Blithe Spirit* 16th June 2000
Dorothy Tutin.	*Are You Sitting Comfortably?* 30th January 1986
Paul Daneman.	*Are You Sitting Comfortably?* 30th January 1986
Caroline Langrishe.	*Talk of the Devil* 6th March 1986; *Private Lives* 25th February 1994
Annette Crosbie.	*Talk of the Devil* 6th March 1986
Jane Lapotaire.	*Double Double* 15th May 1986
Gayle Hunnicutt.	*So Long on Lonely Street* 2nd October 1986
Helen Mirren.	*Madame Bovary* 29th January 1987
Maria Friedman.	*Spin of the Wheel* 5th March 1987
Patsy Byrne.	*Laburnum Grove* 2nd April 1987
Donald Douglas.	*Laburnum Grove* 2nd April 1987
Julian Fellowes.	*Laburnum Grove* 2nd April 1987
Daniel Hill.	*Everything in the Garden* 3rd September 1987; *Queen's English* 3rd November 2005
Amanda Waring.	*Mary Rose* 29th September 1987
Anna Cropper.	*Mary Rose* 29th September 1987

Charlotte Cornwell.	*A Doll's House* 22nd October 1987
John Fortune.	*A Doll's House* 22nd October 1987
Tony Slattery.	*The Cat and the Canary* 26th November 1987
Natalie Forbes.	*The Cat and the Canary* 26th November 1987
Francis Matthews.	*Suite in Two Keys* 28th January 1988
Isla Blair.	*Suite in Two Keys* 28th January 1988, *So Long on Lonely Street* 30th May 1988
Caroline Blakiston.	*Suite in Two Keys* 28th January 1988
John Sessions.	*The Common Pursuit* 3rd March 1988
Stephen Fry.	*The Common Pursuit* 3rd March 1988
Rik Mayall.	*The Common Pursuit* 3rd March 1988
John Gordon-Sinclair.	*The Common Pursuit* 3rd March 1988
Pam Ferris.	*Exclusive Yarns* 8th June 1988.
Sheila Steafel.	*The Gingerbread Lady* 1st September 1988
Sandra Dickinson.	*The Gingerbread Lady* 1st September 1988; *A Perfect Ganesh* 17th May 2002
Peter Skellern.	*In concert* 31st October 1988
Richard Stilgoe.	*In concert* 31st October 1988
Lenny Henry.	*One Man Show* 5th January 1989
Rupert Graves.	*The History of Tom Jones* 26th January 1989
Anna Carteret.	*Diplomatic Wives* 2nd March 1989; *Sitting Pretty* 27th January 2005
Brian Murphy.	*Roll On Friday* 5th October 1989
Don Warrington.	*A Raisin in the Sun* 9th November 1989; *Middle-age Spread* 10th June 1994
Jerry Hall.	*Bus Stop* 25th January 1990
Tim Brooke-Taylor.	*You Must Be the Husband* 1st March 1990
Sue Pollard.	*A Song, a Frock and a Tinkle* 28th March 1990
Philip Franks.	*I Have Been Here Before* 5th April 1990
Frances Barber.	*Over a Barrel* 6th September 1990
Serena Evans.	*Getting On* 4th October 1990
Clive Francis.	*Getting On* 4th October 1990
Eleanor Summerfield.	*Getting On* 4th October 1990
Ruth Kettlewell.	*Getting On* 4th October 1990
Ruby Wax.	*Live Wax* Sunday 21st April 1991
Ronnie Corbett.	*The Seven Year Itch* 6th September 1991
Dr. Evadne Hinge.	*Dick Whittington* 7th December 1991
Helena Bonham-Carter.	*The Barber of Seville* 6th March 1992

Jeremy Sinden.	*On Approval* 12th March 1992
Julian Glover.	*All My Sons* October 2nd October 1992
Edward de Souza.	*The Old Country* 29th January 1993; *Single Spies* 2nd February 1995
Oliver Ford Davies.	*The Old Country* 29th January 1993
Chris Emmett.	Every pantomime from 1990 to 2000 *Black Comedy and the Public Eye* 1st September 1995
Nick Staverson.	*Mother Goose* 10th December 1993; *Cinderella* 8th December 1995; *Puss in Boots* 7th December 1996; *Babes in the Wood* 6th December 1997; *Jack and the Beanstalk* 5th December 1998
Eve Matheson.	*Duet for One* 8th October 1993
Marty Cruikshank.	*A Handful of Dust* 21st January 1994; *Vita and Virginia* 21st April 1999
Marsha Fitzalan.	*Woman in Mind* 30th September 1994
Sara Crowe.	*French Without Tears* 10th November 1995
Jean Boht.	*Kindertransport* 24th May 1996
Diana Quick.	*Kindertransport* 24th May 1996
Louise Germaine.	*Women Laughing* 4th October 1996.
Gemma Jones	*Mrs. Klein* 21st March 1997.
Brian Conley.	*Elton John's Glasses* 16th April 1998
James Fleet.	*The Late Middle Classes* 19th March 1999
Harriet Walter.	*The Late Middle Classes* 19th March 1999
Gemma Craven.	*The Shakespeare Revue* 25th January 2000; *A Taste of Honey* 3rd November 2000
Jane Milligan.	*Three Steps to Heaven* 4th February 2000
Nichola McAuliffe.	*Talking Heads* 18th May 2000
Zena Walker.	*Talking Heads* 18th May June 2000; *The Deep Blue Sea* 1st February 2002
Anne Reid.	*Blithe Spirit* 16th June 2000
Debra Penny.	*Blithe Spirit* 16th June 2000; *Martha, Josie and the Chinese Elvis* 2nd February 2001; *How the Other Half Loves* 31st August 2001; *One Last Card Trick* 2nd March 2006 and *News from the Seventh Floor* in 2003, staged in Clements store
Natalia Makarova.	*Blithe Spirit* 16th June 2000
Matthew Kelly.	*Rough Crossing* 6th October 2000
Belinda Lang.	*Martha, Josie and the Chinese Elvis* 2nd February 2001; *Sitting Pretty* 27th January 2005

Janet Henfrey.	*Perfect Days* 31st October 2001
Philip Madoc.	*The Deep Blue Sea* 1st February 2002
Julia Watson.	*The Deep Blue Sea* 1st February 2002
Greta Scacchi.	*The True Life Fiction of Mata Hari* 8th March 2002
Helen Lederer.	*Full House* and *The Hairless Diva* 12th April 2002
Sandi Toksvig.	*Big Night Out at the Little Palace Theatre* 14th June 2002
Bonnie Langford.	*Big Night Out at the Little Palace Theatre* 14th June 2002
Kim Hartman.	*Sitting Pretty* 27th January 2005
Avril Elgar.	*One Last Card Trick* 2nd March 2006
Germaine Greer.	*An Evening With Germaine Greer* Sunday 10th September 2006

To all of those who should have been included in this list but are not, the author's sincerest apologies.

Epilogue

The year 2008, the centenary year, commenced with a flourish. The selected programme encapsulated the history of activities at the theatre. Variety, an imported production, performances by two amateur societies, a play by the Young People's Theatre and, naturally, the theatre's own productions, the first of which was a new play.

The annual pantomime, which was *Jack and the Beanstalk*, finished on Saturday the 6th January and this was followed by *Ruddigore* by Gilbert & Sullivan presented, as their annual production, by the Abbots Langley Gilbert & Sullivan Society. Then came two performances, on the 25th and 26th of January by the Watford Palace Young People's Theatre, of *Softcops* by Caryl Churchill.

On the 6th February Colonel Bob made a welcome return with his *Top Brass Jazz Orchestra*, always a popular event. Colonel Bob Wheal, a resident of Watford for many years, gathered together many illustrious musicians from big bands of the past to form his Jazz Orchestra and regularly presented programmes full of nostalgia by composers including George Gershwin, Richard Rodgers, Cole Porter and Jerome Kern.

The following evening the American stand-up comedian Rich Hall paid a visit to the theatre and was well received. He was followed on Friday the 8th February by *The Motown Show* and the week concluded with *An Audience with Michael Rosen*, the writer and broadcaster.

The first play of 2008 was *An English Tragedy*, the world premiere of a new play by the acclaimed playwright Ronald Harwood, and told the story of John Amery who was tried for treachery after WWII, found guilty and executed. The story was doubly tragic in that John Amery was the son of a member of Churchill's War Cabinet. This play ran from the 15th February to the 8th March.

For eleven performances including three matinees, from the 13th to the 22nd March, a visiting company, sponsored by Hoipolloi and the theatre Royal Plymouth in association with English Touring Theatre and the Watford Palace Theatre, presented *Doubtful Guest*. At the end of March there were three performances of *A Vampire Story* by Moira Buffini presented by the Hertfordshire County Youth Theatre

Although there had been many performances of plays by Shakespeare at the Palace over the years, only three, which took place in 1965, 1966 and 1967, were 'home produced', the rest had been productions by visiting companies. In 2008 the theatre produced what is believed to be its fourth 'home produced' Shakespeare, *As You Like It*.

Shakespeare was succeeded from the 28th April to the 3rd May by Tim Rice when Watford Operatic Society returned to the theatre for their annual visit to present *Chess* with music by Bjorn Ulvaeus and Benny Andersen, the two male members of the popular Swedish chart-topping singing group from the 1970s and early 1980s, ABBA.

Alan Bennett, ever popular with Watford audiences, was represented by his play *Kafka's Dick* from the 8th to the 31st May. Highly appropriate since it was only three years since what many consider to be Alan Bennett's masterpiece *The History Boys* was filmed, mostly in Watford.

The first half of the centenary year drew towards its close with a one night visit on Sunday the 1st June by Rabbi Lionel Blue. Then the National Theatre of Scotland and Wee Stories brought to Watford *The Emperor's New Kilt*, a re-imagining of the familiar *The Emperor's New Clothes*, and finally, from the 17th to the 24th June, Yellow Earth Theatre Company presented *Running the Silk Road* by Paul Sirett.

The season progressed. The Palace Theatre was now poised to commence its second century. Housed in a building renovated and modernised for the twenty-first century, the theatre is equipped with state-of-the-art technology, yet retaining all the beauty of its Edwardian origins. It provides comfort for the 120,000 people who pass through its doors each year and for its staff. A café and two bars provide refreshment not only when the theatre is open but throughout the day.

Watford has reason to be proud of its theatre and of its history. From modest beginnings, a hundred years ago, today an institution with a national reputation.

The story continues.

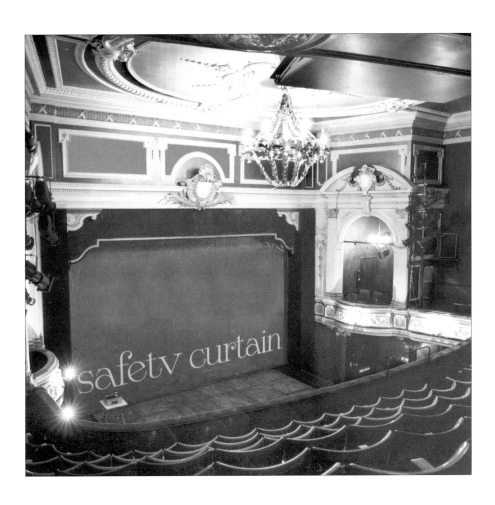

List of Productions
1909-2008

Full list of productions
S denotes Sunday only

1909

4th **Jan.** "The Diver's Luck"

11th **Jan.** Variety

18th **Jan.** "Raffles" presented by Reginald Dane &Powerful Company. Between Acts 3 and 4 scenes from the "Earthquake in Italy" were shown on the Cinematograph - this was also showing next door at the Clarendon Hall along with "Our Army and Our Navy" and the "Famous Animals Entertainment".

25th **Jan.** "The Gay Gordons" Mr. Seymour Hicks Company (for three nights) and for the rest of the week "Grand Variety Co." including Lillo, Otto and Lotto "the World's Greatest Comedy and Trick Cyclists".

1st **Feb.** "Mrs. Dot" for the first three days followed by "Miss Hook of Holland"

8th **Feb.** "Grand Star Vaudeville Company".

15th **Feb.** "As Midnight Chimes" - Sensational Realistic Novel Drama" Played to crowded houses.

22nd **Feb.** Variety, including Peter Goyz, a wrestler who offered £50 to any man who could defeat him within a specified time.

1st **March** Variety "Quite one of the best", but the weather was against good houses. "The Palace Pictures are interesting and the adventures of a dog created a good deal of merriment."

8th **March** "The Sailor's Wedding" - drew large audiences. Produced by Hardie and Van Leer. A new romantic Play of life and love in Sunny Italy.

15th **March** "Two Little Vagabonds" The Most Successful Play of Modern Times. Presented by Hardi and Van Leer's London Company - from the Royal Princes Theatre, London. The two lead male' characters were played by

women.

22nd **March** "Dick Whittington"

29th **March** "An Englishman's Home" by Major du Maurier. London's Latest and Greatest Success. Watford is the only town in the provinces of its size which can boast of An Englishman's Home being performed at its theatre. The management after long and tedious efforts, congratulate themselves on bringing to Watford a production which cannot fail to appeal to all patriotic Englishmen.

5th **April** "The Cingalee", by Lionel Monckton and James T. Tanner. Brilliantly Successful Musical Comedy. Entire production from Daley's Theatre, London. Full Chorus and increased orchestra.

12th **April** Variety "STAIG TROUPE" including George Robey. The first comedian ever to visit Watford and commanded a salary of £300 a week. It seems he gave only one performance at a 'flying matinee'.

19th **April** "When Knights Were Bold".

26th **April** "Swiss Express" - a musical pantomimical comedy.

3rd **May** Variety, including Harry Tate in "Motoring", as played before the King and Queen.

10th **May** "A White Man" by Edwin Milton Royle.

17th **May** "Sergeant Brue", musical comedy from the Strand and Prince of Wales Theatres, London. Very funny.

24th **May** Variety.

31st **May** A-LAD-IN. And Well Out Of It - a play by Mr. W. Bruce Smith - performed by children of Drury Lane Theatre. Children admitted at half price to all parts. "Mr. Smith's rhymed couplets however are somewhat tedious. For one thing puns occur with such exasperating frequency that they cease to amuse."

7th **June** "My Sweetheart", "A Wonderful Woman" and "Fritz and Katrina" - musical comedies.

14th **June** Variety.

21st **June** Variety, including Leonard Barry in his latest great song scena "Ginger's Dream". Bioscope and Leo Merode "Looping the Devil's Loop" - "absolutely the Greatest Sensation in the World. This act is indescribable".

28th **June** Variety including Fred Lindsay (Australian Stock Whip manipulator) and Company.

5th **July** "The Dandy Fifth" - delightful comic opera.

12th **July** "Ruined by Drink" by Hall Caine - thrilling human drama, adapted from Zola's novel "L'Assomoir". (King Edward VII and Queen Alexandra stayed the weekend, 17th July, at The Grove as guests of The Earl and Countess of Clarendon)

19th **July** Variety

26th **July** Variety. The Programme included "A Vision of Japan" - "This oriental scene is perhaps the most beautiful that has ever been staged in Watford".

2nd **Aug.** "At the World's Mercy" by Carr Loates - successful Musical Comedy Drama.

9th **Aug.** Splendid Variety Company - "Some good 'turns' but hardly up to the standard of some previous shows".

16th **Aug.** "The Silver King" melodrama by Henry Arthur Jones. "Greatest Drama of the Past and Present Century". Twenty four years of unbroken popularity. Only fault to be found was that the curtain came down at nearer to 11.30 pm than 11.00.

23rd **Aug.** Variety.

30th **Aug.** "The Christians" by Hall Caine - first three nights, presented by Wentworth Croke in the Lyceum version, direct from Lyceum and Shaftesbury Theatres. Last three nights "Idols" by Roy Horniman, from the Garrick Theatre.

6th **Sept.** "The Way Women Love". Great Domestic Drama by Mrs. Frank Bateman, who played Violet Tremaine.

13th Sept. "The World, The Flesh and The Devil" by Lesser Columbus. "The Greatest Melodrama produced in the last twenty years……The central character manages in every act to horrify the audience with his crimes." "Whether or not you enjoy it depends on your temperament".

20th Sept. "Through the Divorce Court". Great Play of enormous heart interest.

On Saturday 18th Sept. there was a performance by Besses o' the' Barn Band prior to world tour. Sponsored by Baring Bros.

Sept. 27th Variety, including Nellie Wallace.

2nd Oct. *Flying matinee* - Mr. Gaston Myers London Company in "Mrs. Wiggs of the Cabbage Patch".

4th Oct. Variety.

11th Oct. "The Coal King" - the Great Mining Drama.

18th Oct. "The Prodigal Son" by Hall Caine - direct from Drury Lane Theatre, presented by Wentworth Croke.

25th Oct. Variety.

Nov. 1st & 3rd "In the Storm" - Three Act original comedy by W. Strange Hall. Given by the Watford Amateur Players on Monday and Wednesday in aid of The Society for Improving the Conditions of the Watford Poor and on the Wednesday Matinee in aid of Watford District Hospital.

Nov. 2nd, 4th and Nov. 6th "The Prisoner of Zenda" by Anthony Hope - Played over 700 times at the St. James's Theatre, London. "A notable addition to the many successes played at the Palace Theatre.

8th Nov. Variety, including Miss Ella's Wonderful Trained Forest-Bred Lions, also "Something Extra Ordinary".

15th Nov. Variety. " ….probably one of the best that has been given since the theatre was opened. Really the show is so good, that on leaving the first 'house' one almost envied those waiting for the second".

22nd Nov. "At Duty's Call" - Popular Military Play.

29th Nov. "The Belle of New York" given by Bannister Howard's No.1 London Company - from the Shaftesbury Theatre, London, including Frank Lawton as Blinkey Bill.

6th Dec. "The Dairymaids" Great Farcical Play. Full and Powerful Chorus and augmented orchestra.

13th Dec. Variety

From 18th November to 27th December the theatre was closed

27th Dec. A Special Holiday Programme.

1910

3rd Jan. "Under Two Flags" - six nights - Matinee Saturday from Cirdas famous novel. Play a world wide success. On Monday evening a complete copy of the novel was given to any lady paying more than 1s. admission

10th Jan. "The Cingalee" from Daly's Theatre. Musical comedy *Prices:* Orch. Stalls 3/-; Stalls 2/-; Pit 1/-; Dress circle 3/-; Circle 2/-; Gallery 6d.

15th Jan. "Private Secretary" in aid of Watford District Hospital. Prices increased by 1/- on all seats.

24th Jan. "Cinderella" *Prices:* Boxes 15/-; Orch. Stalls 4/-; Stalls 3/-; Pit 1/-; Circle 2/- Gallery 6d. Children admitted at half price at matinee.

5th Feb. "A Girl's Cross Roads" play written and produced by Walter Melville.

21st Feb. "Raffles" Presented by Leonard Boynes West End Company. A great success.

28th Feb. "The Little Damsel" - London's latest production. Had twice received the honour of a command performance before the King and Queen.

14th March "Jack and the Beanstalk" for one week.

21st March Grand Variety. Twice nightly

28th March "Grand Easter Attraction" - Raymond, globe trotting fun maker, magician, humorist and fantasist. The man who puzzled Edison.

4th April Mr. Russell's company in "Lady Huntworth's Experiment". In aid of the Watford & District Bureau for the Employment of Women" - A huge success.

11th April Great Military Play "The Woman of Kronstadt" by Max Pemberton. Direct from the Garrick Theatre. On Friday of that week (15th Feb) there was a performance of "Collaborators" – a One Act Farce, and "Under the Greenwood Tree" the charming romantic comedy. They were performed, perhaps, by a local amateur company.

18th April "The Arcadians" musical comedy with an augmented orchestra.

24th April "The Gay Gordons". Entire and actual Aldwych Theatre production.

9th May Selected company - Tom Costello, Tom York, Rob Gilmore, Lily Elfrida (impersonating Harry Lauder, Marie Lloyd, Vesta Tilly etc.).

21st May "Not Before the Missises" - J.W. Hoolies Musical Comedy.

13th June Grand Variety Company - twice nightly.

18th June "The Gift from Kays" Musical Comedy - Full Chorus. From the Apollo Theatre.

Notice to Patrons. From 28th June until August Bank Holiday the theatre will be open as a High Class Picture Palace at popular prices. Stalls 6d, Circle 4d, Pit 3d and Gallery 1d.

1st Aug. Re-open with Variety Season - twice nightly. Victor Widdicombe & Company in "Her Devonshire Dad"

Box office open 10am till 4pm and 6pm till 10pm.

6th Aug. Grand Star Company. Norman G. Acton and Arthur Keen's company in "A Sister's Honour" Entertainment well up to average with charming songs and dances. Praise given to orchestra.

13th Aug. Variety - Tom Wootwell, Harry Varden, Joe Belmont, Verne and Green, Herbert Shelly.

27th Aug. Variety - The Great Halma, Martin Henderson- blind musician, Ethel Campbell.

3rd Sept. Variety Company - Adam Tomlinson, Maud Courteney, Nora Dean, Very good. Artists and acts.

10th Sept. Carrie Lauries Comedy Company - "Belles of the Kitchen" - Tom Hood, Cissie Tompson, Sisters Edwards. Played to full houses- best audience since theatre opened.

17th Sept. Variety Company - Leo Dryden, Arthur Stacy, Heans & Lux, Cissie Lupino, Mark Hall.

24th Sept. Variety - Yangar - great illusionist, Florence Deighton, Nellie Norway, Harry Brown, Billy Tucker.

1st Oct. Variety - Reg Bolton, Bert Beecham, Devon and Earle. Really enjoyable entertainment.

8th Oct. Variety - Sam Mayo, Hemsley and Ambrose, Miss Alice Hollander (famous Australian Contralto).

15th Oct. Variety - Harry Champion, Crystal & Saville, Spanish Goldinis in great electric act.

22nd Oct. Comedy Sketch - Mr and Mrs Royston Dene in "My Lady's Chamber". The Markies in "The Professor's Studio".

29th Oct. Variety - Van Riene in "Karl's Luck" (Sons and daughter of late Arthur Lloyd - the Arthur Lloyd Trio), the twin sisters Barney Armstrong and Kelly.

5th Nov. Napoleon at Waterloo introducing Dana Royal who offers £20 to any man who can defeat him by three falls in 5 minutes.

Varieties weekly up to 1st January 1911.

1911

9th Jan. A variety bill - Bellew & Stocks, Kitty Wager, Ted Cowan, John Morris, Harry Wenburn etc.

16th Jan. Another variety bill - Fred Eustace, The Sisters Harcourt, Six White Boys, Ruffells, Imperial Bioscope. The critic said this week's bill was not so amusing.

23rd Jan. More variety - George Leyton - Massona, Lyric Hummers. Very good this week - one might be tempted to go three times.

30th Jan. "Cinderella" one week only. More attention should have been paid to the fairy tale but very funny.

6th Feb. Closed for a week,

9th Feb. At the Police Court - Juvenile Performer. Ernest Montefiore of the Willesden Hippodrome was granted a license permitting Sarah Ann Walker aged 12 years and 11 months to perform at the Palace Theatre for the week ending 18ᵗʰ Feb.

13ᵗʰ Feb. Grand Star Variety Company.

20ᵗʰ Feb. Variety again. The Eight Varsity Girls, Ernest, Archie Pitt. Archie Pitt invited his audience to join in the chorus of a song concerning shops which stock "Shot socks with spots".

27ᵗʰ Feb. The Cumberland Troupe of Acrobats topped the bill, also Rex Fox who played a mandolin on a tight-rope.

6ᵗʰ March An amateur singing contest was held as well as Variety - Sam Mayo top of the bill. Competitors asked to impersonate Sam. 25 competitors in final. Cup won by Mr. G. Still, 69 Cardiff Road.

9ᵗʰ March At the Police Court - Juvenile Performer. Licenses were provisionally granted to permit Esther Jukes, 12, of the Empire, Barnsley and Clare Agnes Johnson, 12, of The Pavilion, Newcastle, to perform at the Palace Theatre for one week, commencing13th March.

13ᵗʰ March The Seven Bramusas top of the bill - a family of juvenile musicians.

20ᵗʰ March More Variety - Tubby Edlin, Ernie Leno (son of Dan Leno).

27ᵗʰ March James Fawn - Hammon & Wyatt, etc.

3ʳᵈ April "Chinco" - from the London Palladium. The Boat Race on the Bioscope.

10ᵗʰ April A short play in the Variety bill this week, lasting half an hour, about Sexton Blake. Critic said he was pleased to see a well staged and professionally acted play again even if it lasted only half an hour, and hoped the management would include good sketches in their variety in future.

17ᵗʰ April The Bioscope film this week very thrilling. About Sioux Indians on the banks of the Missouri.

24ᵗʰ April On the Bioscope the 'Cup Final' at Crystal Palace and Manchester.

1ˢᵗ May Gotham Quartette top of the bill this week.

8ᵗʰ May Variety again - nothing special.

15ᵗʰ May A burlesque of the Salvation Army this week, thought by the critic to be in bad taste.

22ⁿᵈ May Bioscope showed German fleet on manoeuvres.

29ᵗʰ May The Bouncing Dillons - comedy gymnasts top of the bill this week. Also a Grand Bouncing Competition for all amateurs over 16 with a grand finale on Friday. Also Bioscope on the Derby

5ᵗʰ June Variety again

12ᵗʰ June Theatre closed for Reconstruction.

16ᵗʰ Oct. Theatre now cosy and beautiful - top of the bill A Military Band. The Legion of Frontiersmen, conducted by Lt. Insen.

23ʳᵈ Oct. A company directed by Fred Karno which included Sydney Chaplin also Harry Champion.

30ᵗʰ Oct. Variety again.

6ᵗʰ Nov. Very varied this week. A sketch "The Pawnbroker", imperson- ations, music and dancing.

13ᵗʰ Nov. Entertainment above average this week.

20ᵗʰ Nov. Variety - nothing special.

27ᵗʰ Nov. The Manager, Lionel G. Holding, is scoring a big success this week, according to the critic, and attracting 'bumper houses'. A well known American comedienne Anna Chandler has delighted the spectators.

4ᵗʰ Dec. Another good bill. The Two Lillies - dancing with mirrors. Mr. Geco, who leads the orchestra, very talented, according to the critic.

11ᵗʰ Dec. No need to visit the City, according to the critic, Watford provides good, reliable and sometimes, sensational turns. Full houses all through the week.

18ᵗʰ Dec. Another capital programme.

26ᵗʰ Dec. "Aladdin" commenced on Boxing Night.

1912

1ˢᵗ Jan. Variety, including sketches by Fred Karno and his company: "Mumming Birds" and "Skating".

8ᵗʰ Jan. Variety, including a Bioscope film of the Delhi Durbar. Bioscop show of football match: Watford 2 Brentford 1

15ᵗʰ Jan. "Dick Whittington"

22ⁿᵈ Jan. Variety, including John Lawson, Wilf Poluski and Rosie Lloyd (a sister of Marie Lloyd) *who wore a Union Jack in an unusual position.*

29ᵗʰ Jan. Variety with a larger musical content than usual.

5ᵗʰ Feb. Variety, including Lottie Lennox, Charles Whittle (Let's all go down the Strand).

12ᵗʰ Feb. Variety.

19ᵗʰ Feb. Variety, including the Ahkmah String Quartette, playing green instruments.

26ᵗʰ Feb. "Cinderella" from the Canterbury Theatre, London.

4ᵗʰ March Variety, including Evie Greene musical comedy star.

11ᵗʰ March The Christians, by Hall Caine. (The production reduced young men to tears. Un-British conduct).

18ᵗʰ March Variety, including the Glazeroff troupe of Russian dancers.

25ᵗʰ March Variety

1ˢᵗ April Variety, including Harry Lauder (I Love a Lassie) and The Boat Race on the Bioscope.

8ᵗʰ April Variety, including Marie Kendall (Grandmother of Kay Kendall) (Just Like the Ivy…). And the Amsterdam Opera Trio.

15ᵗʰ April Variety, including Ernie Lotinga in a farcical sketch "Her Husband"

22ⁿᵈ April Variety, including Charles Coburn (The Man who Broke the Bank at Monte Carlo)

29ᵗʰ April Violet Black and Company in "In the Tube".

4th May Special matinee on 4ᵗʰ May of "The New Boy" in aid of the Lord

Mayor of London's Fund for the TITANIC sufferers.

6ᵗʰ May Variety, including Gertie Gitana (Nellie Dean)

13ᵗʰ May How Bill Adams won the Battle of Waterloo. A musical extravaganza with no recognisable plot but very funny.

13ᵗʰ May Variety, including Barnard's Marionettes, and Ramona, the famous Spanish dancer.

27ᵗʰ May Variety, including Haley's Juvenile Act.

3ʳᵈ June "Convict 99". The celebrated drama, with comic relief, by Horace Kenney.

10ᵗʰ June "Temptress of Paris", with Agnes Collier.

17ᵗʰ June "A King of Crime". Melodrama. Wentworth Croke's Company of London Artists

24ᵗʰ June Variety, featuring an equestrian act, "Rejected remounts".

1ˢᵗ July "Home, Sweet Home" played by Wentworth Croke's Company.

8ᵗʰ July "East Lynne" by Mrs. Henry Wood. During the performance on 9ᵗʰ July an actor was shot in the foot due to a faulty cartridge. Wentworth Croke's Company.

15ᵗʰ July "The Girl who knew a bit". Drama from the Elephant and Castle Theatre.

22ⁿᵈ July "The Stepmother", played by Wentworth Croke's Company.

July 29-Aug.3 Priscilla Runs Away". A farcical comedy adapted from the novel "Princess Priscilla" by Countess von Arnhim, from the Haymarket Theatre.

5ᵗʰ Aug. Variety, including Harry Champion ("Any old iron…") and Harry Anderson ("Beer, beer, glorious beer…").

12ᵗʰ Aug. "The Gentleman Jockey". Sporting drama.

19ᵗʰ Aug. Variety, including a sketch, "The Yellow Fang", set in a 'Frisco opium den.

26ᵗʰ Aug. "The Glad Eye". Comedy, as playing at the Apollo Theatre.

Sept. 1 (Sunday) General Booth Memorial Service, by Watford Corps of the Salvation Army.

2ⁿᵈ Sept. Variety

9ᵗʰ Sept. Variety, Frank Mayo in "The Bargain".

16ᵗʰ Sept. Variety, headed by Karl Hertz (illusionist)

23ʳᵈ Sept. Variety, including the Two Bobs, the original ragtime entertainers.

5ᵗʰ Sept. Variety

7ᵗʰ Oct. "Married to the Wrong Man". Comedy by Frederick Melville.

14ᵗʰ Oct. Variety, including Fred Karno and Company in sketches "Village Sports" and "Mumming Birds".

21st Oct. Variety, headed by Sam Mayo ("The Old Tin Can") and Ada Colley, the Australian Nightingale.

28ᵗʰ Oct. Variety. Ruby Miller and Company.

4th Nov. "The Eternal City" by Hall Caine.

11th Nov. "The Monk and the Woman" by Fredk. Melville, from the Lyceum Theatre

18th Nov. "The Bad Girl of the Family" by Fredk. Melville - drama.

25th Nov. "The Private Secretary" by Charles H. Hawtry, farcical comedy.

2nd Dec. "The Belle of New York". Musical comedy.

9th Dec. Variety, headed by Gertie Gitana (The Idol of the People) and including Naughton & Gold.

16th Dec. Variety.

23rd Dec. "Dick Whittington and his Cat".

30th Dec. Variety, headed by Bransby Williams. Bobby Leach (one of the most thrilling scenes is that depicted on the cinema and personally carried out by Bobby Leach who claims to be the only man in the world who has negotiated Niagara Falls sealed in a steel cask).

Quotations in brackets refer to songs made popular by the performer mentioned.

1913

5th Jan. "Cinderella"

12th Jan. "Aladdin". Mr. Wentworth Croke's Grand Pantomime - Special Scenery and Effects. Full Chorus and Ballet.

19th Jan. "Sinbad the Sailor" Presented by George Brydon Phillips. Special Harlequinade for the children at Matinee.

26th Jan. Grand Star Variety" McLellan & Carson, Roy Wallace, Lottie Lennox. The Trilbies, Harry Tate in "The Perch Club" by Woody and Well.

2nd Feb. "The Woman in the Case" - direct from the Garrick and New Theatres. Miss Olive Warne, Rita Johnson and Edward Harrison.

9th Feb. Variety including "The Coster's Courtship".

16th Feb. Variety, including Rose Hamilton & Co in "Kleptomaniacs"

23rd Feb. "A Country Girl" from Daly's. M. Durrant Swan's No.1 Company presents Miss Ethel Negretti, Mr. Arthur Staples (the famous music comedy)

2nd March Variety - including Fred Karno in "Early Birds" and "Mumming Birds".

9th March Variety

16th March EASTER PROGRAMME - Levin & Pantzer. Jean Harkness, Elsie Faye & Co. Gertrude Clark, Spencer Ward.

23rd March "The Walls of Jericho". Alfred Sutro's Great Play. Presented by Mr. Ernest E. Norris. Miss Ray Parry, Miss Lily O'Donchoo. "Top Top London Company- Special Scenery".

30th March Bransgrove & Slaughter present A. Conan Doyle's "The Speckled Band". C.W. Somerset as Dr. Grubdy. Charles Gibbons.

6th April Bransgrove & Slaughter present Charles Hawtrey's "Inconstant George" . Mr. Slaughter, W. Lester, Frank Mayban.

13th April "The Mysterious Lady in Red". Williams & Warden, Reo Rex. Hendrick & Laura, Jack Lane, Molly Wells, Rosie Archie, H. Upton. "Although the programme is a thoroughly enjoyable one; if it is not quite up to the standard of some previous ones have been".

20th April "Jane" by Charles Hawtrey, produced by Bransgrove & Slaughter. Mr. Sebastion Smith plays William and Miss Jennie Lynn plays Jane, Lionel Ellis. "One of the pleasantest evenings imaginable".

27th April Irma Lorraine, Leo Fields, Daisey Stratton.

4th May Special Holiday Attraction.

11th May "Bunty Pulls the String" by Graham Moffat, produced by Cyril Maude's Company.

18th May "In a Man's Grip" by Chas. Darrell. Wentworth Croke & Herbert Sleath's Company.

25th May "Trilby". Wentworth Croke's Company. Miss Anna Rutland, Juan D'Alberti, Booth Conway.

1st June "The Importance of Being Earnest" by Oscar Wilde. Montague Love, Miss Hilda Glynn, Fred Lester.

8th June "Home Sweet Home". Herbert Lloyd, Frank Ayrton, Madge Seymour, Steven Armitage.

15th June "Under Two Flags". Anna Rutland, Percy Ballard, Frank Ayrton.

22nd June "The Prodigal Parson". Wentworth Croke.

29th June "A Pair of Spectacles". Louis Palgrave, Carter Slaughter.

6th July "East Lynn".

13th July "Called Back",

20th July "A Woman's Past". Anna Rutland, Juan D'Alberti.

27th July "The Four Elles". Gertrude Bibby, Griffith & Carmen, Lawrence Barclay, Edie Veno

3rd Aug. "The Two Bobs". Les Andres, Arthur Woodville, Arthur F. Ward.

10th Aug. "Ready Honey". Edmund F. Kennedy, Chas. Groves.

17th Aug. "The Headmaster". Ch. Windermere, Miss Molly Maitland, Gordon Starkey.

23rd Aug. "Find the Woman" Edmund Kennedy, Rosemary Rees, Dorothy Radcliffe.

30th Aug. "Caste".

7th Sept. "The Barrier". Stanley Bedwell, Henry Nunn, Jessie Belmore.

14th Sept. "Lady Hoggs". Nina Scott-Watson, Humphrey Warden.

21st Sept. "The Lady Slavey". W.T. Thompson, Miss Hilda Stuart.

28th Sept. "Anne" – a modern light comedy. Mary Dandridge, Henry Winn.

5th Oct. Variety. Miss Josephine Davis, Torino, Walton & Lester, Signor Torti, Gret Lumars.

12th Oct. "The Debut" – Beryl Wallace, Spiers, Joyce Wallace, Carlotta Mossetti. "

A White Slave". Joseph Millane, Edith Blande, Agnes Paulton.

19th Oct. "The Glad Eye". Tom Tindall, Gwen Ffrangcon Davies.

26th Oct. "A Member of Tattersalls". Maitland Marler, Louis Palgrave.

2nd Nov. "The New Clown". Albert Simmons, Mr. Wyn Weaver, Margery Brown.

9th Nov. "The Arcadians" George Lane, Ellis Carlyle, Miss Minnie Rayner and J.E. Swinburne.

16th Nov. "Charley's Aunt". D. Price Evans, Mackenzie Rogen, Eric Hemmerde, Miss Leila M. Russell, Ch. E. Thomas.

23rd Nov. "Doormats". Wilfred Manners, Henry Wolston, Percy Marshall, Miss Jane Saville.

30th Nov. Variety - Glazeroff Troupe, Frances & Stewart, Roy Wallace (impressionist) John Donald, Miss Flora Comer.

7th Dec. "The Manxman". Derwent (*sic*) Hall Caine, Lewis Willoughby, Courtney Robinson, Miss Dorothy Stephen.

14th Dec. Variety.

26th Dec. "Babes in the Wood".

1914

5th Jan. "Aladdin and His Wonderful Lamp".

12th Jan "Robinson Crusoe"

19th Jan. "Cinderella".

26th Jan. "A Royal Divorce" with Juan Bonaparte as Napoleon and Octavia Kenmore as Josephine.

2nd Feb. Variety, including thirty artistes originally engaged for the Indian Pageant, Earls Court.

9th Feb. Variety - headed by Gissie Lawson.

16th Feb. 1 Variety - headed by Fred Karno and Company (including Sydney Chaplin) in sketches "The Hydro" and "The New Slavey".

23rd Feb. "Raffles" - the amateur cracksman, with Gerald Alexander.

2nd March "Gee Whiz" Revue.

9th March Variety.

16th March "Hullo! Ragtime". Revue, as played at the London Hippodrome.

23rd March "The Girl in the Taxi". A musical comedy from the Lyric Theatre.

30th March "Leah Kleschna", by C.M.S. McCellan. Drama.

6th April "Tom, Dick and Harry" a farcical comedy from the Comedy and Duke of York's Theatres.

13th April "The Bondman" by Hall Caine. Drama.

The following plays of William Shakespeare were presented by Florence Glossop Harris and Frank Collier and their Company.

20th April "Taming of the Shrew".

21st April "Hamlet".

22nd April "Romeo and Juliet"

23rd April "The Merry Wives of Windsor".

24th April "Macbeth".
25th April "A Midsummer Night's Dream".
26th April "The Merchant of Venice"
27th April "A Child of the Streets". Domestic drama.
4th May "General John Regan", by George A. Birmingham. A rollicking Irish farce from the Apolllo Theatre.
11th May Greater London Variety
18th May "The Dairymaids", by A.M. Thompson and Robert Courtneidge with music by Frank B. Tonks and Paul Reubens.
25th May Variety, headed by Fred Emney and Miss Sydney Fairbrother in a sketch: "A Sister to Assist 'er".

(Note: This Fred Emney was the father of the similarly named comedian who was a popular entertainer in the 1950's and 1960's)

The following seven plays were presented by Messrs. Bransgrove and Slaughter, with different companies. The season was originally advertised for eight weeks.

1st June "The Night of the Party" by Weedon Goldsmith. A farcical comedy as played over 1,000 times at the Avenue Theatre.
8th June "In the Soup", by Ralph Lumley. Farcical comedy from the Strand Theatre.
15th June "Mrs. Gorringe's Necklace", by H.H. Davies. From the Avenue Theatre.
22nd June "Oh! Susanna". Farce, from the Royalty Theatre.
29th June "Samson", by Henry Bernstein, from the Garrick Theatre.
6th July "Dr. Wake's Patient". The Adelphi Theatre success.
13th July "Under Two Flags", by Ouida.
20th July "Little Miss Ragtime". A new musical comedy.
27th July "A Single Man", by Hubert Henry Davies. From the Playhouse Theatre.
3rd Aug. "Baby Mine" by Margaret Mayo.
10th Aug. "A Message from Mars". Comedy, pathos, mysticism.
17th Aug Variety, headed by Carl Hertz, the great American illusionist.
24th Aug. "The Blindness of Virtue", by Cosmo Hamilton. Moral play from the Ambassador's Theatre.
31st Aug. Variety
7th Sept. Variety, headed by Violet Black and Company.
14th Sept, Variety, headed by Mary Neal in a one-act play "A Thief".
21st Sept. "Hindle Wakes" by Stanley Houghton. A Lancashire play.
28th Sept. "The Ever Open Door" by G.R. Sims and H.H. Herbert.
5th Oct. "Mr Wu", by Harry M. Vernon and Harold Owen. An Anglo-Chinese play from the Savoy Theatre.
12th Oct. "The Headmaster" by Cyril Maude. From the Playhouse.
19th Oct. "The Pearl Girl" by Basil

Hood, with music by Hugo Felix and Howard Talbot. A musical comedy from the Shaftesbury Theatre.
26th Oct. "A Pair of Silk Stockings" by Cyril Harcourt. The Criterion Theatre success of 1914.
2nd Nov. Variety, headed by Arthur Roberts in a farcical comedy sketch "The Importance of Being Another Man's Wife".
9th Nov. "Potash and Perlmutter", by Montague Glass. A comedy of human interest.

From this week certain evenings were advertised as Special Military Performances, *starting earlier than usual and quoting finishing times.*

16th Nov. "The Balkan Princess". Musical comedy from the Prince of Wales' Theatre.
23rd Nov. "Eliza Comes to Stay". Farcical comedy, the success at the Criterion Theatre in 1913.
30th Nov. "The Glad Eye" Comedy with Alfred Drayton. From the Globe, Apollo and Royalty Theatres.
7th Dec. "Milestones" by Arnold Bennett and Edward Knoblauch, from the Royalty Theatre.
14th Dec. "Charley's Aunt" Comedy
21st Dec. Grand Variety Company.
28th Dec. "Robinson Crusoe"

1915
11th Jan. "The Lady Slavey". Musical Comedy. Leonard Willoughby's Company.
18th Jan. "A Chinese Honeymoon". Geo. Dance Company.
25th Jan. "The Fatal Wedding".
1st Feb. "Grumpy". Play. Charles Winderene Company.
8th Feb. "Diana of Dobsons". Comedy.
15th Feb. Joe Peterman's Company of Comedians. Halma – Jack Murray – The Junes – Wynn Mentomore – Arthur D'Orville – May O'Connor - Yelta - Bioscope.
22nd Feb. "The French Woman" and Jumping Competition. (Army). Open to members of H.M. Forces.
1st March "The Second Mrs. Tanqueray" Sir Arthur Pinero company. Louise Hampton. Play.
8th March Fred Moul Company. Tom Wootwell - Kisby - Vine and Brewer – The Meades - Signor Torli (Italian Tenor) - Edith Trevor - Clara Pladge.
15th March J.W. Turner English Company:
15th Maritana – Wallace
16th Satanella - Balfe
17th Il Trovatore - Verdi
18th Faust - Gounod
19th Tannhäuser - Wagner
20th The Bohemian Gir - Balfe (Wallace and Balfe were Irish composers both living and working in London during the 1840's)
22nd March (Evenings) "Oh, I Say" Farce (Afternoons) Cinema Lecture "Scott in the Antarctic".

29th March "The Girl with the Wink" play.
5th April "The Queen's Messengers". Mabel Costello
12th April "Every Little Alps". Arthur Rigby & Company. Dolly Lee - Kitty Corrie - J.J. Mannix, the coffee coloured coon.
19th April Grand Variety Company.
26th April Marie Lloyd in New Songs and Paris costumes. Lawrence Barclay - Dainty Doris - Iris Banfield - Hall and Earle –Arthur Leslie - Laurie Wylie in Toy Theatre.
3rd May "Caste or Ordered to the Front". Play of 1868 updated.
10th May Fred Karno's Company.and two comedies - The Hydro and Jack Melville The New Slavey.
17th May Ernie Lotinger Company in Bluebottles.
24th May "In the Ranks". Military drama.
31st May "Chosen by the People". Military drama.
7th June "What Happened to Jones". Comedy.
14th June "Second to None". Play in seven scenes.
21st June "A Bunch of Violets". Play.
28th June "Sowing the Wind". Sydney Grindy and Company.
5th July Variety.
12th July Variety.
19th July "The School". Play.
26th July Variety.
2nd Aug. "Come in Miss". Revue. Madge Fenton.
9th Aug. Gambles Belgian Band.(Special Attraction)
Marcas Draper - The Society Quartette – Abgela Cavene - Barber Harber - Leslie Glencoe –Vera Moore - May Dalton.
16th Aug. "The Flag Lieutenant". Play
23rd Aug. "Why Not Tonight?" Revue. Two Bobs - Bob Adams and Bob Aldon - Jack McKay - The Finders.
30th Aug, "Kitty Grey" Musical comedy.
6th Sept. "Play the Game". Revue.
13th Sept. "The Quaker Girl". Musical comedy. Eric Burton and company.
20th Sept. (Evenings) "Within the Law" Play
(Afternoons) "African Hunt". Play.
27th Sept. "Her Wedding Eve".
4th Oct. "Think of Me". A Musical Revuesical
11th Oct. Joe Petermans & Company in "The Stardresser" and "The Section Master"
18th Oct. "So Long Lucy" Revue.
25th Oct. "The Geisha" Musical comedy.
1st Nov. "The Rosary". Play with John Glendenning and Miss Josie Millward.
8th Nov. Grand Variety Company.
15th Nov. "Hello Watford". Revue.
22nd Nov. "Brewsters Millions" with Emma and Percy Hutchinson.
29th Nov. "Love Birds". Revue. Baxter and Boyden.
6th Dec. "Peg O' My Heart", with

Macdonald and Young.
13th Dec. Grand Variety Company.
20th Dec. "Are You a Mason". Comedy.
24th Dec. "Babes in the Wood".

1916
3rd Jan. "Red Riding Hood".
10th Jan. "Dick Whittington".
13th Jan. "The Stormy Petrel", written by Dr. W. Strange Hall (a local doctor who wrote several plays that were produced in London).
20th Jan. "The Story of Rosary". Play.
27th Jan. "The Passing of the Third Floor Back"
3rd Feb. "Grumpy", with Robertson Hare in the name part, also Harold Wilkinson, who was to join the Melville Players
10th Feb "Eliza Comes to Stay".
17th Feb. Revue.
24th Feb. Revue.
2nd March Variety
9th March "The Count of Luxembourg".
16th March Revue.
23rd March Revue.
30th March "The Cinema Star". Farce
6th April Marie Lloyd
13th April Variety
20th April "The Marriage of Kitty". Farce.
27th April "The Case of Lady Camber". Play.
4th May "Potash and Permutter". Comedy.
11th May "The Marriage Market".
18th May "Hindle Wakes". Play.
25th May "Girl in the Taxi". Musical comedy.
1st June "When Knights were Bold". Comedy.
8th June "Prisoner of Zenda". Play.
15th June "A Cigarette Maker's Romance". Play.
22nd June "Maths". Drama.
29th June "Nell Gwynne". Play.
6th July Review
13th July "Jane". Farce.
20th July "The Ever Open Door". Drama.
27th July "A Take of Two Cities". Drama.
3rd Aug. Revue.
10th Aug. Fred Karno's "Parlex Vous Francais". Syd Walker.
17th Aug. "Tiger's Cub" Drama.
24th Aug. "A Buttterfly on the Wheel". Drama.
31st Aug. "Ye Gods". Farce.
7th Sept. "Bella Donna".
14th Sept. Revue
21st Sept. "The Basker".
28th Sept. "The Man Who Stayed at Home". Play.
5th Oct. "Within the Law".
12th Oct. "The Silver Crucifix". Play.
19th Oct. "Stop Thief". Farce.
26th Oct. "The Rosary".
2nd Nov. Variety.
9th Nov. Variety.
16th Nov. "Please Help Emily". Comedy.

23rd Nov. Variety.
30th Nov. "Peg O' My Heart"
7th Dec. Variety
14th Dec. Variety
21st Dec. "Cinderella".
28th Dec. "Sinbad the Sailor".

1917
4th Jan. Variety.
11th Jan. "Paris to Maidenhead". Revuesical comedy.
18th Jan. "Two Little Vagabonds". Drama.
25th Jan. "The Rotters".
1st Feb. "Lucky Jim".
8th Feb. "The Stormy Petrel".
15th Feb. "The Ware Case".
22nd Feb. "David Garrick". Play.
1st March "The Story of the Rosary".
8th March "Diana of Dobsons".
15th March "Our Flat". Farce.
22nd March Revue.
29th March "Ann". Comedy.
5th April "Beauchamp & Beauchamp. Comedy.
12th April Variety.
19th April Variety.
26th April "The New Boy". Farce.
3rd May Revue.
10th May Variety.
17th May "Our Boys". Comedy.
24th May "Under Two Flags". Play.
31st May "In Cripple Creek". Drama.
7th June "The Slaughraun". Drama.
14th June "The Walk of Jericho". Play.
21st June "Second to None". Play.
28th June "The Lass of Dingley Moor". Drama.
5th July "The Marriage of Kitty". Comedy.
12th July "When the Heart is Young". Drama.
19th July "Ye Gods". Farce.
26th July "Dolly Reforming Herself". Comedy
2nd Aug. Variety.
9th Aug. "The Importance of Being Earnest".. Henry Baynton
16th Aug. "Nobody's Daughter". Comedy.
23rd Aug. "Merely Mary Ann".
30th Aug. "Honour Among Thieves".
6th Sept. "Inside the Lines".
13th Sept. "Kick In". Play
20th Sept. Revue.
27th Sept. "The Double Event". Comedy.
4th Oct. "The Three Musketeers". Play.
11th Oct. "The Misleading Lady". Play
18th Oct. "Jerry". Farce.
23rd Oct. "Cash on Delivery" by Seymour (later 'Sir Seymour') Hicks, for one night only, his new farce with music. Ellaline Terriss (his wife) sang several songs.
25th Oct. "The Muddler". Play
1st Nov. "Mr. Wu".
8th Nov. "The Heart of a Hunchback" written and produced by Tom Taylor (manager of the Palace Theatre). Hunchback played by Henry Baynton.
15th Nov. "Ghosts". The play that was banned for 23 years.

23rd Nov. "Oh, I Say". Farce.
30th Nov. "Seven Days Leave". Play.
6th Dec. Variety.
13th Dec. "Her Only Son". Play
20th Dec. "The Girl from Upstairs". Farce.
27th Dec. "Babes in the Wood".

1918
7th Jan. "Monty's Flapper". By W.E. Ellin. Farce.
14th Jan. "Mother Hubbard".
21st Jan. "Damaged Goods" by Brieux. Play on the social evil.
28th Jan. "The Case of Lady Camber". By Horace Annesley Vachell. Play.
4th Feb. "Three Weeks" by Elinor Glynn. Play from the Strand Theatre.
11th Feb. "The Barton Mystery" by Walter Hackett. Play
18th Feb. "For Sweethearts and Wives" by Arthur Roseberry. Naval Play.
25th Feb. "The Marriage of Kitty" by Cosmo Gordon Lennox. Play.
4th March "The Arcadians". Music by Lionel Monckton. Musical play.
11th March "The Man who Stayed at Home" by Lechmere Worrall and J.E. Harold Terry.
18th March "The Mollusc" by Hubert Henry Davis. Play, the great Criterion success.
25th March "Jane" by William Lestcoq and Harry Nicholls. Farcical comedy.
Four week season by Henry Baynton and company:
1st April "Captain Drew on Leave" by Hubert Henry Davis.
8th April "A Fool's Paradise" by Sydney Grundy
15th April "The Melting Pot" by Israel Zangwill.
22nd April "John Glayde's Honour" by Alfred Surro.
29th April "A Little Bit of Fluff" by Walter W. Ellis. Farce, from the Criterion Theatre.
6th May "The White Slaves of London" by Arthur Shirley. Moral play.
13th May "The Walls of Jericho" by Arthur Sutro.
20th May "The Sleigh Bells". Alsatian drama.
27th May/1st June "The Perplexed Husband" by Arthur Sutro. Play about women's suffrage.
31st May "The Melting Pot" by Israel Zangwill. Single benefit performance for Henry Baynton.
3rd June "All of a Sudden Peggy" by Ernest Denny. Farcical comedy from the Duke of York's Theatre.
10th June "Pygmalion" by George Bernard Shaw. Romance from His Majesty's Theatre.
17th June "The Better 'Ole" by Bruce Bairnsfather and Arthur Elliot. Comedy from the Oxford Theatre
24th June "Somewhere a Voice is Calling". Melodrama.
1st July "The Pride of the Regiment" by Mrs. F.G. Kimberley. Play.
8th July "High Pressure". A revue in

four scenes.
15th July "The Confessions of a Wife" by Joseph Millane. Play.
22nd July "A Woman's Victory" by Herbert Shelley. Play. Mr. Herbert Shelley acted and sang from his repertoire of songs.
29th July "Duty and the Girl" by Clifford Rean. Play – a story for today.
5th Aug. "San Toy". Music comedy from Daly's Theatre.
12th Aug. "The Thief" by Henri Bernstein (translated from the French) from the St. James's Theatre.
19th Aug. "Still Waters Run Deep" by Tom Taylor.
26th Aug. "A Village Priest" by Sydney Grundy.
2nd Sept. "Seven Days Leave" by Walter Howard. Play.
9th Sept. "The Melting Pot" by Israel Zangwill. Play.
16th Sept. "Married on Leave" by Dorothy Mullord. Play.
23rd sept. "Eliza Comes to Stay" by H.V. Esmond. Comedy.
30th Sept. "Annie Laurie" An all Scotch novelty of music, comedy and tragedy, presented by Alfred Denville.
7th Oct. "Leah Kleschna" by C.M.S. McLellan. Psychological play, from the New Theatre.
14th Oct. "All Black". A South American revue with twenty three coloured performers.
21st Oct. "The Rotters" by H.F. Maltby. Farcical comedy, played by Arthur Gibbons' London Company.
28th Oct. "Diplomacy" by Victoria Sardou (translated from the French). Play
4th Nov. "Gayest of the Gay" by Arthur Shirley and Eric Hudson. Great moral drama.
11th Nov. "East Lynne" by Mrs. Henry Wood. Melodrama.
18th Nov. "Reported Missing" by Alfred Denville.
25th Nov. "The Balkan Princess". Musical comedy
2nd Dec. "Oh! Alexander" by Bay Dumaresq. Farce.
9th Dec. "A Soldier's Bride" by Walter Howard. Romantic military drama.
16th Dec. "A Married Man's Sweetheart" by Walter Saltoun. Play
26th Dec. "The Babes in the Wood" by Richard Hearne.

1919
4th Jan. "Dick Whittington and his Cat".
13th Jan. "The Man She Bought" by Walter Saltoun. Play
20th Jan. "Tainted Goods" by Clifford Rean. Play dealing with great social evil and the hidden plague.
27th Jan. "Nell Gwynne". Historical and romantic play.
3rd Feb. "My Sweetheart". A pastoral musical play of heart interest.
10th Feb. "Real Sports". A cheerful, patriotic revue.
17th Feb. "For Sweethearts and Wives" by Arthur Roseberry. Naval play.

23rd Feb. "The Little Brother" by Benedict James. Play, from the Ambassador's Theatre.
3rd March   "The Airman's Wife" by Charles Darrell. An intensely human play.
10th March "The Rosary" by Edward E. Rose. Play.
17th March "The Little Lost Sister" by Edward E. Rose. Play.
24th March "The Lads of the Village". Musical comedy, melodrama in ten scenes.
31st March "The Sealed Door" by Ben Lendeck. Drama.
4th April During the previous week's run a single performance of "East Lynne"
7th April "His Last Leave" by Clifford Rean. Realistic play.
14th April "The Secret Service Girl". Naval play.
21st April "Maid of the South". A new musical comedy.
28th April "Love and the Law" by Charles Darrell. Drama.
5th May "The Lady of Ostend" by Sir Francis Burnard. Farcical comedy.
12th May "The Prince and the Beggar Maid" by Walter Howard. Drama
19th May "Joyland". Revue. The London Hippodrome production.
26th May "Her Love Against the World" by Walter Howard. Play.
2nd June "The Lifeguardsman" by Walter Howard. Romantic modern play.
9th June "Damaged Goods" by Brieux. Play on the great social evil, from St. Martin's Theatre.
16th June "Pygmalion" by George Bernard Shaw. Play.
23rd June "Nights of Gladness". Comedy revue.
30th June "Tiddly Winks". Revue in three Acts.
7th July "White Slaves of London" by Arthur Shirley. Moral drama.
14th July "Hushed Up". Mystery play.
21st July "A Temporary Gentleman" by H.F. Maltby. Comedy.
28th July "The Silver Crucifix" by Walter Howard. Play.
4th Aug. "Rosebuds" by Chris Hamilton. Musical comedy revue.
11th Aug. "A Mill Girl's Wedding" by Herbert Shelley. Lancashire drama.
18th Aug. "A Woman's Victory" by Herbert Shelley. Play.
There then followed four weeks by the Henry Baynton Shakespearean Company.
25th Aug. "Hamlet"
26th Aug. "Merchant of Venice"
27th Aug. "Romeo and Juliet"
28th Aug. "The Sleigh Bells"
29th Aug. "David Garrick"
30th Augst "Romeo and Juliet".st Sept. "The Taming of the Shrew"
2nd Sept. "Hamlet"
3rd Sept. "Twelfth Night"
4th Sept. "Macbeth"
5th Sept. "Twelfth Night"
6th Sept. "The Taming of the Shrew"
8thSept. "Dora Stays the Night"

15th Sept. "Merchant of Venice"
16th Sept. "Othello"
17th Sept. "She Stoops to Conquer"
18th Sept. "King Lear"
19th Sept. "She Stoops to Conquer"
20th Sept. "Othello"
22nd Sept. "The Sleigh Bells"
23rd Sept. "As You Like It"
24th Sept. "The Taming of the Shrew"
25th Sept. "Merry Wives of Windsor"
26th Sept. "David Garrick"
27th Sept. "Merry Wives of Windsor"
29th Sept. "The Greater Love" by Vincent Carlyle. Play
6th Oct. "Five Nights" by Victoria Cross. A love problem.
13th Oct. "The Luck of the Navy" by Clifford Mills.
20th Oct. "Broadway Jones". A scream in four acts. From the Prince of Wales, Lyceum and Princes Theatres.
27th Oct. "rigadier Gerard" by Sir Arthur Conan Doyle. Play.
3rd Nov. "Wit and Wisdom". A super musical burlesque.
10th Nov. "By Pigeon Post" by Austin Page. Play from the Garrick Theatre.
17th Nov. "Temptations" by Cecil Sankey. Musical play.
24th Nov. "Sunshine". A revue in four rays of brightness.
1st Dec. "Na-poo". Revue.
8th Dec. "Oh, Laugh". A novelty revue in five scenes.
15th Dec. "Making Movies" and "Syncopated Schooldays". Great novelty.
22nd Dec. "Coloured Society". An all black South American revue.
29th Dec. "Mother Goose", with Richard Hearne (father of Mr. Pastry – Richard Hearne).

1920
5th Jan. "Jack and Jill".
12th Jan. "Our Mr. Hepplewhite" by Gladys Unger. Play
19th Jan. "Cash on Delivery". Musical comedy.
26th Jan. "Nights of Gladness". Revusical comedy.
2nd Feb. "Lads of the Village". Second edition, presented by I.V.T.A.
9th Feb. "The Silent Watch" by Arthur Roseberry. Naval drama.
16th Feb. " For Sweethearts and Wives" by Arthur Roseberry. Romantic naval play.
23rd Feb. "Honeymoon Express". A musical joyride from the Oxford Theatre, London.
1st March "Discharged with Honour" by Madge Douglas.
8th March "The Lady of Ostend" by Sir Francis Burnand. Comedy.
There followed a week of opera, performed by the J. W. Turner Opera Company:
15th March "Il Trovatore"
16th March "Faust"
17th March "The Bohemian Girl" (Matinee performance)
17th March "Pagliacci" and Cavalleria Rusticana" (Evening performance)
18th March "La Traviata"

19th **March** "Tannhäuser"
20th **March** " Maritana"
22nd **March** "Mr. Tower of London".
Revue with Gracie Fields.
29th **March** Variety.
5th **April** "Maid of the South" Musical
revue.
12th **April** "The Girl in the Taxi".
Musical comedy from the Lyric Theatre.
19th **April** "Disgraced" by Neville
Whitbread and Howard Wagner.
Romantic play.
26th **April** "Parted" by Leonard
Mortimer. Romantic play.
3rd **May** "The Naughty Wife". Comedy
from the Playhouse Theatre.
10th **May** "Hobson's Choice" by Harold
Brighouse. Lancashire comedy.
17th **May** "Maid of the Mountains".
Musical comedy.
Then there followed two weeks of opera by
the Fairbairn Milne Opera Company:
24th **May** "Faust"
25th **May** "Il Trovatore"
26th **May** "Maritana"
27th **May** "Cavalleria Rusticana" and
Pagliacci"
28th **May** "The Bohemian Girl"
29th **May** "Faust"
31st **May** "Cavalleria Rusticana " and
"Pagliacci"
1st **June** "Rigoletto"
2nd **June** "Il Trovatore"
3rd **June** "Faust"
4th **June** "Don Giovanni"
5th **June** "The Bohemian Girl"
7th **June** "My Aunt from New York" by
Herbert Shelley. Farce.
14th **June** "Why Men Love Women" by
Walter Howard.
21st **June** "Death or Glory Boys" by E,
Hill-Michelson. Melodrama.
28th **June** "Inconstant George".
Comedy.
5th **July** "The Prince and the Beggar
Maid" by Walter Howard. Play.
12th **July** "Oh! Alexander" by Barry
Dumaresq. Farce.
19thJuly "The Christians" by Hall
Caine. Drama.
23rd **July** "The White Slaves of
London".
24th **July** "The Christians".
26th **July** "The Sailor's Wedding".
Melodrama.
2nd **Aug.** "Oh! Laugh". Musical
burlesque.
9th **Aug.** "Tiger, Tiger" by Edward
Knoblock. Social play.
16th **Aug.** "Jack in the Box". Revue.
23rd **Aug.** "Daddies" by John L.
Hobble. Comedy.
30th **Aug.** "Nothing Doing". Musical
6th **Sept.** "The Mill Girl's Wedding" by
Herbert Shelley. Drama.
13th **Sept.** "The Man from Toronto".
Comedy.
20th **Sept.** "Wit and Wisdom" Musical
burlesque.
27th **Sept.** "The Jeffersons" by Vincent
Douglas. Comedy.
4th **Oct.** "The Luck of the Navy". Spy
play.

11th **Oct.** "Tatters" by Mrs. Kimberley.
A mixture of comedy, melodrama and
pantomime.
18th **Oct.** "The Temporary Gentleman"
by F.T. Maltby. Play
25th **Oct.** "Mice and Men". Play
1st **Nov.** "Sunshine". Revue.
8th **Nov.** "Great Scott". Revue
15th **Nov.** "Three Wise Fools" by
Austin Strong.
22nd **Nov.** "The Toodle-oo-Girl".
Comedy.
Sun. 28th **Nov.** Herbert Butcher's
Concert Orchestra. Tom Taylor
(mamager of the Palace Theatre) was
asoloist.
Then there followed two weeks by Henry
Baynton and his Shakespeare Company:
29th **Nov.** "Taming of the Shrew"
30th **Nov.** "The Merchant of Venice"
1st **Dec.** "Julius Caesar"
2nd **Dec.** "Macbeth"
3rd **Dec.** "Twelfth Night"
4th **Dec.** "Taming of the Shrew"
6th **Dec.** "Antony and Cleopatra"
7th **Dec.** "Romeo and Juliet"
8th **Dec.** "Hamlet"
9th **Dec.** "As You Like It"
10th **Dec.** "The Merry Wives of
Windsor"
11th **Dec.** "Antony and Cleopatra"
S. 5th **Dec.** Herbert Butcher's Concert
Orchestra.
S.12th **Dec.** Grand Concert.
13th **Dec.** "Pink-a-poo". Musical
comedy revue.
S.19th **Dec.** Scots Guards Octette.
20th **Dec.** "Freedom of the Seas".
Comedy.
S.26th **Dec.** Herbert Butcher's Concert
Orchestra.
27th **Dec.** "Sinbad the Sailor".

1921
S.2nd **Jan** .Palladium Octette
3rd **Jan.** "Aladdin". Most beautiful
production of its type ever to visit
Watford. Crowded houses again.
S. 9th **Jan** .Philip Ritte's Concert Party.
10th **Jan.** "Babes in the Wood". As good
as the two previous ones. Singing good
and humour really humorous.
S. 16th **Jan.** Edmund Maney's orchestra
17th **Jan.** "Jack and the Beanstalk".
Included Claud Ginnett and his
performing horses which had nothing to
do with the story.
23rd **Jan.** "O Betsey" musical comedy
S. 30th **Jan.** Scots Guards Octette.
31st **Jan.** "A White Man's Way" (James
and Stillwell's Company). Hints of
Madame Butterfly.
S. 6th **Feb.** Harry Jackson's London
Concert Party.
7th **Feb.** "Our Flat". A farce - "The
company does not appear to be too
familiar with the context but this is
only a minor detail".
S.13th **Feb** .Ubique Octette of ex-RA
musicians.
14th **Feb.** "See You Later". Very little in
the show but it provides an enjoyable
evening's entertainment. Critic

commented "One felt extremely grateful
to Miss Josie Delmaine for giving a fresh
interpretation of 'Swanee'. The number
of times this song has been murdered in
public by overdone sentiment and
untalented singers is almost past belief".
S. 20th **Feb.** H.M. Grenadier Guards
Sextette.
21st **Feb.** "A Peep Behind the
Curtains" (Lizzie Bateman company).
This play is nothing more nor less than a
frame for a charming children's ballet.
Acting of the adults was not good but
the dialogue was not too well written.
S. 27th **Feb.** The Broomwood Octette.
28th **Feb.** "Roxana" by Avery
Hopwood - comedy
In 1920 the old Skating Rink next door to
the theatre was converted into the Super
Cinema. Watford also had the Empire cinema
in Merton Road.
S. 6th **March** Edmund Maney's
orchestra
7th **Mar** "Her Only Way". Drama. "A
play with possibilities. The villain played
by Rhys Meredith was hissed by the
audience which is a sure sign of his
success. On Tuesday night the lights
failed but the management got the gas
footlights going until the electricity was
restored.
S. 13th **Mar.** Philip Lewis's Palladium
Octette.
14th **March** "Fair and Warmer" by
Avery Hopwood from the Prince of
Wales Theatre, London.
S. 20th **Mar** Band of the Civil Service
Rifles
21st **March** The Lads of the Village".
Great comedy-drama revue.
S. 27th **Mar.** The Broomwood Octette
28th **Mar.** "The Face at the Window".
Melodrama. There was a special
matinee performance on Thurs. 31st
March of "Two Eyes of Grey" in aid of
Earl Haig's Fund for Ex-servicemen.
1st **April** Good Friday concert by Philip
Ritte's Concert Party.

West Herts and Watford Observer issue of 2nd
April announced the showing of a film of the
Oxford and Cambridge Boat Race, including
the sensational finish, at the Super Cinema.

S. 3rd **April** H.M. Scots Guards
Octette - in aid of Warriers' Day Fund.
Theatre packed out.
4th **April** "Find the Lady". Farcical
revuical comedy.
S. 10th **April** The Broomwood Octette
11th **April** "The Yellow Ticket" play.
S. 17th **April** Band of H.M. Irish
Guards.
18th **April** "Two Little Vagabonds".
Famous melodrama by George R. Sims
and Arthur Shirley.
  On Friday 22nd only "East Lynne".
S. 24th **April** Philip Lewis' Palladium
Octette.
25th **April** "A Mother Should Tell" by
Dorothy Mullord and Ivan Patrick Gore.
2nd **May** "The Girl from Ciros".
9th **May** "Nights of Gladness".

16th **May** "Mr. Pim Passes By". Three Act comedy - should not be missed.
23rd **May** "Cupid in Hospital". Comedy - a delightful comedy with very little action.
30th **May** "The Dawn of Happiness". A play of comparatively little merit but drawing large audiences.
6th **June** "The Silent Watch" by Arthur Rosebury. Naval drama - presented at Watford for the fifthtime.(This observation is doubtful. Rosebury's other play "For Sweethearts and Wives" also a naval drama was presented twice, making this production the fifth by Arthur Rosebury.)
"Full of patriotic outbursts which received their measure of appreciation from a responsive audience".
13th **June** "The Far East" - musical comedy drama.
20th **June** "Carminetta" C.A. Stephenson's No1 Company. Comic opera. "Best show of its kind since Maid of the Mountains.
27th **June** "Oh, Harry". A merry musical melange.
4th **July** "Broadway Jones" - farce - played to crowded audiences "a splendid tonic for anyone down in the dumps".
11th **July** "Eliza Comes to Stay". Comedy.
18th **July** "Nothing Doing". The critic said the play belied its title because there was plenty doing. A comedian named Cyril Dunn resembled Charlie Chaplin.
25th **July** "All Black" - Will Garland's South American Revue.
1st **Aug.** "Kick Off" Musical comedy revue, including Dick Ray, comedian.
8th **Aug.** "The Very idea" presented by Haldane Crichton from the St. Martins Theatre. "…belongs to that type of play which might just as well not have been written but now that it has it cannot fail to amuse in its rather unusual line"
15th **Aug.** "The Romance of the Rosary" by Herbert Shelley, presented by the Herbert Shelley Company.
Play set in Lime House "has a great many thrilling moments and an air of mystery. One lady in the Stalls dissolved into tears at frequent intervals and was only brought round by brief spells of rather dull comic relief."
22nd **August** "The Lass of Dingley Moor", presented by the Herbert Shelley Company. A far fetched plot based on the eternal triangle.
29th **Aug.** "Should a Husband Forgive". Mrs. Fred Ormond's Company. "Some of the dialogue is unnecessarily sordid and one wonders what purpose the representation of a disagreeablesubject on the stage can possibly serve".
5th **Sept.** "The Queen's Rival", presented by Arthur Rosebury. Based on the story of Nell Gwynne.
12th **Sept.** "A Week End", farce, played to packed houses - "so genuinely funny that one chuckles all the time and roars with laughter frequently".

19th **Sept.** "Oh! Laugh". Revue.
Sun. 25th **Sept.** Broomwood Octette - *resumption of Sunday League Concerts.*
26th **Sept.** "Daddies". Four act comedy by John L. Hobble, pays a return visit from last year.
Sun. 2nd **Oct** .Headquarters Band of the Comrades of the Great War.
3rd **Oct.** "The Jeffersons". Lancashire play.
Sun. 9th **Oct.** The "Bow Bells" Concert Party.
10th **Oct.** "The Partners". Play. "Similar in context to "The Jeffersons". The author has allowed his predilection for long speeches to become a little too evident." The play had to contend with Charlie Chaplin in The Kid (film) playing next door.
Sun. 16th **Oct.** Frederick Stock's Octette. Record audience was delighted.

During this performance a speech was given on behalf of the Sunday League Concerts saying that a petition was being organised to ban the concerts because audiences were laughing on a Sunday. Profits given to charity.

17th **Oct.** "A Noble Brother" - "thoroughly predictable".
S. 23rd **Oct.** Philip Lewis' Palladiium Octette.
24th **Oct.** "The House of Peril". Play by Horace Annesley Vachell
In the West Herts and Watford Observer issue of the 22nd Oct. 1921 there appeared an announcement of the sale of Cassiobury Estate.
Sun. 30th **Oct.** H.M. Scots Guards Octette.
31st **Oct.** "Great Scott" revue - "plenty of musical numbers, a little dancing and a lot of rather indifferent humour.
Sun. 6th **Nov.** London Orchestral Octette.
7th **Nov.** "When Knights Were Bold" presented by Beresford & Pearce. "The company is one of the most talented we have had here recently".
Sun. 13th **Nov.** Gordon Marsh's London Concert Party.
14th **Nov.** "Tatters" - musical comedy dramatic play. Concerns a child of rich parents brought up in the slums
Sun. 20th **Nov.** Broomwood Octette
21st **Nov.** "The Purple Lady". Musical comedy - more the air of a farce with a few musical numbers thrown in.
Sun. 27th **Nov.** "Bow Bells" Concert Party.
28th **Nov.** "Seven Nights in London" - "It is a succession of events crudely strung together, with a little humour thrown in. Miss Phyllis Claud and Miss Winifred Felix Pitt deserve to be seen in a play of a more attractive nature."
Sun. 4th **Dec.** Grand Concert including Sterndale Bennett.
5th **Dec.** "Soiled" by the company which performed "Seven Nights in London the previous week. "A play of a similar nature" was the critic's only

comment.
Sat 10th **Dec.** at 2.30pm a Shakespearean Lecture - Recital given by Sir Johnston Forbes-Robertson. Organised by Watford Public Library Students' Association.
Sun. 11th **Dec.** Philip Lewis' Palladium Octette - including Ronald Gourley, the blind pianist, who played "When You Come to the End of a Perfect Day" with his back to the piano.
12th **Dec.** Variety, including Countess Olga Petroff, Russian Phenomenal Pianist, **Harry Champion**, Ida Barr and a star variety company, which the critic described as a "welcome change of fare".
Wed. 14th **Dec.** A matinee performance of "The Man Who Stayed at Home".
Sun. 18th **Dec.** Band of H.M. Welsh Guards.
19th **Dec.** "The White Slave's Wedding", except Friday, a surprisingly agreeable play.
Fri. 23rd **Dec.** "The Hooded Death".
26th **Dec.** "Little Red Riding Hood" - pantomime. "Almost impossible to get a seat, so heavy was the advance booking. Beautifully staged and dressed but the show needs livening up".

1922

Sun. 1st **Jan.** Philip Ritte's Concert Party
2nd **Jan.** "Little Bo-Peep" pantomime. "Decided improvement on last week's production"
Sun. 8th **Jan.** P.S. Robinson's Premier English Concertina Band.
9th **Jan.** Aladdin, Dick Ray in the cast.
Sun. 15th **Jan.** The Favourite Octette. The show started at 7.00pm but the Octette and several of the vocalising soloists were delayed at Queen's Park Station due to a blizzard at Queen's Park and did not arrive until 8.45. Meanwhile the audience were kept entertained by the manager, Mr. Tom Taylor with recitations, and other local artists and two members of the cast of Mother Goose.
16th **Jan.** "Mother Goose" presented by Ventom Swift. "Best of the four"
S. 22nd **Jan.** Grand Concert by Favourite Artistes.
23rd **Jan.** "Crossing the Line" - revue. Bright and breezy nautical extravaganza. "It is not cleverly conceived and there are not outstanding individual performances.
S. 29th **Jan.** The Co-Optimists Octette from the Palace Theatre, London.
30th **Jan.** Grand Variety Week, including Sam Mayo, Marie Kendall and others.
S. 5th **Feb.** The Broomwood Octette.
6th **Feb.** "Be Careful Baby" Bedroom farce from the Apollo Theatre.
Sun. 12th **Feb.** London Orchestral Sextette. "The popularity of the concerts given on Sunday evenings under the auspices of the National Sunday League has in no way diminished." Ronald Gourlay again played the piano and managed to impersonate a brass band.

Once again he played the piano with his back to the keyboard.

13th Feb. "Rose Petals" revue based on the theme of roses. The first visit to Watford by Mr. F.H. Fowler and one of his companies. He can be assured of a hearty welcome if he has other productions of this same standard.

S.9th Feb.   Murray Ashford's Margate Concert Party.

20th Feb.   "An Irish Maid" - musical play.

S.26th Feb.   Band of the "Rangers" 12th London Regiment.

27th Feb.   Variety including "A Dress Rehearsal" first performance in England. Part of the author played by Eddie Vogt.

S. 5th Mar.   The London Octette

6th March "All Aboard" - revue.

S. 12th Mar.   Grand Concert

13th March "Go As You Please" - musical extravaganza – "There have been many revues at the Palace Theatre, good, bad and indifferent, but it is difficult to remember one which comes anywhere near this week's production for all round excellence.

S. 19th Mar.   The Broomwood Octette.

20th Mar.   "Kiddie O' Mine". Domestic play by Mrs. Kimberley which   serves as a background for Madame Walker's little kiddies in song and dance. The dialogue is not very clever and the acting could be improved."

S. 26th Mar.   The Favourite Octette. Their visit on 15th January was disrupted by the blizzard at Queen's Park.

27th March   "Charlie Goes East". Original musical farcical comedy revue.

S. 2nd April   Stanley C. Mills London Octette.

3rd April "Keep It Going" - revue.

S. 9th April   Band of the Royal Naval Volunteer Reserve.

10th April "All Put" - revue.

14th April (Good Friday) Grand Operatic Concert given by the Principals of the H.B. Phillips Opera Company.

15th April "Brown Sugar" given by the Bushey Grove Dramatic Society.

17th Feb. "Joy Bells", ideally required a larger stage.

24th April "A Spanish Romance" - musical comedy.

1st May "The Quaker Girl"

8th May "There You Are Then" - revue.

15th May "Bubble and Squeak", starring Charlie Rich.

22nd May "Behind the Scenes" - revue.

27th May Matinee performance of "Iolanthe" by the Operatic Society of the School of Music. Due to heavy booking a second matinee was given.

29th May   Royal Welsh Ladies.

5th June "See You Later" - revue.

12th June "The Wheel of Fortune"

19th June "French Leave". Celebrated West End farce.

26th June "The Skin Game" by John Galsworth.

3rd July "Are You a Mason"

10th July "Polly Put the Kettle on"

presented by Nelson Keys from St. James's Theatre. 'Brilliantly done with a first class cast.'. 'There has been a run of good plays at the Palace Theatre lately and one hopes that such a welcome improvement has met with the financial success it deserves.'

17th July "Daddy Long Legs" - starred the well known London actress Miss Renee Kelly who received a remarkable reception.

24th July "Heads or Tails", comedy. *Because of the General Strike no review of 'Heads or Tails' was published.*

31st July "Eliza Comes to Stay" a play with a theme similar to Pygmalion

7th Aug. "Kick Off" revue with Dick Ray. Popular return visit, played to crowded houses. Dick Ray was especially funny in his burlesque on a footballer, and his references to the Watford team and the new ground.

14th Aug. "The Perfect Woman" presented by Arthur Rosebery, a domestic comedy. The critic said "The dialogue is none too brilliant, nor the characters too convincing".

21st Aug. "More Splashes" - musical revue. "Except for one or two patches of doubtful humour the revue….is an amusing and attractive show".

28th Aug. "A Week End", billed as a hilarious farce presented by Walter Ellis.

4th Sept. "The Buccaneer", musical comedy. Excellent music and effective scenery

11th Sept. Will E. Land, Harry Champion and Jack Cock and Full Variety Company. Jack Cock was an International Football Centre Forward who also played for Chelsea, he is reported as singing with "a pleasant. Natural voice". There is no mention of Will E. Land - perhaps it was the title of the show and a play on words.

18th Sept. "Cheerful Days". Comedy revue. "No one could call 'Cheerful Days' brilliantly written or even excellently produced but all the same it certainly has many strong features'.

25th Sept. "How Do You Do?". Musical comedy revue.

Sun. 1st Oct. Favourite Octette Resumption of Sunday league concerts.

2nd Oct. "Simple Simons Baby". New Lancashire comedy.

S. 8th Oct. Broomwood Octette - Very popular, many could not get seats.

9th Oct. "The Man Who Came Back" play.

S. 15th Oct. The Georgians Concert Party.

16th Oct. "The Red Heads", musical burlesque.

n. 22nd Oct. Grand Concert.

23rd Oct. "A Trip To Paris" musical revue.

S. 29th Oct. The Orientals Concert Party.

30th Oct. "Happy Go Lucky!". The new Pierrotic revue. Poorly attended.

S. 5th Nov. Palladium Octette.

6th Nov. "Bull-Dog Drummond" direct

from Wyndhams Theatre.S

n. 12th Nov. "Bow Bells" Concert Party.

13th Nov. "Hoist Yer Slacks" a nautical revue.

S 19th Nov. London Orchestral Sextette.

20th Nov. "A Social Convenience". Brilliant comedy from Royalty

S. 26th Nov. The Albert Baga Trio

27th Nov. "Pedlars Pie". A new and novel revue.

Sat 2nd Dec. Lecture on Shakespeare by Sir Johnston Forbes-Robertson under the auspices of Watford Public Library Students Association.

S. 3rd Dec. The Favourite Octette.

4th Dec. "Giggles". Burlesque revue.

S 10th Dec. Broomwood Octette

11th Dec. "Seven Days' Leave". Drama from the Lyceum.

S. 17th Dec. Grand Concert.

18th Dec. "Down South" revue.

26th Dec. "Aladdin"

S.31st Dec. The "Georgians" Concert Party.

1923

1st Jan. "Dick Whittington"

S. 7th Jan. Band of the R.N.V.R. (Sunday League)

8th Jan. "Puss in Boots"

S. 14th Jan. Tom Howells Opieros Concert Party.

15th Jan "Three Wise Fools"

22nd Jan. "The Mikado". Watford School of Music - Operatic Society (later re-named Watford Operatic Society.)

25th Jan. "The Merchant of Venice" evening performance and

27th Jan. "Twelfth Night" matinee presented by Watford Public Library Students Association.

29th Jan. "Arabian Love".

S. 28th Jan. Murray Ashford's Margate Concert Party.

S. 4th Feb. Grand Concert.

5th Feb. "Gay Ostend". Musical burlesque.

n. 11th Feb. London Orchestral Sextet.

12th Feb. "Search Me". Musical revue.

S. 18th Feb. Grand Concert.

19th Feb. "A Case of Diamonds!"

S. 25th Feb. Fred Wildons Entertainers (Margate 1922)

26th Feb. "Kick Off". Sporting revue with Dick Ray.

S. 4th Mar. Oriental Concert Party.

5th March "All Pep". Revue in ten scenes.

S. 11th Mar. Grand Concert with Leslie Weston.

12th March "Nuggetts of 1923".

S. 18th Mar. Tom Howelss and his Opieros.

19th March "A Bill of Divorcement".

S. 25th Mar. Concert Party with Robl Easton.

26th March "The Sheikh".

2nd April "Smile Awhile" with Webb and Page.

9th April "Hawley of the High Street".

16th **April** "The Girl in the Taxi".
23rd **April** "If Four Walls Told" from the Savoy Theatre.
30th **April** "You'd Laugh If You Knew".
7th **May** "Drama of Dobsons".
14th **May** "My Pretty Maid".
21st **May** ""A Little Bit of Fluff".
28th **May** "More Splashes". Revue.
6th **June** "Smiling Through".
13th **June** "A Week End".
20th **June** "Would You Believe It",
27th **June** "My Pal Jerry". Lew Lake and Company.
2nd **July** "Joy Bells"
9th **July** "East Lynne"
16th **July** "K'Nights of Joy". Ray Brothers revue.
23rd **July** "Inconstant George".
30th **July** "Skittles".
6th **Aug.** "Eliza Comes to Stay".
13th **Aug.** "Oh, I"
20th **Aug.** Old Time Singers of Popular Songs - Charlie Russell.
27th **Aug.** ":Let's Go".
3rd-5th **Sept.** "Tatters". Musical comedy - Dramatic play.
6th-8th **Sept.** "Kiddie o Mine". Musical comedy - Dramatic play.
10th **Sept.** Grand Variety Week- Dan Leno Jr., son of the great Dan Leno.
17th **Sept.** "Down South" Revue.
24th **Sept.** "Twilfils Night Out". A revue with opera choruses and ten Highland lassies.
1st **Oct.** "Unemployed". Comedy burlesque.
8th **Oct.** Mrs. May Gels (H) in Farce.
15th **Oct.** "Up the River". Musical burlesque.
S. 21st **Oct.** The Versatile Octette.
22nd **Oct.** Grand Variety Programme - Nervo and Knox from the Crazy Gang.
29th **Oct.** Vaudeville.
5th **Nov.** Vaudeville.
12th **Nov.** "Better and Better". Revue.
19th **Nov.** "Quality Street Madona Players".
26th **Nov.** "To Please You". Revue.
3rd **Dec.** "The Gondoliers" -. Watford School of Music Operatic Society
16th **Dec.** "The Man Who Came Back". George Manship Company.
26th **Dec.** "Dick Whittington".

Charles Stafford - Manager

1924
7th **Jan.** "Little Bo Peep".
14th **Jan.** Variety
21st **Jan.** "Wangles of 1924". Musical comedy revue.
28th **Jan.** "A Trip to Paris". Non-stop revue.
4th **Feb.** "Lights Up". Musical comedy revue. Syd Walker in the cast.
11th **Feb.** "London to New York". Musical revue.
Sat. 16th **Feb** at 2.30. "Much Ado About Nothing" presented by The Watford Amateur Players, most of whose members were members of Watford School of Music Operatic Society
18th **Feb.** "One Moment Please".

Variety revue.
25th **Feb.** "Helter Skelter". Musical comedy revue.
3rd **March** "Bluebeard's Eighth Wife" by Arthur Wimperis. Play.
10th **March** Variety. Talbot O'Farrell & Company. (Engaged at biggest salary ever paid to a variety artist in Watford).
17th **March** "Fun Shop". Burlesque.
24th **March** "The Zancigs & Co." (Mind readers) Variety programme.
31st **March** Fred Wildons Famous 1923 Entertainers. ??????
31st **March** Trial By Jury and The Pirates of Penzance. Watford School of Music Operatic Society
7th **April** "The Maid of the Mountains".
14th **April** "Shuffle Along". Cyril Dunn, Gladys Francis, Musical revue.
21st **April** "Hickey's Comedy Circus"

Theatre re-lamped, now double the quantity of light, materially adding to the beauty of the theatre shows.

Visit by the Imperial Opera Company.
28th **April** "Maritana"
29th **April** "The Daughter of the Regiment"
30th **April** "Lily of Killarney".
1st **May** "Il Trovatore"
2nd **May** "Faust".
3rd **May** "The Bohemian Girl".
5th **May** Harry Tate and Company. The greatest and most expensive variety programme ever seen in Watford.
12th **May** "Drawing the Dole". Musical burlesque.
19th **May** Variety, including Charlie Whittle, Penrose and Whitlock.
26th **May** "On the Run". Revue, including Billy Lev, Kathleen Hesketh.
2nd **June** "New Wives for Old". Farcical comedy
9th **June** Variety.
16th **June** Creations Musical Revue. Tom Gamble
23rd **June** Variety. Dr. Walford Bodie, demonstrating the powers of wireless.
30th **June** Variety, including Scott and Whaley.
7th **July** "Ton of Fun". Revue. Arthur Pond, Daisy Crossley, Leonard Morris.
14th **July** Farcical Comedy. Tom, Dick and Harry.
21st **July** Variety. The Two Bobs.
28th **July** "An Interrupted Honeymoon" Mystery play.
4th **Aug.** Varicty. Gus Fowler.
11th **Aug.** "Served Hot". Musical comedy revue.
18th **Aug.** "Round the Town". Musical revue.
25th **Aug.** Variety. Ella Shields.
1st **Sept.** "On the Dole". Comedy revue.
8th **Sept.** "Sign On". Musical revue.
15th **Sept.** Variety. Fred Barnes.
22nd **Sept.** "Pledges". Irish-Jewish musical comedy revue.
29th **Sept.** Variety, including J.W. Rickaby

6th **Oct.** "Our Liz". Musical comedy.
13th **Oct.** "The Side Show". Revue.
20th **Oct.** Variety. Victoria Monks.
27th **Oct.** "Risk It". Comedy revue.
3rd **Nov.** "Some Hustle". Revue.
S. 9th **Nov.** Clarkson Rose and Company.
10th **Nov.** "Rattles". Laughter revue.
17th **Nov.** "The Amazing Samson" - The strongest man in the world. Competition held for strongest man £10 prize.
24th **Nov.** "Princes Own". Romantic play.
1st **Dec.** "Betty". Musical comedy.
8th **Dec.** "Iolanthe". Watford Operatic Society.
15th **Dec.** "Me and My Gal". Comedy.
22nd **Dec.** "Little Jack Horner". Christmas pantomime.
29th **Dec.** "Ton of Money".

1925.
5th **Jan.** Miss Ethel Levy and company.
12th **Jan.** "Babes in the Wood".
19th **Jan.** "The Rainbow Revue"
26th **Jan.** Talbot O'Farrell and Company. (Talbot O'Farrell was King Rat of the Grand Order of Water Rats in 1930)
2nd **Feb.** Variety, headed by the 10 Loonies (a comedy band).
9th **Feb.** "Tonics". Revue.
16th **Feb.** "Stop Flirting". A musical comedy from the Strand Theatre, London.
23rd **Feb.** "The Outsider". A play from St. James's Theatre, London. This play was so popular that people had to be turned away.
2nd **March** Variety. Including Jack Hylton's Band.
9th **March** "10 - 1 On" A sporting revue, including Jimmy James.
16th **March** "The Lure". A play.
23rd **March** "Pins and Needles"
30th **March** "Yeomen of the Guard" - Watford Operatic Society.
6th **April** "The Jog Trot". A cabaret show.
13th **April** "The Whirlwind". Revue.
20th **April** "The Gay City". Revue, including the Jazz Maniacs and a Parisian chorus.
27th **April** Variety
4th **May** "Samson" in feats of strength and a competition with prizes totalling £10 to anyone who can bend an iron bar like Samson.
11th **May** "Snatches". A revue, including 'Keystone Police', a tumbling act.
18th **May** "Sally". From the Wintergarden, London.
25th **May** "Crisps".
1st **June** The famous comedian George Mozart.
8th **June** "On the Panel". A musical comedy.
15th **June** Another revue.
22nd **June** Fred Barnes, another comedian.
29th **June** "Our Liz". Musical comedy.

6th July "What Ho". A nautical revue.

13th July "Models and Muddles". A musical comedy.
20th July The Buffalo Bank of Chicago.
27th July "Sacked Again". Revue.
3rd Aug. "Revelations".
10th Aug. Henry Poynton and company.
17th Aug. "Situation". A revue.
24th Aug. "Posh". A revue.
31st Aug. Ernie Mayne and company.
7th Sept. "Puzzles of 1925" Revue.
14th Sept. "Say When". Revue.
21st Sept. Variety.
28th Sept. "What'll I Do". Revue.
5th Oct. Variety.
12th Oct. "Parish Relief". Revue.
19th Oct. "Tiger Cats". A play in three acts.
26th Oct. "Bed and Breakfast". A burlesque.
2nd Nov. "Here's To You". Florrie Forde - very good.
9th Nov. "Volumes" 20 scenes.
16th Nov. "The Mustard Pot". Comedy revue.
23rd Nov. "The Vortex" by Noël Coward.
30th Nov. "The Creaking Chair". A play.
7th Dec. "One Moment Please". Revue.
14th Dec. "Rack and Ruin". Revue.
21st Dec. Radiana" a machine with mechanical hands - plays piano, shaves etc.
28th Dec. "Uncle Tom's Cabin". A musical version.

1926

S. 3rd Jan. Murray Ashford's Felixstowe Entertainers.
4th Jan. "Puss in Boots".
11th Jan. Variety, including Elsie and Doris Waters
S. 17th Jan. Tom Howel and his Concert Party The Opieros.
18th Jan. "Roses". A new comedy revue. Enormous cast and popular artists. Full Beauty Chorus and Dancers.
25th Jan. Grand Variety Programme. Eight acts including Houston Sisters
1st Feb. "Tonics", a new original revue - 14 doses to be taken twice nightly - cast of ten including Frank Lawson.
8th Feb. "Merrie England" - Watford Operatic Society.
15th Feb. "Coloured Lights". South American Musical. Creole revue.
22nd Feb. "Served Hot". Comedy revue.
1st March Captain Clive Maskelyne - The World Famous Illusionist - direct from Maskelyne Theatre, London. He was a member of the family of illusionists. Nevil Maskelyne was part of the celebrated team of Maskelyne and Devant.
8th March "Nippy".
15th March "The Right Age to Marry".
22nd March "Stop Here". Revue in

seventeen scenes.
29th March "Margate Ped'lers" - caste of a dozen, including Ethel Revnell and Gracie West giving child studies and singing. (This revue is written of as the best entertainment at the Palace for a long time).
5th April Gigantic All-Star Variety Company.
12th April "Apple Sauce". New revue.
19th April Variety with Kate Carney.
26th April "Tarnish". By Gilbert Emery. A play in three acts.
  Margaret St. Barbe West.
3rd May "Mr. Tower of London". Presented and written by Archie Pitt.
10th May Variety with Marie Kendall.
17th May "Speed" – a musical comedy revue.
24th May Variety. Hilda Glyder topping the bill.
31st May "Good Old Sergeant" – revue.
7th June All-Star Variety Programme, Headed by Fred Barnes.
14th June "Revelations". A musical revue
21st June Variety. Talbot O'Farrell, top of the bill.
28th June "Wake Up" starring Jack Gallagher.
5th July All-Star Variety Programme, including Will Hay.
12th July "Green Goddess" billed as 'The Success of two hemispheres.'
19th July Variety.
26th July "Three Bags Full". Musical revue.
2nd Aug. Variety.
9th Aug. "Stuff & Nonsense". Musical revue.
16th Aug. "The Gorilla". Claimed to be 'the Funniest Show on Earth'
23rd Aug. "What Ho!" Nautical Musical Comedy Revue.
30th Aug. "The Golden West" Musical revue. Horses included, also Hylda Baker who was well applauded as a cleve comedienne.
6th Sept.   "Our Liz" . New musical in 3 Acts.
13th Sept.   Variety, including Naughton and Gold, Palladium revue comedians.
20th Sept.   Variety headed by Bransby Williams.
27th Sept.   "Are You Working". Revue in 13   scenes.
S. 3rd Oct.   Murray Ashford's Felixstowe Concert Party.
4th Oct. "Just for Fun", burlesque.
S. 10th Oct. The Famous Roosters Concert Party.
11th Oct. "Crossing the Line".
S. 17th Oct. "Gertrude Mayo's Entertainment.
18th Oct. "Caseys Circus" played by 30 children
S. 24th Oct. Shakespeare-Rutherford Rythmonic Band.
25th Oct. "Broadway Jones" presented by Seymour Hicks. Harry Piddock as "Broadway | ".

S. 31st Oct. Fred Wildon's Margate Entertainers.
1st Nov. The Famous American Boy Star, Tom Douglas and variety company.
S. 7th Nov. Murray Ashford's Herne Bay Concert Party.
8th Nov. "What'll I Do". Revue.
Su. 14th Nov. Tom Howell and his "Opieros" Concert Party
15th Nov. Will Fyffe, the famous comedian from the Palladium and Coliseum.
n 21st Nov. Claude Chandler's Cheltenham Entertainers.
22nd Nov. "The Belle of New York". Musical Comedy.
S. 28th Nov. Songtime Concert Party.
29th Nov. "On Velvet", featuring Wal Langtry.
6th Dec. "Ruddigore". Watford Operatic Society.
S. 12th Dec. Bow Bells – the celebrated London Concert Party.
13th Dec. "Here's Luck". Musical Comedy.
S. 19th Dec. The Clacton Entertainers
20th Dec. The Opieros Concert Party
27th Dec. Holiday Week – an all-star variety programme.

1927

S. 2nd Jan. Roosters Concert Party.
3rd Jan. "Sacked Again". Revue.
S. 9th Jan. Arnold Johnson Octette.
  A week from Henry Baynton and Company.
10th Jan. "She Stoops to Conquer", by Goldsmith
11th Jan. "David Garrick"
12th Jan. "The Rivals" by Sheridan.
13th Jan. "The Rivals" by Sheridan.
14th Jan. "She Stoops to Conquer", by Goldsmith
15th Jan. "David Garrick"
S. 16th Jan. Gwen Lewis's Broadstairs Entertainers.
17th Jan. "Dick Whittington".
S. 23rd Jan. Shakespeare-Rutherford Rhythmic Band.
24th Jan. Variety
S. 30th Jan. Colin Campbell and his Concertina Band.
31st Jan. "The Beggar's Opera". Bucroda Productions.
S. 6th Feb. The Felixstowe Entertainers.
7th Feb. "No. 17", by J. Jefferson Farjeon (A joyous mystery play).
S. 13th Feb. The Favourite Octette; Popular Operatic Concert.
14th Feb. "Winning Ways". A musical adventure.
21st Feb. "Looking Around". Revue.
S. 27th Feb. Royal Artillery Octette.
28th Feb. "The Last Waltz". A musical comedy.
S. 6th Mar. Margate Concert Party and Orchestra.
7th March Kate Carney - burlesque and comedy.
S. 13th Mar. The Maurice Sextette - operatic concert.
14th March "Distinguished Villa", starring Hilda Stuart, from the Little

Theatre, London.
S. 20ᵗʰ Mar.   Margate Entertainers.
21ˢᵗ March   "Alf's Button". A comic play.
S. 27ᵗʰMar.   Roosters Concert Party
28ᵗʰ March   "The Mikado" - Watford Operatic Society.
S. 3ʳᵈ April   Songtime Concert Party, with the Maurice Sextette.
4ᵗʰ April   "The Lie", starring Mary Byron, from the New Theatre, London.
S. 10ᵗʰ April   "Bow Bells". The 56ᵗʰ (London) Division Entertainers.
11ᵗʰ April   "Modern Times". A modern comedy, in ten scenes.
18ᵗʰ April   "The Golden West" . Circus revue.
25ᵗʰ April   Variety
2ⁿᵈ May   Will Catlin's Summer Follies.
9ᵗʰ May   "Raffles - the amateur cracksman", from the Comedy and Wyndham's Theatres, London.
1May   All Star Variety, with Marie Lloyd Jnr.
23ʳᵈ May   "In the Night" a comedy from the St. Martin's Theatre.
30ᵗʰ May   All Star Variety, with Albert Sandler and Jack Byfield (Palm Court Orchestra)
6ᵗʰ June   Le Grande Revuette.
13ᵗʰ June   "Forty Winks". Revue.
20ᵗʰ June   Grand Variety Programme, including Ella Shields.
27ᵗʰ June   "Mr. Tower of London", a revue from the Alhambra.
4ᵗʰ July   Variety, including Volpre's Famour Circus.
11ᵗʰ 13ᵗʰ, 16ᵗʰ July   "Comin' thro' the Rye". Frank Forbes-Robertson and Company.
12ᵗʰ July   "David Garrick". Frank Forbes-Robertson and company.
14ᵗʰ,15ᵗʰ July   "The Call of the Road". Frank Forbes-Robertson and Company.
18ᵗʰ July   All Star Variety Programme, headed by Lily Morris, from the Alhambra , Coliseum and Paladium.
25ᵗʰ July   "Spotlights". Revue with Jack Herbert.
1ˢᵗ Aug.   Gigantic Holiday Programme, headed by Talbot O'Farrell.
8ᵗʰ Aug.   "London Nights". Revue.
15ᵗʰ Aug.   "Something New" with Dixie Minstrels and Kentucky Belles - an all-white cast who work like niggers.
22ⁿᵈ Aug.   Murray, the Australian Escapologist, and supporting variety programme.
29ᵗʰ Aug.   "In the Next Room", by Eleanor Robson and Harriet Fox, from St. Martin's Theatre.
5ᵗʰ Sept.   "Grumpy" by Horace Hodges and T. Wigney Percyval, from the New and Criterion Theatres.
12ᵗʰ Sept.   "White Cargo".
19ᵗʰ Sept.   Estelle Brady (Mademoiselle from Armentieres) and full supporting programme.
26ᵗʰ Sept.   Variety
3ʳᵈ Oct.   "Here and There". London's latest revue.
10ᵗʰ Oct.   "Twelve Miles Out", from the Strand Theatre.

S. 16ᵗʰ Oct.   Colin Campbell and his concertina band.
17ᵗʰ Oct..   "A Cuckoo in the Nest", from the   Aldwych Theatre.
S. 23ʳᵈ Oct.   Ernie Rutherford and his rhythmic dance band.
24ᵗʰ Oct.   "The Big House". Revue.
S. 30ᵗʰ Oct.   The Songtime Concert Party.
31ˢᵗ Oct.   "The Rat". Story of an American Apache.
S. 6ᵗʰ Nov.   Harry Brandon's All Star Concert Party.
7ᵗʰ Nov.   Variety.
S. 13ᵗʰ Nov.   The Mountebanks Concert Party.
14ᵗʰ Nov.   "The New Splinters" by L Arthur Rowe.
S. 20ᵗʰ Nov.   The Clacton Entertainers.
21ˢᵗ Nov.   "No. No, Not Yet!", a musical, revusical burlesque.
S. 27ᵗʰ Nov.   The Londoners Concert Party.
28ᵗʰ Nov.   "Rookery Nook", from the Aldwych Theatre.
S. 4ᵗʰ Dec.   The Felixstowe Entertainers.
5ᵗʰ Dec.   "It Pays to Advertise". (Kept London laughing for over 600 performances).
S. 11ᵗʰ Dec.   Eddie Hepworth's Family Entertainers.
12ᵗʰ Dec.   "Princess Ida" - Watford Operatic Society.
19ᵗʰ Dec.   "Pensions", a new comedy.
26ᵗʰ Dec.   Variety.

1928

Hugh D. Wilson appointed manager from 25ᵗʰ June.
S. 1ˢᵗ Jan.   Tom Howell and the Opieros Concert Party.
2ⁿᵈ Jan.   Dick Whittington
S. 8ᵗʰ Jan.   Murray Ashford's Entertainers (of Margate and Westcliff fame)
9ᵗʰ Jan.   Robinson Crusoe
S. 15ᵗʰ Jan.   Gwen Lewis's Broadstairs Entertainers
16ᵗʰ Jan.   Variety, with the Houston Sisters.
S. 22ⁿᵈ Jan.   Eastbourne Entertainers
23ʳᵈ Jan.   Scotch Broth, a revue nicely seasoned and beautifully flavoured.
S. 29ᵗʰ Jan.   Harry Brandon's all-star concert party.
30ᵗʰ Jan.   "The Ringer", by Edgar Wallace - from Wyndham's Theatre.
S. 5ᵗʰ Feb.   Metropolitan Police Band with singers, usually five items from the programme were advertised.
6ᵗʰ Feb.   Johnson Clark (ventriloquist) and full supporting company.
S. 12ᵗʰ Feb.   Exmouth Concert Party.
13ᵗʰ Feb.   "The Laugh Mixture", a comedy concoction.
S. 19ᵗʰ Feb.   George Cameron's Entertainers (The Curiosities).
20ᵗʰ Feb.   Variety.
S. 26ᵗʰ Feb.   Hamilton Spencer and his New Plaza Band.
27ᵗʰ Feb.   "Maria Martin" or "The Murder in the Red Barn" from the

Elephant Theatre, London.
S. 4ᵗʰ Mar.   The Melody Makers.
5ᵗʰ March   "Scenes and Screams", a new novel musical show.
S. 11ᵗʰ Mar.   Harry Gibbs' Entertainers and the Margate Jetty Band.
12ᵗʰ March   Variety.
S. 18ᵗʰ Mar   Lloyd Shakespeare and his Band.
19ᵗʰ March   Variety, including Lingh-Singh, the Royal Indian Magician and Zoman, the psychic phenomenon.
S. 25ᵗʰ Mar.   The Grotrian Entertainers.
26ᵗʰ March   "The Merchant Prince", music by J.J. Sterling Hill, book by A.B. Cox.
2ⁿᵈ April   "Surprises", a new comedy burlesque.
9ᵗʰ April   Variety, headed by Albert Whelan.
16ᵗʰ April   Variety, headed by Bransby Williams.
23ʳᵈ April   "The Terror" , by Edgar Wallace - from the Lyceum Theatre.
30ᵗʰ April   "The 100ᵗʰ Chance", by Ethel M. Dell.
7ᵗʰ May   "The Joker", a detective play from the Royalty and Comedy Theatres.
14ᵗʰ May   Variety, headed by Naughton and Gold.
21ˢᵗ May   "The Haunted House", by Stanley Brighton.
28ᵗʰ May   Grand Holiday Attraction, headed by Clive Maskelyne, with a selection of "Maskelyne Mysteries".
4ᵗʰ June   "The Goods of 1928" a real revue.
11ᵗʰ June   Variety, headed by Princess Sunita (Indian Mystic).
18ᵗʰ June   Variety, headed by P.T. Selbit (illusionist).
25ᵗʰ June   "Who Goes There", the great military burlesque.
2ⁿᵈ July   "Dracula", as played at four London theatres.
9ᵗʰ July   Variety, headed by Arthur Prince (ventriloquist).
16ᵗʰ July   "Results", a comedy revue.
23ʳᵈ July   Veteran Stars of Variety.
30ᵗʰ July   "Family Affairs", the domestic comedy revue.
6ᵗʰ Aug.   "Is Zat So?" The brilliant comedy from the Apollo Theatre.
13ᵗʰ Aug.   "Something New". As 15ᵗʰ August 1927.
20ᵗʰ Aug.   "The Spice of Life", a new musical revue.
27ᵗʰ Aug.   Variety, including the Welsh Miners' Quartette.
3ʳᵈ Sept.   "Searchlights", revue.
10ᵗʰ Sept.   "Paint and Powder", revue.
17ᵗʰ Sept.   "The Cat Burglars", revue.
24ᵗʰ Sept.   "The Wrecker", by Arnold Ridley.
1ˢᵗ Oct.   "Seven Keys to Baldpate", a thriller, by George M. Cohan.
S. 7ᵗʰ Oct.   Ernest Rutherford and his band.
8ᵗʰ Oct.   "The Fanatics" a play for the broadminded
S. 14ᵗʰ Oct.   The Famous Daniels Instrumental Trio".
15ᵗʰ Oct.   "The Silent House", from the

Comedy Theatre.
S. 21st Oct. Hamilton Spencer and his New Plaza Band.
22nd Oct. "Come to the Show", revue.
S. 28th Oct. Colin Campbell and his concertina band.
29th Oct. "Sweeny Todd, the Demon Barber of Fleet Street".
S. 4th Nov. Jessie Filer's Ladies Band.
5th Nov. "Mrs. 'arris", a family affair in three tiffs.
S. 11th Nov. Clacton Entertainers.
12th Nov. "The Best People", a comedy success from the Lyric Theatre.
S. 18th Nov. Felixstowe 1928 Entertainers.
19th Nov. "All Smiles", revue.
S. 25th Nov. Gwen Lewis's Broadstairs Entertainers.
26th Nov. "Hi Diddle Diddle", revue.
S. 2nd Dec. Dorothy Sturdy's Ladies Orchestra.
3rd Dec. "The Crooked Billet", the mystery sensation by Dion Titherage, from the Royalty Theatre.
S. 9th Dec. Victor Vorzanger's Orchestra.
10th Dec. "Tom Jones", Watford Operatic Society.
S. 16th Dec. The Melody Makers.
17th Dec. "Steady Trade", revue.
S. 23rd Dec. Lloyd Shakespeare and his band.
24th Dec. "Jack and Jill"
S. 30th Dec. Royal Artillery Band String Octette.
31st Dec. "Dick Whittington and his Cat".

1929

Manager: Hugh D. Wilson
S. 6th Jan. Hamilton Spencer and the New Plaza Band.
7th Jan. "Aladdin".
S. 13th Jan. Bainbridge Robinson and his band.
14th Jan. "The Haunted Light", a comedy mystery of the sea.
S. 20th Jan. Haidie de Rance and her orchestra.
21st Jan. "Casey's Court", Music Hall from the New Oxford Theatre, London.
S. 27th Jan. Jimmy Parsons and his band.
28th Jan. "Going Strong", revue.
S. 3rd Feb. The Band of the London Fire Brigade.
4th Feb. "On Parade". A musical revusical burlesque.
S. 10th Feb. Dorothy Sturdy's Ladies Band.
11th Feb. "The Twister". A new thriller with an abundance of laughs.
S. 17th Jan. Ernest Rutherford and his band.
18th Feb. "Introduce Her". A novel American cabaret.
S. 24th Feb. Evelyn Hardy's Ladies Band.
25th Feb. "Ha! Ha! Ha!" Revue.
S. 3rd Mar Victor Vorzanger's Octette.
4th March "Mercenary Mary". Musical comedy from the LondonHippo drome.

S. 10th March Bainbridge Robinson and his band with Harry Hemsley (child impersonator).
11th Mar "One Damn Thing After Another". Revue from the London Pavilion.
S. 17th Mar Lloyd Shakespeare and his band.
18th March "Trial by Jury" and "H.M.S. Pinafore". Watford Operatic Society.
S. 24th Mar Sydney Jerome's orchestra.
25th Mar "Get Busy", revue.
S. 31st Mar Peggy Wildon's Ladies' Band.
1st April "Our Cabaret 1929". Revue.
8th April "Burlesques of 1929"
15th April "The Terror" by Edgar Wallce, from the Lyceum Theatre.
22nd April "Back Your Fancy", musical comedy revue.
29th April "The Blue Train". Musical comedy from the Prince of Wales Theatre.
6th May "Seven Days Leave". Drama from the Lyceum Theatre.
13th May "Round the World", revue.
20th May "Evening Stars", revue.
26th May "Hot Ice", revue.
3rd June "Seaside Frolics", revue.
10th June "The Man Who Came Back". A play of love and passion.
17th June "The Ghost Train" by Arnold Ridley, from the Garrick Theatre.
24th June "Blackmail". A thrilling play from the Globe Theatre.
1st July "By Whose Hand". A play with Sir Jacob Epstein's model Dolores.
8th July "Whispering Wires", Crook-play, from the Apollo Theatre.
15th July "The Passing of the Third Floor Back", revue by Jerome K. Jerome, in which Frank Forbes-Robertson played the Stranger, his most famous role also in the cast Miss Sydney Thornton.
22nd July "Lost Property", a comedy from the Duke of Yorks Theatre, with Myra Ansell.
29th July "Square Crooks", a comedy from the Prince of Wales and Globe Theatres, with Enid Shelly.
5th Aug. "Work", a revue.
12th Aug. "Switch", a musical burlesque.
19th Aug. "The Black Spider", from the Lyric, Strand and Savoy Theatres, with Evelyn Hope.
26th Aug. "The Killing of Anthony Drake", by Cedric Lewes.
2nd Sept. "So This is London", a comedy as played at the Prince of Wales and Savoy Theatres.
9th Sept. "The Red Lamp". Musical Comedy with Wal Langtry.
16th Sept. "The Farmer's Wife", by Eden Phillpots. From a three year run at the Royal Court Theatre.
23rd Sept. "Mr. Bingle", a mixture of mirth and music.
30th Sept. "The Constant Nymph", by Margaret Kennedy and Basil Doon. From the New and GarrickTheatres.

S. 6th Oct. Bransby Williams and supporting cast.
7th Oct. "High Words", revue.
S. 13th Oct. Ernest Rutherford and his band.
14th Oct. "One of the Best", revue.
S. 20th Oct. Will Rodwell and his band.
21st Oct. "When Blue Hills Laughed". Comedy adventure from the Criterion Theatre.
S. 27th Oct. Haidee de Rance and her Ladies Band "The Microphonians"
28th Oct. "The Trial of Mary Dugan" from the Queen's Theatre, with Dorothy Heave.
S. 3rd. Oct. Evelyn Hardy's Ladies Band.
4th Oct. "Bird in Hand", by John Drinkwater. Comedy.
S. 10th Oct. Lloyd Shakespeare and his band.
11th Oct. "Up with the Lark". Musical comedy from the Adelphi Theatre.
S. 17th Oct. Dorothy Sturdy and her Ladies Band.
18th Oct. "Speed and Sparkle", revue.
S. 24th Oct. New Bow Bells.
25th Oct. "Sop the Wedding". A play of life, love and laughter.
S. 1st Dec. An all star concert.
2nd Dec. "The Speed Show", revue.
S. 8th Dec. Song time.
9th Dec. Variety, headed by Attalia, an escapologist.
S. 15th Dec Jimmy Parsons and his Octette.
16th Dec. "Form Fours". A comedy revue in 14 parades.
23rd Dec. Variety.
S. 29th Dec. Jessie Wildon and her Margate Jetty band.
30th Dec. "Little Red Riding Hood".

1930

S. 5th Jan. Grand Concert.
6th Jan. "Babes in the Wood".
S. 12th Jan. The Band of the London Fire Brigade, with Elsie and Doris Waters.
13th Jan. "The Lido Follies". The cabaret revue.
S. 19th Jan. Television. A cast of seven, including Harry Hemsley.
20th Jan. "The Burglar", by Terence Byron. A comedy thriller.
S. 26th Jan. Ernest Rutherford and his band.
27th Jan. "Casey's Court". New songs, new sketches, new ideas.
S. 2nd Feb. Grand Concert.
3rd Feb. "This Thing Called Love". A comedy.
S. 9th Feb. The Opieros. Concert party.
10th Feb. "Mumming Birds" Variety by Fred Karno's Company.
S. 16th Feb. Grand Concert.
17th Feb. "The Sketch Book", revue.
S. 23rd Feb. Lloyd Shakespeare and his band.
24th Feb. "The Rebel Maid". Watford Operatic Society.
S. 2nd March The Band of the London

Fire Brigade.

3rd March "The Sugar Baby". Revue.

S. 9th March Grand Concert.

10th March "August 1914". Burlesque revue.

S. 16th March Felgate King and his party.

17th March "The Sacred Flame", by W. Somerset Maugham, with Gladys Cooper and a strong West End cast.

S. 23rd March Fred Wildon and his party.

A week by Henry Baynton and his company

24th March "Bulldog Drummond", the famous thriller

25th March "The Speckled Band" by Conan Doyle

26th March "The Invisible Foe" by Walter Hackett

27th March "Witness for the Defence" by A.E.W. Mason

28th March "The Melting Pot" by Israel Zangwill

29th March "Bulldog Drummond", the famous thriller

S. 30th Mar Murray Ashford and his 1929 party (sic).

31st March West End Variety, headed by Joe Boganny and his college boys.

S. 6th April "The Microphonians".

7th April "Young Woodley" An entrancing love story, from the Savoy Theatre.

14th April "Rogues and Vagabonds". Variety with Hetty King.

21st April "Brown Sugar". Famous laughter play from the Garrick and Duke of York Theatres.

28th April "Yellow Sands" by Eden and Adelaide Phillpots, from the Theatre Royal Haymarket.

5th May "Crack a Jacks". A laughter salad with musical dressing.

12th May "Bill of Divorcement", by Clemence Dane, with Max Jerome, from St. Martin's Theatre.

19th May "By Candlelight". A joyous naughty comedy, with Yvonne LeDain, from the Criterion Theatre.

26th May "A Sunburst in Vaudeville", Signor Arvi's burlesque show.

2nd June "Wife Tamers", a comedy mixture starring Jack Stanley.

9th June West End Vaudeville, headed by Samson, the amazing strongman.

16th June "Just a Minute". A musical burlesque.

23rd June "Journey's End", by R.C. Sherriff.

30th June "Playtime". Variety, featuring Nora Bancroft, vocalist.

7th July "The Singing Clown". A story of laughter and tears, with the Lancashire comedian Joe Moss.

14th July "The Tiny Town Follies". Twenty midget artists from The Tower, Blackpool; The Winter Gardens. Berlin and The Palace, New York.

21st July "The Golden Melody". Musical revue.

28th July "The Bells" by Henry Irving, with Henry Baynton.

4th Aug. Vaudeville, featuring Robb Wilton in a sketch: "His Journey".

11th to 16th August: Closed for redecorating and reseating. Seats in the Pit replaced by tip-up seats, which could be booked in advance.

18th Aug. "The Mirth Parade". Revue, featuring Fred Morgan.

25th Aug. Variety, headed by Billy Merson.

1st Sept. "Frankenstein". Played by Hamilton Deane and his company.

8th Sept. "Painted Dolls". Variety

15th Sept. "Going the Pace". Revue.

22nd Sept. "Symphony in Two Flats" by Ivor Novello. From the Apollo and New Theatres.

29th Sept. "Down Our Street", comedy from the Vaudeville Theatre.

S. 5th Oct. Jack Gold's Octette.

6th Oct. West End Variety.

S. 12th Oct. Victor Vorzanger's Octette.

13th Oct. "The Laugh Parade". Revue.

S. 19th Oct. The Band of the London Fire Brigade.

20th Oct. West End Variety.

S. 26th Oct. Evelyn Hardy's Ladies Band.

27th Oct. "The Dug Out Melody". A Great War comedy.

S. 2nd Nov. George Thomas and his party.

3rd Nov. A Military Pickle. Musical burlesque.

S. 9th Nov. Ernest Rutherford and his band.

10th Nov. "There's No Argument". Musical revue with a plot.

S.16th Nov. "Regional Calling". With Kenneth and George Western (The Western Brothers)

17th Nov. Variety, headed by Horace Goldin, illusionist.

S.23rd Nov. Jack Bruske and rhythmic band.

24th Nov. "French Leave" by Reginald Berkeley. A war comedy from the Vaudeville Theatre.

S.30th Nov. Jessie Wildon and her band.

1st Dec. Variety, headed by the Hai Yung Family, acrobats, jugglers and equilibrists.

S. 7th Dec. Wilby Lunn's Felixstowe Party.

8th Dec. "Love Liars". Revue.

S.14th Dec. "Bow Bells", with Elsie and Doris Waters.

15th Dec. Folies Bergère Revue. From the Folies Bergère Theatre, Paris and the Victoria Palace.

S.21st Dec. Fred Wildon's Party, from Margate.

22nd Dec. "Charley's Aunt" by Brandon Thomas.

S.28th Dec. "Songtime".

29th Dec. "Cinderella".

1931

S. 4th Jan. Jack Bruske and his rhythmic band.

5th Jan. "Happy Days". A revue with Jack Young.

S. 11th Jan. Lloyd Shakespeare and his band

12th Jan. "Goldilocks and the Three Bears".

S. 18th Jan. The Microphonians.

19th Jan. Lido Follies of 1931.

S. 25th Jan. All-star Concert.

26th Jan. West End Vaudeville Company.

S. 1st Feb. Murray Ashford and his party.

2nd Feb. "Almost a Honeymoon". The daring but really funny farce, now playing at the Garrick Theatre.

S. 8th Feb. The London Fire Brigade Band.

9th Feb. "Night Revels" Revue.

S.15th Feb. Regional Calling.

16th Feb. "The Cat's Cradle". Exquisite comedy, with Sybil Arundale, from the Criterion Theatre.

S.22nd Feb. Ernest Rutherford and his band.

23rd Feb. "Veronique". Watford Operatic Society.

S.1st Mar Jack Gold and his band.

2nd Mar "Irish Smiles". The 100% Irish Revue.

S. 8th Mar George Thomas's 1930 Ramsgate Party.

9th Mar "Alf's Button" (re-polished) with Lew Lake as "Alf".

S. 15th Mar Fred Wildon's Party.

16th March Casino de Paris. Revue from Paris.

S. 22nd Mar Jack Bruske and his rhythmic band.

23rd Mar "Third Time Lucky" by Arnold Ridley. London's funniest play.

S. 29th Mar Leonard Henry's Little Show.

30th March "High Toppers". Revue.

6th April West End Variety Company.

13th April "A Warm Corner". Farcical comedy with Enid Cooper.

18th April Matinee performance by pupils of local schools of dancing. In aid of the NSPCC and Dr. Barnardo's Homes.

20th April "The Man in Possession" by H.M. Harwood, with Terence Duff, from the Ambassadors Theatre.

27th April Vintage Variety.

4th May "Blackberries". The greatest coloured show.

11th May. "All Right on the Western Front". Comedy revue, featuring Tom Gambe.

18th May "(K)nights of Gladness". Revue featuring Len Jackson.

25th May "Something Sensational". Revue with Victor Duprez and his band.

1st June "Traffic". A thriller with Katherine Tremaine, from the Lyceum Theatre.

8th June "Joy-Time". The laughable music show.

15th June Vaudeville Menu.

22nd June "Beauty Spots". A revue, clean, cute and comical.

29th June. "London Revels".

6th July "It's a Boy". Farce, with Margaret Standley. Now in its tenth month at the Strand Theatre.

13th July "The Silent Witness". Mystery play.
20th July "Talkie Stars". Revue.
27th July "Paradise Island". A play of romance and adventure.
3rd Aug. West End Vaudeville Company.
10th Aug. "A Murder Has Been Arranged". A ghost story from the St. James's Theatre.
17th Aug. "The Second Man". An ultra modern comedy with Jack Tully and Ethel Cadman. From the Playhouse and Embassy Theatres.
24th Aug. "A Little Bit of Fluff", by Walter Ellis, with Sydney Hale. A farce from the Criterion Theatre.
31st Aug. "Something New", featuring the Dixie Minstrels and the Kentucky Belles.
7th Sept. "West End Revue Company" headed by Ethel Revnel and Gracie West.
14th Sept. "Just Married", with Herbert Mansfield. From the Comedy Theatre.
21st Sept. "Tiny Town Follies". The world's most marvellous midgets.
28th Sept. "West End Vaudeville Company", headed by Flanagan and Allen.
5th Oct. "Why Go to Paris" . A daring new revue.
12th Oct. "Fine and Dandy". A vaudeville bill.
S.18th Oct. George Thomas's 1931 Ramsgate Concert Party.
19th Oct. "Sez You". The international revue.
S.25th Oct. The Band of the London Fire Brigade.
26th Oct. "The Co-Optimists", with Phyllis Monkman and Stanley Holloway.
S.1st Nov. Ernest Rutherford and his band.
2nd Nov. "The Outside Inn". An original revusical burlesque.
S.8th Nov. Dorothy Sturdy and her band.
9th Nov. "West End Vaudeville", headed by Jack Lewis and his Rolling Stones.
S.15th Nov. Victor Vorzanger's Octette.
16th Nov. "Marry the Girl", a new farce from the Aldwych Theatre.
S.22nd Nov. Concert Party of Margate Favourites.
23rd Nov. "Sunburst in Vaudeville". Signor Arvi's non-stop sparkling revue (1931).
S.29th Nov. Jack Bruske and his Elstree Orchestra.
30th Nov. "West End Vaudeville" headed by King and Benson.
S.6th Dec. "A Modern Entertainment", directed by Leslie Sarony.
7th Dec. "My Wife's Family". The funniest play in the world, with Fred Duprez. The Garrick Theatre success.
S.13th Dec. The Watford Military Band.
14th Dec. "The Song of the East". A new musical production.

21st Dec. "One Big Smile" A great comedy with Little Jimmie Leslie and Maia Barrie.
28th Dec. "Robinson Crusoe".

1932.

4th Jan. Vaudeville, headed by Holden's Mannikins (Puppets)
11th Jan. "Casey's Court". An entirely new show.
18th Jan. "Room for Two", a crook farcical comedy.
25th Jan. Vaudeville, headed by Elsie Bowers and Billy Rutherford.
1st Feb. "Follies of 1932". Comedy musical attraction.
8th Feb. "West End Vaudeville Company", including a lightning return of Bowers and Rutherford.
15th Feb. "The Vagabond King", Watford Operatic Society
22nd Feb. "Crooks in Clover". Musical show of laughter and thrills.
29th Feb. "West End Vaudeville Company".
7th March "Follies Masquerade". A huge joke with music.
14th March "Happy Snaps". A big new revue.
21st March "Don't Tell the Wife". The funniest play for years with Marie Brooke.
28th March Vaudeville, headed by Linga Singh, assisted by Miss Lakhami, presenting real oriental mysteries.
4th April "West End Vaudeville Company", headed by Jane Ayr and Eddie Leslie, including a singing or dancing competition (over 15), judged by the audience. Final held during 9pm performance on Saturday: Prizes £10; £6; £3 and £1
11th April "The Lido Follies of 1932", including Raymond Bennett and Fai Robins.
18th April "London Wall", by John van Druten. From the Duke of York's Theatre.
25th April "The Crimes of Burke and Hare". Melodrama from the New Theatre, with Tod Slaughter.
2nd May "Springtime Cabaret", headed by Lydia Kyasht, the world famous ballerina, with a small corps de ballet. Also Tommy Trinder performing burlesque dances.
9th May Vaudeville Menu and Paris a la nuit, a dance-cabaret show.
16th May "West End Vaudeville Company", including football on bicycles, with audience competing for a top prize of £3.
23rd May "Important People", with Zillah Bateman and Gerald Ames.
30th May "West End Vaudeville Company".

The Denville Players were the resident company from 6th June until 6th May 1933

6th June "Story of the Rosary", as played at the Prince's Theatre.
13th June "Paddy, the Next Best

Thing". A thousand laughs without a single blush. From the Savoy Theatre.
20th June "The Black Moth". Thrilling mystery play.
27th June "The Yellow Ticket". From the Playhouse Theatre, London.
4th July "Tilly of Bloomsbury", from the Apollo Theatre, with Audrey Wilson.
11th July "Spring Cleaning", by Frederick Lonsdale. The brilliant comedy from the St. Martin's Theatre, London. Special engagement of Kim Peacock.
18th July "Polly with a Past", by George Middleton and Guy Bolton. Famous comedy from St. James's Theatre, London.
25th July "The Squall". The daringly outspoken play, with Betty Nelson.
1st Aug. "The Middle Watch" by Ian Hay and Stephen King-Hall. A naval comedy, ran for over twelve months at the Shaftsbury Theatre.
8th Aug. "Lady Windermere's Fan" by Oscar Wilde, with Betty Nelson.
15th Aug. "The Man from Toronto" by Douglas Murray, from the Duke of York's Theatre, with Donald Edwards.
22nd Aug. "The Last of Mrs. Cheyney", with Betty Nelson.
29th Aug. "The Fake" by Frederick Lonsdale.
5th Sept. "Three Wise Fools" by Austin Strong. The great success from the Comedy Theatre, London.
12th Sept. "A Woman of No Importance" by Oscar Wilde. A play in four acts, with Dora Fanshaw and Barbara Reynolds.
19th Sept. "Miss Hobbs", by Jerome K. Jerome. A comedy drama in four acts.
26th Sept. "A Butterfly on the Wheel" by Ed. H. Hemmerde, K.C., and Frances Neilson. The great play of the Divorce Court from the Globe and Queen's Theatre London.
3rd Oct. "Lord Richard in the Pantry" by Sidney Blow and Douglas Hoare. Screamingly Funny Comedy from the Criterion Theatre, London.
10th Oct. "A Pair of Silk Stockings" by Cyril Harcourt. Excruciatingly Funny Comedy from the Criterion Theatre, London.
17th Oct. "Fair and Warmer" by Avery Hopwood. A farcical comedy in three acts. As produced at the Prince of Wales Theatre, London.
24th Oct. "On the Spot", Edgar Wallace's Greatest Play. After a year's run at Wyndham's Theatre, London and six months at the Forrest Schubert Theatre, New York.
31st Oct. "The Hypocrites" by Henry Arthur Jones, author of the "The Silver King". Starred artiste Nancy Taylor.
7th Nov. "Her Past" by Frederick Jackson. Alice Delysia's dark, daring comedy from the Shaftsbury Theatre. Starred artiste Audrey Stevens.
14th Nov. "Proof or a Celebrated Case", the magnificent play. Adapted for the English Stage by Sir F.C. Burnand.

21st **Nov.** "The Under Dog" by Walter Howard. A play of Rhodesian life from the Princes Theatre, London. Starred Peter Murray-Hill and Annette Peacock.
28th **Nov.** "Jane" by W. Lestocq and H. Nicholls. The Rollicking Farcical Comedy from the Comedy Theatre, London. As played by Sir Charles Hawtrey.
5th **Dec.** "The Lie" by Henry Arthur Jones. A play in four acts.
12th **Dec.** "A Sinner in Paradise" by Val Gurney in four acts. By special request of numerous patrons. A Play that will make you talk for weeks.
19th **Dec.** "Rookery Nook" by Ben Travers. The Exhilarating Farcical Comedy, Popularised by Ralph Lynn and Tom Walls at the Aldwych Theatre, London.
26th **Dec.** "A Christmas Carol", adapted from Dickens Immortal Story.

1933

2nd **Jan.** "Tom, Dick and Harry", an uproariously funny comedy. Specially produced for the delectation of the children.
9th **Jan.** "Come Out of the Kitchen", a comedy in three acts. Adapted by A.E. Thomas from the story of the same name by Alice Duer Miller. As produced at the Strand Theatre, London.
16th **Jan.** "9.45" by Owen Davis and Sewell Collins. The Greatest of All Mystery Plays. The Play That Baffled Scotland Yard.
23rd **Jan.** "Carnival" - Matheson Lang's Great Success. Adapted from the Italian Play "Sirocco" by C.M. Harding and Matheson Lang. Music, Life and Laughter. Members of the Alfieri Theatre Company and Revellers.
30th **Jan.** "Baby Mine" by Margaret Mayo. The 100% Laughterpiece, from the Criterion Theatre.
6th **Feb.** "The Silver King" by Henry Arthur Jones. William Barrett's masterpiece. Five acts and fourteen scenes.
13th **Feb.** "The Naughty Wife" by Frederick Jackson. A comedy in Three acts made famous by Sir Charles Hawtry and Miss Gladys Cooper.
20th **Feb.** "Monsieur Beaucaire". Watford Operatic Society
S.26th **April** Sunday Concert at 7.00pm by West End Artistes. (Inc Herschel Henlere)
27th **Feb.** "Grumpy" by Horace Hodges and T. Wighey Percyval. Cyril Maudes famous play from the New Theatre, London.
S. 5th **Mar** Sunday Concert at 7.00pm by West End Artistes. (Rio Marino Band)
6th **March** "Nell Gwyn". The Fascinating Romantic Play Especially Written for Mr. Alfred Denville.
S.12th **Mar** Sunday Concert at 7.00pm by West End Artistes. (Al Kendall and his Mayfair Band)
13th **March** "The Silent House" by G.

Brandon and George Pickett. A play in four acts, from the Comedy Theatre, London.
S.19th **Mar** Sunday Concert at 7.00pm by West End Artistes. (Jack McDermott and his Covent Garden Band)
20th **March** "If Four Walls Told" by Edward Percy. A Village Tale in Three acts. On Friday night only, Jerry the Tramp, Alfred Denville (himself) will appear in his famous part of 'Jerry'.
S.26th **Mar** Sunday Concert at 7.00pm by West End Artistes. (Alan Parsons and his Gaumont British Band)
27th **March** "The Rat" by David Lestrange. A Romantic Story of Modern Parisian Life. Produced by arrangement with Ivor Novello. Starred Barbara Reynolds, Nancy Taylor, Violet Hollis.
S. 2nd **April** Sunday Concert at 7.00pm by West End Artistes. (Olly Aston and his 1933 Band)
3rd **April** "The Best People" by David Grey and Avery Hopwood. A comedy in Two acts. As produced at the Lyric Theatre..
S. 9th **April** Sunday Concert at 7.00pm by West End Artistes. (Mlle. Majinsky and her Hungarian Ladies Gipsy Band, with Hal Wright, the famous troubadour)
10th **April** "The First Mrs. Fraser" by St.John Ervine. A comedy in three acts from the Haymarket Theatre, where it ran for eighteen months.
S.16th **April** Sunday Concert at 7.00pm by West End Artistes. (Al Kendall and his Mayfair Band)
17th **April** "The Prince and the Beggar Maid" by Walter Howard. The Great Military Drama.
S.23rd **April** Sunday Concert at 7.00pm by West End Artistes.
24th **April** "When Knights Were Bold" by Charles Marlowe. A comedy in three acts.
S.30th **April** Sunday Concert at 7.00pm by West End Artistes. San Marino Accordion Band
1st **May** "Seven Days' Leave" by Walter Howard. The celebrated Lyceum melodrama in five acts, for four days only. On Friday and Saturday:
  "Facing the Music" An Uproariously Funny Comedy.

This concluded the season by the Premier Denville Players which ran for 47 weeks.
Plays produced by Edwin J. Collins
Manager: Conrad E. Stratford
Stage Managers: Audrey Wilson and Eastern Pickering
Scenic Artist: Oliver Richardson
(For Alfred Denville)

S. 7th **May** Hal Ross and his music masters
15th **May** "Piccadilly Nights" Revue with Fred Ropner's midgets
22nd **May** "Piccadilly Nights" Revue with different acts.
29th **May** "The Folliss Masquerade". Revue in eighteen scenes, with Teddy

White, the "Clown Prince" of Lancashire.
5th **June** Variety, headed by Mexano Accordion Band.
12th **June** "It's a Girl" by Austin Melford. Comedy.
19th **June** "While Parents Sleep", by Anthony Kimmins. Comedy from the Royalty and Garrick Theatres.
26th **June** "Military Pickles". Revue.
3rd **July** "Road House Revels", a Vaudeville cocktail.
10th **July** West End Vaudeville Company.
17th **July** "Hello Everybody!". The Novelty Show of 1933
24th **July** "Her Cardboard Lover". Farcical Comedy..
31st **July** Nine O'Clock Revue and Cabaret, headed by Maria Minetti, direct from the Café Anglais and Beno Leopold from Borsta.
7th **Aug.** West End Vaudeville Company
14th **Aug.** "Ladies and Laughter". Revue.
21st **Aug.** "A Cup of Happiness" by Eden Phillpotts, from the Garrick Theatre.
28th **Aug.** West End Revue Company, headed by Murray, the famous Australian escapologist.
4th **Sept.** Variety, headed by the Five Sherry Brothers and the Three Sherina Sisters.
11th **Sept.** "Pleasure Cruise". Comedy from the Apollo Theatre, with Rene Dress.
18th **Sept.** "The Gipsy Princess" . Musical comedy from the Prince of Wales and Strand Theatres, with Doris Francis.
25th **Sept.** "The Spice of Paris", a fascinating dancing revue in 34 stupendous scenes and 100 people on stage.
2nd **Oct.** "It's You I Want". Farce, playing at Daly's Theatre.
9th **Oct.** "The Casey's in Society". New burlesque in ten scenes of pure, original, clean comedy.
S.15th **Oct.** Al Kendall's Mayfair Band.
16th **Oct.** West End Revue Company, including the Andos family, Japanese entertainers; and Jose A'Beckett, Watford's phenomenal girl violinist.
S.22nd **Oct.** Anton Marenna and his Argentine Gitanos band.
23rd **Oct.** "Fresh Fields" by Ivor Novello. Running at the Criterion Theatre.
S.29th **Oct.** Laurie Page and his Band.
30th **Oct.** "Paris on Parade". Sparkling revue.
S. 5th **Nov.** Edward Bell and his band.
6th **Nov.** West End Vaudeville Company, headed by Maloitz, the Dutch singing telepathist.
S.12th **Nov.** Olly Aston and his 1933 band.
13th **Nov.** "Paris by Night". Exotic revue.
S.19th **Nov.** Band of the London Fire Brigade.

20th **Nov.** West End Modern Vaudeville, headed by Chris Charlton *conjuror to HM King George V.*
S.26th Nov. De Cassin and his gipsy band.
27th Dec. "Magic Nights". A new supreme Wonder Pageant with lions, monkeys, birds, etc. Presented by the Great Carma.
S.3rd Dec. The Luton Band.
4th Dec. "'The Ringer" by Edgar Wallace. Amateur production by the Aldenham Players.
S.10th Dec. Carl Carroll and his rhythm band.
11th Dec. West End Vaudeville Company, including Dan Grey and his rhythm band, also Hammersley & Hunter and company in a comedy sketch.
S.17th Dec. Mexano's Accordion Band
18th Dec. "Cock Crows". Variety bill.
S.24th Dec. Ralph Jeffrey and his Radio Paris band.
26th Dec. "Jack and the Beanstalk"
S.31st Dec. Zaharhoff and his International band.

1934

1st Jan. "The Chocolate Soldier" by Oscar Strauss.
S.7th Jan. Desmonde and his blue rhythm and Hawaiian band.
8th Jan. "Robinson Crusoe".
S.14th Jan. Olly Aston and his 1934 band
15th Jan. "Hullo Laughter". A musical revusical burlesque.
S. 21st Jan. Robert Saunders and his band.
22nd Jan. West End Vaudeville Company.

Forty three weeks Watford Season by the Arthur Gibbons Popular Players:
(N.B. Sunday evening concerts continued until 6th May)

29th Jan. "Thark" by Ben Travers.
5th Feb. "Autumn Crocus" by C.L. Anthony.
12th Feb. "Almost a Honeymoon" by Walter Ellis.
19th Feb. "Eight Bells" by Percy G. Mandley
26th Feb. "Hindle Wakes" by Stanley Houghton.
5th March "Merrie England". Watford Operatic Society.
12th March "The Sign on the Door" by Channing Pollock.
19th March "A Bill of Divorcement" by Clemence Dane.
26th March "The Rotters" by H.F. Matby. Personal appearance of Arthur Gibbons.
2nd April "Eliza Comes to Stay" by H.V. Esmond.
9th April "The Case of the Frightened Lady" by Edgar Wallace.
16th April "Daddy Long Legs" by Jean Webster.
23rd April "Tons of Money" by Will

Evans and Valentine.
30th April "The Land of Promise" by W. Somerset Maugham.
7th May "East Lynne", the evergreen drama.
14th May "Bulldog Drummond" adapted by "Sapper" and Sir Gerald Du Maurier from the famous novel.
21st May "Ambrose Applejohn's Adventure" by Walter Hackett.
28th May "Sixteen" by Aimee and Philip Stuart.
4th June "The Trial of Mary Dugan".
11th June "The Chinese Bungalow" by Marion Osmond and James Corbet.
18th June "Proscenium" by Ivor Novello.
25th June "The Patsey" by Barry Conners.
2nd July "The Barratts of Wimpole Street" by Rudolph Besier.
9th July "Sowing the Wind", Sydney Grundy's Greatest Comedy Drama. Personal appearance of Arthur Gibbons.
16th July "Up in the Air" by Roger Wheeler and Terence Neill.
23rd July "The Man at Six" by Jack Celestine and Jack de Leon.
30th July "Private Room" by Naomi Royde-Smith.
6th Aug. "Are You a Mason?". The World Famous Farcical Comedy.
13th Aug. "The Thief". George Alexander's Famous Comedy-Drama.
20th Aug. "Our Betters" by W. Somerset Maugham.
27th Aug. "The Green Pack". The last thriller by Edgar Wallace.
3rd Sept. "Milestones" by Arnold Bennett and Edward Knoblock.
10th Sept. "Good Morning Bill" by P.G. Wodehouse, the King of Laughter-makers.
17th Sept. "Blackmail" by Charles Bennett.
24th Sept. "Meet the Wife" by Lyn Starling.
1st Oct. "The Luck of the Navy" by Clifford Mills.
S.7th Oc. Sunday Concert with Tommy Hunt and Smiling Billy Mason.
8th Oct. "Sunshine Sisters" by Ivor Novello.
S.14th Oct. Sunday Concert.
15th Oct. "The Midnight Wedding" by Walter Howard.
S 1st Oct. Sunday Concert. Edna Cecil's Royal Accordion Band.
22nd Oct. "Counsel's Opinion" by Gilbert Wakefield.
S 28th Oct. Sunday Concert. Max Swart and his band with Arthur Lavis and Violet, Victoria and Paul Carlyle.
29th Oct. "Apron Strings" by Dorrance Davis.
5th Nov. "The Private Secretary" by Charles Hawtrey.
S.11th Nov. Sunday Concert. Bernard Ash and his wonder band with Little Tommy Mackintosh, the boy wonder vocalist.
12th Nov. "Under Cover" by Roi Cooper Megrew.

S.18th Nov. Sunday Concert. Hal Swain the Canadian Saxophonist
19th Nov. "Old Heidelberg", the romantic story of the student prince.
S.25th Nov. Sunday Concert. Neville Ravell and his Zouave Orchestra and Jack Royce, England's Paul Robeson.
26th Nov. "Nothing but the Truth" by James Montgomery.
S 2nd Dec. Sunday Concert. Alan Selby and his Murray's Club Orchestra.
3rd Dec. West End Vaudeville Company.
S. 9th Dec. Ralph Jeffrey and his Radio Paris band.
10th Dec. West End Vaudeville Company, headed by Anton Dolin, Wendy Toye and supporting dancers.
S.16th Dec. Olly Aston and his 1934 band.
17th Dec. "London Scandals". Revue.
24th Dec. "Red Riding Hood"
S.30th Dec. Ray Novella and his band.
31st Dec. Variety, including Fred Ropner's midgets, animal acts, clowns and acrobats.

1935

Licensee and Manager: David Shenstone
Assistant Stage Manager: Michael Wilding
Musical Director and Hostess: Phyllis Norman-Parker, LRAM.

S.6th Jan. Al Smith and his band.
7th Jan. "Alf's Button", a modern version of Aladdin.
S.13th Jan. Max Seener and his band.
15th Jan. "The Ringer" by Edgar Wallace. *(No performance on Monday 14th Jan.)*

Winifred and Andrew Melville managed the theatre as the Watford Repertory Company until 4th May prior to taking over the full management of the theatre in 1939.

S.20th Jan. Sunday Concert. Zarahoff and his International Band with Sutherland Felce.
21st Jan. "The Late Christopher Bean" by Rene Fauchois (translated by Emlyn Williams). *The play was to have been "Clothes and Woman" but was cancelled due to the indisposition of Miss Dorothy Holmes-Gore.*
S.27th Jan. Sunday Concert. Helen Raymond, the BBC Crooner with Philip Martel and his band, Hilda Meacham -Personality singer, Bart Brady (entertainer), Andre Ledor presents "Music Out of the Air".
28th Jan. "The Drummer" by Evan John, produced by the author.
S.3rd Feb. Max Swart and his band. Neville Sydney and his full supporting company.
4th Feb. "The Nelson Touch" by Neil Grant.
S.10th Feb. Hugo Cavolli and his band.
11th Feb. "Dear Brutus" bu J.M. Barrie.
S.17th Feb. Percy Bush and his famous broadcasting band.

18th **Feb.** "Cock Robin" by Elmer Rice and Philip Barry.

S.24th **Feb.** Dawn Daris and her Radio Rhythm Band

25th **Feb.** "This Woman Business". Ben W. Levy's amusing comedy.

S.3rd **Mar** Norman Long, Sydney James's Band, Barbara Domaire.

4th **Mar** "On the Spot" by Edgar Wallace.

S.10th **Mar** Sunday Concert. The Western Brothers (Kenneth and George). Jessie Wildon's Band and supporting artistes.

11th **Mar** "The Desert Song". Watford Operatic Society.

18th **Mar** "Three for Luck" by Mabel Constanduras.

S.24th **Mar** Fourth "Radio Star" Concert. Bertha Wilmot, Brian Lansbury, Cyril Wheeler's orchestra.

25th **Mar** "Murder on the Second Floor" by Frank Vosper.

S.31st **Mar** Fifth "Radio Star" Concert. Leonard Henry, Phyllis Norman-Parker and her "Qualitone" Band of eleven

1st **April** "The Outsider" by Dorothy Brandon.

S.7th **April** Sixth "Radio Star" Concert. Charles Hayes, Helena Millais, Dorothy Sturdy and her Ladies Band.

8th **April** "The Sport of Kings" by Ian Hay.

S 4th **April** Seventh "Radio Star" Concert. Nora Brightwell and her Ladies Band. Stainless Stephen.

15th **April** "Outward Bound" by Sutton Vans.

S 1st **April** Grand Easter Sunday Concert. Phyllis Norman-Parker and her "Qualitone" band of eleven, Alec McGill and Gwen Vaughan.

22nd **April** "Dangerous Corner" by J.B. Priestley.

29th **April** "Lucky Dip" by Frank Vosper. *Final week of the Watford Repertory Company. Farewell night 4th May.*

6th **May** "Jubility". Revue

13th **May** "Spring Song". Revue.

20th **May** "Life Begins at Clarendon Road". Revue.

27th **May** "East in East". Revue, with the **Western Brothers**.

3rd **June** "America Goes Over". Revue, with the Cole Brothers.

10th **June** "Navy Blues". Revue.

17th **June** "Honi soit qui Watford Palace". Revue, with **Herschel Henlere**.

24th **June** "Honi soit qui Watford Palace" Revue with **Robb Wilton**

1st **July** "Crazy Week" Revue with **Lily Morris**.

8th **July** "Crazy Week" with Claude Dampier and Billie Carlyle.

Donald Edwards and Betty Nelson took leading roles in productions from 15th July. The company was advertised as the Edward Nelson Players from 5th August.

15th **July** "Peg o' My Heart", by J. Hartley Manners.

22nd **July** "The Man in Possession" by J.M. Harwood.

29th **July** "While Parents Sleep" by Anthony Kimmins.

5th **Aug.** "It's a Boy" by Sydney Howard and Leslie Henson.

12th **Aug.** "Loose Ends" by Dion Titherage.

19th **Aug.** "The Cat and the Canary" by John Willard.

26th **Aug.** "Worse Things Happen at Sea" by Keith Winter.

2nd **Sept.** "Brown Sugar" by Lady (Arthur) Lever.

9th **Sept.** "Laburnam Grove" by J.B. Priestley.

16th **Sept.** "The Happy Ending" by Ian Hay.

23rd **Sept.** "Little Women" by Louisa M. Alcott.

30th **Sept.** "High Temperature" by Wilson Collison.

7th **Oct.** "The Letter" by W. Somerset Maugham.

14th **Oct.** "Paddy the Next Best Thing" by W. Gayer Mackay and Robert Ord, from the novel by Gertrude Page.

21st **Oct.** "By Candlelight" adapted by Harry Graham from the German of Siegfried Gever.

28th **Oct.** "The Blindness of Virtue" by Cosmo Hamilton

4th **Nov.** "Mr. Wu" (Matheson Lang's great success). An oriental drama in 3 acts.

11th **Nov.** "Billeted" by F. Tennyson Jesses and H.M. Harwood.

18th **Nov.** "The Passing of the Third Floor Back" by Jerome K. Jerome.

25th **Nov.** "Charley's Aunt" by Brandon Thomas .

2nd **Dec.** "Grumpy" by Horace Hodges and T. Wigney Percyval (For three nights)

5th **Dec.** "The Patsey" by Harry Connors. (Thurs, Fri and Sat.)

9th **Dec.** "The Middle Watch" The Aldenham Players.

16th **Dec.** Grand Variety Bill featuring Les Militaires.

26th **Dec.** "Babes in the Wood"

1936

Licensee and General Manager: David Shenstone

6th **Jan.** Maurice Chester's 1936 Stage Circus.

13th **Jan.** Fred Rapner's Productions "Skylarks". A revue performed by midgets.

20th **Jan.** Jubilee Revels.

27th **Jan.** "Fools and Angels". Revue.

3rd **Feb.** "The Wind and the Rain" by Merton Hodge.

S.9th **Feb.** George Jackley, Doris Palmer and Frank Fletcher and his band.

10th **Feb.** "Ten Minute Alibi" by Anthony Armstrong.

S.16th **Feb.** Haver and Lee, Eddy Bayes, Frank Stewart and his Betta Entertainment from the BBC.

17th **Feb.** "Vintage Wine" Seymour Hick's Great Comedy from the French.

S.23rd **Feb.** Ronald Gourley, Arthur Askey, Raymond de Courcy and his band.

24th **Feb.** "Sweet Aloes" by Jay Mallory.

S. 1st **Mar** Northfleet Silver Band and stars from the George Robey Radio Party.

2nd **Mar** "A Warm Corner" an adapted farce by A. Wimperis and Laurie Wylie.

S.8th **Mar** Special return visit of Natana and his San Romaine Band. Stanley and Young, Bunny Doyle.

9th **Mar** "Rose Marie" Watford Operatic Society.

16th **Mar** "Escape Me Never" by Margaret Kennedy.

S. 22nd **Mar** Stainless Stephen, Richard Hassett, Frank Fletcher and his band.

23rd **Mar** "Full House" by Ivor Novello.

S.29th **Mar** The Four Aces 'The Vocal Orchestra', Eddy Bayes, John Stein and his novelty Tzigane orchestra.

30th **Mar.** "The Two Mrs. Carrolls" by Martin Vale.

S.5th **April** Sutherland Felce, Billie Lockwood and Gordon Whelan. Charles Grossman and his 'Elstree Recorders' orchestra.

6th **April** "The Skin Game" by John Galsworthy.

S.12th **April** Danny Walters and his Rhythm Boys, Ronald Frankau, Nora Williams.

13th **April** "The Best People" by Avery Hopwood and David Grey.

20th **April** "The First Year" by Frank Craven.

27th **April** "Nina" adapted from the German by Bruno Frank.

4th **May** "The Greeks Had a Word for It" by Zoe Akins.

11th **May** "The Monkeys Paw" and "The £12 Look". Two great plays in one evening.

18th **May** "The Unguarded Hour" from the German by Bernard Merivale.

25th **May** "The Family Upstairs" by Harry Delf.

1st **June** "Just Married" by Adelaide Matthews and Anne Nichols.

8th **June** "Over the Hill" by Henriette Brown.

15th **June** "Eliza Comes to Stay" by H.V. Esmond.

22nd **June** "The Jade God" by William E. Barry.

29th **June** "The Last of Mrs. Cheyney" by Frederick Lonsdale.

6th **July** "Tread Softly" by Peter Traill.

13th **July** "Daddy Longlegs" by Jean Webster.

20th **July** "Rope" by Patrick Hamilton.

27th **July** "The Man from Toronto" by Douglas Murray.

A performance of 'The Man from Toronto' was broadcast on London Regional Radio on 16th August

3rd **Aug.** "Tilly of Bloomsbury" by Ian Hay.

10th **Aug.** "Moths" by Ouida.

17th **Aug.** "Yellow Sands" by Eden and

Adelaide Phillpots.
24ᵗʰ Aug. "French Salad" by Max Catto.
31ˢᵗ Aug. "Dusty Ermine" by Neil Grant
7ᵗʰ Sept. "White Cargo" by Leon Gordon
14ᵗʰ Sept. "Her Past" by Frederick Jackson
21ˢᵗ Sept. "Spooks", A new thriller by Robert J. Sherman
28ᵗʰ Sept. "A Little Bit of Fluff" by Walter Ellis.
S.4ᵗʰ Oct. Sunday Concert. The Marie Lloyd Family, Stanford and Taylor, Howard Baker's Astorians.
5ᵗʰ Oct. "Two Seconds" by Elliott Lester. The first production of this play outside America.
S.11ᵗʰ Oct. Sunday Concert. Ronald Frankau, Helen Trix, Jules Adrian and his band.
12ᵗʰ Oct. "The School for Husbands" by Frederick Jackson.
S.18ᵗʰ Oct. Sunday Concert. Lily Morris, Scott Saunders, Paul Clifford and his 'Master Musicians'.
19ᵗʰ Oct. "Potiphar's Wife" by Edgar Middleton.
S.25ᵗʰ Oct. Sunday Concert. Denis O'Neil and Harry Hudson, Bertha Wilmot. The Friary Band (26 performers).
26ᵗʰ Oct. "Love from a Stranger" by Frank Vosper.
S.1ˢᵗ Nov. Sunday Concert. Stainless Stephen, David Jenkins & Suzette Tarri, Alan Green and his band from the Hammersmith Palais deDance.
2ⁿᵈ Nov. "He Walked in Her Sleep".
S.8ᵗʰ Nov. Sunday Concert. Morris Motors Band, Doris Collette, Talbot O'Farrell.
9ᵗʰ Nov. "Miss Smith" by Henry Barnard.
S.15ᵗʰ Nov. Sunday Concert. Phylllis Norman-Parker and her Qualitone Band of Eleven. Ward and Draper, Albert Whelan.
16ᵗʰ Nov. "Twin Beds" by Margaret Mayo.
S.22ⁿᵈ Nov. Sunday Concert. Arthur Askey, Eddy Bayes, Phil Hudson and his Sylvans Band.
23ʳᵈ Nov. "Someone at the Door" (Author not mentioned)
S.29ᵗʰ Nov. Sunday Concert. Rupert Hazel and Elsie Ray, Mario de Pietro, Olly Aston and his Melody Makers.
30ᵗʰ Nov. "Spring Cleaning" by Frederick Lonsdale.
S.6ᵗʰ Dec. Sunday Concert. Haver and Lee, Pat Hyde, Paul Clifford and his 'Master Musicians Band'.
7ᵗʰ Dec. "Private Lives" by Noël Coward.
S.13ᵗʰ Dec. Sunday Concert. Clarkson Rose, Cecil Johnson, John Stein and his Tzigane Orchestra.
14ᵗʰ Dec. "The Dominant Sex" by Michael Egan.
S.20ᵗʰ Dec. Sunday Concert Alec McGill and Gwen Vaughan, Leonard

Henry, Danny Walters and his band from the Chiswick Empire.
26ᵗʰ Dec. "Dick Whittington and his Cat".

1937
11ᵗʰ Jan. "Splinters". Hal Jones and 'Les Rouges et Noires' an all male chorus from France.
S.17ᵗʰ Jan. Ronald Frankau, Olly Aston and his 'Melody Masters'.
18ᵗʰ Jan. "The Astonished Ostrich" by Archie N Menzies. *Advertised as the farewell performance by David Shenstone (Licensee and General Manager).*
25ᵗʰ Jan. Closed for redecoration.
Licensee and General Manager: Donald B. Edwards
Business Manageress: Nora Gordon, Musical Director Jack Hall.
1ˢᵗ Feb. "Peg O' My Heart" by J. Hartley Manners.
S.7ᵗʰ Feb. Andre and his band, Florence Oldham, Stanford and McNaughton.
8ᵗʰ Feb. "Winter Sunshine" by G.A. Thomas.
S.14ᵗʰ Feb. Jack Hart and his band, Dick Henderson, Nora Savage and Jane Wentworth.
15ᵗʰ Feb. "Anthony and Anna" by St.John G. Ervine.
S.21ˢᵗ Feb. Marcus and his band, Kenneth Blain, The Southern Sisters.
22ⁿᵈ Feb. "Sally Who?" by Dion Titheradge.
S.28ᵗʰ Feb. Alf Freid and his band, Geoffrey Briggs, Ann Penn.
1ˢᵗ Mar "The Elusive Mr.Yen".
S.7ᵗʰ Mar Edie Mendoza and his Rhythm Swingers, Stanley and Young, Tessie O'Shea.
8ᵗʰ Mar "The Student Prince". Watford Operatic Society.
15ᵗʰ Mar "Mademoiselle" by Jacques Deval.
S.21ˢᵗ Mar Paul Clifford and his Master Musicians, Vic Oliver, Edith Price.
22ⁿᵈ Mar "The Rosary" by Edward E. Ross.
S.28ᵗʰ Mar The Roosters (The Greatest Party of All), Sutherland Felce.
29ᵗʰ Mar "The Gold Diggers" by Avery Hopwood.
S.4ᵗʰ April Paul Stein and his Novelty Tzigane Orchestra, Albert Whelan, Mary Rose.
5ᵗʰ April "Busman's Honeymoon" by D.L. Sayers and M. St.Clare Byrne.
S.11ᵗʰ April Frank Stewart and his band, Peggy Cochrane, Gordon Whelan.
12ᵗʰ April "Little Miss Bluebeard" by Avery Hopwood.
19ᵗʰ April "Aloma", a colourful tale of the South Seas.
26ᵗʰ April "Heart's Content" by W. Chetham Strode.
3ʳᵈ May "The Rotters" by H.F. Maltby. *(Note in the programme - The King's Speech will be broadcast throughout the theatre on Wednesday 12ᵗʰ May)*
10ᵗʰ May "An Apple a Day" by Ralph Timberlake.
17ᵗʰ May "Ladies' Night" by Avery

Hopwood.
24ᵗʰ May "Interference" by Harold Dearden and Roland Pertwee.
31ˢᵗ May "The Shadow" by H.F. Maltby.
7ᵗʰ June "Glass Houses" by Walter Ellis.
14ᵗʰ June "Marigold" by Allen Harker and F.R. Pryor.
21ˢᵗ June "It's You I Want" adapted from the French, Seymour Hick's Rollicking Farce.
28ᵗʰ June "Keepers of Youth" by Arnold Ridley.
5ᵗʰ July "Fallen Angels" by Noël Coward.
12ᵗʰ July "My Old Dutch" by Arthur Shirley and Albert Chevalier.
19ᵗʰ July "Fred E. Rayne's North Regional Follies, the Famous Broadcasting Show.
26ᵗʰ July "Kit Walter's' Crazy Follies", the Concert Party de Luxe, with its own stage band.
2ⁿᵈ Aug. "Nightie Night" by Martha M. Stanley and Adelaide Matthews.
9ᵗʰ Aug. "Wise Tomorrow" by Stephen Powys.
16ᵗʰ Aug. "The Ruined Lady" by Ann Wynn.
23ʳᵈ Aug. "And the Music Stopped" by Noël Scott.
30ᵗʰ Aug. "Lord Babs" by Keble Howard.
6ᵗʰ Sept. "The Last Coupon" by Ernest A. Bryan.
13ᵗʰ Sept. "Tovarich" by Jacques Deval, adapted by Robert Sherwood.
20ᵗʰ Sept. "Devonshire Cream" by Eden Phillpotts.
27ᵗʰ Sept. "Love on the Dole" by Arthur Greenwood.
4ᵗʰ Oct. "Lass o' Laughter" by Edith Carter and Ian Marriott Watson
11ᵗʰ Oct. "Late Night Final" by Louis Weitzenkorn.
18ᵗʰ Oct. "Three for Luck" by Mabel Constanduros.
25ᵗʰ Oct. "To Have and to Hold" by Lionel Brown.
1ˢᵗ Nov. "While Parents Sleep" by Anthony Kimmins.
8ᵗʰ Nov. "Journey's End" by R.C. Sherriff.
15ᵗʰ Nov. "Escape Me Never" by Margaret Kennedy.
22ⁿᵈ Nov. "The Ghost Train" by Arnold Ridley.
29ᵗʰ Nov. "Three Wise Fools" by Austin Strong.
6ᵗʰ Dec. "High Temperature" by Avery Hopwood and Laddie Cliff.
13ᵗʰ Dec. "Brown Sugar" by Lady (Arthur) Lever.
20ᵗʰ Dec. "Cinderella". Amateur production by the Star School of Dancing.
27ᵗʰ Dec. "Alice in Wonderland" by Lewis Carroll adapted by William Sherwood.

1938
Licensees: New Watford Productions Ltd.
Directors: Kenneth Duffield (Managing

Director), E.A. Gilham, O.T. Hedges, O.S. Marshall, C.E. Robinson.
Chairman and Secretary: A.E. Millett
Business Manager: Nora Gordon.
Orchestra under the direction of Jack Hall.

3rd **Jan.** "Robinson Crusoe".
10th **Jan.** Derrickson-Brown Road Show.
17th **Jan.** "Casey's Court".
24th **Jan.** The Ridgeway Parade of 1938.
31st **Jan.** "Sunshine Sally"
7th **Feb.** *Closed.*
14th **Feb.** "The Amazing Dr. Clitterhouse" by Barrie Lyndoh.
21st **Feb.** "Tonight at 8.30" with Ian Fleming.
"Ways and Means", "Fumed Oak" and "Hands Across the Sea".
28th **Feb.** "Housemaster" by Ian Hay.
7th **March** "Victoria and Her Hussar". Watford Operatic Society.
14th **March** "Queer Cargo" by Noël Langley.
21st **March** "Pride and Prejudice" by Helen Jerome.
28th **March** "Living Dangerously" by Reginald Simpson and Frank Gregory.
4th **April** "Intimate Relations" by C. Stafford Dickens.
11th **April** "Double Error" by John Lee Thompson.
18th **April** "The Late Christopher Bean" by Emlyn Williams.
25th **April** "Night Must Fall" by Emlyn Williams.
2nd **May** "Aren't Men Beasts" by Vernon Sylvaine.
9th **May** "Fresh Fields" by Ivor Novello.
16th **May** "Lover's Leap" by Philip Johnson.
23rd **May** "Candida" by Bernard Shaw.
30th **May** "Black Limelight" by Gordon S. Sherry.
6th **June** "Spring Tide" by J.B. Priestley and George Billam.
13th **June** "The Three Pigeons" by Anthony Armstrong and Roland Crossley, with Donald Wolfit and Isla Bardi.
20th **June** "Eden End" by J.B. Priestley.
27th **June** "Mile Away Murder" by Anthony Armstrong.
4th **July** "Quinneys'" by H.A. Vachell.
11th **July** "Autumn" by Margaret Kennedy and Gregory Ratoff.
18th **July** "The Man Who Changed His Name" by Edgar Wallace.
25th **July** "London Wall" by John Van Druten.
1st **Aug.** "Tell Me the Truth" by Leslie Howard.
8th **Aug.** "The Joker" by Noël Scott.
15th **Aug.** "Bird in Hand" by John Drinkwater.
22nd **Aug.** "For the Love of Mike" by H.F. Maltby.
29th **Aug.** "Suspect" by Rex Judd.
5th **Sept.** "Mrs. Gorringe's Necklace" by Hubert Henry Davies.
12th **Sept.** "The Green Pack" by Edgar Wallace.

19th **Sept.** "The Whole Town's Talking" by John Enerson and Anita Loos.
26th **Sept.** "The Magic Cupboard" by Percy Walsh.
3rd **Oct.** "I Killed the Count" by Alec Coppell.
10th **Oct.** "Young Woodley" by John Van Druten.
17th **Oct.** "Third Time Lucky" by Arnold Ridley.
24th **Oct.** "Lucky Dip" by Frank Vosper.
31st **Oct.** "Whiteoaks" by Mazo De La Roche.
7th **Nov.** "The Shining Hour" by Keith Winter.
14th **Nov.** "George and Margaret" by Gerald Savory.
21st **Nov.** "Time and the Conways" by J.B. Priestley.
28th **Nov.** "Comedienne" by Ivor Novello.
5th **Dec.** ""Black Swans" by Geoffrey Kerr.
12th **Dec.** "Yes and No" by Kenneth Horne.
19th **Dec.** "Canaries Sometimes Sing" by Frederick Lonsdale.
26th **Dec.** "Aladdin" by Margaret Carter. The Star Amateur Musical Comedy and Pantomime Society.

1939

2nd **Jan.** "Babes in the Wood"
16th **Jan.** "Lilac Time". Music by Franz Schubert, with Darroll Richards, Rite Mackay, Edgar Owen, Sinclair Cotter. (A Leon Underwood Production).
23rd **Jan.** "Intrigue" by Walter Hackett.
30th **Jan.** "Too Young to Marry" by Martin Flavin (Adapted by Emile Littler).
6th **Feb.** "George and Margaret" by Gerald Savory.
13th **Feb.** "Square Crooks" by James P. Judge.
20th **Feb.** "Jane Eyre" by Helen Jerome - from the novel by Charlotte Bronte.
27th **Feb.** "I Have Been Here Before" by J.B. Priestley.
6th **March** "Show Boat" Watford Operatic Society.
13th **March** "Touch Wood" by Dodie Smith. *First production under the direction of the Melvilles*
20th **March** "For Services Rendered" by Somerset Maugham.
27th **March** "Pygmalion" by George Bernard Shaw.
3rd **April** "Outward Bound" by Sutton Vane.
10th **April** "Death on the Table" by Guy Beauchamp and Michael Pertwee.
17th **April** "People in Love" by Arthur Reid.
24th **April** "The Creaking Chair" by Allene Tupper Wilkes.
1st **May** "Hyde Park Corner" by Walter Hackett.
8th **May** "Recipe for Murder" by Arnold Ridley .
15th **May** "Bulldog Drummond Hits Out" by "Sapper" and Gerald Fairlie.

22nd **May** "Double Door" by Elizabeth McFadden.
29th **May** "Lot's Wife" by Peter Blackmore.
5th **June** "Poison Pen" by Richard Llewellyn.
12th **June** "Call it a Day" by Dodie Smith.
19th **June** "The Wind and the Rain" by Merton Hodge.
26th **June** "To What Red Hell" by Percy Robinson.
3rd **July** "The Rising Generation" by Wyn Weaver and Laura Leycester.
8th **July** Matinee *An Amateur Variety show in aid of the Thetis (submarine) Fund.*
10th **July** "The Terror" by Edgar Wallace.
17th **July** "Storm in a Teacup" by James Bridie.
24th **July** "Arms and the Man" by George Bernard Shaw.
31st **July** "Frankenstein" by Peggy Webling.
Licensee and General Manager: Andrew Melville. The Melville Players.
7th **Aug.** "Private Lives" by Noël Coward.
14th **Aug.** "They Fly by Twilight" by Paul Dornhurst.
21st **Aug.** "Polly with a Past" by George Middleton and Guy Bolton.
28th **Aug.** "Ask Beccles" by Cyril Campion and Edward Dignon.
4th **Sept.** *Closed* "Baby Mine" had been advertised.
11th **Sept.** "Baby Mine" by Margaret Mayo.
18th **Sept.** "Hay Fever" by Noël Coward.
25th **Sept.** "High Temperature" by Avery Hopwood and Laddie Cliff.
2nd **Oct.** "French Without Tears" by Terence Rattigan.
9th **Oct.** "Sweet Aloes" by Jay Mallory.
16th **Oct.** "French Leave" by Reginald Berkeley.
23rd **Oct.** "Goodness, How Sad" by Robert Morley.
30th **Oct.** "The Barretts of Wimpole Street" by Rudolph Besier.
6th **Nov.** "The Sport of Kings" by Ian Hay.
13th **Nov.** "Tony Draws a Horse" by Lesley Storm.
20th **Nov.** "When We Are Married" by J.B. Priestley.
27th **Nov.** "The Ware Case" by George Pleydell.
4th **Dec.** "Design for Living" by Noël Coward.
11th **Dec.** "The Man in Possession" by H.M. Harwood.
26th **Dec.** "Beauty and the Beast" by Walter and Frederick Melville. This programme also stated that "The theatre is disinfected throughout with Jeyes Fluid".

1940

5th **Feb.** "Theatre Royal" by Edna Ferber and George Kaufmen
12th **Feb.** "Grouse in June" by N.C.

Hunter.

19th Feb. "While Parents Sleep" by Anthony Kimmins.

26th Feb. "Robert's Wife" by St. John Ervine.

4th March "Rookery Nook" by Ben Travers.

11th March "Pygmalion" by George Bernard Shaw.

18th March "If Four Walls Told" by Edward Percy.

25th March "Three Men on a Horse" by J.C. Holm and George Abbott.

1st April "White Cargo" by Leon Gordon.

8th April "Little Ladyship" by Ian Hay.

15th April ""A Murder Has Been Arranged" by Emlyn Williams.

22nd April "Maid of the Mountains". Watford Operatic Society.

29th April "The Hardy Family" by Aurania Rouvel and Emile Littler.

6th May "The Astonished Ostrich" by Archie N. Menzies.

13th May "Clive of India" by W.P. Lipscombe and R.J. Minney.

20th May "Saloon Bar" by Frank Harvey Jnr.

27th May "The Bishop Misbehaves" by Frederick Jackson.

3rd June "Dear Octopus" by Dodie Smith.

10th June "The Torch-Bearers" by George Kelly.

17th June "Mary Rose" by J.M. Barrie.

24th June "The Last of Mrs. Cheyney" by Frederick Lonsdale.

1st July "The Improper Duchess" by J.B. Fagan.

8th July "Lot's Wife" by Peter Blackmore.

15th July "Quiet Wedding" by Esther McCracken.

22nd July ""George and Margaret" by Gerald Savory.

29th July "Happy Circle" - a new song and laugh show for a summer season. (A complete change of programme weekly)

19th Aug. "Happy Circle" - a new song and laugh show. Staged and produced by Eddie Henderson and Andrew Melville.

28th Oct. "Private Lives" by Noël Coward.

4th Nov. "Fresh Fields" by Ivor Novello.

11th Nov. "Rebecca" by Daphne Du Maurier. (The Melville Players were the first repertory company to perform this play.

18th Nov. "French Without Tears" by Terence Rattigan.

25th Nov. "Robert's Wife" by St. John Ervine.

2nd Dec. "The School for Husbands" by Frederick Jackson.

9th Dec. "The Light of Heart" by Emlyn Williams.

16th Dec. "A Party for Christmas" by Norman C. Hunter. Comedy.

26th Dec. "Queen of Hearts" by Walter and Frederick Melville.

1941

3rd Feb. "The Rising Generation" by Wyn Weaver and Laura Leycester.

10th Feb. "Gas Light" by Patrick Hamilton.

17th Feb. "Nothing But the Truth" by James Montgomery.

24th Feb. "Dangerous Corner" by J.B. Priestley.

3rd March "See Naples and Die" by Elmer Rice.

10th March "Call it a Day" by Dodie Smith.

17th March "Night Must Fall" by Emlyn Williams.

24th March "Thark" by Ben Travers.

31st March "French for Love" by Marguerite Steen and Derek Patmore.

7th April "I Have Been Here Before" by J.B. Priestley.

14th April "While Parents Sleep" by Anthony Kimmins.

21st April "The Importance of Being Ernest" by Oscar Wilde.

28th April "Soring Cleaning" by Frederick Lonsdale.

5th May "The Rose Without a Thorn" by Clifford Bax.

12th May "Room for Two" by Gilbert Wakefield. A farcical comedy.

19th May "White Oaks" by Mazo de la Roche.

26th May "Tovarich" by Jacques Deval.

2nd June "When We Are Married" by J.B. Priestley.

9th June "Love From a Stranger" by Frank Vosper.

16th June "Bluebeard's Eighth Wife" by Arthur Wimperis (from the French by Alfred Savoir).

23rd June "Housemaster" by Ian Hay.

30th June "They Walk Alone" by Max Catto

7th July "Arms and the.Man" by George Bernard Shaw.

14th July "By Candle Light" adapted by Harry Graham from the play by Siegfried Geyer.

21st July "The Late Christopher Bean" by Emlyn Williams.

28th July "Heroes Don't Care" by Margot Neville.

4th Aug. "Tony Draws a Horse" by Lesley Storm.

11th Aug. "Love on the Dole" by Ronald Gow and Walter Greenwood.

18th Aug. "The Little Dog Laughed" by Geoffrey Thomas.

25th Aug. "Spring Tide" by George Billam and J.B. Priestley.

1st Sept. "White Cargo" by Leon Gordon

8th Sept. "Indoor Fireworks" by Arthur Macrae.

15th Sept. "Design for Living" by Noël Coward.

22nd Sept. "Berkeley Square" by John L. Balderson in collaboration with J.C. Squire.

29th Sept. "The Best People" by David Grey and Avery Hopwood.

6th Oct. "Young Madame Conti" by Bruno Frank, Hubert Griffith and Benn

Levy.

13th Oct. "Hay Fever" by Noël Coward.

20th Oct. "The Barretts of Wimpole Street" by Rudolph Besier.

27th Oct. "The Patsy" by Barry Conners.

3rd Nov. "Once a Crook" by Evadne Price and Ken Attiwell.

10th Nov. "High Temperature" by Avery Hopwood and Laddie Cliff.

17th Nov. "Jane Eyre" by Helen Jerome from the novel by Charlotte Bronte.

24th Nov. "I Lived With You" by Ivor Novello.

1st Dec. "The Blue Goose" by Peter Blackmore.

8th Dec. "French Leave" by Reginald Berkeley.

15th Dec. "It's a Boy" by Austin Melford.

26th Dec. "Puss in Boots"

1942

2nd Feb. "Rope" by Patrick Hamilton.

S.8th Feb. Home Guard All-Star Variety Concert. (All profits to Comfort Fund 23rd Company, 10th Herts Battalion Home Guard).

9th Feb. "Painted Sparrows" by Guy Paxton and Edward V. Hoile.

16th Feb. "Cottage to Let" by Geoffrey Kerr.

23rd Feb. "Saint Joan" by George Bernard Shaw.

2nd March "Storm in a Tea Cup" by James Bridie.

9th March "The Squall" by Jean Bart.

16th March "Even Stephen" by Howard Irving Young.

23rd March "Bird in Hand" by John Drinkwater.

30th March "People at Sea" by J.B. Priestley.

6th April "George and Margaret" by Gerald Savory

13th April "On the Spot" by Edgar Wallace.

20th April "The Flashing Stream " by Charles Morgan.

27th April "Good Men Sleep at Home" by Walter Ellis.

4th May "Jupiter Laughs" by Dr. A.J. Cronin (Creator of Dr. Finlay).

11th May "The Wrong Man" by Daniel N. Rubin.

18th May "Cornelius" by J.B. Priestley.

25th May "Charley's Aunt" by Brandon Thomas.

1st June "Little Women" adapted for the stage by Marian de Forest from the book by Louisa M. Alcott.

8th June "Evacuation Peace" by Margaret Macleod.

15th June "Worth a Million" by Vernon Sylvaine.

22nd June "I Killed the Count" by Alec Coppel.

29th June "The Young Idea" by Noël Coward.

6th July "Hyde Park Corner" by Walter Hackett.

13th July "Strange Orchestra" by

Rodney Ackland.
20th **July** "Yellow Sands" by Eden and Adelaide Philpotts.
27th **July** "Black Limelight" by Gordon Sherry.
3rd **Aug.** "Tons of Money" by Will Evans and Valentine.
10th **Aug.** "The Trial of Mary Dugan" An Outstanding Attraction.
17th **Aug.** "Ladies Into Action" by Ivor Novello.
24th **Aug.** "Distinguished Gathering" by James Parish.
31st **Aug.** "Sweet Nell of Old Drury" by Paul Kester.
7th **Sept.** "Without a Prince" by Philip King.
14th **Sept.** "Interference" by Roland Pertwee and Harold Dearden.
21st **Sept.** "The Rotters" by H.F. Maltby.
28th **Sept.** "Hobson's Choice" by Harold Brighouse.
5th **Oct.** "You Can't Take it With You" by George S. Kaufman and Moss Hart.
12th **Oct.** "Whistling in the Dark" by Laurence Gross and Edward C. Carpenter.
19th **Oct.** "Baby Mine" by Margaret Mayo.
26th **Oct.** "Death Takes a Holiday" – Special attraction.
2nd **Nov.** "Sweet Aloes" by Jay Mallory.
9th **Nov.** "The Letter" the sensational play by W. Somerset Maugham.
16th **Nov.** "Billeted" by F. Tennyson Jesse and H.M. Harwood – Brilliant Comedy.
23rd **Nov.** "Camille". Translation of Alexander Dumas' masterpiece "The Lady of the Camellia's" by Edith Reynolds and Nigel Playfair.
30th **Nov.** "Spring Meeting" by J.M. Farrell and John Perry.
7th **Dec.** "Ladies in Retirement" by Edward Percy and Reginald Denham.
14th **Dec.** "Fallen Angels" by Noël Coward.
26th **Dec.** "Dick Whittington".

1943
1st **Feb.** "The Wind and the Rain" by Merton Hodge.
8th **Feb.** "The Bread Winner" by W. Somerset Maugham.
15th **Feb.** "The Light of Heart" by Emlyn Williams.
22nd **Feb.** "The First Mrs. Fraser" by St. John Ervine.
1st **March** "It's a Wise Child" by Larry E. Johnson.
9th **March** "Viceroy Sarah" by Norman Ginsbury.
15th **March** "Full House" by Ivor Novello.
22nd **March** "Biography" by S.N. Behrman.
29th **March** "Other People's Houses" by Lynne Dexter.
5th **April** "The Two Mrs. Carrolls" by Martin Vale.
12th **April** "Quiet Wedding" by Esther McCracken.

19th **April** "The Passing of the Third Floor Back" by Jerome K. Jerome.
26th **April** "He Walked in Her Sleep" by Norman Cannon.
3rd **May** "Gas Light" by Patrick Hamilton.
10th **May** Noël Coward Week - Three one act plays - "Fumed Oak", "Family Album" and "Red Peppers".
17th **May** "The Family Upstairs" by Harry Delf.
The programme shows that from 17th May the theatre was under the management of Winifred Melville.
24th **May** "The Corn is Green" by Emlyn Williams.
31st **May** "Ma's Bit o' Brass" by Ronald Gow.
7th **June** "Doctor Brent's Household" by Edward Percy.
14th **June** "Fair and Warmer" by Avery Hopwood.
21st **June** "Thunder Rock" by Robert Ardrey.
28th **June** "Mary's Other Husband" by Larry E. Johnson.
5th **July** "Candida" by George Bernard Shaw.
12th **July** "No Time for Comedy" by S.N. Behrman.
19th **July** "Grandpa Sees it Through" by John Taylor.
26th **July** "Rebecca" by Daphne Du Maurier.
2nd **Aug.** "The Bishop Misbehaves" by Frederick Jackson.
9th **Aug.** "Eliza Comes to Stay" by H.V. Esmond.
16th **Aug.** "The Shining Hour" by Keith Winter.
23rd **Aug.** "Jam Today" by Dennis Waldock and Roger Burford.
30th **Aug.** "To Have and to Hold" by Lionel Brown.
6th **Sept.** "Love in a Mist" by Kenneth Horne.
13th **Sept.** "Murder Without Crime" by J. Lee Thompson.
20th **Sept.** "Skylark" by Samson Raphaelson.
27th **Sept.** "Behold We Live" by John Van Druten.
4th **Oct.** "Lot's Wife" by Peter Blackmore.
11th **Oct.** "Suspect" by Edward Percy and Reginal Denham.
18th **Oct.** "Mother Be Good" by Max Murray.
25th **Oct.** "Men in Shadow" by Mary Haley Bell (Lady [John] Mills)
1st **Nov.** "Square Pegs" by Lionel Brown.
8th **Nov.** "Lifeline" by Norman Armstrong.
15th **Nov.** "Just Married" by Adelaide Matthews and Anne Nichols.
22nd **Nov.** "The Little Foxes" by Lillian Hellman.
29th **Nov.** "The Good Young Man" by Kenneth Horne.
6th **Dec.** "Play With Fire" by Edward Percy.
13th **Dec.** "The Whole Town's Talking"

by John Emerson and Anita Loos.
27th **Dec.** "Jack and the Beanstalk"

1944
31st **Jan.** "Nothing but the Truth" by James Montgomery.
7th **Feb.** "Grumpy" by Horace Hodges and T. Wigney Percyval.
14th **Feb.** "Theatre Royal" by Edna Ferber and George Kaufman.
21st **Feb.** "The Fur Coat" by A.G. Macdonell.
28th **Feb.** "The Rose Without a Thorn" by Clifford Bax.
6th **March** "The Middle Watch" by Ian Hay and Stephen King Hall.
13th **March** "Hawk Island" by Howard Irving Young.
20th **March** "Private Lives" by Noël Coward.
27th **March** "Kind Lady" by Edward Chodorov.
3rd **April** "The Peaceful Inn" by Denis Ogden.
10th **April** "Daddy-Long-Legs" by Jean Webster.
17th **April** "The Man in Dark Glasses" by Mabel L. Tyrrell.
24th **April** "The Case of the Frightened Lady" by Edgar Wallace.
1st **May** "Fresh Fields" by Ivor Novello.
8th **May** "Living Room" by Esther McCracken.
15th **May** "The Man Who Came to Dinner" by George B. Kaufman and Moss Hart.
22nd **May** "Double Door" – a new kind of thriller by Elizabeth McFadden.
29th **May** "Tilly of Bloomsbury" by Ian Hay.
5th **June** "Third Party Risk" by Gilbert Lennox and Gisela Ashley.
12th **June** "When We Are Married" by J.B. Priestley.
19th **June** "Lottie Dundass" by Enid Bagnold.
26th **June** "Sleeping Out" by Walter Ellis.
3rd **July** "Love from a Stranger" by Frank Vosper.
10th **July** "Her Past". A comedy in three acts by Alice Delysia.
17th **July** "Strangers Road" by W. Chetham Strode.
24th **July** "They Walk Alone" by Max Catto.
31st **July** "Polly Wish a Past" by George Middleton and Guy Bolton.
7th **Aug.** "Tony Draws a Horse" by Lesley Storm.
14th **Aug.** "Watch on the Rhine" by Lillian Hellman.
21st **Aug.** "Charity Begins…." By Ireland Wood.
28th **Aug.** "Death on the Table" by Guy Beauchamp and Michael Pertwee.
4th **Sept.** "Libel" by Edward Wooll.
11th **Sept.** "This Time It's Love" by Louis Verneuill.
18th **Sept.** "Dear Brutus" by J.M. Barrie.
25th **Sept.** "Blithe Spirit" by Noël Coward.

2nd Oct. "Winter Sunshine" by G.A. Thomas.

9th Oct. "The Man Who Changed His Name" by Edgar Wallace.

16th Oct. "The Chinese Bungalow" by Marian Osmond and James Corbet.

23rd Oct. "The Torch Bearers" by George Kelly.

30th Oct. "The Doctor's Dilemma" by George Bernard Shaw.

6th Nov. "The Best People" by David Grey and Avery Hopwood.

13th Nov. "Indian Summer" by Lionel Brown.

20th Nov. "Whiteoaks" by Mazo de la Roche.

27th Nov. "The First Year" by Frank Craven.

4th Dec. "The House of Jeffreys" by Russell Thorndike.

11th Dec. "The Rising Generation" by Wyn Weaver and Laura Leycester.

26th Dec. "Robinson Crusoe".

1945

29th Jan. "Lover's Leap" by Philip Johnson.

5th Feb. "Jupiter Laughs" by Dr. A.J. Cronin.

12th Feb. "A Soldier for Christmas" by Regina Beckwith.

19th Feb. "The Outside" by Dorothy Brandon.

26th Feb. "The Improper Duchess" by James Bernard Fagan.

5th March "They Came to a City" by J.B. Priestley.

12th March "My Mother Had Three Sons by Richard Sargent.

19th March "Claudia" by Rose Franken.

26th March "Outward Bound" by Sutton Vane.

2nd April "When Knights Were Bold" by Charles Marlowe.

9th April "This Happy Breed" by Noël Coward.

16th April "Young Madame Conti", adapted by Benn Levy and Hubert Griffith from the play by Bruno Frank.

23rd April "Residents Only" by Alexander Gordon and James Pratt.

30th April "The Barretts of Wimpole Street" by Rudolph Besier.

7th May "Bed Without Breakfast" by Stanley Russell and Allan Barnes.

14th May "Even Stephen" by Howard Irving Young.

21st May "What Happened to Jones" by George H. Broadhurst.

28th May "Without Witness" by Anthony Armstrong and Harold Simpson.

4th June "Acacia Avenue" by Mabel and Denis Constanduros.

11th June "This Was a Woman" by Joan Morgan.

18th June "Jane Steps Out" by Kenneth Horne.

25th June "After the Dance" by Terence Rattigan.

2nd July "The Naughty Wife" by Fred. Jackson.

9th July "The Morning Star" by Emlyn Williams.

16th July "High Temperature" by Avery Hopwood and Laddie Cliff.

23rd July "Mr. Wu" by Harold Owen and H.M. Vernon.

30th July "Children to Bless You" by G. Sheila Donisthorpe.

"Children to Bless You! The last programme in the collection to show Winifred as sole manager."

6th Aug. "Are You a Mason?" , adapted by Emanuel Lederer.

13th Aug. "Wuthering Heights" by John Davison.

20th Aug. "Snobbery with Violence" by Mackenzie Usill.

27th Aug. "White Cargo" by Leon Gordon.

3rd Sept. "Apron Strings" by Dorrance Davis.

10th Sept. "Ten Little Niggers" by Agatha Christie.

17th Sept. "Eve" by Lionel Brown.

24th Sept. "Flare Path" by Terence Rattigan.

1st Oct. "Home and Beauty" by W. Somerset Maugham.

8th Oct. "This is My Life" by R.L. Delderfield and Basil Thomas.

15th Oct. "The Tolerant Husband" by Dudley Harcourt and Elena Cleary-Fox.

22nd Oct. "Uncle Harry" by Thomas Job.

29th Oct. "How Are They at Home" by J.B. Priestley.

5th Nov. "The Price of Wisdom" by Lionel Brown.

12th Nov. "Aren't We All" by Frederick Lonsdale.

19th Nov. "The Creaking Chair" by Allene Tupper Wilkes.

26th Nov. "Wasn't it Odd?" by Kenneth Horne.

3rd Dec. "A Murder Has Been Arranged" by Emlyn Williams.

10th Dec. "Flat to Let" by Arthur Macrea.

17th Dec. *Theatre closed for one week.*

26th Dec. "Cinderella".

1946

4th Feb. "While Parents Sleep" by Anthony Kimmins.

11th Feb. "A Cuckoo in the Nest" by Ben Travers.

18th Feb. "Dangerous Corner" by J.B. Priestley.

25th Feb. "Fountain of Youth" by Lance Hamilton.

4th March "Another Love Story" by Frederick Lonsdale.

11th March "Rebel Maid". Watford Operatic Society.

18th March "You Never Can Tell" by George Bernard Shaw.

25th March "Art and Mrs. Bottle" by Benn W. Levy.

1st April "Rope" by Patrick Hamilton.

8th April "Great Day" by Lesley Storm.

15th April "I Have Been Here Before" by J.B. Priestley .

22nd April "A Little Bit of Fluff" by

Walter Ellis.

29th April "Pink String and Sealing Wax" by Roland Pertwee.

6th May "French for Love" by Marguerite Steen and Derek Patmore.

13th May "And the Music Stopped" by Noel Scott.

20th May "There's Always Tomorrow" by Lionel Brown.

27th May "The Last of Mrs. Cheyney" by Frederick Lonsdale.

3rd June "Quiet Wedding" by Esther McCracken.

10th June "Quiet Week-end" by Esther McCracken.

17th June "Laura" by Vera Caspary and George Skylar.

24th June "Housemaster" by Ian Hay

1st July "The Fake" by Frederick Lonsdale.

8th July "While the Sun Shines" by Terence Rattigan (?).

15th July "A Man About the House" by John Perry.

22nd July "Good Men Sleep at Home" by Walter Ellis.

29th July "The Wind of Heaven" by Emlyn Williams.

5th Aug. "Blythe Spirit" by Noël Coward.

12th Aug. "The Police Are Anxious" by James Parrish.

19th Aug. "Marigold" by Allen Harker and F.R. Pryor

26th Aug. "The Crime of Margaret Foley" by Percy Robinson and Terence de Marney

2nd Sept. "Cut for Partners" by Lionel Brown.

9th Sept. "Duet for Two Hands" by Mary Hayley Bell.

16th Sept. "Bird in Hand" by John Drinkwater.

23rd Sept. "I Killed the Count" by Alec Coppel.

30th Sept. "The Druid's Rest" by Emlyn Williams.

7th Oct. "Autumn" by Margaret Kennedy and Gregory Ratoff.

14th Oct. "Young Mrs, Barrington" by Warren Chetham Strode.

21st Oct. "Hobson's Choice" by Harold Brighouse.

28th Oct. "Give Me Yesterday" by Edward Percy and Reginald Denham.

4th Nov. "Tomorrow the World" by James Gow and Arnaud D'Usseau.

11th Nov. "We Laugh and Live" by Edwin Henderson.

18th Nov. "Jane Eyre" by Dorothy Brandon, adapted from the novel by Charlotte Bronte.

25th Nov. "Almost a Honeymoon" by Walter W. Ellis.

2nd Dec. "Error of the Moon" by Joyce Harwood, in collaboration with Ferdy Mayne.

9th Dec. "Sweet Aloes" by Jay Mallory.

26th Dec. "Babes in the Wood".

1947

3rd Feb. "George and Margaret" by Gerald Savory.

10th **Feb.** "The Ghost Train" by Arnold Ridley.
17th **Feb.** "The Years Between" by Daphne Du Maurier.
24th **Feb.** "Ladies in Retirement" by Edward Percy and Reginald Denham.
3rd **March** "Payment Deferred" by Jeffery Dell.
10th **March** "The Vagabond King". Watford Operatic Society.
17th **March** "Fit For Heroes" by Harold Brooke and Kay Bannerman.
24th **March** "The Hasty Heart" by John Patrick.
31st **March** "Frieda" by Ronald Miller.
7th **April** "Is Your Honeymoon Really Necessary" by E.V. Tidmarsh.
14th **April** "Laburnum Grove" by J.B. Priestley.
21st **April** "The Importance of Being Ernest" by Oscar Wilde.
28th **April** "The Sacred Flame" by W. Somerset Maugham.
5th **May** "The Man in Possession" by H.M. Harwood.
12th **May** "No Medals" by Esther McCracken.
19th **May** "Murder on the Second Floor".
26th **May** "The Private Secretary" by Charles Hawtry.
2nd **June** "The Gleam" by Warren Chetham Strode.
9th **June** "The Dover Road" by A.A. Milne.
16th **June** "The Silver Cord" by Sidney Howard.
23rd **June** "The Farmer's Wife" by Eden Philpotts.
30th **June** "Portrait in Black" by Ivan Goff and Ben Roberts.
7th **July** "This Land of Ours" by Lionel Brown.
14th **July** "Petticoat Influence" by Neil Grant.
21st **July** "The Amazing Dr. Clitterhouse" by Barrie Lyndon.
28th **July** "Desert Highways" by J.B. Priestley.
4th **Aug.** "Madame Louise" by Vernon Sylvaine.
11th **Aug.** "Lady from Edinburgh" by Aimee Stuart.
18th **Aug.** "Arsenic and Old Lace" by Joseph Kesselring.
25th **Aug.** "And No Birds Sing" by Jenny Laird and John Fernald.
1st **Sept.** "Lady Frederick" by W. Somerset Maugham.
8th **Sept.** "The Squall" by Jean Bart.
15th **Sept.** "Yellow Sands" by Eden and Adelaide Philpotts.
22nd **Sept.** "The Circle" by W. Somerset Maugham.
29th **Sept.** "Indoor Fireworks" by Arthur Macrae.
6th **Oct.** "The Young Idea by Noël Coward.
13th **Oct.** "We Proudly Present" by Ivor Novello.
20th **Oct.** "The Missing Years" by Leslie Sands.
27th **Oct.** "Fools Rush In" by Kenneth

Horne.
3rd **Nov.** "See How They Run" by Philip King.
10th **Nov.** "Grand National Night" by Dorothy and Campbell Christie.
17th **Nov.** "The Dominant Sex" by Michael Egan.
24th **Nov.** "Night of January 16th" by Ayn Rand.
1st **Dec.** "On Approval" by Frederick Lonsdale.
8th **Dec.** "The Cure for Love" by Walter Greenwood.
15th **Dec.** "By Candlelight" by Harry Graham.
26th **Dec.** "Sleeping Beauty"

1948

2nd **Feb.** "Whistling in the Dark" by Laurence Gross and Edward G. Carpenter.
9th **Feb.** "Candida" by George Bernard Shaw.
16th **Feb.** "Miss Tulip Stays the Night" by Nan Marriott-Watson and John O'Douglas.
23rd **Feb.** "Jane" by S.N. Behrman.
1st **March** "The Guinea Pig" by Warren Chetham Strode.
8th **March** "Bitter Sweet" by Noël Coward – Watford Operatic Society.
15th **March** "Message for Margaret" by James Parish. John Le Mesurier was in the cast.
22nd **March** "The Shop at Sly Corner" by Edward Percy.
29th **March** "The Winslow Boy" by Terence Rattigan.
5th **April** "Other People's Houses" by Lynn Dexter.
12th **April** "And So to Bed" by J.B. Fagan.
19th **April** "Deep Are the Roots" by Arnaud D'Usseau and James Gow.
26th **April** "A Play for Ronnie" by W. Chetham Strode.
3rd **May** "Love in Idleness" by Terence Rattigan.
10th **May** "Bats in the Belfry" by Diana Morgan and Robert MacDermot.
17th **May** "The Man from the Ministry" by Madeleine Bingham.
24th **May** "Saint Joan" by George Bernard Shaw.
31st **May** "Nine Till Six" by Aimee and Philip Stuart.
7th **June** "The Blue Goose" by Peter Blackmore.
14th **June** "To Have and To Hold" by Lionel Brown.
21st **June** "Separate Rooms" by Joseph Carole and Alan Dinehart.
28th **June** "An Inspector Calls" by J.B. Priestley.
7th **July** "Clutterbuck" by Benn W. Levy.
14th **July** "London Wall" by John Van Druten.
21st **July** "Behold We Live" by John Van Druten.
28th **July** "High Horse" by Gerard Tyrrell.
2nd **Aug.** "Baby Mine" by Margaret

Mayo.
9th **Aug.** "The Family Upstairs" by Harry Delf.
16th **Aug.** "Ladies in Action" by Ivor Novello.
23rd **Aug.** "Trespass" by Emlyn Williams.
30th **Aug.** "The First Mrs. Fraser" by St. John Ervine.
6th **Sept.** "The Right to Strike" by Percy Robinson.
13th **Sept.** "Flowers for the Living" by Toni Block.
20th **Sept.** "This Happy Breed" by Noël Coward.
27th **Sept.** "Romance" by Edward Sheldon.
4th **Oct.** "La Jalousie" by Sacha Guitry.
11th **Oct.** "The Indifferent Shepherd" by Peter Ustinov.
18th **Oct.** "Love in a Mist" by Kenneth Horne.
25th **Oct.** "Peg o' My Heart" by Hartley Manners.
1st **Nov.** "The Lass of Richmond Hill" by W.P. Lipscombe.
8th **Nov.** "Death Dawdles Daintily" by Felix Deebank.
15th **Nov.** "Time and the Conways" by J.B. Priestley.
22nd **Nov.** "Present Laughter" by Noël Coward.
29th **Nov.** "The Girl Who Couldn't Quite" by Leo Marks.
6th **Dec.** "Fly Away Peter" by A.P. Dearsley.
13th **Dec.** "A Soldier for Christmas" by Reginald Beckwith.
27th **Dec.** "Ali Baba and the Forty Thieves".

1949

24th **Jan.** "Peace Comes to Peckham" by R.F. Delderfield.
31st **Jan.** "The Blind Goddess" by Patrick Hastings.
7th **Feb.** "The Linden Tree" by J.B. Priestley.
14th **Feb.** "Hay Fever" by Noël Coward.
21st **Feb.** "His House in Order" by Arthur Pinero.
28th **Feb.** "The Magic Cupboard" by Percy Walsh.
7th **March** "The Yeomen of the Guard". Watford Operatic Society.
14th **March** "While the Sun Shines" by Terence Rattigan.
21st **March** "Life With Father" by Clarence Day.
28th **March** "The Flashing Stream" by Charles Morgan.
4th **April** "Design for Living" by Noël Coward.
11th **April** "What Anne Brought Home" by Larry E. Johnson.
18th **April** "The First Gentleman" by Norman Ginsbury.
25th **April** "Without the Prince" by Philip King.
2nd **May** "The Paragon" by Roland and Michael Pertwee.
9th **May** "No Medals" by Esther

McCracken.

16ᵗʰ May "Fifty-Fifty" by Larson Brown.

23rd May "Dr. Angelus" by James Bridie.

30ᵗʰ May "No Time for Comedy" by S.N. Behrman.

6ᵗʰ June "Miranda" by Peter Blackmore.

13ᵗʰ June "Breach of Marriage" by Dan Sutherland.

20ᵗʰ June "Acacia Avenue" by Mabel and Denis Constanduros.

27ᵗʰ June "Dear Murderer" by St. John L. Clowes.

4ᵗʰ July "Easy Money" by Arnold Ridley.

11ᵗʰ July "Summer in December" by James Liggat.

18ᵗʰ July "Too Young to Marry" by Martin Flavin.

25ᵗʰ July "Night Must Fall" by Emlyn Williams.

1ˢᵗ Aug. "Room for Two" by Gilbert Wakefield.

8ᵗʰ Aug. "Mr. Bolfry" by James Bridie.

15ᵗʰ Aug. "Eden End" by J.B. Priestley.

22ⁿᵈ Aug. "Full House" by Ivor Novello.

29ᵗʰ Aug. "Shooting Star" by Basil Thomas.

5ᵗʰ Sept. "Musical Chairs" by Ronald Mackenzie.

12ᵗʰ Sept. "Third Time Lucky" by Arnold Ridley.

19ᵗʰ Sept. "Little Lambs Eat Ivy" by Noel Langley, from his book "Cabbage Patch".

26ᵗʰ Sept. "The Pay-off" by Barbara S. Harper.

3rd Oct. "Spring Tide" by J.B. Priestley and George Billam.

10ᵗʰ Oct. "School for Spinsters" by Roland Pertwee.

17ᵗʰ Oct. "Born Yesterday" by Garson Kanin.

24ᵗʰ Oct. "Tons of Money" by Will Evans and Valentine.

31ˢᵗ Oct. "Terence Rattigan's Playbill" - two plays, "The Browning Version" and "A Harlequinade".

7ᵗʰ Nov. "Ten Minute Alibi" by Anthony Armstrong.

14ᵗʰ Nov. "The Chiltern Hundreds" by William Douglas Home.

21ˢᵗ Nov. "Why Not Tonight" by C. Stafford Dickens.

28ᵗʰ Nov. "Jeannie" by Aimee Stuart.

5ᵗʰ Dec. "The Perfect Woman" by Wallave Geoffrey and Basil Mitchell.

12ᵗʰ Dec. "Lover's Leap" by Philip Johnson.

26ᵗʰ Dec. "Puss in Boots"

1950

23rd Jan. "Eliza Comes to Stay" by H.V. Esmond.

30ᵗʰ Jan. "Rain on the Just" by Peter Watling.

6ᵗʰ Feb. "French Without Tears" by Terence Rattigan.

13ᵗʰ Feb. "The Happiest Days of Your Life" by John Dighton.

20ᵗʰ Feb. "For Dear Life" by Lionel Brown.

27ᵗʰ Feb. "Young Wives' Tales" by Ronald Jeans.

6ᵗʰ March "March Hares" by Harry Wagstaff Gribble.

13ᵗʰ March "Chu Chin Chow". Watford Operatic Society.

20ᵗʰ March "The Gioconda Smile" by Aldous Huxley.

27ᵗʰ March "Master of Arts" by William Douglas Home.

3rd April "The Patsy" by Barry Conners.

10ᵗʰ April "Off the Record" by Ian Hay and Stephen King-Hall.

17ᵗʰ April "Maiden's Prayer" by Robert Charles.

24ᵗʰ April "Dusty Ermine" by Beil Grant.

1ˢᵗ May "Mountain Air" by Ronald Wilkinson.

8ᵗʰ May "Edward My Son" by Robert Morley and Noel Langley.

15ᵗʰ May "Love in Albania" by Eric Linklater.

22ⁿᵈ May "Ten Little Niggers" by Agatha Christie.

29ᵗʰ May "Three Blind Mice" by Stephen Powys.

5ᵗʰ June "The Millionairess" by George Bernard Shaw.

12ᵗʰ June "To-morrow's Child" by John Coates.

19ᵗʰ June "Bright Shadow" by J.B. Priestley.

26ᵗʰ June "The Lady Purrs" by Ted Willis.

3rd July "Pink String and Sealing Wax" by Roland Pertwee.

10ᵗʰ July "The Green Pack" by Edgar Wallace.

17ᵗʰ July "Canaries Sometimes Sing" by Frederick Lonsdale.

24ᵗʰ July "The Foolish Gentlewoman" by Margery Sharp.

31ˢᵗ July "He Walked in Her Sleep" by Norman Cannon.

7ᵗʰ Aug. "Top Secret" by Alan Melville.

14ᵗʰ Aug. "Before the Party" by Rodney Ackland.

21ˢᵗ Aug. "Just Married" by Adelaide Matthews and Anne Nichols.

28ᵗʰ Aug. "Mr. Gillie" by James Bridie.

4ᵗʰ Sept. "Claudia" by Rose Franken.

11ᵗʰ Sept. "Chelsea Reach" by Vincent McConnor and Cecil Madden.

18ᵗʰ Sept. "Twenty to One" by L. Arthur Rose. Lupino Lane in the cast.

25ᵗʰ Sept. "On Monday Next" by Philip King.

2ⁿᵈ Oct. "Wishing Well" by E. Eynon Evans.

9ᵗʰ Oct. "Chain Mail" by A.R. Rawlinson and Michael Pertwee.

16ᵗʰ Oct. "The Late Edwina Black" by William Dinner and William Morum.

23rd Oct. "A Pig in a Poke" by Mabel and Denis Constanduros.

30ᵗʰ Oct. "Heaven and Charing Cross" by Aubrey Danvers-Walker.

6ᵗʰ Nov. "Skin Deep" by Ernest Enderline.

13ᵗʰ Nov. "Background" by Warren Chetham-Srode.

20ᵗʰ Nov. "Madame Tic-Tac" by Falkland L. Cary and Philip Weathers.

27ᵗʰ Nov. "Lovely to Look At" by Philip Johnson.

4ᵗʰ Dec. "Busman's Honeymoon" by Dorothy L. Sayers and M. St. Clare Byrne.

11ᵗʰ Dec. "Sweethearts and Wives" by Gilbert and Margaret Hackforth-Jones.

26ᵗʰ Dec. "Beauty and the Beast" by Walter and Frederick Melville.

1951

22ⁿᵈ Jan. "See How They Run" by Philip King.

29ᵗʰ Jan. "Murder at the Vicarage" dramatised by Moie Charles and Barbara Hoy from Agatha Christie's thriller.

5ᵗʰ Feb. "Mary Bonaventure" by Charlotte Hastings.

12ᵗʰ Feb. "The Poltergeist" by Frank Harvey Jnr.

19ᵗʰ Feb. "Black Chiffon" by Lesley Storm.

26ᵗʰ Feb. "Random Harvest" by James Hilton, dramatised by Moie Charles and Barbara Toy.

5ᵗʰ March "New Moon". Watford Operatic Society.

12ᵗʰ March "The Heiress" by Ruth and Augustus Goetz.

19ᵗʰ March "To See Ourselves" by E.M. Delafield.

26ᵗʰ March "One Wild Oat" by Vernon Sylvaine.

2ⁿᵈ April "After All" by John Van Druten.

9ᵗʰ April "Castle in the Air" by Alan Melville.

16ᵗʰ April "Miss Mabel" by R.C. Sherriff.

23rd April "Sugar Plum" by Arthur Macrae.

30ᵗʰ April "If This Be Error" by Rachel Grieve.

7ᵗʰ May "Travellers Joy" by Arthur Macrae.

14ᵗʰ May "Love's a Luxury" by Guy Paxton and Edward V. Hoile .

21ˢᵗ May "The Shadow" by H.F. Maltby.

28ᵗʰ May "Harvey" by Mary Chase.

4ᵗʰ June "The Man With a Load of Mischief" by Ashley Dukes.

11ᵗʰ June "The Third Visitor" by Gerald Anstruther.

18ᵗʰ June "Captain Carvallo" by Denis Cannon.

25ᵗʰ June "Home at Seven" by R.C. Sherriff.

2ⁿᵈ July "The Isle of Umbrellas" by Mabel R. Tyrre and Peter Coke.

9ᵗʰ July "But for the Grace of God" by Frederick Lonsdale. A.E. Matthews in the cast.

16ᵗʰ July "A Lady Mislaid" by Kenneth Horne.

23rd July "Dangerous Corner" by J.B. Priestley.

30ᵗʰ July "Larger than Life" by Guy Bolton. Jessie Matthews was in the cast.

6th **Aug.** "Charley's Aunt" by Brandon Thomas.

13th **Aug**. "Don't Listen Ladies" adapted from Sacha Guitry's comedy by Stephen Powys and Guy Bolton.

20th **Aug.** "The Cure for Love" by Walter Greenwood.

27th **Aug.** "The Bishop Misbehaves" by Frederick Jackson.

3rd **Sept.** "The Chiltern Hundreds" by William Douglas-Home. A.E.Matthews in the cast

10th **Sept.** "Night Was Our Friend" a new play by Michael Pertwee.

17th **Sept.** "The Anonymous Lover" by Vernon Sylvaine.

24th **Sept.** "The Family Upstairs" by Harry Delf.

1st **Oct.** "Many Happy Returns" by Roland Pertwee and Noel Streatfeild. Helen Haye and Irene Handl were in the cast.

8th **Oct.** "Brittania of Billingsgate" by Christine Jope-Slade and Sewell Stokes.

15th **Oct.** "Four Days" by Monckton Hoffe.

22nd **Oct.** "High Temperature" by Avery Hopwood.

29th **Oct.** "Hindle Wakes" by Stanley Houghton.

5th **Nov.** "Love in Idleness" by Terence Rattigan. Jessie Matthews in the cast.

12th **Nov.** "Square Pegs" by Lional Brown.

19th **Nov.** "Indoor Fireworks" by Arthur Macrae.

26th **Nov.** "The Holly and the Ivy" by Wynward Browne.

3rd **Dec.** "Rookery Nook" by Ben Travers. Ralph Lynn was in the cast.

10th **Dec.** "It Won't Be a Stylish Marriage" by A.P. Dearsley.

22nd **Dec.** "Mother Goose" written and produced by Andrew Melville

1952

21st **Jan.** "Flat to Let" by Arthur Macrae.

28th **Jan.** "The Fifty Mark" by Dan Sutherland. Derek Oldham was in the cast.

4th **Feb.** "The Cat and the Canary" by John Willard.

11th **Feb.** "And This Was Odd" by Kenneth Horne.

18th **Feb.** "Count Your Blessings" by Ronald Jeans.

25th **Feb.** "A Streetcar Named Desire" by Tennessee Williams.

3rd **March** "The Three Musketeers". Watford Operatic Society.

10th **March** "Suspect" by Edward Percy and Reginald Denham.

17th **March** "His Excellency" by Dorothy and Campbell Grey.

24th **March** "Is Your Honeymoon Really Necessary" by E.V. Tidmarsh. Ralph Lynn was in the cast.

31st **March** "The Duke in Darkness" by Patrick Hamilton.

7th **April** "For the Love of Mike" by H.F. Maltby.

14th **April** "Will Any Gentleman?" by Vernon Sylvaine.

21st **April** "Anna Christie" by Eugene O'Neill.(The first recorded appearance of Gwen Watford in the cast).

28th **April** "The Shop at Sly Corner" by Edward Percy. Irene Handl in the cast.

5th **May** "Release" by Alfred Shaughnessy.

12th **May** "Relations Are Best Apart" by Edwin Lewis.

19th **May** "Who Goes There!" by John Dighton.

26th **May** "Black on Magenta" by Ronald Adam.

2nd **June** "Who is Sylvia" by Terence Rattigan.

9th **June** "The Bat" by Mary Roberts Rinehart and Avery Hopwood.

16th **June** "Blithe Spirit" by Noël Coward.

23rd **June** "While Parents Sleep" by Anthony Kimmins.

30th **June** "The Light of Heart" by Emlyn Williams.

7th **July** "Master Crook" by Bruce Walker.

14th **July** "The Fourposter" by Jan de Hartog. (The story of a marriage in six scenes - played by Gwen Watford and George Selway)

21st **July** "The School for Husbands" by Frederick Jackson.

28th **July** "Private Lives" by Noël Coward.

4th **Aug.** "Baby Mine" by Margaret Mayo.

11th **Aug.** "The Magic Cupboard" by Percy Walsh.

18th **Aug.** "Waggonload o' Monkeys" by R.F. Delderfield.

25th **Aug.** "The Robinson Family" by Jonquil Antony.

1st **Sept.** "Red Letter Day" by Andrew Rosenthal.

8th **Sept.** "Love from a Stranger" by Frank Vosper.

15th **Sept.** "George and Margaret" by Gerald Savory.

22nd **Sept.** "To Kill a Cat" by Roland Pertwee and Harold Dearden.

29th **Sept.** "The Late Christopher Bean" by Emlyn Williams.

6th **Oct.** "Johnny Belinda" by Elmere Harris.

13th **Oct.** "Up in Mabel's Room" by Wilson Collison and Otto Harbach.

20th **Oct.** "Black Coffee" by Agatha Christie.

27th **Oct.** "Pick-up Girl" by Elsa Shelley.

3rd **Nov.** "Worms Eye View" by R.F. Delderfield.

10th **Nov.** "To Dorothy a Son" by Roger MacDougall.

17th **Nov.** "Maiden Ladies" by Guy Paxton and Edward V. Hoile.

24th **Nov.** "The White Sheep of the Family" by L. du Garde Peach and Ian Hay.

1st **Dec.** "Checkmate" by Victor Lucas.

8th **Dec.** "Meet the Wife" by Lynn Starling.

15th **Dec.** "Love in a Mist" by Kenneth Horne.

6th **Dec.** "Aladdin" written and produced by Andrew Melville.

1953

26th **Jan.** "Fools Rush In" by Kenneth Horne.

2nd **Feb.** "The Constant Wife" by W. Somerset Maugham.

9th **Feb.** "The Hollow" by Agatha Christie.

16th **Feb.** "The Seventh Veil by Muriel and Sydney Box.

23rd **Feb.** "School for Spinsters" by Roland Pertwee.

2nd **March** "Winter Journey" by Clifford Odets.

9th **March** "Magyar Melody". Watford Operatic Society.

16th **March** "Daughter of My House" by Barry Phelps.

23rd **March** "Housemaster" by Ian Hay.

30th **March** "Easy Money" by Arnold Ridley.

6th **April** "Just Married" by Adelaide Matthews and Anne Nichols.

13th **April** "King of the Castle" by Mabel and Denis Constanduros.

20th **April** "The Crooked Billet" by Dion Titheradge.

27th **April** "Rebecca" by Daphne Du Maurier.

4th **May** "A Little Bit of Fluff" by Walter Ellis.

11th **May** "The Man in Grey" by Barbara Toy and Moie Charles.

18th **May** "The First Mrs. Fraser" by St. John Ervine.

25th **May** "Good Men Sleep at Home" by Walter Ellis.

1st **June** "The Sport of Kings" by Ian Hay.

8th **June** "Candida" by George Bernard Shaw.

15th **June** "White Cargo" by Leon Gordon.

22nd **June** "Almost a Honeymoon" by Walter Ellis.

29th **June** "Gaslight" by Patrick Hamilton.

6th **July** "September Tide" by Daphne Du Maurier.

13th **July** "A Woman's Place" by Wendy Grimwood.

20th **July** "A Guardsman's Cup of Tea" by Thomas Browne.

27th **July** "Mystery at Greenfingers" by J.B. Priestley.

3rd **Aug.** "The Happiest Days of Your Life" by John Dighton.

10th **Aug.** "Tons of Money" by Will Evans and Valentine.

17th **Aug.** "Little Women" adapted by Marian de Forest from the book by Louisa M. Alcott.

24th **Aug.** "Third Time Lucky" by Arnold Ridley.

31st **Aug.** "The Middle Watch" by Ian Hay and Stephen King-Hall.

7th **Sept.** "Ambrose Applejohn's Adventure" by Walter Hackett.

14th **Sept.** "Relative Values" by Noël

Coward.

21st Sept. "Manhandled" by Stuart Ready.

28th Sept. The Day's Mischief" by Lesley Storm.

5th Oct. "Laura" by Vera Caspary and George Skylar.

12th Oct. "The Young in Heart" by Derek Benfield.

19th Oct. "Wuthering Heights" by John Davison (from the novel by Emily Bronte)

26th Oct. "When We Are Married" by J.B. Priestley.

2nd Nov. "Ordeal by Fire" by Ivan Butler.

9th Nov. "Painted Sparrows" by Guy Paxton and Edward V. Hoile.

16th Nov. "The Deep Blue Sea" by Terence Rattigan.

23rd Nov. "The Martin's Nest" by Joan Morgan.

30th Nov. "The Uninvited Guest" by Mary Haylet Bell.

7th Dec. "Goodness, How Sad" by Robert Morley.

14th Dec. "It's You I Want" by Maurice Braddell.

26th Dec. "Babes in the Wood".

1954

25th Jan. "Glad Tidings" by R.F. Delderfield.

1st Feb. "The Bad Samaritan" by William Douglas Home.

8th Feb. "Devonshire Cream" by Eden Philpotts.

15th Feb. "Murder Mistaken" by Janet Green.

22nd Feb. "My Wife's Lodger" by Dominic Roche.

1st March "Murder on the Nile" by Agatha Christie.

8th March "The Student Prince". Watford Operatic Society.

15th March "The Noble Spaniard" by W. Somerset Maugham.

22nd March "Meet Mr. Callaghan" by Gerald Verner.

29th March "The Happy Times" by Samuel Taylor.

5th April "The Naughty Wife" by Frederick Jackson.

12th April "Intent to Murder" by Leslie Sands.

19th April "Bed, Board and Romance" by Harry Jackson.

26th April "Four Winds" by Alex Atkinson.

3rd May "Half Seas Over" by Roy Plomley.

10th May "Mademoiselle" by Jacques Deval, adapted by Audrey and Waveney Carton.

17th May "Me and My Girl" by L. Arthur Rose, Douglas Furber and Noel Gay. The *Non-musical* version with Lupino Lane in the cast.

24th May "The Ticking Clock" by Ivan Butler and Kenneth Watson.

31st May "Petticoat Fever" by Mark Reed.

7th June "Widows Are Dangerous" by

June Garland Thomas.

14th June "Someone at the Door" by Dorothy and Campbell Christie.

21st June "We Took a Cottage" by Mary Harris.

28th June "Why Not Tonight?" by C. Stafford Dickens.

5th July "Friendly Relations" by James Liggat.

12th July "The Gift" by Mary Lumsden.

19th July "Trial and Error" by Kenneth Horne.

26th July "It's a Boy" by Austin Melford.

2nd Aug. "Off the Record" by Ian Hay and Stephen King-Hall.

9th Aug. "Peg o' My Heart" by J. Hartley Manners.

16th Aug. "See How They Run" by Philip King.

23rd Aug. "Smilin' Through" by Allan Langdon Martin.

30th Aug. "Without the Prince" by Philip King.

6th Sept. "While the Sun Shines" by Terence Rattigan.

13th Sept. "Dial 'M' for Murder" by Frederick Knott.

20th Sept. "Not So Dusty" by Wally Patch and Frank Atkinson.

27th Sept. "A Priest in the Family" by Keiran Tunney and John Synge.

4th Oct. "Come Back Peter" by A.P. Dearsley. The first appearance of **Jimmy Perry** in the cast.

11th Oct. "Someone Waiting" by Emlyn Williams.

18th Oct. "For Better, For Worse" by Arthur Watkin.

25th Oct. "Down Came a Blackbird" by Peter Blackmore.

1st Nov. "Escapade" by Roger MacDougall.

8th Nov. "Because I am Black" by Earl Couttie.

15th Nov. "The Dashing White Sergeant" by Charles Campbell Gairdner and Rosamund Pilcher.

22nd Nov. "Golden Rain" by R.F. Delderfield

29th Nov. "Shadow of a Man" by Paul Erickson.

6th Dec. "Love's a Luxury" by Guy Paxton and Edward V. Hoile.

13th Dec. "Here We Come Gathering" by Philip King and Anthony Armstrong.

27th Dec. "Dick Whittington"

1955

24th Jan. "Seagulls Over Sorrento" by Michael Hamilton.

31st Jan. "We Must Kill Toni" by Ian Stuart Black.

7th Feb. "The Wise Children" by Ivan Butler.

14th Feb. "Mate in Three" by L. Du Garde Peach.

21st Feb. "Affairs of State" by Louis Verneuil.

28th Feb. "Blind Alley" by Jack Popplewell.

7th March "Song of Norway". Watford Operatic Society.

14th March "A Question of Fact" by Wynyard Browne.

21st March "A Call on the Widow" by James Doran.

28th March "Beside the Seaside" by Leslie Sands.

4th April "The Paper Chain" by Falkland L Carey and Ivan Butler.

11th April "The Little Hut" by Andre Roussin, adapted by Nancy Mitford.

18th April "Waiting for Gillan" by Ronald Miller.

25th April "Angels in Love" or "The Perils of Purity" by Hugh Mills.

2nd May "It's Never to Late" by Felicity Douglas.

9th May "The Wooden Dish" by Edmund Morris.

16th May "Joking Apart" by Ivan Butler, who was producer at the Palace for many years.

23rd May "The Secret Tent" by Elizabeth Addyman.

30th May "As Long As They're Happy" by Vernon Sylvaine.

6th June "The Cat and the Canary" by John Willard.

13th June "Both Ends Meet" by Arthur Macrae.

20th June "Job for the Boy" by Dennis Driscoll.

27th June "The Moon is Blue" by F. Hugh Herbert.

4th July "The Man" by Mel Dinelli.

11th July "By Candle Light" by adapted by Harry Graham from the German of Siegfried Geyer.

18th July "Dead Secret" by Michael Clayton Sutton.

25th July "Where There's a Will" by R.F. Delderfield.

1st Aug. "Reluctant Heroes" by Colin Morris.

8th Aug. "Sabrina Fair" by Samuel Taylor.

15th Aug. "Lace Up Her Petticoat" by Aimee Stuart.

22nd Aug. "Up the Garden Path" by Hugh Beresford.

29th Aug. "A Gentleman's Daughter" by Aimee Stuart.

5th Sept. "My Wife's Lodger" by Dominic Roche.

12th Sept. "Late Love" by Rosemary Casey.

19th Sept. "Bob's Your Uncle" by Austin Melford.

26th Sept. "Book of the Month" by Basil Thomas.

3rd Oct. "To Dorothy a Son" by Roger MacDougall.

10th Oct. "Young Wives Tales by Ronald Jeans.

17th Oct. "Simon and Laura" by Alan Melville.

24th Oct. "The Alibi Game" by Patrick Cargill.

31st Oct. "The Love Match" by Glen Melvyn.

7th Nov. "Murder Without Crime" by J. Lee Thompson.

14th Nov. "High Temperature" by Avery Hopwood.

21st **Nov.** "Dear Charles". A comedy by Alan Melville.

28th **Nov.** "Dangerous Corner" by J.B. Priestley.

5th **Dec.** "The Family Upstairs" by Harry Delf.

12th **Dec.** "Lover's Leap" by Philip Johnson.

26th **Dec.** "Cinderella" written and directed by Andrew Melville.

1956

23rd **Jan.** "The Rotters" by H.F. Maltby.

30th **Jan.** "Worm's Eye View" by R.F. Delderfield.

6th **Feb.** "The Lady Asks for Help" by James Parish.

13th **Feb.** "Talk of the Town Hall" by Barbara Smith and Hans Keuls.

27th **Feb.** "The Manor of Northstead" by William Douglas-Home. A.E. Matthews was in the cast.

5th **March** "The Dancing Years". Watford Operatic Society

12th **March** "Fallen Angels" by Noël Coward.

19th **March** "Honey Pot" by Helen and Edward V. Hoile.

26th **March** "Springtime for Henry" by Benn Levy.

2nd **April** "Witness for the Prosecution" by Agatha Christie.

9th **April** "My Three Angels" by Sam and Bella Spewak.

16th **April** "May I Borrow Your Wife" by H.F. Maltby and Vera Gray

23rd **April** "Dial 'M' for Murder" by Frederick Knott.

30th **April** "I am a Camera" by John Van Druten.

7th **May** "Ring Twice" by Falkland L. Cary.

14th **May** "Lucky Strike" by Michael Brett.

21st **May** "All for Mary" by Harold Brooke and Kay Bannerman.

28th **May** "The Whole Truth" by Philip Mackie.

4th **June** "Birthday Honours" by Paul Jones.

11th **June** "He Walked in Her Sleep" by Norman Cannon.

18th **June** "Love in a Mist" by Kenneth Horne.

25th **June** "Black Chiffon" by Lesley Storm.

2nd **July** "For Pete's Sake" by Leslie Sands.

9th **July** "Dead on Nine" by Jack Popplewell.

16th **July** "Bell, Book and Candle" by John Van Druten.

23rd **July** "The Anonymous Lover" by Vernon Sylvaine.

30th **July** "Seagulls Over Sorrento" by Hugh Hastings.

6th **Aug.** "Hippo Dancing" by Robert Morley.

13th **Aug.** "Tabitha" by Arnold Ridley and Mary Cathcart Borer.

20th **Aug.** "Waggonload o' Monkeys" by R.F. Delderfield.

This was the last production by Andrew Melville at the Palace Theatre, Watford. New proprietors The Watford Theatre Co. Ltd., Lessees and Licensees: James and Gilda Perry, Secretary Theresa Bridgland.

27th **Aug.** *Closed*

3rd **Sept.** "See How They Run" by Philip King.

10th **Sept.** "Ten Little Niggers" by Agatha Christie.

17th **Sept.** "Ma's Bit o' Brass" by Ronald Gow.

24th **Sept.** "Dracula" by Hamilton Deane.

1st **Oct.** "Small Hotel" by Max Frost.

8th **Oct.** "My Wife's Family" by Fred Duprez.

15th **Oct.** "Rope" by Patrick Hamilton.

22nd **Oct.** "It Won't be a Stylish Marriage" by A.P. Dearsley.

29th **Oct.** "Ladies in Retirement" by Edward Percy and Reginald Denham.

5th **Nov.** "Why Not Tonight?" by C. Stafford Dickens.

12th **Nov.** "The Hollow" by Agatha Christie.

19th **Nov.** "French Without Tears" by Terence Rattigan.

26th **Nov.** "Ask Your Dad" by Edwin Lewis.

3rd **Dec.** "Me and My Girl" by L. Arthur Rose, Douglas Ferber and Noel Gay.

10th **Dec.** "The Constant Wife" by W. Somerset Maugham.

26th **Dec.** "Mother Goose"

1957

21st **Jan.** "A Likely Tale" by Gerald Savory

28th **Jan.** "The Case for Silence" by Kate Lindsay.

4th **Feb.** "For the Love of Mike" by H.F. Maltby.

11th **Feb.** "Between Ourselves" by Parnell Bradbury and Richard Norman.

18th **Feb.** "Rookery Nook" by Ben Travers.

25th **Feb.** "Inlaws and Outlaws" by Anne Sherwin and Gerard Hely.

4th **March** "Show Boat". Watford Operatic Society.

11th **March** "Murder When Necessary" by Philip Levene.

18th **March** "Doctor in the House" by Ted Willis, from the novel by Richard Gordon.

25th **March** "Murder at the Vicarage" by Agatha Christie.

1st **April** "The Flying Saucer" by John Hargrave.

8th **April** "The Love Match" by Glenn Melvyn.

15th **April** "The Man in Grey" dramatised by Barbara Toy and Moie Charles from the novel by Lady Eleanor Smith.

22nd **April** Old Time Musical Hall by the resident company. "The Drunkard"

29th **April** "The Men in Possession" by H.M. Harwood.

6th **May** "Mystery at Greenfingers" by J.B. Priestley.

13th **May** "Pyjama Tops" by Mawby Green and Ed. Feilbert. (Based on the French farce "Moumou" by Jean Letrez).

20th **May** "Payment Deferred" by Jeffrey Dell.

27th **May** "Charley's Uncle" by Dennis Staveley.

3rd **June** "The Archers" by E.J. Mason and G. Webb.

10th **June** "The Little Hut" by Andre Roussin (adapted by Nancy Mitford).

17th **June** "Love on Easy Terms" by Stuart Ready.

24th **June** "Double Image" by Roger MacDougall and Ted Allan. (based on a story by Roy Vickers)

1st **July** "Watford Rock" Revue - an evening of laughs, songs and dance.

8th **July** "A Policeman's Lot" by Christopher Bond.

15th **July** "This Happy Home" by Michael Brett.

22nd **July** "A Bit o' Peace and Quiet" by John Vickers.

29th **July** "To Settle for Murder" by Stuart Ready.

5th **Aug.** "Honeymoon Beds" by Cedric Richards.

12th **Aug.** "Tons of Money" by Will Evans and Valentine.

19th **Aug.** "Peg o' My Heart" by J. Hartley Manners.

26th **Aug.** "The Magic Cupboard" by Percy Walsh.

2nd **Sept.** "Reluctant Heroes" by Colin Morris.

9th **Sept.** "Spider's Web" by Agatha Christie.

16th **sept.** "Yorkshire Relish" by Austin Steele.

23rd **Sept.** "Reluctant Debutant" by William Douglas Home.

30th **Sept.** "Old Time Music Hall No.2", melodrama "The Farmer's Daughter" by Ivan Butler.

7th **Oct.** "Come On, Jeeves" by P.G. Wodehouse and Guy Bolton.

14th **Oct.** "The Touch of Fear" by Dorothy and Campbell Christie.

21st **Oct.** "The Prince of Portobello" by Alan Haines (Alan John).

28th **Oct.** "Watford Rock",,"The Red Pullover" was postponed due to the indisposition of Edward Evans.

4th **Nov.** "The Gay Deceiver" by Neville Brian.

11th **Nov.** "Look Back in Anger" by John Osborne.

18th **Nov.** "The Plaintiff in a Pretty Hat" by Hugh and Margaret Williams.

25th **Nov.** "The Red Pullover".

2nd **Dec.** "While Parents Sleep" by Anthony Kimmins.

9th **Dec.** "School for Husbands" by Frederick Jackson.

26th **Dec.** "Jack and the Beanstalk", written and produced by James and Gilda Perry.

1958

20th **Jan.** "Mate in Three" by L. Du

Garde Peach.
27ᵗʰ **Jan.** "Subway in the Sky" by Ian Main.
3ʳᵈ **Feb.** "Miranda" by Peter Blackmore.
10ᵗʰ **Feb.** "Love from a Stranger" by Agatha Christie, adapted by Frank Vosper.
17ᵗʰ **Feb.** "A Bed for Two" by Cedric Richards.
24ᵗʰ **Feb.** "Four Winds" by Alex Anderson.
3ʳᵈ **March** "Wild Violets". Watford Operatic Society.
10ᵗʰ **March** "Look Back in Anger" by John Osborne.
17ᵗʰ **March** "Silver Wedding" by Michael Clayton Hutton.
24ᵗʰ **March** "The House by the Lake" by Hugh Mills.
31ˢᵗ **March** "Odd Man In" by Claude Magnier.
7ᵗʰ **April** "Towards Zero" by Agatha Christie.
14ᵗʰ **April** "Love's a Luxury" by Guy Paxton and Edward V. Hoile.
21ˢᵗ **April** "Summer of the Seventeenth Doll" by Ray Lawler.
28ᵗʰ **April** "Dodo's in Love" by Harold Brooke and Kay Bannerman.
5ᵗʰ **May** "Night Must Fall" by Emlyn Williams.
12ᵗʰ **May** "French for Love" by Marguerite Steen and Derek Patmore.
19ᵗʰ **May** "Claudia" by Rose Franklin.
26ᵗʰ **May** "My Wife's Lodger" by Dominic Roche.
2ⁿᵈ **June** {"The Respectable Prostitute" by Jean Paul-Satre,
{"The Proposal" by Anton Tchekoff.
9ᵗʰ **June** "Actresses Will Happen" by Walter Ellis.
16ᵗʰ **June** "The Man in the Mirror" by Jean Brampton.
23ʳᵈ **June** "Paddle Your Own Canoe" by Max Regnier and Andre Gillois, (adapted by Lucienne Hill).
30ᵗʰ **June** "Poet and Peasant" by Willis Hall and Lewis Jones.
7ᵗʰ **July** "Sweet Madness" by Peter Jones.
14ᵗʰ **July** *Theatre closed for redecoration and new seating.*
21ˢᵗ **July** "Teahouse of the August Moon" by John Patrick.
28ᵗʰ **July** "The Shop at Sly Corner" by Edward Percy.
4ᵗʰ **Aug.** "Dry Rot" by John Chapman. Rodney Bewes by this time a regular member of the cast.
11ᵗʰ **Aug.** "The Ghost Train" by Arnold Ridley.
18ᵗʰ **Aug.** "Jane Steps Out" by Kenneth Horne.
25ᵗʰ **Aug.** "Something to Hide" by Leslie Sands.
1ˢᵗ **Sept.** "Sailor Beware" by Philip King and Falkland Cary.
8ᵗʰ **Sept.** "The Bride and the Batchelor" by Ronald Miller.
15ᵗʰ **Sept.** "Pink String and Sealing Wax" by Roland Pertwee.
22ⁿᵈ **Sept.** "Touch it Light" by Robert

Sharrow.
29ᵗʰ **Sept.** "Dear Delinquent" by Jack Popplewell.
6ᵗʰ **Oct.** "Verdict" by Agatha Christie.
13ᵗʰ **Oct.** "Doctor in the House" by Ted Willis from the novel by Richard Gordon.
20ᵗʰ **Oct.** "Yes and No" by Kenneth Horne.
27ᵗʰ **Oct.** "It Pays to Advertise" by Walter Hackett and Roi Cooper Megrue.
3ʳᵈ **Nov.** "The Girl Who Couldn't Quite" by Leo Marks.
10ᵗʰ **Nov.** "The Entertainer" by John Osborne.
17ᵗʰ **Nov.** "Hot and Cold in All Rooms" by Max Reitman.
24ᵗʰ **Nov.** "He Walked in Her Sleep" by Norman Cannon.
1ˢᵗ **Dec.** "The Late Edwina Black" by William Dinner and William Morum.
8ᵗʰ **Dec.** "This Happy Home" by Michael Brett.
15ᵗʰ **Dec.** "Always Friday Night" by Peter Hogben and Cecil Widdows.
26ᵗʰ **Dec.** "Robinson Crusoe" written and produced by James and Gilda Perry.

1959
26ᵗʰ **Jan.** "Gang Show" S.W. Herts Scouts. Words and music by Ralph Reader.
2ⁿᵈ **Feb.** "Honeymoon Beds" by Cedric Richards.
9ᵗʰ **Feb.** "Come Back Peter" by A.P. Dearsley.
16ᵗʰ **Feb.** "They Fly by Twilight" by Paul Dornhurst.
23ʳᵈ **Feb.** "The Modern Generation" by Max Reitman.
2ⁿᵈ **March** "Oklahoma". Watford Operatic Society.
9ᵗʰ **March** "The Happy Marriage" by John Clements.
16ᵗʰ **March** "An Air for Murder" by Falkland L. Cary and Philip King.
23ʳᵈ **March** "The Reluctant Debutant" by William Douglas-Home.
30ᵗʰ **March** "Peril at End House" by Agatha Christie.
6ᵗʰ **April** "You Too Can Have a Body" by Fred Robinson. Bill Maynard in the cast.
13ᵗʰ **April** "Whiteoaks" by Mazo De La Roche
20ᵗʰ **April** "Speaking of Murder" by Audrey and William Roos.
27ᵗʰ **April** "Gigi" by Colette and Anita Loos.
4ᵗʰ **May** "Grand National Night" by Dorothy and Campbell Christie.
11ᵗʰ **May** "The Tunnel of Love" by Joseph Field and Peter DeVries.
18ᵗʰ **May** "Charley's Aunt" by Brandon Thomas.
25ᵗʰ **May** "A Girl Called Sadie" by Eugene Hamilton.
1ˢᵗ **June** "Man For the Job" by Dennis Driscoll. Terry Scott in the cast.
8ᵗʰ **June** "Flare Path" by Terence Rattigan.
15ᵗʰ **June** "This Thing Called Love" by

Michael Brett.
22ⁿᵈ **June** "Keeping Up With the Joneses" by Max Reitman.
29ᵗʰ **June** "By a Hand Unknown" by C. Neilson Gattey and Z. Bramley-Moore.
6ᵗʰ **July** "The Perfect Woman" by Wallace Geoffrey and Basil Mitchell.
13ᵗʰ **July** "Ghosts" by Henrik Ibsen.
20ᵗʰ **July** "Four in Hand" by Michael Brett.
27ᵗʰ **July** "Bus Stop" by William Inge.
3ʳᵈ **Aug.** "Worm's Eye View" by E.M. Delderfield.
10ᵗʰ **Aug.** "Breath of Spring" by Peter Coke.
17ᵗʰ **Aug.** "A Day in the Life of…" by Jack Popplewell.
24ᵗʰ **Aug.** "The Long and the Short and the Tall" by Willis Hall.
31ˢᵗ **Aug.** "Black Coffee" by Agatha Christie.
7ᵗʰ **Sept.** "Break Out" by Bill Owen.
14ᵗʰ **Sept.** "The Patsy" by Barry Conners.
21ˢᵗ **Sept.** "Not in the Book" by Arthur Watkin.
28ᵗʰ **Sept.** "Gilt and Gingerbread" by Lionel Hale.
5ᵗʰ **Oct.** "George Dillon" by John Osborne and Anthony Cheighton.
12ᵗʰ **Oct.** "Murder on the Nile" by Agatha Christie.
19ᵗʰ **Oct.** "Easy Money" by Arnold Ridley.
26ᵗʰ **Oct.** "Dry Rot" by John Chapman.
2ⁿᵈ **Nov.** "Present Laughter" by Noël Coward. Judy Parfitt in the cast.
9ᵗʰ **Nov.** "The Pony Cart" by Roger Garis.
16ᵗʰ **Nov.** "Wolf's Clothing" by Kenneth Horne.
23ʳᵈ **Nov.** "Murder on Arrival" by George Batson.
30ᵗʰ **Nov.** "It's a Boy" by Austin Melford.
7ᵗʰ **Dec.** "Sauce for the Goose" by Archie Douglas.
14ᵗʰ **Dec.** "Your Obedient Servant" by Diana Morgan.
26ᵗʰ **Dec.** "Babes in the Wood" written and Produced by James and Gilda Perry. Bob Grant in the cast.

1960
18ᵗʰ **Jan.** "Gang Show". S.W. Herts Scouts.
25ᵗʰ **Jan.** "Gaslight" by Patrick Hamilton.
1ˢᵗ **Feb.** "The French Mistress" by Robert Monro.
8ᵗʰ **Feb.** "A Doll's House" by Henrik Ibsen.
15ᵗʰ **Feb.** "Private Lives" by Noël Coward.
22ⁿᵈ **Feb.** "The Pirates of Penzance" First production by Abbots Langley G&S Society at the Palace.
29ᵗʰ **Feb.** "The Merry Widow". Watford Operatic Society.
7ᵗʰ **March** Ballet Rambert.
14ᵗʰ **March** "Pretty as Paint" A musical

farce by Alan Haines.
21st March "Dial 'M' for Murder" by
Frederick Knott
28th March "A View from the Bridge"
by Arthur Miller.
4th April "Basinful of the Briny" by
Leslie Sands.
11th April "The Man Who Changed
His Name" by Edgar Wallace.
18th April "The Unexpected Guest" by
Agatha Christie.
25th April "The Danger Line" by
Stuart Ready.
2nd May "The TV Murders" by Frank
Williams.
9th May "The Sound of Murder" by
William Fairchild.
16th May "High Temperature" by Avery
Hopwood.
23rd May "Hot Summer Nights" by Ted
Willis.
30th May "Sailor Beware" by Philip
King and Falkland Cary.
6th June "Twenty to One" by Arthur
Rose, Arthur English was in the cast.
13th June "Witness for the
Prosecution" by Agatha Christie.
20th June "Roar Like a Dove" by
Lesley Storm.
27th June "The Grass is Greener" by
Hugh and Margaret Williams.
4th July "The Pleasure of His
Company" by Samuel Taylor.
11th July "Five Finger Exercise" by
Peter Schaffer.
18th July "Suddenly it's Spring" by Jack
Popplewell.
25th July "Black Chiffon" by Lesley
Storm.
1st August "Why Not Tonight?" by C.
Stafford Dickens.
8th August "Murder at the Vicarage" by
Agatha Christie.
15th August "The Tender Trap" by Max
Shulman and Robert Paul Smith.
22nd August "Separate Tables" by
Terence Rattigan.
29th August "The More the Merrier"
by Ronald Milleer.
5th Sept. "Alibi" by Agatha Christie.
12th Sept. "Meet Me by Moonlight" by
Anthony Lesser.
19th Sept. "A Clean Kill" by Michael
Gilbert.
26th Sept. "When We Are Married" by
J.B. Priestley.
3rd Oct. "A Shred of Evidence" by
R.C. Sherriff.
10th Oct. "Birthday Honours" by Paul
Jones.
17th Oct. "Friends and Neighbours" by
Austin Steele.
24th Oct. "Podrecca Piccoli Theatre".
(Marionettes).
31st Oct. "A Taste of Honey" by
Shelagh Delaney.
7th Nov. "Spider's Web" by Agatha
Christie.
14th Nov. "The Sacred Flame" by W.
Somerset Maugham.
21st Nov. "A Guardsman's Cup of Tea"
by Thomas Browne.
28th Nov. "See How They Run" by

Philip King.
6th Dec. "Hamlet" by William
Shakespeare.
24th Dec. "Dick Whittington".

1961
16th Jan. S.W. Herts Scouts "Gang
Show"
23rd Jan. "Annie Get Your Gun".
Rickmansworth Players (Ricky Players
first show at the Palace)
30th Jan. Elsbeth Douglas Reid (One
woman theatre).
6th Feb Ballet Rambert.
13th Feb. "The Boy Friend" by Sandy
Wilson. For two weeks.
27th Feb. "The Gondoliers". Abbots
Langley Gilbert & Sullivan Society.
6th March. "Pink Champagne".
Watford Operatic Society.
13th March "Roots" by Arnold Wesker.
20th March "The Geese Are Getting
Fat" by Arthur Watkin.
27th March "Laburnham Grove" by J.B.
Priestley.
3rd April "The Hollow" by Agatha
Christie.
10th April "The Brides of March" by
John Chapman.
17th April "Anastasia" by Marcelle
Maurette.
24th April "Matilda Shouted Fire" by
Janet Green.
1st May "The Substitute" by Frank
Williams.
8th May "Pools Paradise" by Philip
King.
15th May "Tea and Sympathy" by
Robert Anderson.
22nd May "Love from a Stranger" by
Agatha Christie, adapted by Frank
Vosper.
29th May "Rookery Nook" by Ben
Travers.
5th June "This Year, Next Year" by Jack
Ronder.
12th June "Murder at Quay Cottage"
by Simon Amberley.
19th June "Two Dozen Red Roses" by
Kenneth Horne.
26th June "The Last Word" by Jack
Popplewell.
3rd July "Love in a Mist" by Kenneth
Horne.
10th July "Dracula" by Hamilton
Deane.
17th July "The Story of Mike", a
musical play by Ralph Reader, with a
cast of 70 members of the Boy Scouts
Association.
24th July "Laura" by Vera Caspary and
George Skylar.
31st July "The Cat and the Canary" by
John Willard.
7th Aug. "Beside the Seaside" by Leslie
Sands.
14th Aug. "Ten Little Niggers" by
Agatha Christie.
21st Aug. "The Seven Year Itch" by
George Axelrod.
28th Aug. "The Hostage" by Brendan
Behan.
4th Sept. "Watch it Sailor" by Philip

King and Falkland L. Cary.
11th Sept. "The Bargain" by Michael
Gilbert.
18th Sept. "Fallen Angels" by Noël
Coward.
25th Sept. "The Bride Comes Back" by
Ronald Miller.
2nd Oct. "Peril at End House" by
Agatha Christie.
9th Oct. "Settled Out of Court" by
Cecil Hunt and William Saroyan.
16th Oct. "Cat Among the Pidgeons"
by Duncan Greenwood.
23rd Oct. "Podrecca Piccoli Theatre"
(Marionettes).
30th Oct. "The Caretaker" by Harold
Pinter.
6th Nov. "Go Back for Murder" by
Agatha Christie.
13th Nov. "While the Sun Shines" by
Terence Rattigan.
20th Nov. "The Crime of Margaret
Foley" by Percy Robinson and Terence
de Marney.
27th Nov. "A Likely Tale" by Gerald
Savory.
4th Dec. "Murder Delayed" by Duncan
Greenwood.
11th Dec. Closed
18th Dec. Closed
26th Dec. "Mother Goose"

On the night of 19th/20th October
there wasa "Midnight Matinee" in aid of
the Palace Theatre appeal held in the
Main Assembly Room of Watford Town
Hall. Taking part were Terry Scott, Beryl
Reid, Jon Pertwee, Diane Todd, Bob
Grant, The Palace Company (extracts
from "The Boy Friend"), Spanish
Dancers and members of the S.W. Herts
"Gang Show".

1962
15th Jan. S.W. Herts "Gang Show"
22nd Jan. "Doctor in the House" with
Jill Browne and the cast of the Television
programme "Emergency Ward 10.
29th Jan. "Brigadoon". Rickmansworth
Players.
5th Feb. "Salad Days" by Dorothy
Reynolds and Julian Slade. Performed by
the resident company with Billy Durrant
at the piano. For two weeks.
19th Feb. For three nights – "Giselle"
and "Façade". Performed by Ballet
Rambert.
22nd Feb. For three nights – "Pas des
Deesses, "Death and the Maiden",
"Judgement of Paris", "Winter Night"
and Act 3 of "Coppelia". Performed by
Ballet Rambert.
26th Feb. "The Yeomen of the Guard".
Abbots Langley Gilbert & Sullivan
Society.
5th March "Summer Song". Watford
Operatic Society.
12th March "Billy Liar" by Keith
Waterhouse and Willis Hall.
19th March "Black Coffee" by Agatha
Christie.
26th March "Love Locked Out" by
David Kirk. Sydney Crooke at the piano

before each act.

2nd April "Time to Kill" by Diana Morgan.

9th April "The Gazebo" by Alec Coppel.

16th April "Don't Tell Father" by Harold Brooke and Kay Bannerman.

23rd April "Hot and Cold in All Rooms" by Max Reitemann. Colin Bean in the cast.

30th April "The Irregular Verb to Love". By Hugh and Margaret Williams.

7th May "Towards Zero" by Agatha Christie.

14th May. "Hocus Pocus" by Jack Popplewell.

21st May "The Shadow Witness" by Falkland L Cary and Phillip Weathers.

28th May "Hay Fever" by Noël Coward.

4th June "The Devil Was Sick" by Kenneth Horne.

11th June "Simple Spyman" by John Chapman.

18th June "The Big Killing" by Phillip Mackie.

25th June "Murder By Accident" by Alan Peters and Campbell Singer.

2nd July "Don't Listen Ladies" by Sacha Guitry

9th July "Time to Speak" by Sylvia Rayman.

16th July "A Bill of Divorcement" by Clemence Dane.

23rd July "Cup and Saucer" by Gerald Savory.

30th July "The Amorous Prawn" by Anthony Kimmins.

6th Aug. "Saturday Night at the Crown" by Walter Greenwood.

13th Aug. "Doctor at Sea" by Ted Willis adapted from the book by Richard Gordon.

20th Aug. "Murder at the Vicarage" by Agatha Christie.

27th Aug. "George and Margaret" by Gerald Savory.

3rd Sept. "After My Fashion" by Diana Morgan.

10th Sept. "The Happy Man" by Hugh and Margaret Williams.

17th Sept. "The Man With a Load of Mischief" by Phillip Dukes.

24th Sept. "Guilty Party" by George Ross and Campbell Singer.

1st Oct. "Double Yoke" by Hugh and Margaret Williams.

8th Oct. "Dear Charles" by Alan Melville.

15th Oct. "Murder at Midnight" by Peter Hoar.

22nd Oct. "The Holly and the Ivy" by Wynyard Browne.

29th Oct. "Open Verdict" by Falkland L. Cary and Phillip Weathers.

5th Nov. "Young Wives Tale" by Ronald Jeans.

12th Nov. "The Dover Road" by A.A. Milne.

19th Nov. "Johny Belinda" by Elmer Harris.

26th Nov. "Verdict" by Agatha Christie.

3rd Dec. "Merrie England" by Cassio

Operatic Society

10th Dec. "Old Time Musical Hall".

26th Dec. "Cinderella"

N.B. "Bingo Sessions" were held at the theatre at 3pm on Wednesdays and 7pm on Sundays from 14th May to 8th October 1962.

1963

21st Jan. "The District Gang Show" South West Herts Boy Scouts Association.

28th Jan. "The Pyjama Game". Rickmansworth Players.

4th Feb. "The Boy Friend" by Sandy Wilson.

11th Feb. "Salad Days" by Dorothy Reynolds and Julian Slade.

18th Feb. "Ballet Rambert".

25th Feb. "The Cadet Show". Two hours of fabulous and free entertainment by national stars of stage and television presented by the makers of Cadet Cigarettes.

4th March "Princess Ida". Abbots Langley Gilbert & Sullivan Society.

11th March "Bless the Bride". Watford Operatic Society.

18th March "Photo Finish" by Peter Ustinov.

25th March "Kill 2 Birds" by Philip Levene.

1st April "Rock-a-bye Sailor" by Philip King and Falkland L. Cary. Hailed as the funniest of the "Sailor" series.

8th April "Joy of Living" by W.P. Lipscombe.

15th April "Alibi" by Agatha Christie.

22nd April "Belinda" by A.A. Milne.

29th April "The Telescope" by R.C. Sherriff.

6th May "Signpost to Murder" by Monte Doyle.

13th May "The Blue Goose" by Peter Blackmore.

20th May "The Seventh Veil" by Muriel and Sydney Box"

27th May "Miss Pell is Missing" by Leonard Gershe.

3rd June "The Importance of Being Ernest" by Oscar Wilde.

10th June "Policy for Murder" by Jack Popplewell.

17th June "The Silver Soldier".

Close until 5th August for financial reasons.

5th Aug. "Pyjama Tops" by Mawby Green and Ed Feilbert.

12th Aug. "Murder on the Nile" by Agatha Christie.

19th Aug. "Goodnight Mrs. Puffin" by Arthur Lovegrove.

26th Aug. "Brush With a Body" by Maurice McLoughlin.

3rd Sept. "Semi-Detached" by David Turner.

S.9th Sept. John Layton presents, for one night:

The Caravelles - Houston Wells and the Marksmen

Tommy Quickly - Sons of the Piltdown

Men

Cherry Holland - The Velvets - Gary and Lee

Long John Baldry - Cyril Davies and the Rhythm and Blues All Stars.

10th Sept. "Amateur Means Lover" by Dodie Smith.

17th Sept. "Come Blow Your Horn" by Neil Simon.

24th Sept. "How Are You Johnny?" by Philip King..

1st Oct. "The Tulip Tree" by N.C. Hunter.

8th Oct. "Double Trouble" by Michael Brett.

15th Oct. "The Unexpected Guest" by Agatha Christie.

22nd Oct. "The Private Ear and the Public Eye" by Peter Shaffer.

29th Oct. "The Long Sunset" by R.C. Sherriff. Michael Knowles in the cast.

5th Nov. "Norman" by Frank Harvey.

12th Nov. "The Lodger" by Anthony Skene.

19th Nov. "See How They Run" by Philip King.

25th Nov. "The Magic Box" - Tricks and Twist, Magic, Comedy and Music.

2nd Dec. "Rose Marie". Cassio Operatic Society.

9th Dec. "Old Time Music Hall" for one week. Including Randolph Sutton and Billy Danvers.

26th Dec. "Aladdin".

N.B. The theare was used for wrestling on alternate Mondays and for Bingo during 1963.

1964

20th Jan. ""The District Gang Show" South West Herts Boy Scouts Association.

27th Jan. "Kiss Me Kate. Rickmansworth Players.

3rd Feb. "Simple Man With a Rattle" by Charles Ryer.

10th Feb. "Harlequin Ballet" in a programme of classical, modern and folk ballets, by Harlequin Ballet Trust Ltd.

17th Feb. "Stop the World I Want to Get Off" by Leslie Bricusse and Anthony Newley For two weeks.

2nd March "The Mikado". Abbots Langley Gilbert & Sullivan Society.

9th March "Kismet". Watford Operatic Society.

16th March "Distinguished Gathering" by James Parish. Vic Oliver in the cast.

23rd March "This Happy Home" by Michael Brett. Bob Grant in the cast.

30th March "Spider's Web" by Agatha Christie.

6th April "The Hot Tiara" by Janet Allen

13th April "Trap for a Lonely Man" by Robert Thomas. Mystery drama.

20th April "Everybody's Making Money - Except Shakespeare" by Roy Plumley.

27th April "The Shot in Question" by Michael Gilbert. A tense thriller.

4th May "Jane Steps Out" by Kenneth

Horne.
11th May "No Time for Love" by James Ligggat.
18th May "Woman in a Dressing Gown" by Ted Willis.
25th May "Mary Mary" by Jean Kerr. The Queen's Theatre.
The last play of the season – the theatre re–opened on Monday 3rd August.
3rd Aug. "Flat Spin" by Derek S. Royle.
10th Aug. "A Shot in the Dark". Adapted by Harry Kurnotz from "L'Idiote" by Marcel Achard.
17th Aug. "Out of Bounds" by Arthur Walkyn.
24th Aug. "Peril at End House" by Agatha Christie.
31st Aug. "The Happiest Days of Your Life" by Jogn Dighton.
7th Sept. "Murder Without Crime" by J. Lee Thompson.
14th Sept. "The Wings of a Dove" by Christopher Taylor from the novel by Henry James.
21st Sept. "Make Me a Widow" by David Ellis.
28th Sept. "Separate Rooms" by Joseph Carole and Alan Dinehart in collaboration with Alex Gottlieb and Edmund Joseph.
5th Oct. "Billy Liar" by Keith Waterhouse and Willis Hall. Adapted from the novel by Keith Waterhouse.
12th Oct. "Murder at the Vicarage" by Agatha Christie.
19th Oct. "Wuthering Heights" by Emile Bronte. Adapted for the stage by John Davidson.
26th Oct. "Taste of Honey" by Shelagh Delaney.
2nd Nov. "The Little Hut" "La Petite Hutte" by Andre Roussin, adapted by Nancy Mitford.
9th Nov. "Gaslight" by Patrick Hamilton.
16th Nov. "Black Coffee" by Agatha Christie. *James and Gilda Perry's farewell Repertory production.*
23rd Nov. "Person Unknown" with West End cast including Anna Neagle. For two weeks.
30th Nov. "Carousel". Cassio Operatic Society.
7th Dec. "Good Old Days" James and Gilda Perry & Company. When variety went with a swing.
14th Dec. Closed
26th Dec. "Sleeping Beauty"

1965
18th Jan. "Gang Show" by South West Herts Boy Scouts Association.
25th Jan "Show Boat". Rickmansworth Players.
1st Feb. "Hello Watford Goodbye".
8th Feb. Ballet Rambert
15th Feb. "HMS Pinafore". Abbots Langley Gilbert & Sullivan Society.
22nd Feb. "Kings Rhapsody" by Ivor Novello. Watford Operatic Society.

Immediately following this production the Palace became a Civic theatre.

There then followed programmes which changed every two weeks.

30th March "Around the World in 80 Days" by Jules Verne. Re-opening play.
13th April "Blithe Spirit" by Noël Coward
27th April "Alfie" by Bill Naughton
11th May "Macbeth" by William Shakespeare.
25th May "One for the Pot" by Ray Cooney and Tony Hilton
7th June "The Reluctant Debutante" by William Douglas Home.
21st June "From Rush Hour with Love" by Glyn Winslip and Richard Stilgoe and "A Resounding Tinkle" by M.F. Simpson – a double bill.
6th July "Pygmalion" by George Bernard Shaw. Jane Asher in the cast.
20th July "Return Ticket" by William Conlett.
3rd Aug. "Born Yesterday" by Garson Kanin.
17th Aug. "Everything in the Garden" by Giles
30th Aug. "Love From a Stranger" by Frank Vosper.
14th Sept. "Sweet Fanny" by John Gould and Chris Miller.
S.19th Sept. Sunday Night Special – "Gilbert & Sullivan for all".
28th Sept. "The Piccadilly Bushman" by Ray Lawler.
S.10th Oct. Sunday Night Special – Dame Peggy Ashcroft and Julian Bream.
12th Oct. "Uncle Vanya" by Anton Chekov.
26th Oct. "Twelfth Night" by William Shakespeare.
9th Nov. "Devil May Care" by Alan Melville.
S.14th Nov. "The Hollow Crown". A collection of writings, humorous, sad and musical by and about the Kings and Queens of England. Has been played with success all over the world by the Royal Shakespeare Company.
22nd Nov. "The Gipsy Princess" by Emmerich Kalman. Cassio Operatic Society.
29th Nov. Antonia and Marino – the two famous Spanish dancers, present their intoxicating and exciting programme.
6th Dec. "A Christmas Carol" by Charles Dickens.
27th Dec. "Babes in the Wood" James and Gilda Perry in their tenth spectacular pantomime.

1966
24th Jan. "The Gang Show 1966". South West Herts Boy Scouts Asociation.
1st Feb. "The Marriage-Go-Round" by Leslie Stevens. Gwen Watford and Richard Bebb in the cast.
14th Feb. "South Pacific" by Richard Rodgers and Oscar Hammerstein. Rickmansworth Players.
21st Feb. "Ruddigore" by Gilbert & Sullivan. Abbots Langley Gilbert & Sullivan Society.

28th Feb. "The Most Happy Fella". Watford Operatic Society
8th March "Chu Chin Chow". Bushey Operatic Society.
15th March "The Life of Henry the Fifth" by William Shakespeare.
29th March "A Man for All Seasons" by Robert Bolt.
S.3rd April Michael MacLiammoir in "The Importance of Being Oscar".
12th April "Semi-detached" by David Turner.
26th April "A Victorian Evening" including Mrs. Henry Wood's immortal "East Lynne".
10th May "The Constant Wife" by W. Somerset Maugham.
S.15th May "Aspects of Life" a programme of poetry and music devised by John Carron.
24th May "Dial 'M' for Murder" by Frederick Knott.
7th June "The Importance of Being Ernest" by Oscar Wilde .
S.12th June "Set By Swann". A musical evening with Donald Swann (piano) Marion Studholme (Soprano) Ian Wallace (bass baritone) William Elvin (baritone).
21st June "Present Laughter" by Noël Coward.
S.26th June "Opera Favourites" with Elizabeth Fretwell (Soprano) Alberto Remedios (tenor) Evan Thomas (baritone) John D. Parry (piano). Supported by Watford Operatic Society.
5th July "The Glass Menagerie" by Tennessee Williams. Bessie Love in the cast
19th July "Conversation at Night" by Friedrich Durrenmatt, and "High Fidelity" by John Gould a new musical with Ian Wallace. Double bill.
2nd Aug. "Who's Afraid of Virginia Woolf" by Edward Albee.
16th Aug. "A Severed Head" by Iris Murdoch and J.B. Priestley.
30th Aug. Giles Havergal presents "Our Summer Review" – Jane Lows - Marina McConnell – Frances Barlow – Jonathan Elsom – George Howell.
13th Sept. "Entertaining Mr. Sloane" by Joe Orton. John Savident in the cast.
27th Sept. "The Silk Room" by Maureen Duffy.
S.2nd Oct. "Gilbert & Sullivan for All" (Second Edition).
11th Oct. "Rattle of a Simple Man" by Charles Dyer.
25th Oct. "The Gentle Avalanche" by Bill Corlett.
8th Nov. "As Dorothy Parker Once Said". World Premiere. Libby Morris in cast.
23rd Nov. "The Queen and the Rebels" by Ugo Betti. Gwen Watford and Richard Bebb in the cast.
S.4th Dec. "Ballet for All" with dancers from the Royal Ballet.
12th Dec. "The Pirates of Penzance" by Gilbert & Sullivan, Abbots Langley Gilbert & Sullivan Society.
26th Dec, "Cinderella".

1967

23rd Jan. "Gang Show 1967" South West Herts District Scout Council.
31st Jan. "The Anniversary" by Bill Macilwraith.
14th Feb, "The Caretaker" by Harold Pinter.
28th Feb. "The Seagull" by Anton Chekov.
13th March "The Vagabond King". Watford Operatic Society.
21st March "The Picture of Dorian Grey" by Christopher Gable, adapted from the novel by Oscar Wilde.
4th April "The Killing of Sister George" by Frank Marcus. Patricia Burke in the cast.
18th April "Oklahoma" by Rogers and Hammerstein. Rickmansworth Players.
25th April "Jane Eyre" adapted from the novel by Charlotte Bronte. Brigit Forsyth and Liz Gebhardt in the cast
9th May "The Knack" by Anne Jellicoe. Introduced Maureen Lipman. (Her stage debut)
23rd May "The Merry Widow". Bushey Operatic Society.
30th May "A Song at Twilight" by Noël Coward.
S.4th June "A Funny Kind of Evening" with David Kossoff.

Theatre closed 12th June to 25th July for redecoration and a new lighting board installed with a grant from the Arts Council of Great Britain.

25th July "The Country Wife" by William Wycherley, with Anthony Booth and Frances Barlow in the cast.
8th Aug. "The Owl and the Pussycat" by Bill Manhoff. Kevin Lindsay and Jane Bolton in the cast.
22nd Aug. "Irma La Douce". Lynda Baron and David Kernan in the cast.
5th Sept. "The Private Ear and the Public Eye" by Peter Shaffer.
18th Sept. "Pinocchio"
26th Sept. "Wuthering Heights" by Mary Miller. Maureen Lipman in the cast.
9th Oct. "Dance with a Dolly" by Jack Pulman. A new play with Constance Cummings and William Lucas in the cast.
23rd Oct. "Ballet for All". The Royal Ballet.
30th Oct. "The King and I". Cassio Operatic Society
7th Nov. "The Merchant of Venice" by William Shakespeare.
21st Nov. "The Waiters" by Norman Bogner. Patricia Burke and Frank Williams in the cast.
4th Dec. "Iolanthe". Abbots Langley Gilbert & Sullivan Society

11th to 23rd Dec. Theatre closed

26th Dec. "Aladdin" with Amanda Barrie and Maureen Lipman in the cast.

1968

22nd Jan. "Gang Show 1968". South West Herts District Scout Council.
30th Jan. "A Taste of Honey" by Shelagh Delaney.
13th Feb. "She Stoops to Conquer" by Oliver Goldsmith.
26th Feb. "Love from Judy", a musical play based on Jean Webster's "Daddy Long Legs". Watford Operatic Society.
5th March "A Streetcar Named Desire" by Tennessee Williams.
19th March "Loot" by Joe Orton. Maureen Lipman and Kevin Lindsay in the cast.
1st April "Guys and Dolls". Rickmansworth Players.
9th April "The Three Musketeers" by H. Marshall, from Alexander Dumas.
23rd April "A Day in the Death of Joe Egg" by Peter Nichols.
6th May "Orpheus in the Underworld". Bushey Operatic Society.
14th May "Private Lives" by Noël Coward. Amanda Barrie and Robin Hunter in the cast.
28th May "The Rehearsal" by Jean Anouilh. Helen Cherry, Elspet Gray and Celia Bannerman in the cast.
10th June   *Theatre closed*
30th July "Candida" by George Bernard Shaw. Moira Redmond and Charles Tingwell in the cast. This was an Yvonne Arnaud Theatre, Guildford production, directed by Giles Havergal.
3rd Aug. "Fracas at the Palace" – for one night only at 10.30pm. A bright new University based revue. Five men and a girl, all former students of Watford and Bushey Grammar Schools.
13th Aug. "I am a Camera" by John Van Druten. Polly James and Philip Lowrie in the cast
27th Aug. "The Indian Wants the Bronx" by Israel Horovitz.
9th Sept. "Three-To-One-On" by Terence Brady. Revue from the Edinburgh Festival.
16th Sept. "The Thwarting of Baron Bollingrew" by Robert Bolt.
24th Sept. "Inadmissible Evidence" by John Osborne. Steven Murray in the cast.
8th Oct. "The Spoils" by Caryl Brahms and Ned Sherrin. World premiere. Maxine Audley and Angela Pleasance in the cast.
21st Oct. Ballet Rambert
29th Oct. "Little Malcolm And His Struggle Against the Eunuchs" by David Halliwell.
11th Nov. "The Student Prince" by Sigmund Romberg. Cassio Operatic Society.
19th Nov. "Sweet Bird Of Youth" by Tennessee Williams. Bessie Love, Vivien Merchant (wife of Harold Pinter) and John Savident in the cast.
2nd Dec. "Patience" by Gilbert & Sullivan. Abbots Langley Gilbert & Sullivan Society.
24th Dec. "Beauty And The Beast"

1969

27th Jan. "South West Herts Gang Show".
4th Feb. "The Homecoming" by Harold Pinter. Harold Pinter, John Savident, Larry Noble and Maurice Kaufmann in the cast
10th Feb "The Hogarth Puppets" – matinees only.
17th Feb. "Oliver!" by Lionel Bart. Watford Operatic Society
25th Feb. "The Guardsman" by Frank Marcus. William Lucas in the cast.
11th March "Wise Child" by Simon Gray. Kevin Lindsay and Cleo Sylvestre in the cast.
S.16th Mar "Gilbert & Sullivan For All"
24th Mar "Calamity Jane". Rickmansworth Players.
1st April "Hobson's Choice" by Harold Brighouse. Mary Miller in the cast.
15th April "A Doll's House" by Henrik Ibsen.
28th April "Song of Norway". Bushey Operatic Society.
6th May "Look Back in Anger" by John Osborne.
20th May "Arms and the Man" by George Bernard Shaw.
24th May Special Late Show at 10.30pm "The Scaffold"
    End of Season
29th July "Two For the Seesaw" by William Gibson. Jane Merrow and Philip Bond in the cast of two.
12th Aug. "Happy Family" by Giles Cooper.
26th Aug. "The Hotel in Amsterdam" by John Osborne. Ann Firbank and Kevin Lindsay in the cast.
9th Sept. Charles Dyer's 'Staircase'. James Beck in the cast.
22nd Sept. "Ballet For All"
30th Sept. "Spring and Port Wine" by Bill Naughton.
14th Oct. "Pinocchio" by Brian Way.
28th Oct. "The Italian Girl" by James Saunders and Iris Murdoch.
10th Nov. "Camelot" by Lerner and Loewe. Cassio Operatic Society.
18th Nov. "Relatively Speaking" by Alan Ayckbourn.
1st Dec. "The Yeomen of the Guard" by Gilbert & Sullivan. Abbots Langley Gilbert & Sullivan Society.
8th – 19th Dec. *Theatre closed.*
20th Dec. "Dick Whittington".

1970

19th Jan. "The Au Pair Man" by Hugh Leonard.
26th Jan. "Gang Show" South West Herts Scouts.
2nd Feb. "What the Butler Saw" by Joe Orton.
17th Feb. "The Daughter-in-law" by D.H. Lawrence.
2nd March "Mr Fair Lady" by Lerner and Loewe. Watford Operatic Society.
10th March "A Midsummer Night's Dream" by William Shakespeare.
24th Mar "A Boston Story" by Ronald Gow, adapted from the novel by Henry

James.
6th **April** "The Desert Song" by Sigmund Romberg. Rickmansworth Players.
14th **April** "In Celebration" by David Stacey.
28th **April** "Black Comedy" by Peter Shaffer and
 "The Lover" by Harold Pinter.
11th **May** "La Belle Hélène" by Offenbach. Bushey Operatic Society.
19th **May** "Zigger Zagger" by Peter Terson. Youth Theatre production.
26th **May** "Wait Until Dark" by Frederick Knott.
 3rd June Theatre Closed
28th **July** "Say Who You Are" by Keith Waterhouse and Willis Hall.
11th **Aug.** "On Approval" by Frederick Lonsdale.
25th **Aug.** "Cat on a Hot Tin Roof" by Tennessee Williams.
8th **Sept.** "Out of the Crocodile" by Giles Cooper.
22nd **Sept.** "Hedde Gabler" by Henrik Ibsen.
28th **Sept.** "A Face for All Seasons" by Michael Darlow. Bill Maynard in the cast.
6th **Oct.** "Beeston Craig" by Michael Lawrence. World premiere. William Lucas in the cast.
20th **Oct.** "Love for Love" by William Congreve (1690)
26th **Oct.** Northern Dance Theatre.
3rd **Nov.** "Under Milk Wood" by Dylan Thomas.
9th **Nov.** "The Mixture as Before". Theatre in Education team.
17th **Nov.** "Old King Cole" by Ken Campbell. A new kind of pay for children
23rd **Nov.** Olde Time Music Hall.
30th **Nov.** "White Horse Inn". Cassio Operatic Society.
7th **Dec.** "The Gondoliers". Abbots Langley Gilbert & Sullivan Society.
22nd **Dec.** "Mother Goose".

1971
19th **Jan.** "Ritual for Dolls" by George MacEwan Green, and
 "The Real Inspector Hound" by Tom Stoppard.
1st **Feb.** "The Gang Show". South West Herts Scouts.
9th **Feb.** "It's a Two Feet Six Inches Above Ground Level World" by Kevin Laffan. World premiere.
15th **Feb.** "The Scaffold" Three man pop music group from Liverpool
22nd **Feb.** "Half a Sixpence". Watford Operatic Society.
2nd **March** "Julius Caesar" by William Shakespeare.
16th **March** "The Odd Couple" by Neil Simon.
22nd **March** Traditional Music Hall.
30th **March** "Tenderloin". Rickmansworth Players.
6th **April** "An Ideal Husband" by Oscar Wilde.
27th **April** "The Prime of Miss Jean

Brodie" by Jay Presson Allan.
10th **May** "Kismet". Bushey Operatic Society.
18th **May** "The Superannuated Man" by Kevin Laffan. World premiere.
8th **June** "Oh, What a Lovely War". Palace Theatre for Youth.
.
The theatre then closed for the planned summer break. Following a disagreement with the Trust over future policy, Miss Gardner resigned suddenly at the end of June. The season, due to recommence with "Palace Roundabout" from 23rd to 28th August was cancelled. Stephen Hollis was appointed Artistic Director from 15th September. A separate post of Business Manager was created and filled later (after re-advertisement). Initially it was intended to present an autumn series of plays but this was abandoned. The Palace Theatre was closed for 21 weeks.

8th **Nov.** "Paint Your Wagon". Cassio Operatic Society.
29th **Nov.** "The Mikado". Abbots Langley Gilbert & Sullivan Society.
22nd **Dec.** "Jack and the Beanstalk"

1972
24th **Jan.** "The Gang Show". S.W. Herts Boy Scouts.
2nd **Feb.** "Don Juan" by J.B.P. de Molière. (Translated from the French).
21st **Feb.** "Grumbold" by Martin Carter.
28th **Feb.** "The Merry Widow". Watford Operatic Society.
8th **March** "Romeo and Juliet" by William Shakespeare. Angharad Rees and John Savident in the cast.
29th **March** "The Erpingham Camp" by Joe Orton.
17th **April** "Pickwick". Rickmansworth Players.
26th **April** "The Bacchae" by Euripides. (Translated from Greek).
8th **May** "Die Fledermaus". Bushey Operatic Society"
17th **May** "Ladies in Retirement" by Edward Percy and Reginald Denham. Rose Hill in the cast.
7th **June** "Orpheus Descending" by Tennessee Williams.
27th **June** "Watford on Stage - a celebration for Jubilee Year" - Theatre for Youth production
3rd - 10th July Theatre closed.
11th **July** "The Sound of Music" by Rogers and Hammerstein. Watford Operatic Society. For two weeks.
 23rd July - 5th Sept Theatre closed.
6th **Sept.** "The Ballad of the False Barman" by Colin Spencer. Cheryl Campbell in the cast. (Advertised as "a rather vulgar musical").
27th **Sept.** "Saved" by Edgar Bond. Cheryl Campbell in the cast.
S.8th **Oct.** "The Scaffold". (Different cast from the March 1971 group) A week of experimental theatre.
16th & 17th **Oct.** Ken Campbell's Road Show.

18th **Oct.** Mike D'Abo and Demick Armstrong.
19th **Oct.** Bruce Lacey and the Alberts.
20th **Oct.** London School of Contemporary Dance.
21st **Oct.** Plays for rubber go-go girls, presented by Portable Theatre.
23rd **Oct.** "Music Man". Cassio Operatic Society
1st **Nov.** "Mother Courage" by Berthold Brecht. Miriam Karlin and Cheryl Campbell in the cast. in the cast
20th **Nov.** "Princess Ida". Abbots Langley Gilbert & Sullivan Society.
29th **Nov.** "Charley's Aunt" by Brandon Thomas. Cheryl Campbell in the cast.
23rd **Dec.** "Cinderella".

From September 1972, drinks and snacks were available at the theatre bar at lunch time. Complaints from local publicans were reported in the Watford Observer for 15th September. The issue of 22nd September reported a twenty minute play (with cast of two) entitled "The Strip Game". No further reference is available but the presentation probably continued until November.

1973
22nd **Jan.** "Gang Show" . South West Herts Scouts.
31st **Jan.** "Alpha Beta" by E.A. Whitehead. Sian Phillips and Daniel Massey in the cast. Daniel Massey was the son of Raymond Massey, brother of Anna Massey and nephew of Vincent Massey, Governor General of Canada.
21st **Feb.** "The Provoked Wife" by Sir John Vanbrugh. Prunella Scales, Trevor Peacock, Zoe Wanamaker in the cast.
 24th **Feb** "Hogarth Puppets" (Daytime performances).
12th **March** "Finian's Rainbow". Watford Operatic Society.
21st **March** "Dutch Uncle" by Simon Gray.
1st **April** "East of Eden"
11th **April** "The Hostage" by Brendan Behan.
30th **April** "Fiddler on the Roof". Rickmansworth Players.
9th **May** "The Royal Hunt of the Sun" by Peter Shaffer.
28th **May** "La Vie Parisienne" by Offenbach. Bushey Operatic Society.
4th **June** "Glasstown" by Noel Robinson. Robert Powell and Anne Stallybrass in the cast
20th **June** "The Letter" by W. Somerset Maugham. Jill Bennett in the cast.
Theatre closed.
5th **Sept.** "Butley" by Simon Gray.
24th **Sept.** "Captain Pugwash" (Daytime)
3rd **Oct.** "The Milk Train Doesn't Stop Here Anymore" by Tennessee Williams. Maxine Audley in the cast.
22nd **Oct.** "Bitter Sweet" by Noël Coward. Cassio Operatic Society.
31st **Oct.** "The Tempest" by William Shakespeare, with rock music by Henry Gow. Philip Jackson in the cast.
12th **Nov.** Hogarth Puppets. (Daytime)

19th **Nov.** "HMS Pinafore". Abbots Langley Gilbert & Sullivan Society.
28th **Nov.** "A Patriot for Me" by John Osborne. Marianne Faithful and John Savident in the cast
24th **Dec.** "Aladdin".
8th **Sept – 1st Dec.** LUNCH TIME THEATRE Saturdays and most Fridays.

1974
21 **Jan.** "Sooty's Super Show". (Daytime)
23rd **Jan.** Fumble   } Pop music concerts
25th **Jan.** Kiki Dee } at 8.30pm
28th **Jan.** "Gang Show" S.W. Herts Scouts
6th **Feb.** "Fallen Angels" by Noël Coward. Fenella Fielding, Rose Hill and Penelope Keith in the cast.
27th **Feb.** "Captain Pugwash" Theatre in Education, given mainly for schools.
18th **March** "Kiss Me Kate". Watford Operatic Society.
27th **March** "She Stoops to Conquer" by Oliver Goldsmith.
17th **April** "Forget-Me-Not Lane" by Peter Nichols.
6th **May** "Hello Dolly". Rickmansworth Players.
15th **May** "The Corn is Green" by Emlyn Williams. Joanna van Gyseghem and Gwen Watford in the cast.
S.9th June Silverhead in Concert, with Casablanca (Revised date).
18th **June** Ballet Rambert in two hour programme:-
'Tis Goodly Sport,
Ricercare
Judgement of Paris
Embrace Tiger and Return to Mountain.
4th **Sept.** "Three Sisters" by Anton Chekov. Pauline Moran in the cast
2nd **Oct.** "The Threepenny Opera" by Berthold Brecht. Pauline Moran in the cast.
8th **Oct.** "Grumbold and the Smugglers". Theatre in Education. Performed mainly for schools.
4th **Nov.** "Annie Get Your Gun". Cassio Operatic Society.
11th **Nov.** "Ruddigore". Abbots Langley Gilbert & Sullivan Society.
20th **Nov.** "Candida" by George Bernard Shaw. William Lucas in the cast.
21st **Dec.** "Babes in the Wood". Anita Dobson in the cast.

1975
20th **Jan.** "Gang Show" South West Herts Scouts. 25th Jubilee and Farewell.
29th **Jan.** "Tonight at 8.30" by Noël Coward. Anita Dobson in the cast.
25th **Feb.** Royal Ballet Company presents "Ballet for All".
3rd **March** "Robert and Elizabeth". Watford Operatic Society.
13th **March** "Happy As A Sandbag". A musical by Ken Lee. Anita Dobson in the cast
17th **April** "Hello, Hollywood, Hello". A musical by Ken Lee. World premiere.

Anita Dobson in the cast.
14th **May`** "Bus Stop" by William Inge.
4th **June** "French Without Tears" by Terence Rattigan.
1st **July** "Indians" by Arthur Kopit. Watford Palace Theatre for Youth production.
10th **Sept.** "Irma La Douce". Una Stubbs in the cast.
8th **Oct.** "Out On the Lawn" a new play by Don Taylor. Dinah Sheridan, T.P. McKenna, Rosemary Leach, Frank Middlemass in the cast
3rd **Nov.** "Call Me Madam" by Irving Berlin. Cassio Operatic Society.
12th **Nov.** "Variation on a Theme" by Terence Rattigan. Adrienne Corri and William Lucas in the cast.
19th **Nov.** "Hans, the Witch and the Gobbin" by Alan Cullen. A Theatre in Education production. Matinees only.
8th **Dec.** "Iolanthe". Abbots Langley Gilbert & Sullivan Society
20th **Dec.** "Dick Whittington and his Cat" by John Moffatt and Peter Mackriel.

1976
21st **Jan.** "Pygmalion" by George Bernard Shaw. Jan Waters and Margaretta Scott in the cast
17th **Feb.** "Ballet for All" with dancers of The Royal Ballet.
25th **Feb.** "The Merchant of Venice" by William Shakespeare (Prior to International Tour). Jan Waters played Portia. John Savident, Shylock, Donald Pickering Antonio.
22nd **March** "The Card". Watford Operatic Society.
1st **April** "Leave Him to Heaven" by Ken Lee. Anita Dobson and Brian Protheroe in the cast.
28th **April** "Family Matter" by Noel Robinson. Premiere with Rupert Davis (Maigret) and Jane Baxter.
26th **May`** "The Fenella Fielding Show".
15th **June** "A Bit Between the Teeth" Hugh Lloyd and Trevor Bannister in the cast.
21st **June** "Olde Tyme Musical Hall". Sandy Powell ('Can you hear me mother') and Kim Kordell.
28th **June** "The Dracula Spectacular". Palace Theatre for Youth.
8th **Sept.** "Guys and Dolls" by Frank Loesser. Bennie Lee in the cast.
8th **Oct.** "The School for Scandal" by Richard Brinsley Sheridan.
1st **Nov.** "Rose Marie". Cassio Operatic Society
10th **Nov.** "Getting On" by Alan Bennett. Paul Eddington and Barbara Lott in the cast.
17th **Nov.** "Mystery at the Mill" written and directed by Stephen Boyce. (Morning and afternoon matinees only). Theatre in Education.
Dec. Cox and Box and The Sorcerer. Abbots Langley Gilbert & Sullivan Society
20th **Dec.** "Jack and the Beanstalk" by

Peter John.

1977
19th **Jan.** "Hay Fever" by Noël Coward. Renee Asherson in the cast.
S.30th Jan. "A Funny Kind of Evening". David Kossoff.
15th **Feb.** "Ballet for All" by the Royal Ballet Company.
23rd **Feb.** "Mrs. Warren's Profession" by George Bernard Shaw. Selina Cadell and Valentine Dyall in the cast.
S.6th Mar Jazz Concert with Annie Ross and Eddie Thompson.
21st **March** "Fiddler on the Roof". Watford Operatic Society.
30th **Marchl** "Miss Julie" by August Strindberg.
4th **April** Monday, Thursday and Saturday at 11.00a, and 2.30pm "Kovari" Mystery and Magic from a master of the art.
S.10th April "Move Along Sideways" with Ron Moody.
19th **April** "A Long March to Jerusalem" by Don Taylor. Presented by Theatre for Youth.
S.8th May Dennis Waterman in concert.
28th **April** "Foxy", a new musical. Book by Roger Deeley, lyrics by Jill Racy, music by Tony Sharp. Bernard Bresslaw in the cast
25th **May** "Sleuth" by Anthony Shaffer. Anthony Woodruff in the cast.
20th **June** Clown Cavalcade in "Clown for a Day".
28th **June** Alexander Roy London Ballet Theatre.
7th **Sept.** "Blithe Spirit" by Noël Coward. Irene Handl and Amanda Reiss in the cast.
3rd **Oct.** Theatre des Amandiers Nanterre "les farceurs" in "As the Caravan Barks the Dog Passes". Advertised as "An evening of visual hilarity". Mostly mime and slapstick comedy with some French dialogue.
12th **Oct.** "Equus" by Peter Shaffer.
S.23rd Oct. "So You Think You Don't Like Opera". Watford Operatic Society, with Ray Woodland (Soprano) and Thomas Round (Tenor).
31st **Oct.** "No, No, Nanette". Cassio Operatic Society.
9th **Nov.** "Molly" by Simon Gray. British Premiere. Mary Miller and Raymond Francis in the cast
16th **Nov.** "Space Trap" by Clive Flint. Matinees only. Theatre in Education.
5th **Dec.** "The Yeomen of the Guard". Abbots Langley Gilbert & Sullivan Society.
19th **Dec.** "Cinderella"

1978
Until 21st Jan. "Cinderella" by Peter John.
9th **Jan** Miriam Karlin (at 9.00pm) in Liselotte, A one woman show.
16th **Jan** "A Little Night Exposure" (at 9pm). A late night musical revue.
25th **Jan.** "Relatively Speaking" by Alan

Ayckbourn. Lana Morris and Geoffrey Chater in the cast.
21st Feb. "Ballet for All" with dancers from the Royal Ballet.
27th Feb. "Brigadoon". Watford Operatic Society.
8th March "Comedians" by Trevor Griffiths.
6th April "Cabaret" by Joe Masteroff, John Kandler and Fred Edd (based on stories by Christopher Isherwood). Anna Sharkey and Pamela Cundell in the cast.
10th May "The Lady from the Sea" by Henrik Ibsen. Alison Fiske in the cast.
7th June "Rain" by John Bolton and Clemence Randolph from the short story "Miss Thompson" by W. Somerset Maugham. Gloria Grahame in the cast.
5th July "Corsican Brothers" by John Bowen. Theatre for Youth.
7th Sept. "You Never Can Tell" by George Bernard Shaw. Diana Fairfax in the cast.
9th Sept. Children's Theatr,. at 11am.
5th Oct. "Otherwise Engaged" by Simon Gray.
30th Oct. "Gigi" by Lerner and Loewe. Cassio Operatic Society.
9th Nov. "The Late Christopher Bean" by Rene Fauchos. Dora Bryan and Pamela Cundell in the cast.
4th Dec. "The Pirates of Penzance". Abbots Langley Gilbert & Sullivan Society.
S.10th Dec. Georgie Fame and the Blue Flames.
18th Dec. "Aladdin" by Peter John.

1979

Until 20th Jan. "Aladdin" by Peter John.
23rd Jan. "Ballet for All" with dancers from the Royal Ballet.
   Four performances: Tchaikovsky and his Ballets;
   Four performances: The Dream Era.
1st Feb. "Loot" by Joe Orton.
26th Feb. "Hello Dolly". Watford Operatic Society.
S.4th Mar "Heathcliffe" - a tribute to Elvis.
8tht Mar "Side by Side by Sondheim" - an evening of music and wit.
14th Mar "Treasure Quest" by Hilary Cullow. Presented by Theatre in Education. Day time performances.
S.1st April "Salute to Satchmo"
5th April "The Autumn Garden" by Lillian Hellman. (British Premiere). Mary Peach in the cast.
S.29th April Robin Hall and Jimmy McGregor.
3rdh May "Bedroom Farce" by Alan Ayckbourne. Terence Longdon and Amanda Reiss in the cast.
S.27th May George Melly.
S.10th June Jonathan Miller. Talk on directing Shakespeare.
31st May "Summer" by Hugh Leonard. (British Premiere).
S.24th June Terry Lightfoot and his Band.
27th June "The Apprentices" by Peter

Terson. Watford Palace Theatre for Youth.
Theatre closed.
6th Sept. "The Fat Show" by Ken Lee. (World Premiere). A musical.
S.30th Sept. Abbots Langley Gilbert & Sullivan Society, selections from musicals and operas.
4th Oct. "The Glass Menagerie" by Tennessee Williams.
29th Oct. "Me and My Girl". Cassio Operatic Society.
S.4th Nov. National Youth Jazz Orchestra.
8th Nov. "Rosencrantz & Guildenstern Are Dead" by Tom Stoppard.
14th Nov. "The Playboard Puppets". Afternoons only. The adventures of Mo and Hedge.
3rd Dec. "The Gondoliers". Abbots Langley Gilbert & Sullivan Society.
S.9th Dec. Roy Hudd's Music Hall.
17th Dec. "Babes in the Wood" by Peter John.

1980

Until 19th Jan. "Babes in the Wood" by Peter John.
21st Jan. London City Ballet.
S.27th Jan. Acker Bilk and his Paramount Jazz Band.
31st Jan. "Night Must Fall" by Emlyn Williams. Joyce Carey in the cast.
25th Feb. "Carousel". Watford Operatic Society.
S.2nd Mar "The Marriage of Figaro". Operabout.
6th Mar "What the Butler Saw" by Joe Orton.
S.30th Mar "Instant Sunshine".
3rd April "Habeas Corpus" by Alan Bennett. Farce. June Brown (Dot Cotton in Eastenders) in the cast.
1st May "My Fat Friend" by Charles Lawrence. Comedy. Philip Bretherton in the cast
26th May "Outside Edge" by Richard Harris. Imogen Hassell, Norman Rossington, Amanda Richardson and James Ellis in the cast
S.26th June Humphrey Lyttelton and his band.
25th June "The Wings of Time". Theatre for Youth.

Three Evenings as part of Watford Show Week:

Thurs. 28th Aug. A Champagne Variety Bill, alias the Barry Manning Show.
Fri. 29th Aug. Olde Tyme Music Hall.
Sat. 30th Aug. Final of Post-Echo "Young Talent '80" Competition.
8th Sept. "Crown Matrimonial" by Royce Ryton, with Margaret Ashcroft. (a Malcolm Knight production on National Tour). Dillie Keane in the cast.
15th Sept. Roy Hudd's Music Hall.
Sat. 20th Sept at 3pm. "White's Wonders Magic Lantern Show" (for 6-10 year olds)
S.21st Sept. "White's Wonders Magic

Lantern Show" with "all the flavour of the Victorian Music Hall"
S.28th Sept. Victoria Wood and Geoff Durham's "The Great Soprendo" and Funny Magician".
2ndh Oct. "The Girl in Melanie Klein" by James Saunders (Premiere) Frank Finlay, Susan Penhaligon, Renee Asherson and Robert Flemying in the cast
10th Oct. *Appeal launched for funds for restoration.*
27th Oct. "Showboat" by Jerome Kern and Oscar Hammerstein II. Cassio Operatic Society.
S.2nd Nov. Annie Ross and Harry South Quartette.
6th Nov. "Absurd Person Singular" by Alan Ayckbourn.
S.23rd Nov. Marion Montgomery and Richard Rodney Bennett in "Just Good Friends", songs of the 20's to the present day.
11th Nov. "Sleeping Beauty" Playboard Puppet Company. Morning and afternoon performances.
1st Dec. "Patience". Abbots Langley Gilbert & Sullivan Society.
S.7th Dec. "Telephone Bill and the Smooth Operators". An acoustic group - ranging from Punk to cabaret.
15th Dec. "Dick Whittington" by Peter John.

1981

Until 17th Jan. "Dick Whittington" by Peter John.
19th Jan. London City Ballet.
S.25th Jan. George Melly and John Chilton's Feet warmers (Jazz)
29th Jan. "Design for Living" by Noël Coward. Maureen Lipman and Jeremy Clyde in the cast.
23rd Feb. "Song of Norway". Watford Operatic Society.
S.1st Mar "The Vienna of Johann Strauss". Operabout.
5th Mar "Night and Day" by Tom Stoppard. Gwen Taylor in the cast.
14th Mar "The Tinder Box". A musical entertainment for children by Malcolm Sircom based on a story by Hans Christian Anderson. Mornings and afternoons.
S.29th Mar Jonathan Cohen and Co-operation dancing, barbershop harmonies and songs from the 20's and 30's. In aid of the Palace Theatre Appeal.
2nd April "Local Affairs" by Richard Harris. Irene Handl in the cast.
29th April "Grinling Gibbons and the Plague of London" by Brian May. Watford Palace Theatre for Youth production.

Theatre closed for restoration, to designs by Clare Ferraby.

18th Nov. "The Importance of Being Earnest" by Oscar Wilde. Dame Wendy Hiller, Gabrielle Drake and Gary Bond in the cast.
25th Nov. Formal re-opening by the

Mayor Cllr. Ted Amey and Sir John Mills.
14th Dec. "Cinderella" by Peter John.

1982

Until 16th Jan. "Cinderella" by Peter John.
18th Jan. London City Ballet.
S.24th Jan. Roy Castle and artistes from the Players Theatre present an evening of Victorian Music Hall.
28th Jan. "Terra Nova" by Ted Tally. Robert Powell as Capt. Scott and Stephanie Beacham in the cast.
 22nd Feb. "Camelot". Watford Operatic Society.
S.28th Feb. Mr. Acker Bilk and his Paramount Jazz Band.
4th Mar "Once a Catholic" by Mary O'Malley.
13th Mar "The Secret Garden" .World premiere of a musical play for children, based on the novel by Frances Hodgson Burnett. Morning and afternoon performances.
S.28th Mar Prunella Scales and Richard Jackson in "An Evening with Queen Victoria".
1st April "The Big Knife" by Clifford Odets. Ian McShane and Gwen Taylor in the cast.
S.25th April George Melly with John Chilton's Feetwarmers (Jazz).
29th April "How the Other Half Loves" by Alan Ayckbourn. Terence Longdon and Karen Lewis in the cast.
S.23rd May "La Belle Hélène" by Offenbach, presented by Operabout.
26th May "Kas" by Barry Hines and Allan Stronach. Double bill with "Waking Up" by Dario Fo. Presented by Theatre in Education.
3rd June "Time Gentlemen Please" – Old Time Musical Hall with Roy Castle.
7th June "Deathtrap" by Ira Levin
        Theatre closed
2nd Sept. "Having a Ball" by Alan Bleasdale.
S.26th Sept .George Chisholm, an evening of Louis Armstrong and Fats Waller music.
30th Sept. "Veronica's Room" by Ira Levin. (British Premiere) Margaret Tyzack in the cast.
25th Oct. "My Fair Lady". Cassio Operatic Society.
S.31st Oct. "A Funny Kind of Evening" with David Kossoff.
4th Nov. "Sweeney Todd" by Stephen Sondheim. A musical.
4th Nov. "Mr. Spoon and Button Moon". Playboard Puppet Theatre. Morning and afternoon performances.
29th Nov. "The Mikado". Abbots Langley Gilbert & Sullivan Society.
13th Dec. "Jack and the Beanstalk" by Peter John.

1983

Until 15th Jan. "Jack and the Beanstalk" by Peter John.
17th Jan. London City Ballet.
27th Jan. "Romantic Comedy" by

Bernard Slade. (British Premiere). Pauline Collins, Jan Holden and Simon Callow in the cast.
21st Feb. "La Belle Hélène" by Offenbach. Watford Operatic Society.
S.27th Jan. Humphrey Lyttelton and his band.
3rd Mar "Wedding Song" by James Robson. (World Premiere).
12th Mar "Heidi and Peter", a musical play for children adapted from the novel by Johanni Spyri (World Premiere). Mornings and afternoons.
31st March "Educating Rita" by Willy Russell
S.24th April "Gilbert & Sullivan for All". Presented by Watford Rotary Club.
29th April "Little Lies" by Joseph George Caruso, adapted from "The Magistrate" by Arthur Pinero. (Premiere). Sir John Mills, Anthony Bate, Connie Booth and Paul Hardwick in the cast.
8th June "Toad of Toad Hall" by A.A. Milne. Theatre for Youth Drama Club.
        Theatre closed
31st Aug. "The Beautiful Part of Myself" by Tom Kempski. Warren Mitchell in the cast.
S.25th Sept George Chisholm. An evening of Louis Armstrong and Fats Waller music. Vocals by 'Sweet Substitute'.
29th Sept. "Some of My Best Friends Are Husbands" by Hugh Leonard (based on "Celimare, Le Bien Aime" by Eugene Labiche). Tony Britton, Rosemary Leach, Hugh Paddick and Roy Barraclough in the cast.
1st Oct. "Red Riding Hood". Playboard Puppet Theatre. Morning and afternoon performances.
24th Oct. "Perchance to Dream". Cassio Operatic Society.
3rd Nov. "Body and Soul" by Roy Kendall. (World Premiere). Gwen Watford, Patrick Stewart and Helen Ryan in the cast
28th Nov. "Princess Ida". Abbots Langley Gilbert & Sullivan Society.
12th Dec "Mother Goose" by Peter John, with the author in the title role.

1984

Until 14th Jan. "Mother Goose" by Peter John.
17th Jan. Janet Smith and dancers.
S.22nd Jan. The Temperance Seven (Jazz)
26th Jan. "Taking Steps" by Alan Ayckbourn.
20th Feb. "Oklahoma". Watford Operatic Society.
S.26th Feb. Jimmy Perry and his Hi-de-hi Gang with the St. Peter Players in Old Tyme Music Hall.
1st Mar. "On The Spot" by Edgar Wallace. Simon Callow and James Warwick in the cast.
12th Mar. "Raj", presented by Theatre in Education. Mornings and afternoons only.
5th April "Cider With Rosie" by Laurie

Lee.
3rd May "Mornings at 7" by Paul Osborn. Teresa Wright, Margaret Tyzack, Faith Brooke, Peter Jones, Andre Melly and Doreen Mantle in the cast.
31st May "The Caucasian Chalk Circle" by Berthold Brecht. Presented by the Theatre in Youth Drama Club.
Extension built during the summer on part of the Carlton Cinema site.

3rd Sept. *Extension, including the Green Room Bistro, opened.*
6th Sept. "Raffles - The Amateur Cracksman" by E.W. Horning and Eugene Presbrey. Simon Cadell and Alan Dobin in the cast.
4th Oct. Trumpets and Raspberries" by Dario Fo. (British Premiere)   Griff Rhys Jones and Gwen Taylor in the cast.
S 7th Oct. "Wilfred Owen". A play devised and performed by Nigel Bowden.
23rd Oct.   "Button Moon and the Tin Can Band". Playboard Puppet Theatre. Morning and afternoon performances.
8th Nov. "Chance Visitor" by Aleksei Arebuzov, translated from the Russian by Ariadne Nicolaeff. (British Premiere).
26th Nov. "Calamity Jane". Cassio Operatic Society.
3rd Dec.   "Trial by Jury" and "HMS Pinafore". Abbots Langley Gilbert & Sullivan Society.
17th Dec. "Aladdin" by Peter John.

1985

Until 19th Jan. "Aladdin" by Peter John.
22nd Jan. Janet Smith and dancers.
31st Jan. "Natural Causes" by Eric Chappell. (World Premiere). Ian Lavender and Michael Robbins in the cast.
25th Feb "Oliver!". Watford Operatic Society.
7th Mar. "A Private Treason" by P.D. James, Robert Eddison and Susannah York in the cast.
Sat. 9th Mar "On The Road", with Brian Cant and Jonathan Cohen. Performances at 11am and 2.30pm, for children from 6 to 60.
Sat. 1 Sat. 6th Mar "On The Road", with Brian Cant and Jonathan Cohen. Performances at 11am and 2.30pm, for children from 6 to 60.
11th April "Lulu" by Frank Wedekind. Translated by Peter Tegel and adapted by Leon Rubin.
2nd May   "I Do Not Like Thee Doctor Fell" by Bernard Farrell. (British Premiere).
29th May Youth Theatre Festival. Performances by four age groups:
  "Spring Awakening" (17-25)
"Splitting Images"   (10-13)
  "Dream Date"   (14-16)
"Mr. Sweet Steeler" (6-9)
    Theatre closed
5th Sept. "Lady Windermere's Fan" by Oscar Wilde.

Sat.29th Sept. The David Wood Magic and Music Show (for children).
3rd Oct. "The Decorator" by Donald Churchill. (World Premiere).
22nd Oct. "Blast Off Button Moon" presented by Playboard Puppet Theatre. Morning and afternoon performances.
31st Oct. "Toys in the Attic" by Lillian Hellman. Gwen Watford, Hayley Mills, Lysette Anthony and Barbara Murray in the cast.
S.10th Nov. Book Publishers Jonathan Cape, in conjunction with Eastern Arts, invite the audience to meet well known writers and hear them talk about their work.
25th Nov. "Annie". Cassio Operatic Society.
2nd Dec. "Iolanthe". Abbots Langley Gilbert & Sullivan Society.
11th Dec. "Paddington Bear". Daytime performances only.
20th Dec.-18th Jan." Seasons Greetings" by Alan Ayckbourn.

1986
Until 11th Jan. "Paddington Bear"
Until 18th Jan. "Seasons Greetings"
20thJan. "The Real Thing" by Tom Stoppard. Touring production with Christopher Timothy and Paula Wilcox in the cast.
30th Jan.
"Are You Sitting Comfortably?" by Sue Townsend. Dorothy Tutin and Paul Daneman in the cast.
12th Feb. "Colonel Chumbley and Toni Arthur". Performances morning and afternoon for 4-10 year olds.
24th Feb. "Bitter Sweet" by Noël Coward. Watford Operatic Society.
6th March "Talk of the Devil" by Mary O'Malley. (World Premiere). Annette Crosby and Caroline Langrishe in the cast.
12th 1 12th April "Wonderful Town" Music by Leonard Berstein. Maureen Lipman, Lesley Joseph in the cast. Prior to the West End.
15th May "Double Double" by Roger Rees and Eric Elice. (World Premiere). Jane Lapotaire in the cast
4th Sept. "Just Between Ourselves" by Alan Ayckbourn.
2nd Oct. "So Long On Lonely Street" by Sandra Deer. Gayle Hunnicutt in the cast.
31st Oct. "The Seagull" by Anton Chekov. Prunella Scales in the cast.
24thh Nov. "Carousel". Cassio Operatic Society.
4th Dec. "There Was An Old Woman…" by David Wood. Mainly daytime performances.
19th Dec "Spotted Dick" by Ben Travers. Paula Wilcox in the cast.

1987
Until 3rd Jan "There Was An Old Woman…."
Until 11th Jan. "Spotted Dick".
19th Jan. "Ruddigore". Abbots Langley

Gilbert & Sullivan Society.
29th Jan. "Madame Bovary" by Gustave Flaubert. Helen Mirren in the cast. (World Premiere of a new adaptation by Edna O'Brien).
7th Feb. "Mr. Spoon on Button Moon". Playboard Puppet Theatre. Performances 11am and 2.30pm.
25th & 26th "The Tail of the White Giant". Northern Black Light Theatre Feb. Company (Puppets). Performances 11am and 2.30pm.
23rd "The King and I". Watford Operatic Society.
5thMarch "Spin of the Wheel" by Geoff Morrow and Timothy Praeger. World Premiere of a new musical. Maria Friedman in the cast.
2ndApril "Laburnam Grove" by J.B. Priestley. Patsey Byrne, Trevor Peacock, Donald Douglas and Julian Fellowes in the cast
8th May "A Thousand Clowns" by Herb Gardner.

Theatre closed

3rd Sept. "Everything in the Garden" by Giles Cooper. Paula Wilcox and Daniel Hill in the cast.
29th Sept. "Mary Rose" by J.M. Barrie. Amanda Waring and Anna Cropper in the cast.
17th Oct. "Button Moon - Tina's Surprise". Playboard Puppet Theatre. Daytime performances.
22nd Oct. "A Doll's House" by Henrik Ibsen. Susan Penhaligon, Charlotte Cornwall and John Fortune in the cast.
16th Oct. "Viva Mexico". Cassio Operatic Society.
26th Nov. "The Cat and the Canary" by John Willard. Tony Slattery and Natalie Forbes in the cast.
10th Dec. "Pinocchio". A new version by Lou Stein. Mainly daytime performances.

1988
Until 9th Jan. "The Adventures of Piocchio"
Until 16th Jan. "The Cat and the Canary".
18th Jan. "The Yeomen of the Guard". Abbots Langley Gilbert & Sullivan Society.
28th Jan. "Suite in Two Keys" by Noël Coward. Francis Matthews, Isla Blair and Caroline Blakiston in the cast.
17th & 18th Feb. "Go On The Road". Brian Cant and Jonathan Cohen. Performances 11am and 2pm for 5-10 year olds.
22nd Feb. "Fiddler on the Roof". Watford Operatic Society.
3rd March "The Common Pursuit" by Simon Gray. Stephen Fry, Rik Mayall and John Gordon-Sinclair in the cast
31st March "Winter in the Morning" by Jacqui Sharpiro. (World Premiere). Lesley Joseph in the cast.
28th April "The Price" by Arthur Miller.

30th May "So Long On Lonely Street" by Sanda Deer. Isla Blair in the cast. Prior to national tour
8th June "Exclusive Yarns" by Gary Lyons and StewartPurmutt. Susie Blake, Pam Ferris and Lesley Joseph in the cast.

Theatre closed

1st Sept. "The Gingerbread Lady" by Neil Simon. Sheila Steafel and Sandra Dickinson in the cast.
S.18th Sept. Michael Attenborough interviews Sir John Mills. In aid of the Palace Theatre and Watford Scanner Appeals.
29th Sept. "Mrs Dot" by W. Somerset Maugham.
24th Oct. "The Card". Cassio Operatic Society.
26th & 27th Oct. "The Christopher Lillicrap Show" (for 4 - 10 year olds) Mornings and afternoons.
31st Oct. Peter Skellern and Richard Stilgoe in concert.
10th Nov. "Woman Overboard" by Adrian Mitchell. (World Premiere of a sparkling new musical).
16th Dec. "The Patchwork Girl of Oz" by Adrian Mitchell. Based on the novel by L. Frank Baum (which was a sequel to his "Wizard of Oz").

1989
Until 14th Jan. "The Patchwork Girl of Oz"
5thJan Lenny Henry One Man Show
16th Jan. "The Gondoliers". Abbots Langley Gilbert & Sullivan Society.
26th Jan. "The History of Tom Jones" by Henry Fielding, adapted by Andrew Wickes. RuperGraves in the cast.
20th Feb. "Half a Sixpence". Watford Operatic Society.
2nd March "Diplomatic Wives" by Louise Page. (World Premiere).
30th March "Awake and Sing". By Clifford Odets.
27th April "Two for the Seesaw" by William Gibson.
Sat. 29th April "Holiday on Button Moon". Playboard Puppets. Performances 12.30pm and 3.30pm.
Theatre closed
7th Sept. "Candle-Light" by P.G. Wodehouse.
5th Oct. "Roll on Friday" by Roger Hall. Brian Murphy in the cast.
14th Oct. Watford Arts Festival.
30th Oct "Hans Anderson". Cassio Operatic Society.
9th Nov. "A Raisin in the Sun" by Lorraine Hansbury. Don Warrington in the cast.
9th Dec. "Cinderella" by John Moffatt and Tudor Davies.

1990
Until 13th Jan. "Cinderella" directed by Wendy Toye
15th Jan. "The Pirates of Penzance". Abbots Langley Gilbert & Sullivan

Society.
25th Jan. "Bus Stop" by William Inge. Jerry Hall in the cast. Transferred to the Lyric Theatre, Shaftesbury Avenue. 27th **Feb.–31st March 1990**
19th Feb. "The Boy Friend" by Sandy Wilson. Watford Operatic Society.
1th March "You Must Be the Husband" by Colin Bostock-Smith. Tim Brooke-Taylor and Brigit Forsyth in the cast.
28th March Sue Pollard in her one woman show: A Song. A Frock and a Tinkle.
5th April "I Have Been Here Before" by J.B. Priestley.
3rd May "Tartuffe" by Molière. World Premiere of a new translation by David Bryer.
Theatre closed
6th Sept. "Over a Barrel" by Stephen Bill. (World Premiere) Frances Barber in the cast.
4th Oct. "Getting On" by Alan Bennett. Serena Evans (Thin Blue Line), Clive Francis, Eleanor Summerfield and Ruth Kettlewell in the cast.
29th Oct. "Music Man". Cassio Operatic Society.
8th Nov. "Period of Adjustment" by Tennessee Williams.
8th Dec. "Jack and the Beanstalk" by Roy Hudd.

1991
Until **12th Jan.** "Jack and the Beanstalk" by Roy Hudd
14th Jan. "The Mikado". Abbots Langley Gilbert & Sullivan Society.
24th Jan. "Conjugal Rites" by Roger Hall. Nicky Henson and Gwen Taylor in the cast.
18th Feb.. "Cabaret". Watford Operatic Society.
28th Feb. "The Marriage of Figaro". World Premiere of a new translation by Ranjit Bolt of the play by Beaumarchais.
28th March "Widowers' Houses" by George Bernard Shaw.
S.21st April "Live Wax". Ruby Wax in her own show.
25th April "The Odd Couple" by Neil Simon.
26, 27th April
3,4,10,11th May Young Jazz Musicians performing in the Green Room Bar during the evening.
23rd May "Abiding Passions" by Emile Zola. Gwen Watford in the cast.
Theatre closed
27th Aug. "The Devils" by Fyodor Dostoevsky. In Russian by the Novgorod Regional Theatre.
S.1st Sept. The Jiving Lindy Hoppers.
6th Sept. "The Seven Year Itch" by George Axelrod. Ronnie Corbett in the cast.
S.29th Sept. The Featherstonehaughs Dance Company.
4th Oct. "The Complainsant Lover" by Grahame Green. Susan Penhaligon in the cast.
23rd Oct. "Fun and Games on Button

Moon". Playboard Puppets. 11am and 2.30pm.
28th Oct. "The Merry Widow". Cassio Operatic Society.
S.3rd Nov. Jaleo Flamenco
8th Nov. "The Picture of Dorian Gray" by Oscar Wilde.
S 10th Nov. Roy Hudd's Music Hall. A one man show.
7th Dec. "Dick Whittington and his Cat" by Roy Hudd. Dr. Evadne Hinge (a.k.a. George Logan) in the cast.

1992
Until **11th Jan.** "Dick Whittington and his Cat".
13th Jan. "The Sorcerer". Abbots Langley Gilbert & Sullivan Society.
21st J 21st Jan. "Hooray for Hollywood" – Paul Jones and Elaine Delmar in concert.
S.26th Jan. "The Jiving Lindy Hoppers present "The Harvest Moon Ball".
31st Jan. "Me and Mamie O'Rourke" by Mary Agnes Donaghue. (World Premiere).
24th Feb. "Kiss Me Kate". Watford Operatic Society.
6th March "The Barber of Seville". World Premiere of a new translation by Ranjkit Bolt of the play by Beaumarchais. Helena Boham Carter in the cast.
S.29th March "Time Cycle" An Indian dance drama by Kathak Dance, with Nahid Siddiqui.
3rd April "Stitched Up" by Stephen Bill.
Tues. 14th April "Mr. Spoon on Button Moon" Playboard Puppets. 11am and 2.30pm.
1st May "The Baby" by John Canter. (World Premiere).
S.24th May Adventures in Motion Pictures. A dance company.
4th Sept. "The Case of the Frightened Lady" by Edgar Wallace.
2nd Oct. "All My Sons" by Arthur Miller. Julian Glover in the cast.
26th Oct. "Fiddler on the Roof". Cassio Operatic Society.
9th N9 9th Nov. "A Month in the Country" by Ivan Turgenev.
5th Dec. "Aladdin" by Roy Hudd.

1993
11th HMS Pinafore/Zoo. Abbots Langley Gilbert & Sullivan Society
29th Jan. "The Old Country" by Alan Bennett.
1st March "Finian's Rainbow". Watford Operatic Society
12th March "On Approval" by Frederick Lonsdale. Paula Wilcox and Jeremy Sinden in the cast.
16th April "Ghosts" by Ibsen.
14th May "One for the Road" by Willy Russell.
11th June "Salsa Celestina" conceived and directed by Lou Stein.
3rd Sept. "The Real Inspector Hound" and "Dogg's Hamlet" both by Tom Stoppard. Trevor Bannister and

Terence Longdon in the cast.
8th Oct. "Duet for One" by Tom Keminski. Eve Matheson in the cast.
1st Nov. "Anything Goes" Cassio Operatic Society
17th Nov "The Trip to Bountiful" by Horton Foote, presented by The Delaware Theatre Company.
10th Dec. "Mother Goose" by Roy Hudd. Chris Emmett and Nick Staverson in the cast.

1994
10th Jan. "Patience". Abbots Langley Gilbert & Sullivan Society
21st Jan. "A Handful of Dust", in association with Cambridge Theatre Company by Evelyn Waugh. Marty Cruikshank in the cast.
14th Feb. "La Cage aux Folles". Watford Operatic Society.
25th Feb. "Private Lives" by Noël Coward. Caroline Langrishe in the cast.
2nd April "The Return of A.J. Raffles" by Graham Green.
29th April "Desire Under the Elms" by Eugene O'Neill.
10th June "Middle-Age Spread" by Roger Hale. Don Warrington in the cast.
2nd Sept. "Great Expectations", in association with Oxford Stage Company, by Charles Dickens.
30th Sept. ."Woman in Mind" by Alan Ayckbourn. Marsha Fitzalan in the cast.
31st Oct. "Oklahoma" Cassio Operatic Society.
11th Nov. "The Office Party" by John Godber.
9th Dec. "The Sleeping Beauty" by Roy Hudd. Chris Emmett and Nick Staverson in the cast.

1995
16th Jan. "Iolanthe". Abbots Langley Gilbert & Sullivan Society
2nd Feb. "Single Spies" by Alan Bennett. Edward de Souza in the cast
27th Feb. "Wolfboy" by Brad Fraser.
6th March "Seven Brides for Seven Brothers" Watford Operatic Society.
16th March "Borders of Paradise" by Sharman Macdonald
20th April "Loot" by Joe Orton.
25th May "Good Morning, Bill" by P.G. Wodehouse. Philip Bretherton in the cast.
1st Sept. "Black Comedy & the Public Eye" by Peter Shaffer. Chris Emmett in the cast.
6th Oct. "Anna Karenina" by Tolstoy
30th Oct. "Hello Dolly" . Cassio Operatic Society
10th Nov. "French Without Tears" by Terence Rattigan. Sara Crowe in the cast.
S.19th Nov. "A Talent to Amuse". Peter Greenwell (Noël Coward's accompanist)
8th Dec.. "Cinderella" by Roy Hudd. Chris Emmett, Nick Staverson and Pamela Cundell in the cast.

1996
15th Jan. "Yeomen of the Guard".

Abbots Langley Gilbert & Sullivan Society.
2nd Feb. "Foreign Lands" by Karen Hope.
26th Feb. "West Side Story". Watford Operatic Society.
8th March "Charley's Aunt" by Brandon Thomas
10th April "FACE The Musical With Bottle" by Bob Carlton and Whitchurch. Music by Julian Littman. Lyrics by Bob Eaton. In association with Queens's Theatre, Hornchurch, the Nuffield Theatre, Southampton and the Belgrade Theatre, Coventry
13th May. "Follies". Cassio Operatic Society
24th May "Kindertransport" by Diane Samuels. Jean Boht and Diana Quick in the cast.
21st June "Beethoven's Tenth" by Peter Ustinov. Philip Bretherton and Christopher Holt in the cast.
6th Sept. "Happy Families" by John Godber
4th Oct. "Women Laughing" by Michael Wall. Louise Germaine in the cast
28th Oct "Guys and Dolls" Cassio Operatic Society
7th Nov. "Court in the Act" original idea by Peter Wear.
7th Dec. "Puss in Boots" by Roy Hudd. Chris Emmett and Nick Staverson in the cast.

1997
13th Jan. "Ruddigore". Abbots Langley Gilbert & Sullivan Society.
31st Jan. "Kind Hearts and Coronets", adapted by Giles Croft from screen play by Robert Hamer.
24th Feb. "Jack the Ripper" Watford Operatic Society.
21st March "Mrs Klein" by Nicholas Wright. Gemma Jones in the cast.
18th April "Frankie & Tommy" by Garry Lyons
19th May "Barnum". Cassio Operatic Society
30th May "Elton John's Glasses" by David Farr.
27th June "Outward Bound" by Sutton Vane
5th Sept. "Absurd Person Singular" by Alan Ayckbourn
3rd October "Edmund Kean" musical.
27th Oct.. "My Fair Lady". Cassio Operatic Society.
7th Nov. "Sive" by John B. Keane
6th Dec. "Robin Hood And His Merry Men in Babes in the Wood" by Roy Hudd. Chris Emmett and Nick Staverson in the cast.

1998
Jan. "The Gondoliers". Abbots Langley Gilbert & Sullivan Society.
30th Jan. "Wait Until Dark" by Frederick Knott. Andrew Melville in the cast.
23rd "South Pacific". Watford Operatic Society.

13th Mar. "Roots" by Arnold Wesker.
16thApril "Elton John's Glasses" by David Farr (prior to West End run). Brian Conley in the cast.
1st May "Gasping" by Ben Elton.
25th "Annie". Cassio Operatic Society
5th June "Schippel, The Plumber" by C.P. Taylor.
4th Sept. "Dead Funny" by Terry Johnson
2nd Oct. "The Talented Mr. Ripley" by Phyllis Nagy.
26th Oct. "Crazy for You". Cassio Operatic Society.
2nd Nov. "The Glass Menagerie" by Tennessee Williams.
5th Dec. "Jack and the Beanstalk" by Roy Hudd. Chris Emmett also director, Pamela Cundell and Nick Staverson in the cast.

1999
11th Jan. "Pirates of Penzance". Abbots Langley Gilbert & Sullivan Society
29th Jan.. "Darkness Falls" by Jonathan Holloway. Philip Bretherton in the cast.
24th Feb. "Women on the Verge of HRT" by Marie Jones
6th March "Me and My Girl". Watford Operatic Society
19th March "The Late Middle Classes" by Simon Gray. James Fleet, Harriet Walte Walter and Angela Pleasance in the cast. Directed by Harold Pinter Pinter.
21st April "Vita and Virginia" by Eileen Atkins. Marty Cruikshank in the cast
17th May "Half a Sixpence". Cassio Operatic Society
28th May "Emma" by Jane Austen, adapted by Martin Miller and Doon MacKichan.
25th June "Passport to Danger" by Peter Wear.
2nd Sept. "Talent" by Victoria Wood and "Between Mouthfuls" by Alan Ayckbourn.
1st
2n 1st Oct. "Broken Glass" by Arthur Miller. Joint production with Salisbury Playhouse.
25th Oct. "Hot Mikado". Cassio Operatic Society.
5thNov. "Dangerous Corner" by J.B. Priestley
4th Dec. "Robinson Crusoe" by Roy Hudd. Chris Emmett in the cast and director. Pamela Cundell also in the cast.

2000
10th Jan. "Princess Ida". Abbots Langley Gilbert & Sullivan Society.
25th Jan. "The Shakespeare Revue" starring Gemma Craven
4th Feb. "Three Steps to Heaven" by David Cosgrove. Jane Milligan (daughter of Spike) in the cast.
6th March "The Matchgirls". Watford Operatic Society
21st March "Women on the Verge of HRT Get Away" by Marie Jones
14th April "Translations" by Brian Friel
18th May "Talking Heads" by Alan

Bennett. Dora Bryan, Nichola McAuliffe and Zena Walker in the cast.
16th June "Blithe Spirit" by Noël Coward. Paula Wilcox, Anne Reid, Debra Penny and Natalia Makarova in the cast
1st Sept. "Cor. Blimey" by Terry Johnson.
6thOct. "Rough Crossing" by Tom Stoppard. Matthew Kelly in the cast.
3rd Nov. "A Taste of Honey" by Shelagh Delaney. Gemma Craven in the cast
2nd Dec. "Aladdin" by Roy Hudd.

2001
15th Jan. "The Mikado". Abbots Langley Gilbert & Sullivan Society.
2nd Feb. "Martha, Josie and the Chinese Elvis" by Charlotet Jones. Belinda Lang and Debra Penny in the cast.
26th Feb. "Mack & Mabel" Watford Operatic Society
16th March "Neville's Island" by Tim Firth.
20th April "Morning Glory" by Diana Samiels. Brigid Forsyth in the cast.
1 14th May "Oliver!". Cassio Operatic Society
23rd May "Barefoot in the Park" by Neil Simon.
13th June "The Importance of Being Earnest" by Oscar Wilde a new interpre-tation.
31st Aug. "How the Other Half Loves" by Alan Ayckbourn. Debra Penny in the cast.
27th Sept. "A Different Way Home" by Jimmie Chinn. Starring Roy Barraclough.
22nd Oct. "42nd Street". Cassio Operatic Society.
31st Oct. "Perfect Days" by Liz Lochead. Janet Henfrey in the cast.
1st Dec. "Dick Whittington" by Roy Hudd. David Nellist in the cast.
1st1st Directed by Chris Emmett.

2002
14th Jan. "HMS Pinafore/Zoo". Abbots Langley Gilbert & Sullivan Society.
1st Feb. "The Deep Blue Sea" by Terence Rattigan. Philip Madoc, Julia Watson, Zena Walker in the cast.
25th Feb. "Sweet Charity". Watford Operatic Society.
8th March "The True Life Fiction of Mata Hari" by Diane Samuels. Greta Scacchi in the cast.
12th April "Full House" and "The Hairless Diva" the fomer by John Mortimer and the second his translation of the Eugene Ionesco play. Helen Lederer in the cast.
6th May "Camelot" Cassio Operatic Society.
17th May "A Perfect Ganesh" by Terence McNally. Sandra Dickinson in the cast.
14th June "Big Night Out at the little palace theatre" by Sandi Toksvig and Dillie Keane both in the cast and

Bonnie Langford.

After this, the theatre closed for rebuilding and refurbishment until October 2004.

2003
Theatre closed for rebuilding

2004
8th Oct· "The Country Wife" a Restoration Comedy by William Wycherley, adapted by Tanika Gupta.
1st Nov. "The King & I". Cassio Operatic Society
9th&10th Nov. "Mother Courage and her Children" by Berthold Brechtt.
12th&13th Nov. "Lord of the Flies" by William Golding, presented by Hertfordshire County Youth Theatre.
22nd&23rd Nov. "Sing-a-long-a-ABBA" in concert
24th Nov. "Sing-a-long-a Elvis"
3rd Dec. "Mother Goose" by Lawrence Till.

2005
27th Jan. "Sitting Pretty" by Amy Rosenthal (daughter of Maureen Lipman). Belinda Lang, Anna Carteret, Kim Hartman in the cast.
14th Feb. "Yeomen of the Guard" Abbots Langley Gilbert & Sullivan Society.
24th Feb. "I Have Been Here Before" by J.B. Priestley.
31st March "Flying Under Bridges" adapted by Sarah Daniels from the novel by Sandi Toksvig.
S.17th Mar. "Roy Hudd's exceedingly entertaining evening"
26th April "Pyrenees" by David Greig
9th May "Copacabana" by Barry Manilo. Watford Operatic Society
27th May "Alfie" a new musical, based on the novel by Bill Naughton.
30th June "Get Ken Barlow" by Ian Kershaw.
15th Sept.. "The Memory of Water" by Shelagh Stephenson
10th Oct. "Fear And Misery In The Third Reich" by Bertolt Brecht.
17th Oct. "Fiddler On The Roof" Cassio Operatic Society
28th& 9th Oct. "Ghetto" presented by Hertfordshire County Youth Theatre
S.13th Nov. "The Ella Fitzgerald Songbook" with the Tommy Whittle Quartet
3rd Nov. "Queen's English" by Vanessa Brooks. Daniel Hill in the cast.
3rd Dec. "Cinderella".

2006
20th–21st Jan. "More Light" presented by Watford Palace Young People's Theatre.
23rd Jan. "The Pirates of Penzance". Abbots Langley Gilbert & Sullivan Society.
2nd Feb. "The Beauty Queen of Leenane" by Martin McDonagh
2nd Mar. "One Last Card Trick" by Stewart Permutt. Avril Elgar and Debra

Penny in the cast.
S.28th Mar. Humphrey Lyttelton and His Band
3rd April "The Impostor" freely adapted from Molière's 'Tartuffe',
10th April "Them With Tails" entertainment for children
21st April "Paradise Lost" by John Milton adapted by Ben Power.
8th May "Kiss Me Kate" Watford Operatic Society. Premiere of the up-dated version.
18th May "Blue/Orange" by Joe Penhall.
15th June "Hiding" by Francis Turnley. Presented by Birkbeck University of London.
20th June" A Touch of the Sun" by N.O. Hunter. Presented by Salisbury Playhouse.
31st Aug. "Daughter-in-Law" by D.H. Lawrence.
S.10th Sept. "An Evening with Germaine Greer"
28th Sept. "Copenhagen" by Michael Frayn.
16tht Oct. "Jesus Christ Superstar". Cassio Operatic Society
27th&28th Oct. "Great Expectations" by Charles Dickens. Hertfordshire County Youth Theatre.
13th Nov. "The Ella Fitzgerald Songbook"
2nd Nov. "Top Girls" by Caryl Churchill.
S.19th Nov. "The Gershwin Years"
2nd Dec "Aladdin"

2007
19th Jan. "The Birds" by Aristophanes. Presented by Watford Palace Young People's Theatre.
22nd Jan. "The Gondoliers" Abbots Langley Gilbert & Sullivan Society.
1st Jan. Barry Cryer – The First Farewell Tour.
1st Feb. Eric Knowles Antiques Antics
2nd Feb. Ola Onabule with his band
3rd Feb. The Cotton Club Revue.
S.25th Feb. Tommy Whittle's Allstars
8th Feb "Enjoy" by Alan Bennett
5th Mar. "The Hound of the Baskervilles" by Sir Arthur Conan Doyle. Presented by Peepolykus, Neal Street Productions and West Yorkshire Playhouse.
22nd Mar. "Heartbreak House" by George Bernard Shaw
19th April "We That Are Left"
14th May "Annie" Watford Operatic Society
24th May "Blithe Spirit" by Noël Coward
29th June "Mortimer's Miscellamy". Sir John Morrtimer and Gabrielle Drake.
28th July "Herge's Adventures of Tintin"
3rd Sept. "Still Alive" Barry Cryer.
10th Sept. "A Midsummer Night's Dream" Dash Arts production for one week.
21st Sept. "A Small Family Business"

by Alan Aykbourn.
S.30th Sept Frank Skinner
15th Oct. "The Hired Man". Cassio Operatic Society
26th & 27th Oct. "Arabian Nights" Hertfordshire County Youth Theatre.
29th & 30th Oct. "Arturo Ui".
5th Nov. A Glimpse of Stocking.
7th Nov. Voulez Vous.
9th Nov. Let's Talk to Barry.
10th Nov. Subtopia.
13th Nov. The Arab and the Jew.
15th Nov. Nisbat.
16th Nov. An Evening of Spoken Word.
17th Nov. Zoe Rahman.
18th Nov. Russell Howard - Adventures.
29th Nov. "Jack and the Neanstalk".

2008
14th Jan. "Ruddigore" Abbots Langley Gilbert & Sullivan Society.
25th Jan. "Softcops" by Caryl Churchill. Watford Palace Young People's Theatre.
6th Feb. "Top Brass Jazz Orchestra"
7th Feb. Rich Hall.
8th Feb. "The Motown Show".
9th Feb. An Audience with Michael Rosen.
15th Feb. "An English Tragedy" by Ronald Harwood. World Premiere.
13th March "The Doubtful Guest". Presented by Hoipolloi and the Theatre Royal Plymouth in association with English Touring Theatre and Watford Palace Theatre.
28th March "A Vampire Story" by Moira Buffini. Presented by Hertfordshire County Youth Theatre.
4th April "As You Like It" by William Shakespeare
28th April "Chess". Watford Operatic Society
8th May "Kafka's Dick" by Alan Bennett.
S. 1st June "Rabbi Lionel Blue.
12th June "The Emperor's New Kilt". Presented by National Theatre of Scotland and Wee Stories.
17th June "Running the Silk Road"/. Presented by Yellow Earth Theatre Company.

Index